Espionage in the Ancient World

Espionage in the Ancient World

An Annotated Bibliography of Books and Articles in Western Languages

R.M. Sheldon

foreword by Thomas-Durrell Young

McFarland & Company, Inc., Publishers
Jefferson, North Carolina, and London

The present work is a reprint of the library bound edition of Espionage in the Ancient World: An Annotated Bibliography of Books and Articles in Western Languages, *first published in 2003 by McFarland.*

LIBRARY OF CONGRESS CATALOGUING-IN-PUBLICATION DATA

Sheldon, R.M., 1948–
Espionage in the ancient world : an annotated bibliography of books and articles in Western languages / [by] R.M. Sheldon ; foreword by Thomas Durrell-Young.
p. cm.
Includes index.

ISBN 978-0-7864-3768-9
softcover : 50# alkaline paper ∞

1. Intelligence service—History—To 1500—Bibliography.
2. Espionage—History—To 1500—Bibliography. I. Title.
Z6724.I7S54 2008
[JF1525.I6]
016.32712'09'01—dc21 2002012224

British Library cataloguing data are available

Manufactured in the United States of America

McFarland & Company, Inc., Publishers
Box 611, Jefferson, North Carolina 28640
www.mcfarlandpub.com

In Memorium

Philip Henry De Sellem
(April 1, 1947–July 29, 2000)
Librarian, Performer, Friend

Aquí la alma navega
Por un mar de dulzura, y finalmente
En él así se anega,
Que ningún accidente
Extraño o peregrino oye o siente

Here the soul sails through a sea of sweetness,
And finally dissolves into it in such a way
As not to feel nor hear any strange
Or wandering sensation

—Fray Luis de Leon, *Oda a Francisco Sainis*
[translation by Kathleen Bulger-Barnett]

Acknowledgments

An historian of intelligence needs the expertise and counsel of all sorts of specialists: translators, epigraphers, numismatists, experts in the history of religion, Greek and Latin philology, archaeologists, historians, and last but not least, librarians and archivists. I owe a debt of gratitude to a good many librarians and scholars all over the United States and Europe for lending their expertise and helping me to assemble this material. First and foremost, and closest to home, is the staff of the Preston Library at the Virginia Military Institute, in particular Lt. Col. Janet Holly, and Mrs. Elizabeth Hostetter whose work load in inter-library loan services was no doubt doubled by me. I also thank Captain Kenneth Winter who provided reference services and helped in navigating internet resources. My colleague Alan Baragona also sent a never ending stream of leads over the Internet. I wish to thank the staff at the Marshall Library at the Virginia Military Institute, for helping me wend my way through the Friedman Collection, an indispensable tool for anyone doing research on historical cryptography. To my colleagues in the Modern Language Department and numerous friends I owe thanks for checking over translations: Michael Harris and Yvonne Emerson in French, and Kathleen Bulger-Barnett in Spanish. Other translators included Robert Schonberger, Arend von Heemskerck, Inge Hynes, Anna Crockett of VMI. Also Roger Crockett at Washington and Lee helped with the German. Jan Kortmulder helped with the Dutch translation, and my colleague Elena Andre'eva and Mrs. Natalia Sverdlova translated from the Russian, Gerogian, Persian and Arabic. I am indebted to students Magnus Nordenmann of VMI and Erin Frautschy of the University of Minnesota for tracking down a rare title in Minneapolis.

Thanks also go to our neighbors next door in Lexington, Barbara Brown and the staff at the Leyburn Library at Washington and Lee University in Lexington. I am also indebted to Mary Sue Forrest of the Bookery in Lexington for helping me locate books, and to Trevor Cox at Harvard University for tracking down sources. Across the mountain at the University of Virginia in Charlottesville I would like to thank the staffs at the

Fine Arts Library, the Engineering Library, the Law Library, and the Alderman Graduate Library.

In Philadelphia, I wish to thank Daniel Traister and John Pollack of the Annenberg Rare Book and Manuscript Library for help with the Mendelsohn Collection, a treasure-trove of books on cryptography. Thanks also to friends Ralph and Rosemary Hoegermeyer for helping with travel logistics in Philadelphia.

In Washington, D.C., I have relied extensively on the staff of the Library of Congress. My greatest regret is that one of its best librarians, Philip De Sellem, did not survive the completion of this manuscript. At George Washington University I wish to thank the library staff; and Chair of the Classics Department Elizabeth Fisher along with the late Robert Hadley for their help, encouragement and hospitality. The staff of Catholic University was particularly helpful with inscription collections, and my thanks goes to Victoria Erhart for taking the time to show me around the collection. The staffs of the Georgetown University Library and the Center for Hellenic Studies were helpful as always. I am particularly indebted to the former Librarian of the Center, Inge Hynes, whose help with the translation of the German entries has made them much more accurate. Ann Macy Roth of Howard University supplied guidance in all areas Egyptological. My thanks to Alice-Mary Talbot, Director of Medieval and Byzantine Studies at Dumbarton Oaks, and Mark Zapataka in the Library at Dumbarton Oaks for their gracious hospitality and help in locating Byzantine materials. In Baltimore I wish to thank the staffs of the Eisenhower Library of the Johns Hopkins University and the Peabody Library.

I owe thanks to several European scholars. In Athens, Nancy A. Winter, Librarian of the American School of Classical Studies at Athens, helped track down Greek sources In Germany I was greatly helped by Chrystina Häuber of the University of Bonn who helped with German periodicals. In Paris, Cashman Prince of Brown University retrieved items from the Bibliothèque Nationale. And finally, I thank the staff of the British Library at St. Pancras, who were extremely patient in helping me track down many an obscure reference in a very short time period. I am deeply indebted to the Travel and Research Committee of the Virginia Military Institute for funding my trip to London, and Ms. Anne Wells for her kind suggestions on navigating research at the British Library.

In New York, I thank the staff at the New York Public Library; my work there brought back fond memories of writing my master's thesis in the same reading room in 1976. Also in New York, the staff of the Law Library at Columbia University helped locate and reserve for me the only copy of Hans Fischl's book, *Die Brieftaube in Altertum* in this country. The book seemed to be almost as extinct as the passenger pigeon it described.

Acknowledgments

Financial support was provided by the VMI Department of Hist
in the form of travel money and release time. An additional grant fron
the Faculty Development Committee of the Dean's office at VMI was instrumental in covering the expenses of travel, accommodations, and xeroxing.

Many colleagues and friends helped with suggestions and supplied much needed references. Frank Russell of Transylvania University, Robert Dise of the University of Northern Iowa, and Gary Johnson of the University of Southern Maine. I would like to thank the following readers for perusing the manuscript for errors and making useful suggestions: Elizabeth Fisher of George Washington University, Michael Harris, Paul Pierpaoli, and Kenneth Koons of the Virginia Military Institute, and Victoria Erhart of Strayer University. All errors of fact, judgment, or transcription remain mine.

Many members of the Association of Former Intelligence Officers have been supportive over the years. I would be remiss in not thanking them, although I must note with great sorrow that many of them have passed away before this book was published. David Atlee Phillips encouraged me to write this book so that it might take its place among the other histories of intelligence which were much more rare in the 1970s. Col. Russell Bowen and George Constantinides always gave good advice about intelligence matters and bibliography. And I thank Walter Pforzheimer whose salon always included the most interesting writers and intelligence people. In light of the events of September 11, 2001, our discussions on the importance of HUMINT come to mind quite frequently.

Last but not least, I would like to thank my husband, Jeffrey Aubert, for his patience and good humor during the writing of this book, and for his handling of the logistics of this project which made the work and travel possible, easier, safer, and eminently more enjoyable.

Contents

Foreword

It is a regrettable fact of life that all too often compilers of bibliographies get short shrift for their efforts. In academe, typically, the innovative, the flashy, the apparently "new" authors and their works, are adorned with rapt attention and effusive adulation, while those who take the time and energy to compile a bibliography are often judged as having undertaken an unimportant project. But who in academe has not greatly benefited from the existence of a published comprehensive bibliography on his or her field of work?

The challenge of compiling and then organizing this much material for an audience that spans many of the more well-established faculties and government institutions means it is bound to displease someone. While many proclaim the importance of inter-disciplinary studies, there remains considerable institutional prejudice, which is a pity. As demonstrated in this wonderfully extensive, if not, exhaustive compilation, scholars from the classics, history (possibly even social history) politics and security studies (another academic fatherless child), and intelligence studies themselves will benefit from this work being made available for reference.

Professor Sheldon is unusually well qualified to have prepared this bibliography. She has the requisite training and expertise, and truly "knows" the literature on intelligence in antiquity. She is a thoroughly educated classicist whose scholarship reflects Lord Acre's admonition to avoid "monoglot illiteracy." What is remarkable about Professor Sheldon's published scholarship is that she has succeeded in balancing an almost impossible number of disparate subject areas, a feature of her work that is also manifest in this bibliography. This wonderfully expansive compilation includes scholarship from the classics, history (including social history), politics, security studies, and intelligence studies. Scholars working in all of these fields will benefit from this exhaustive reference work, and they will especially appreciate the copious detail and extensive annotations.

Researchers will be thankful that Professor Sheldon has explored the relevant literature in the key modern Western European languages, as well as the ancient languages of Latin and Greek, and that the bibliography includes sources covering medieval Europe, Russia, Africa, India, and China. The volume is user friendly for readers from any field. The author has divided the book into sections based on geographical areas and time periods for easy reference: the Ancient Near East, Classical Greece, the Hellenistic World, The Roman Republic, The Roman Empire, The Byzantine Empire, The Medieval West, the Islamic World, and a catch-all section on Russia, China, India and Africa. The author provides a detailed index which will help readers find intelligence specialties. This makes jumping to sections on specific fields of intelligence quite easy. Readers interested in counterintelligence will find numerous entries, as will those interested in codes and ciphers, secret writing, dead drops, and many other specialties of tradecraft. Readers will be surprised at how many modern-sounding intelligence techniques were used by the ancients. There is an entire section on the worlds oldest unsolved cryptogram. The subjects are far ranging and Professor Sheldon has throw out a very large net to bring in all the available material that might be connected with intelligence activities. She has even provided notations about where very rare books may be found. The index also lists modern authors, ancient place names, intelligence techniques, and ancient authors. This allows the reader to access the information from many different perspectives.

This work is more than a bibliography; it provides the most comprehensive documentation and commentary on the literature on intelligence in antiquity. All libraries building collections in these fields should possess this indispensable reference work.

Dr. Thomas-Durell Young
North American Editor,
Small Wars and Insurgencies

Center for Civil-Military Relations
Naval Postgraduate School
Monterrey, California

Preface

Why a reference book on historical intelligence sources? The short answer is because there are very few people who read *Classical Review, The International Journal of Intelligence and Counterintelligence, The Journal of Roman Studies, Cryptologia, Hesperia,* the *Journal of Military History,* and *L'Année Philologique.* The worlds of Classical Studies, the Military, and the Intelligence Community inhabit separate *niches,* each with its own journal, its own jargon, and its own abbreviations and acronyms. A scholar of one might easily become lost in the arcane knowledge of the other when looking for information on historical intelligence. This book is offered as a Rosetta Stone. It provides, for the first time, a comprehensive guide to the literature of ancient intelligence in one handy volume. Scholars of all three communities have studied aspects of ancient intelligence activities, but very few have crossed over to delve into the secondary literature of the other two groups. There are, of course, exceptions.

Readers with an interest in cryptography, counterintelligence, tradecraft, collection and analysis of intelligence or just simply a general interest in military intelligence can, in this volume, find out what has been published on the subject over the last two centuries. One of the barriers which prevents this from being a comprehensive collection on these subjects is that the literature spans so many languages. I have covered only the major European languages. A companion volume might just as easily be published on the Chinese, Japanese, or Indian sources. Another barrier is gaining access to these works, many of which are in obscure journals, out-of-print sources, or rare book rooms. Inter-library loan services are invaluable if one does not live near a major research library. In cases where volumes are available in one library only, I have indicated where they may be found. With one or two exceptions, all the books can be located at libraries in the United States. I have also noted which volumes are held by the Friedman Collection at the George C. Marshall Library, which houses over 3,004 items, on the campus of the Virginia Military Institute, and the 350-volume Mendelsohn Collection in the Annenberg Rare Book

Collection at the University of Pennsylvania. Both collections are unique and include invaluable sources of information on cryptography. We must be grateful to these two benefactors and their life-long collecting for making these unique collections available to the public.

Choices had to be made in limiting the size of this volume. Some of the subsections I have included could be expanded into bibliographies of their own. As examples, the Bacon cipher, the Sator-Rebus puzzle, and the Tironian notes, all have a vast bodies of literature of their own. For subjects such as these, I have included the major works and indicated the remaining literature may be found. This book was originally designed to cover only the works of Greco-Roman antiquity and the ancient Near East, but since no bibliography covering the period between the fall of Rome and the Renaissance exists, I decided to include works from the Medieval world both East and West, Africa, Russia, India and China.

I have tried to make this volume as user-friendly as possible. I have spelled out the names of journals rather than use abbreviations, and I have included as much bibliographical information as possible so that readers might easily trace these works on World Cat, OCLC, PCI or other major bibliographical search engines. I have included book reviews of the major works so that readers might judge for themselves how well the book was received, and alternative points of view. I have examined all but two works listed in this bibliography: Hemming Forelius's *Dissertatio de modis occulte scribendi et praecibue de scytala Laconica,* (Holmiae, 1697) and Georg Caspar Klauer's *Disputatio historico-philologica de Scytala Lacedaemoniorum,* (Altdorf, 1695) which were not available in this country. I am certain there are many works I have left out, and I would appreciate any help from readers in locating works that will allow me to update this volume for a second edition. I have not included any websites, although they are beginning to proliferate; their addresses tend to change so quickly that any list of them becomes obsolete as soon as the list appears.

When citing ancient sources I have generally listed the Loeb Classical Library editions since these are the easiest way to access the original text and a decent English translation. Classicists whose knowledge of Greek and Latin allow them to read the texts in the original can, of course, go to the Cambridge or Budé editions or the Teubner texts. I have listed the major ancient authors from whom we get our information on intelligence activities, but I have not listed every relevant passage. This is primarily a bibliography of secondary sources. I am compiling a second volume as a guide to the primary sources with translations of the relevant passages. Finally, there are many excellent works on the military of the Greeks, Romans and others that simply do not mention the intelligence function. A cursory glance through the indexes of many otherwise fine works frequently turns up nothing on intelligence, scouting, spies, messengers, signaling, or communications. Such books are becoming rarer as scholars realize that intelligence activities, however primitive, were an integral part of every army and every empire.

The summaries of all these works were meant to be just that, short summaries. I have occasionally indulged an opinion about a work, but I have also tried to indicate where the alternative opinions may be found. All errors in fact, judgment and citation remain mine. Cross references have been added to help the reader see that almost every issue discussed in this book has been debated, sometimes over centuries. Ancient history is never static, and this bibliography is intended as a reference work and a starting point for those who wish to continue the debate or for the reader who just wishes to know what has already been done.

Introduction

The literature of ancient intelligence has never been collected in a single volume. I have already mentioned one of the reasons in the Preface: the subject overlaps at least three major disciplines: military history, intelligence history, and ancient history or classics. Another reason is that over the last three decades, the professionals in these fields have had, at best, a stormy relationship with one another. It has not been unusual to hear military historians berate intelligence history as unreliable because of a lack of good sources. Military history itself for a long time came to be treated as the bastard stepchild that only a few diehards wished to acknowledge. And if military history was unfashionable, then intelligence history is downright dangerous. It has often been condescended to as little more than an *apologia* for an intelligence community that wished to justify its nefarious deeds by giving itself a legitimate history. A perfect example of this is the word tradecraft, which is seminal to intelligence studies yet conjures up only images of pottery making to archaeologists. The point was driven home when one of the readers of my doctoral dissertation wished to strike the word from my study of intelligence gathering in ancient Rome because it "degraded the English language to use such government jargon" (see R.M. Sheldon, "Tinker, Tailor, Caesar, Spy: Espionage in Ancient Rome," University of Michigan, 1987). It is not uncommon for authors on intelligence subjects to deny in the preface to their books any connection to intelligence services.

Shuffling between these communities over the last fifteen years has been, as one military pol put it, "like being in a dog-eat-dog world and wearing milk-bone underwear." This book attempts to bridge the gap between these often hostile factions and put before the general reader for the first time, a guide to both the ancient and modern literature of intelligence activities in the ancient and medieval worlds. It is by no means an exhaustive study, but it will get any reader started on a journey into the world of ancient espionage.

Readers should know the fact that what is referred to as "intelligence activities" is in reality a whole range of subjects that are only loosely bound by the fact that modern intelligence services practice those arts. The ancients certainly did not have our technology, and they rarely used the same terminology. Our modern intelligence services simply do not have ancient equivalents, and to suggest they did would be anachronistic. Yet to use a term like HUMINT is not inaccurate when describing the collection of intelligence by human means. It was done then, it is done now. A spy is a spy is a spy, and eavesdropping is eavesdropping whether done by a human ear or an electronic device. Ancient governments, like modern ones, realized that to keep their borders safe, to control their populations and to keep abreast of political developments abroad, they needed a means to collect the intelligence which enabled them to make informed decisions. Intelligence activities have always been an integral part of statecraft. And we are made painfully aware daily of the damage spies can do. One has merely to peruse the names of the last few years—Pollak, Hanson, Ames, or Walker to realize how one small, insignificant cog in the wheel, with enough access, can destroy systems backed up and supposedly kept secure by billions of dollars of technical equipment. The tragic bombing of the Pentagon and the World Trade Center, which occurred during the final stages of preparing this manuscript, has brought up an entirely new discussion of the importance of having human resources on the ground.

My definition of the intelligence process is a simple one. It is what is commonly referred to as the intelligence cycle, and I do not believe this process has changed over the millennia. Whether we are talking about a single commander, an autocracy, a democratic government, or an oligarchy, the steps in the cycle are always the same. One targets the geographic area on which one needs the intelligence; one collects the information as best as one can; one processes the raw data into a coherent picture, and then one disseminates the finished product to the consumer or decision maker who will act on it. All of this must be done in a timely manner that will make the intelligence useful. It would not be unusual in an ancient world much simpler than ours for one person to accomplish all these steps by himself. On the other hand, Near Eastern bureaucracies had entire departments in the palace dedicated to these activities by the second millennium BC (see Jack Sasson, *The Military Establishment at Mari).*

Readers may be surprised to discover how much intelligence activity went on in the ancient world. Indeed, finding spies in the ancient authors is not nearly as difficult as tracking down some of the secondary literature. Articles and books on aspects of ancient intelligence activities have appeared all over the globe in more languages than one author could ever hope to read. The entries in this collection therefore, represent those items which were read and translated from English, French, German, Italian

Spanish, Polish and Dutch periodicals, the authors of which all pepper their prose liberally with Greek and Latin. Much more may exist in Russian, Chinese, Japanese, Hebrew or Slavic periodicals to which I had no access.

I have tried to cover thoroughly the areas of intelligence collection (both political and military), counterintelligence, espionage, tradecraft and covert action. What constitutes intelligence activities is, of course, debatable even today. Is covert action a legitimate intelligence activity or should it be classified as a strictly military activity? The CIA and the Defense Department will have to sort that problem out by themselves. In the meantime, I have covered all varieties of covert action in this study. Tradecraft, too, takes in a long list of activities which could generate a literature by itself. Cryptography is a perfect example. Each cryptographic study leads to ten more; where does one draw the line? I have limited my list to studies on Greek and Latin cryptography which explain secret codes and ciphers. I have stayed away from numerology or studies of, as yet, undeciphered languages like Linear A or studies of now deciphered languages that still seemed like ancient "codes" to earlier scholars whose work predated the decipherment (Mayan glyphs, Egyptian hieroglyphics, Etruscan).

I have limited this collection to works dealing specifically with tactical intelligence and have studiously avoided general battle studies. Similarly I have covered discussions of strategic intelligence gathering but not general discussions of foreign policy. Strategical and tactical surprise qualify as legitimate topics of concern since one cannot achieve surprise without advanced intelligence. Examples of the former are rare but not impossible to find.

I have included both internal security and policing as important activities. These topics include the activities of secret services run by a central government even including crowd control. When discussing intelligence activities, one must pay close attention to proper definitions of ancient and modern terms. Police forces, as we understand them, are a modern invention; keeping law and order is not. In the ancient world, it was not unusual for many different officials to be responsible for some aspect of collecting intelligence, enforcing laws, arresting people, or transporting information. The authority of military and civilian officials often overlapped, which led to a great deal of ad hoc decision making as a consequence. To give just one example, the *agentes in rebus* of the late Roman empire delivered dispatches, helped to collect taxes, guarded prisons, escorted bishops and sometimes even assassinated people. No single modern agency could be responsible for conducting this many disparate activities.

Some activities, therefore, can be linked to intelligence gathering only tangentially. As the saying goes, espionage is practiced sometimes by spies and all the time by neighbors, relatives and colleagues. I have tried to keep the focus on topics that were of national or international importance. I have avoided the topics of ancient magic, mythology, numerology, or religious practices unless they illustrate a practice that also had military or political applications.

I have listed only books and articles that are completely within the purview of the intelligence enterprise. Snippets of many books discuss, in a few pages, topics touched upon by these works, and I have tried to refer to them in the text. If the section of the book was relatively large, i.e. several chapters, I gave it a separate entry. That the literature of ancient intelligence is so large should not come as a surprise. Espionage is, after all, the world's second oldest profession. As such, it is a topic that has fascinated people for centuries. This collection is a modest representation of what people have written about the spying activities of the ancients.

Glossary

Agentes in Rebus—Part of the intelligence and police system of the late Roman empire. A passage in Aurelius Victor suggests that it was Diocletian who founded the service to replace the notorious *frumentarii* who had been disbanded because of their abuses of power. The *agentes* took over the job as overseers of the *cursus publicus*, and as secret agents of the central government. The new corps also abused their power, and legal action was taken to curb their excesses. They were put under the direction of the *magister officiorum* rather than the *magister militum* to keep too much power from accruing to the latter.

Angaroi—Royal messengers of the Persian postal system. Mentioned in Herodotus 8.98 who gives the famous description of them as being "stayed neither by snow, nor rain, nor heat, nor darkness from accomplishing their appointed course with all speed." *Angaros* (pl. *angaroi)* is a Babylonian word which passed in to Greek and later Roman usage. This suggests that such riders had been in existence for a very long time.

Beneficiarii consularis—*Beneficiarii* was a term used during the time of Caesar for soldiers specifically attached to a particular commander and so freed from ordinary duty by his *beneficium*. Under the Principate, the term came to mean a specific grade of staff officer within each military *officium*. During the early empire the *beneficiarii* were often elected from among the *frumentarii* and no doubt collected intelligence as the *frumentarii* did.

Beneficiarii consularis were also posted to stations along main roads and junctions in the empire. They supervised traffic acted as a police force, collected intelligence, levied customs duties and controlled local markets. They also performed courier services between the *territorium legionis* and the *territorium coloniae*. Their link with the *cursus publicus* was their principal duty in the Late Empire.

Curiosi—Certain high-ranking members of the *agentes in rebus* were given the responsibility of overseeing the *cursus publicus*. Several authors (Blum, Sinnigen, Hirschfeld, Clauss) believe that they constitute part of the Roman Secret Service. Others (Paschoud, Purpura) believe they did not.

Cursus publicus—The *cursus publicus* was the public road system with the accompanying postal service that acted as the arteries of a vast intelligence network which kept the emperor informed of events throughout his domain. Scholars disagree on whether Augustus was inspired by the pre-Roman systems of the Persians, the Greeks, and Ptolemaic Egypt or whether he invented the *cursus publicus* simply because the Roman empire needed a communications system.

Delatores—Under the reign of Augustus, a group of informers arose named *delatores* who turned in influential men on treason charges. They were notorious for making false accusations in the hope of enriching themselves. Some scholars believe that such men did not appear only in the empire, but that there was a republican tradition of informing. Such men were used in the treason trials under Tiberius.

Exploratores—Scouts who were formally part of the Roman cavalry but were attached from their units to go on missions. Their primary job was to locate the enemy. First attested in Caesar, we do not know how many scouts made up a scouting party, but there were usually at least two but not more than ten. Caesar always speaks of them in the plural. Under the empire there were ten attached in each legion.

Frumentarii—Roman military bureaucrats often dubbed 'the Roman Secret Service." Sinnigen suggests the Roman Secret Service was developed out of a basic reform instituted by Domitian (see Sinnigen, "Origins of the *frumentarii*") in the G-4 or supply section of the imperial general staff—the *praetorium*. The reforms involved the use of non-commissioned officers and sometimes centurions. Stated simply, the Roman Secret Service was staffed by supply sergeants whose original function had been the purchase and distribution of grain (*frumentum*), thus their name—*frumentarii*.

Logothete of the Drome—The official responsible for supervising the inspectors of the Byzantine imperial post which carried military intelligence between the emperor and his provincial governors. In the eighth century, this official became director of the Post itself.

Magister Officiorum—No modern parallel for this office exists. The Magister Officiorum's sphere of activities was made up of an aggregation of various powers which brought him into touch with many branches of government. Of great importance to intelligence gathering was his overseeing of the *agentes in rebus*, the *cursus publicus*, and the *scrinia* or the three secretarial bureaux responsible for imperial correspondence. In many ways his job resembled a Minister of Information.

Notarii—Imperial stenographers and secretaries of the late empire.

Being privy to imperial correspondence, put them in the position to handle a great deal of intelligence. Sinnigen referred to them as one of the two branches of the late imperial secret service (Sinnigen, *AJPh* 80 (1959) q.v.). *Notarii* were sometimes used for duties similar to the *agentes in rebus* usually in high level political cases.

Regendarius—Roman officers mentioned in the *Notitia Dignitatum* who were control officers drawn from the *agentes in rebus*.

Sator rebus—A word square that is considered one of the oldest unsolved cryptograms. It consists of five words: SATOR, AREPO, TENET, OPERA and ROTAS. The words form a palindrome. No universally accepted solution has ever been found.

Scytale—Traditionally described as a method of encrypting messages used by the Spartans. In the standard interpretation it consisted of a stick of known diameter around which a piece of leather or paper was wound. A message was written along the length of the stick. When the leather or paper was unwound, the message became unreadable until it was wound around an identical stick kept by the recipient. There is debate as to whether it was meant to conceal the content of a message that fell into enemy hands or prove the authenticity of the delivered message. Many later authors used the term to describe any secret or hidden message, even without the use of sticks.

Speculatores—*Speculatores* were military troops used as spies and scouts. Their primary role was to deliver dispatches (*litterae*) both between camps and from camps to Rome. Each of Caesar's legions had ten *speculatores* under the general staff. Under Augustus, they were used as couriers on the *cursus publicus*. While in Rome they were housed in the *Castra Pererinorum* along with the *frumentarii*. Although we know there were ten *speculatores* per legion, we do not know how many of them were detached to Rome, but they seem to have formed the second largest group in the camp. They were also used as assassins, arresting officers and spies. In Mark 6.27 it is a *speculator* who accompanies Saint Paul to Rome. Most of their policing duties were later taken over by the *frumentarii*.

Sycophants—Usually defined as a private informer in ancient Athens who turns people in for money. Some scholars have argued that sycophancy was a vitally important part of the nature and running of the Athenian democracy. In this view, sycophants prosecuted aristocrats who refused to do their full share politically and financially to support the governmental structure. Private litigation took from these rich men what they should have voluntarily given to the state and thus spread the money around. To others, they are just annoying snitches. Either way, they are a source of intelligence for whoever waned to use them.

Tabellarii—The magistrates in Rome used *tabellarii*, who were freedmen or slaves employed as couriers. These should not be confused with the *tabellarii* employed by the *publicani* whose letter-bearers also exercised the function of modern tax collectors. These latter *tabellarii* often carried private mail for important men, and, to reduce costs, friends often shared the services of a courier. These couriers were one of the few ways of sending intelligence in the Roman republic.

Tradecraft—An intelligence term for the skills taught to field agents in the espionage business. Running spy networks, using dead drops, the techniques of secret writing, flaps and seals, and escape and evasion. Except for our technical advances, examples of most of these techniques, or at least primitive versions of them, are found in the ancient world.

Veredarii—The *agentes in rebus* were, like their predecessors the *frumentarii*, organized as a military unit. They were classified like the palace guards as a *schola*. Their various recorded ranks suggest a cavalry unit, and they were often known by the name *veredarii*, or "dispatch riders." See *C.Th.* 8.5.17, AD 364.

Espionage—General

None of the entries in this section is specific to any one culture of the ancient world. The entries cover either all of antiquity or broad themes touched upon in all the other sections.

1. Dorjohn, Alfred P., "Smoke-Screens in Ancient Warfare," *Classical Bulletin* 35 (1959), p. 33.

Dorjohn discusses several examples of escape and evasion or smokescreens being used as diversions or deceptive signals to fool the enemy. The examples are taken from Polyaenus, the second-century Macedonian rhetorician who compiled eight books of stratagems for the emperors Marcus Aurelius and Lucius Verus as they set out for their Parthian campaign in AD 163.

2. Dorjohn, Alfred P., "Some Ancient Military Stratagems," *Classical Bulletin* 36 (1960), pp. 61–63.

Polyaenus, the second-century Macedonian rhetorician, compiled eight books of stratagems to serve as a guidebook for military leaders. He dedicated the book to the emperors Marcus Aurelius and Lucius Verus as they set out for their Parthian campaign in AD 163. Dorjohn highlights a few of the 833 extant examples of military stratagems. Sixty-three of them were attributed to Iphicrates, the fourth century Greek general.

3. Dvornik, Francis, *The Origins of Intelligence Services*, New Brunswick, N.J.: Rutgers University Press, 1974, 334 pp.

"The origins of intelligence services lie in the beginnings of human civilization and political organization; they are by no means a modern invention." With this idea, Dvornik goes on to write what still remains the only single-volume, English-language history of intelligence services in antiquity. He covers the ancient Near East and the Greeks, the Roman Empire, Byzantium, the Arab Muslim Empires, the Mongol Empire and finally the Muscovy State. The greater part of the book is devoted to late Rome and the Byzantine Empire with which the author is most familiar.

Father Dvornik demonstrates how rulers developed intelligence services for the defense of their countries, for political expansion, and for the security of the state and its dynasties. Rulers protected themselves against domestic and foreign threat, and used internal spying as the basic method of controlling their subjects. These empires operated at a time when they could neglect or ignore the social and economic welfare of their subjects. REVIEWED IN: Ludvik Nemec, *Annals of the American Academy of Rome* 416 (Nov 1974), pp. 197–198; *Choice* 11 (Nov. 1974) p. 1364; Frank Wozniak, *Balkan Studies* 17 (1976), pp. 399–400; Bertold Spuler, *Slavic Review* 34:1 (March 1975), p. 138.

4. Laquer, Walter, "Spying and Democracy. The Future of Intelligence," *Current Affairs* (March/April 1986), pp. 25–34.

One of the best articles on the craft of intelligence and its role in a democracy. Although it was written in the 1980s, Laquer's discussion of the role of a modern intelligence community is still relevant. His conclusions about how to maintain a good intelligence service is as applicable to the ancient world as it is to the modern: recruit promising individuals, use careful personnel evaluation, thorough assignment, extensive and systematic training in relevant subjects, a constant search for better means of collection, and the pursuit of efficiency with a minimum of bureaucratic procedure. There is no panacea for providing better intelligence, no sensational breakthroughs or approaches of which no one has thought before. These measures may seem prosaic, but time and again not following them has led to disaster. Had these rules been followed, Aldrich Ames would be not even a footnote in history, and September 11, 2001, might just be another date.

5. Neilson, Keith & McKercher, B.J.C., *Go Spy the Land. Military Intelligence in History*, Westport, CT.: Praeger, 1992, 208 pp.

A series of articles from various periods of history on the nature of military intelligence. Contributions include an introductory essay by Christopher Andrew on "The Nature of Military Intelligence," "Roman Military Intelligence," by Arther Ferrill, "Intelligence in the Hundred Years War," by Christopher Allmand, "The European Intelligence Community and the Spanish Armada, by Geoffrey Parker, "Diplomatic Cryptography and Universal Languages in the 16th and 17th centuries," by Gerhard F. Strasser, "Military Intelligence Gathering in the Second Half of the Eighteenth Century, 1740–1792 by Gunther Rothenberg, "Lord Salisbury, Secret Intelligence, and British Policy toward Russia and Central Asia, 1874–1878," by John Ferris, "Security Intelligence in Canada, 1864–1945: The History of a "National Insecurity State," by Wesley K. Wark, and a concluding essay on "Intelligence in Historical Perspective," by Michael Handel. REVIEWED BY: R.M. Sheldon, *Journal of Military History* (1994), pp. 139–140.

6. Pekáry, Thomas, "Nachrichtenwesen," *Lexicon der Alten Welt*, Zurich and Munich: Artemis Verlag, 1990, pp. 2052–2054

An encyclopedia entry on the movement of information in the ancient world. Pekary discusses military intelligence, optical signaling, postal systems, propaganda and espionage.

7. Piekalkiewicz, Janusz, *Weltgeschichte der Spionage: Agenten, Systeme, Aktionen*, Munich: Sudwest Verlag, 1988. English translation by William H. Henhoeffer and Gerald L. Liebenau. Translation privately printed by the National Intelligence Book Center, 1999, with a Preface by Dr. Richard Meier, Former President of the Federal Office for the Protection of the Constitution.

A translation of the classic work by Piekalkiewicz which is a history of espionage from earliest times to the present. Includes early chapters on the pharaohs, the Phoenicians and the Hittites, the Babylonians and the Assyrians, the Trojan War, ancient China, Persia, the Greeks, Rome and the Punic Wars, the Roman Empire, the Byzantine Empire, the Age of Islam and the Mongols.

The book was published privately after the author's death, and is "unfinished and only briefly edited" by the editors' own admission. The misspelling of the first word of the German title (*Weltgeschichte*) on the first page should be a forewarning of the editing problems.

8. Reincke, E.C., "Nachrichtenwesen" in Pauly-Wissowa, *Real-encyclopaedie der classischen Altertumswissenschaft*, Supplementband 4 (1924), col. 1495–1542.

A general overview of communications systems, both civilian and military, in the ancient world. Reincke begins by noting the differences between ancient and modern communications and the terms used for them. He then covers scouting and reconnaissance, signaling and telegraphy, official announcements both oral and written publication, the postal systems of Persia, the Ptolemies and the *cursus publicus* in Rome. He finishes with business and commercial communications. This is an excellent summary, but for a more detailed treatment, see Wolfgang, Riepl, *Das Nachrichtenwesen des Altertums* (no. **9**).

9. Riepl, Wolfgang, *Das Nachrichtenwesen des Altertums*, mit besonderer Rücksicht auf die Römer, Leipzig: B.G. Teubner, 1913, 478 pp.

This work is still the great grand-daddy of all books on intelligence activities in the classical world. Meticulously documented from the ancient sources, Riepl covers every aspect of the movement of information. Starting from its collection and transmission, he discusses signaling by means of fire smoke, flags, transmission across roads by foot and animal, and telegraphy of all kinds. He has several sections on secret writing and the use of codes and ciphers. He discusses internal security, secret police, private informers, espionage and counter-espionage, and covers both political and military topics. This book is essential for any collection on intelligence in the ancient world. It should be the very first source one consults.

10. Sheldon, R.M. "Toga and Dagger," *The Washington Post*, July 16, 1985 A 15. Reprinted in *Signal* (September 1985), pp. 55–57.

A short op-ed piece on the long history of intelligence activities. "Intelligence gathering is as old as civilization itself." So are spying, covert action, the problems of internal security vs. human rights and questions about the role intelligence activities play in a democracy.

The author concludes that the study of ancient intelligence would be useful to contemporary intelligence professionals because such research would provide the philosophical underpinnings for their profession. Similar study would be useful to academics to make them familiar with the historical background of intelligence and to show that such activities are not likely to go away. Intelligence history is a legitimate field of study that needs more work in different historical periods. Cooperation between academia and the intelligence profession in scholarship might help bridge the gap that separated them during the Cold War.

11. Wheeler, Everett L. *Stratagem and the Vocabulary of Military Trickery*, Mnemosyne Supplement 108, Leiden: Brill, 1988, 124 pp.

An exhaustive study of the word *stratagema*, or stratagems in Greek and Latin including an analysis of the attitude of ancient writers toward the use of stratagem and trickery. Two problems immediately occur. For the classicist, his jumping around indifferently from archaic to Byzantine Greece seems to give equal credibility to all sources. Does the Livian account of tricks used by Hannibal tell us about the Second Punic War, or attitudes from the Augustan Age? Secondly, traditions from very late writers are sometimes so dubious as to be completely worthless. (See the review of this book by J. F. Lazenby, *JHS*, p. 249.)

From the intelligence standpoint, the thesis that military trickery is millennia old, and that despite their propaganda to the contrary, both the Romans and the Greeks used it willingly, should come as no surprise. The same is true for the discovery that stratagem permits more to be accomplished without arms than with them—a truism known to anyone who has read Sun Tzu. Practitioners all recognize the theory; putting it into practice is the problem. And the observance that "a contrivance must have a reasonable rate of success to qualify as a stratagem" (or else they call it a screw-up?) seems self-evident. I certainly would give the ancients credit for knowing that if a stratagem failed, it should not be included in a book on examples worthy of imitation.

If one can get beyond these naive attempts to reinvent the wheel, this is the best study of the meaning of the word stratagem. Remember, however, that it is a study of vocabulary, not of the stratagems themselves. This book is promised as a *prologomenon* to a much Larger work on the history of the concept of stratagem in ancient military theory and international law. REVIEWED IN: Christopher Tuplin, *Classical Review* 40 (1990), pp. 403–404; J. Lazenby, *Journal of Hellenic Studies* 110 (1990), pp. 248–249; Labarbe, *Antiquité Classique* (1990), pp. 416–417.

Road Building, Communications, and Tradecraft

How intelligence, or for that matter news in general, traveled in the ancient world is a long and intricate subject far beyond the scope of this book.* As a metaphorical image of how fast information could travel, we might turn to Vergil's *Aeneid* (4.173; 7.144; 4.203) where he tells us *rumor volat*—rumor flies.

The Hittites, the Assyrians, the Persians, the Romans, the Byzantines and the Muslims each built upon the road system of their predecessors.

*For a study on Roman civilian and military transport, see Giuseppina Pisani Sartorio, *Messi di trasporto e traffico published by the Museo della Civiltà Romana* (Rome: Edizioni Quasar, 1988).

Postal systems sprang up on these roads and they carried intelligence to all corners of the empire. These were not the private postal services of modern times, but military intelligence networks that kept the emperor or king informed of activities along his borders and in potentially rebellious provinces. News traveled by means of fire signals, semaphore, voice signals, water clocks, carrier pigeon, telegraphy, runners, and heliographs. Transportation might be provided by horses, camels, mules, oxcarts, carriages and ships powered by oars or sails.

Governments spent almost as much time trying to prevent the flow of information as they did making the information flow. The introduction of writing was followed very closely by the invention of secret writing, or to use the word from the Greek, cryptography. Messages were kept secret by codes and ciphers, invisible writing, or by simply hiding the messages. In an age when the rate of literacy was quite low, was easy to put intelligence beyond the reach of the average citizen. Readers interested in rare books on cryptography should avail themselves of two marvelous collections. The Friedman Collection in the Marshall Library at the Virginia Military Institute houses over 3,000 books and articles on the subject of cryptography. William Friedman was a cryptographer during the Second World War, and his estate gave the collection to the Marshall Library. Friedman's interests ran from decipherment of military intelligence traffic to ancient languages and civilization. Charles Jastrow Mendelsohn, on the other hand, possessed a Ph.D in classical languages; he did his dissertation on Studies in Word-Play in Plautus.* He served as a cryptographer in the First World War. His collection is more strictly limited to military cryptography but he included volumes from the 16th and 17th century. His collection contains over 350 books and articles and is housed in the Annenberg Rare Book and Manuscript Library at the University of Pennsylvania.

Before the decipherment of Egyptian hieroglyphics, cuneiform, Etruscan, Mayan glyphs or Mycenaean Linear B, those languages were treated as "encoded" by many authors. Now that we can read them, they are simply ancient writing systems and so I have not included the literature which predates their decipherment, such as Bertainis', *Essai de déchiffrement de quelques inscriptions étrusques* (Leipzig, 1860). Another example would be the work of Giovanni Piero Valeriano Bolzani on Egyptian hieroglyphics (French edition 1576)—a work described as "more imagination than judgment." I have included, however, works about encipherment in ancient languages that we can now read. The Egyptians, for example, have a type of secret writing that is encoded even if one reads hieroglyphics and

*Penn dissertation, 1907. A copy is in the Mendelsohn Collection.

therefore I have included the literature on this secret writing. Languages that remain undeciphered or only partially deciphered such as Linear A or Etruscan, might still be considered unbroken codes.

Oppressed minorities sometimes found it necessary to communicate clandestinely or to recognize each other while staying undetected by the authorities. Just one example of Christian ingenuity in the Roman empire was the Sator-Rebus which has yet to be satisfactorily deciphered.

Certain authorities use the word *Sheshash* in Jeremiah 25:26 and 51:41 as proof of the utilization of ciphers by the early Hebrews. According to their interpretation these are examples of the use of the device, *Atbash*, whereby the last letter of the Hebrew alphabet is substituted for the first, the second-last for the second, etc. so that the word Babel is written cryptographically Sheshash. However, this interpretation has much opposition among authorities. For more information on this and similar Biblical ciphers see the article "Sheshash" by J. A. Selbie in Hastings, *A Dictionary of the Bible*, Charles Scribner and Sons, 1902, vol. 4, pp. 492–493; Joseph Halévy, *Mélanges d'Épigraphie et d'archéologie Sémitiques*, Paris 1874, p. 245. There is no room in this study for a treatment of cryptographic systems that are linked to Kabbalistic numerology.

12. Amit, Moshe, "Les moyens de communications et la défense de l'empire romain," *La Parola del Passato* 20 (1965), pp. 207–222.

The defense of the Roman empire depended on the government's ability to communicate with the provinces. To counteract the centrifugal tendencies that might tear the empire apart, the emperors devised a communications system that would tie the capital at Rome to each province, region and frontier of the empire.

Amit starts with a discussion of the *cursus publicus*. The Augustan system allowed for the provisioning of the army and the transportation of troops to places where revolts broke out. This system worked well for the first two hundred years of relative peace. After the time of Marcus Aurelius when revolts and invasions became more frequent, emperors were faced with the problems of fighting wars on two fronts. Emperors spent less and less time in Rome; only irresponsible leaders like Commodus or Elagabalus spent their entire reign in the capital.

Once one looks at the distances involved in transporting, provisioning and communicating with the army, one sees why there were problems in the later empire. These problems led to multiple emperors, the designation of new capitals, and a new military doctrine that would produce the total reorganization of the army.

13. Aschoff, Volker, *Geschichte der Nachrichtentechnik*. Beitäge zur Geschichte der Nachrichtentechnik von ihren Anfängen bis zum Ende des 18 Jahrhunderts. Berlin, Heidelberg, Tokyo, New York: Springer-Verlag, 1984.

A history of communications from the ancient world to the end of the eighteenth century. Aschoff includes the texts of the ancient writers Like Aeneas Tacticus, Polybius, Polyaenus, Sextus Julius Africanus, Vegetius etc. and discusses all the major forms of optical signaling in classical Greece and Rome and the Near East. He devotes chapters to the Greeks, the Romans, the Persians and Byzantine fire signaling as reported by Leo the Mathematician. A good analysis of the sometimes confusing and fragmentary sources. The book includes excellent drawings of the systems as they may have appeared and charts calculating how they would have worked.

14. Aschoff, Volker, *Aus der Geschichte der Telegraphen-Codes*, Opladen: Westdeutscher Verlag, 1981, 59 pp.

A history of the use of telegraphic codes in antiquity and from the invention of the telescope. Volker explains the telegraphing signaling systems described in Polybius (no. **51**) (ascribed to Kleoxenos and Demokleitos) and the one described by Julius Africanus in his *Kestoi* (no. **386**). He provides illustrations.

15. Aschoff, Volker, "Optische Nachrichtenübertragung im klassischen Altertum," NTZ (Nachrichtentechnische Zeitschrift) 30 (1977), pp. 26–31.

Short article on the optical transmission of communications in the classical world and a consideration of the sources upon which our knowledge is based. A summary of his book *Aus der Geschichte der Telegraphen-Codes* (no. **14**).

16. Belloc, Alexis, *La Télégraphie historique depuis les temps les plus reculés jusqu'à nos jours,* Paris: Librairie de Firmin-Didot et Cie, 1894, 2nd edition, 343 pp.

The first section covers telegraphy in antiquity including Egypt, India, China, Persia, Greece, Carthage, Rome and Byzantium. Section two then goes on to discuss telegraphy in France and the modern age.

This is a rare book. Dibner Library at the Smithsonian Institution and the University of Minnesota have copies.

17. Birt, Theodor, *Die Buchrolle in der Kunst. Archaeologisch-Antiquarische Untersuchungen zum antiken Buchwesen,* Leipzig: B. G. Teubner, 1907, 352 pp; New edition Hildesheim, New York: Olms, 1976, 352 pp.

A discussion of the *skytale* on pp. 274–275, with a line drawing that makes the *skytale* look suspiciously like a candy cane wrapped in leather.

18. Borza, Eugene N. *Travel and Communications in Classical Times. A Guide to the Evidence*, University Park, Pa., Pennsylvania State University, 1969, 158 pp.

A collection of evidence relating to travel and communication in antiquity. Five authors were examined: Herodotus, Thucydides, Xenophon, Livy and Strabo. Besides being a useful reference work for calculating the time it took to get from point A to point B, it allows us to consider the possibilities of what intelligence may have been obtained by a ruler or commander at any given moment. Borza uses the example of Alexander's burning of Persepolis and whether he knew of the Greek rebellion led by Agis III of Sparta before he did it. If it could be shown that Alexander knew of Agis' defeat before the destruction of the palace (assuming it was a deliberate act of policy) then the range of possible motives for the burning can be narrowed.

19. Casson, Lionel. "Speed under Sail of Ancient Ships," *Transactions and Proceedings of the American Philological Association* 82 (1951), pp. 136–148.

In calculating how fast news (and intelligence) could travel in the ancient world, one needs to know the speed of ancient sailing ships. Casson, an expert in this subject, reviews previous literature and shows why calculations by previous scholars may have been off the mark.

One of his suggestions is that one must classify voyages according to the winds encountered *en route*. Secondly, he suggests that voyages where it is likely that oars played a part should not be included in the calculations. His table of ancient voyages shows a consistent picture: In a favorable wind, a fleet could log between two and three knots. With unfavorable winds, a fleet usually could do no better than one to one and a half knots.

20. Crown, Alan D., "Messengers and Scribes: The *Sopher* and *Mazkir* in the Old Testament," *Vetus Testamentum* 24 (1974), pp. 366–370.

Crown discusses evidence from the Tell el-Amarna tablets on the role of messengers (*mar sipri*). They are seen in a full range of duties from carrying intelligence to transporting prisoners. They had considerable status and were privy to the innermost thoughts and confidences of the monarchs. The function of message carrying seems to have been institutionalized and message carriers were given the title *sopher*. Such messengers carried intelligence that was too sensitive to be set down in writing and thus had to be transmitted orally.

21. Crown, Alan D., "Tidings and Instructions: How News Travelled in the Ancient Near East," *Journal of the Economic and Social History of the Orient* 17 (1974), pp. 244–271.

A summary of the Hebrew, Egyptian and Akkadian evidence for messengers carrying intelligence. Crown distinguishes between "object communication" (e.g. the sending of items such as animal bodies"), fire signals or flag signals. He distinguishes between simple messages where speed was of the essence, and those of such complexity that more than simple signals had to be used. He also discusses the transmission of intelligence (specifically cypher messages) over long distances using fire, flag or trumpet blast.

22. de Witte, J., *Descriptions des antiquités et objets d'art qui composent le cabinet de Feu M. Le Chevalier E. Durand*, Paris: Didot Frères, 1836.

On p. 76, Lenormant identifies a *skytale* on a vase. Since this was a sale catalogue, the location of the vase is not known. It is not in the Louvre. Anyone knowing of its whereabouts should please contact the author.

23. Diels, Hermann, *Antike Technik,* B. G. Teubner Verlag: Leipzig and Berlin, 1914.

One of the early classics on ancient technology including doors and locks, artillery, pumps, etc. Of interest to students of intelligence is chapter four which covers ancient telegraphy. Diels discusses the *skytale* (although see the more recent discussions by Kelly no. **221**, and West no. **231**), the code inventions of Aeneas Tacticus (no. **144**) including drawings; the fire signaling system of the Persians, the water telegraph and other systems of telegraphy from Policies (no. **51**). In a later chapter, Dials discusses Greek fire.

24. Echols, Edward, "Military Dust," *Classical Journal* 47 (1952), pp. 285–288.

One of the many imponderables of war, according to Echols, is dust. It can be the sign of an approaching enemy or it may be used as an effective smoke screen when created by cavalry. Indeed, the use of dust to deceive an enemy is not uncommon in classical annals. Echols lists stratagems involving dust used by Ptolemy, Caesar, Epaminondas, Hannibal, and Marius.

25. Fischl, Hans, *Fernsprech-und Meldewesen in Altertum mit besonderer Berücksichtigung der Griechen und Römer*, Schweinfurt, 1904.

Part one contains a discussion of communications by telegraphy among the Greek and Romans: fire signals in the Persian War, the telegraphic methods mentioned in Polybius, and a myriad of references from other classical authors.

Part two of this work, *Die Brieftaube im Altertum und im Mittelalter* (Schweinfurt, 1909), covers the history of the carrier pigeon in classical and medieval times. Called the "engel der Könige" the carrier pigeon has a long history as a conveyer of messages beginning with Noah sending a dove to find land, making it the first documented example of aerial reconnaissance.

26. Fleissner von Wostrowitz, Eduard B., *Handbuch der Kryptographie. Anleitung zum Chiffriren und Dechiffriren von Geheimschriften*, Wien: L. W. Seidel & Sohn, 1881, 189 pp.

A general study of cryptography in which the work of is frequently commented upon. It stresses methods of deciphering. He gives Caesar's cipher and includes examples in the back of the book on which one can practice. He also discusses the use of codes among the Hebrew and Chinese. The second section contains an historical survey on ciphers from Caesar through Napleon.

Friedman Collection, No. 200; Mendelsohn Collection 652M F624.

27. Forbes, R. J. *Studies in Ancient Technology*, Leiden: E.J. Brill, 1965, Vol. 2, part 3. Land transport, pp. 131–190. (3rd edition 1993).

A detailed account of land transport in the ancient world. Included are discussions of the Persian Postal System, the Roman *cursus publicus*, and the Greek use of fire signals. Forbes also covers the medieval world, and Mauryan India.

28. Frend, W. H.C., "A Third Century Inscription Relating to Angareia in Phrygia" *Journal of Roman Studies* 46 (1956), pp. 46–56.

This inscription records three stages in a long drawn-out dispute between the Phrygian villages of Anossa and Antimacheia, which were both part of a great imperial estate in Turkey in the Third Century AD. The dispute concerned the allocation of the *angareia* for the *cursus publicus* which each of the villages was required to provide. This entailed the supply of animals for transport to move individuals and goods on behalf of the state (Holmberg no. **378**).

The inscription is important because of the light it sheds on the administration of the *angareia*. This was one of the legacies of the Persian and Hellenistic rulers to the administration of the Roman Empire (Rostovtzeff, "Angariae" no. **437**; Seeck, "Angareia" no. **445**). A text from Suidas (Bernhardy, 1853 ed. vol. 1, p. 46) shows that it continued to be levied in Byzantine territory as late as AD 1000. Thus it was an enduring factor in the lives of the peasants in Asia Minor for some 1,500 years, and was responsible for the movement of information in the empire for all that time. What is known about the details of its regulation and the basis for its assessment on individual communities comes from inscriptions such as these.

29. Galland, Joseph S. *An Historical and Analytical Bibliography of the Literature of Cryptology*, Evanston, Il., Northwestern University Studies in the Humanities, No. 10, 1945.

Freidman Collection—No. 617.

As the title suggests, a listing of the major works in cryptography with commentary and cross references. Includes entries on ancient authors, Aeneas Tacticus, Dio Cassius, Herodotus, Suetonius, etc. For students of cryptology in later periods, there are very useful entries on Trithemius.

30. Gallende Díaz, Juan Carlos, "Introducción a la criptografía histórica," *Boletin de la Sociedad Castellonense de Cultura* 69, 4 (1993), pp. 501–530.

An historical survey of crytography from classical times to the nineteenth century especially in Spain. Diaz describes each method starting with Julius Caesar's substitution cipher and then continues to the Benedictine method, the Richelieu cipher, transpositional ciphers, double substitutions, Masonic methods, and the systems of Trithemius, Alberti (1404–1472), and Cardano, etc. With illustrations.

31. Gardthausen, Viktor Emil, "Geheimschrift," in Pauly-Wissowa, *Realencyclopaedie der classischen Altertumswissenschaft*, Supplementband 4 (1924), pp. 517–521.

Encyclopedia entry on secret writing in antiquity. Examples described are the so-called Spartan *skytale* (see Leopold no. **223**, West no. **231**, Kelly no. **221**), Caesar's substitution cipher, mirror writing, numerical systems, etc. with listing of major nineteenth century bibliography.

32. Gruterus, Janus, *Inscriptiones antique totius orbis romani in absolutissimum corpus redactae olim auspiciis Iosphi Scaglieri et Marci Velseri, industria autem et diligentia Iani Gruteri* ... Amstelaedami, excudit F. Halma, 1707. 4 vol. In-fol.

All editions of this work contain engravings of the various arbitrary characters that are used in cryptographic schemes. The first edition, Heidelberg 1602, contains the complete list of Tironian notes collected by Gruter. For information on the author and his work see *Allgemeine Deutsche Biographie*, Vol. 10, pp. 68–71 and *Biographie Universelle*, Vol. 17, pp. 645–646. See also Giry, *Manuel de diplomatique*, p. 520; Prou, *Manuel de paléographie latine et française*, p. 48.

33. Harlow, Alvin F., *Old Post Bags*, New York: D. Appleton & Co., 1928.

A history of sending letters in ancient and modern times. The author distinguishes between intelligence sent by governmental officials and that sent by private citizens. He traces written communications from the earliest organized postal systems in Persia, Ptolemaic Greece, Rome and China. Chapter 3 deals with the Middle Ages in the West; Chapter 4 with the great medieval systems of China, Japan and Baghdad. Chapters 6–19 cover the modern world. With no footnotes, it is difficult to trace Harlow's sources, and he does not seem to use them critically. On page 22, for example, one would like to know where he found the reference to carrier pigeons being used on the *cursus publicus*.

34. Haswell, John H. "Secret Writing. The Ciphers of the Ancients and Some of Those in Modern Use," *The Century Illustrated Monthly Magazine*, Vol. 85, no. 1 (November, 1912), pp. 83–92.

Mendelsohn Collection 652M H277.

He gives as the oldest example of a cipher the Greek *skytale* as described by Plutarch. He also mentions Histiaeus and the slave with the tattoo on his head. His brief survey covers the classical and medieval worlds and the cipher of Sir Francis Bacon.

35. Hennig, Richard, *Die Älteste Entwicklung der Telegraphie und Telephonie*, Leipzig: Johann Ambrosius Barth, 1908, 199 pp.

The earlier chapters cover telegraphy in the ancient world. Section one is on fire signaling among the Greeks; Section two, the telegraph system described by Aeneas Tacticus; Section three is on the telegraphic system described by Polybius. Four and five cover Roman fire signaling. There are three sections on the Middle Ages, then sections ten to sixty-one cover the modern world. A solid work that shows the historical development of this important communications technology.

36. Hershbell, J. P., "The Ancient Telegraph." *Communication Arts in the Ancient World.* ed. Eric A. Havelock and J.P. Herschbell, New York: Hastings House, 1978, pp. 84–85.

Hershbell traces the use of fire signaling and the optical telegraphing systems discussed by Polybius, Aeneas Tacticus and Julius Africanus. He discusses not only military applications and innovations spawned by war, but also the connection between the development of the telegraph and the spread of literacy.

Recent work has cast doubt on whether any of these systems were actually put into use. Many may have been invented on paper but never implemented. Hershbell is rather accepting of the sources. Use of the term "telegraph" may be giving a coherence to these systems that they actually lacked in antiquity. Cf. Riepl, *Das Nachrichtenwesen des Alterrums*. For the technical requirements of ancient telegraphy, see entries for Volker Aschoff nos. **13–15**.

37. Isidorus (Saint, Bishop of Seville, d. AD 636), *Etymologiae*, ed. W. M. Lindsay, Oxford: The Clarendon Press, (1911), 2 vols.

Bk. I, ch. 24 contains references to Roman signs and abbreviations used in military documents to note casualties, mortalities, payment schedules, etc. See Lange and Soudart, *Traité de cryptographie* (no. **42**, p. 18, J. Galland, no. **29**, p. 96).

38. Kahn, David, *The Codebreakers. The Story of Secret Writing*, New York: Macmillan, 1967, pp. 1164; revised edition Scribner, 1996, 1181 pp.

The second chapter, entitled "The First 3,000 Years," is an excellent short summary on the history of cryptography. It covers Egypt, where the earliest mention of strange hieroglyphic writing was found. (See Drioton nos. **91**, **93**, Darnell no. **86**, and Deveria no. **87**.) He also discusses the Chinese, the Indians, the Mesopotamians, the Greeks and the Romans. Although there has been much work published on the Greek encryption system called the *skytale*, Kahn did not incorporate this material into the 1996 edition. See the *skytale* section under Ancient Greece.

39. Kahn, David, "On the Origin of Polyalphabetic Substitution," *Isis* 71,1; 256 (1980) 122–127.

The most widely used cipher system in the world is polyalphabetic substitution. In 1940, Charles J. Mendelsohn traced this cipher's first appearance to Leon Battista Alberti (1404–1472). Kahn investigates the source of Alberti's idea. He suspects that the source was the medieval Catalan mystic Ramon Lull (c. 1232–1315) who devised a mechanism for combining letters that stood for philosophical concepts in groups of three. Kahn goes on to describe the system in detail. There is apparently no document stating that Alberti knew of Lull, but the close resemblance of their disk systems suggests that there was borrowing. Kahn also discusses theories about where Lull might have gotten his inspiration.

40. Lacroix, Paul (Pseud. Bibliophile Jacob), *Les secrets de nos pères: La cryptographie, ou l'Art d'écrire en chiffres*, Paris: Adolph Delahays, 1858, 251 pp.

History of early cryptography, pp. 1–17; discusses the *skytale* on pp. 6–11. There is a bibliography on pp. 242–251.

Friedman Collection No. 88.

41. Lang, George B. (Pseud. Excalibur), "Ancient and Modern Cryptography," *The Cryptogram*, Burton, Ohio (June 1932), No. 3, pp. 2–3; (Feb. 1933), No. 7 pp. 7–8; (April 1933), No. 8, p. 1.

More modern than ancient, this work does not go beyond the Spartan *skytale* and Caesar's cipher in the ancient world. It includes biblical references to cryptography in Jeremiah.

42. Lange, André et Soudart, E.A., *Traité de cryptographie*, Paris: Librairie Félix Alcan, 1925, 366 pp. New edition 1935.

One of the standard French works on cryptography. It gives the history of cryptography, theories on ciphering, and examples and methods of deciphering codes. Most useful is the bibliographical list of about 100 items.

Friedman Collection—210.

43. Leighton, Albert C. "Secret Communications among the Greeks and Romans," *Technology and Culture*, 10, 2 (April 1969), pp. 139–154.

An excellent summary of the attempts by the Greeks and Romans to deny information to any but intended recipients. These technological feats required a high degree of ingenuity. Not just confined to cryptography, Leighton covers the entire field of secret communications, which in an age of such high illiteracy might even mean writing itself. Leighton suggests the possibility, although he admits proof is lacking, that the ancients possessed more sophisticated and secure methods of communication than are described in the surviving evidence. He wisely observes that persons and governments that have occasion to communicate secretly are unlikely to permit any excessive dissemination of their private secrets ... even to historians. Those privy to the "secrets of government" would not reveal them in literary works.

Topics are divided into transportation of information (runners, riders, bird couriers and the *cursus publicus*), hidden messages, invisible writing, bush telegraph, heliographs, fire signals, telegraphs, cryptography, secret writing and ciphers. On the *scytale*, see more recently: Kelly no. **221** and West no. **231**.

44. Lerville, Edmond, *Les cahiers secrets de la cryptographie*, Monaco: Éditions du Rocher, 1972, 318 pp.

A history of ancient cryptography and the process of decipherment from the Rosetta Stone through the Middle Ages, the Renaissance and the introduction of printing, Trithemius, Sir Francis Bacon, and the two world wars.

45. Meier, Samuel, *The Messenger in the Ancient Semitic World* (HSMS 45), Atlanta: Scholar's Press, 1988, 269 pp.

This is not a thorough analysis of all data with regard to messengers in the ancient Near East, but is confined to the *mal ak* of the west Semitic world and the *mar sipri* of Akkadian down to the Persian period.

The job of messenger was open to all, male or female, rich or poor, stranger or relative, prince, slave or scribe. Meier discusses passports required to travel along roads while delivering messages and road security. See also section on "documents written to deceive," pp. 174–7. What Meier does not cover is the possibility that messengers were also used as spies. In this Near Eastern context see J. L. Cunchillos, "*La'ika, mal'ak* et en semitique nord-occidental," *Rivista di Studi Fenici* 10 (1982), p. 160 who describes the *mal'ak* as "*le transmetteur de messages, l'espion,* [italics mine], l'auteur d'actions aussi disparates que la destruction d'une armée, le fait d'amener une femme ou de tirer quelqu'un d'une citerne."

46. Merriam, Augustus Chapman, "Telegraphing Among the Ancients," *Papers of the Archaeological Institute of America,* Classical Series 3, no. 1 (1890), pp. 1–32.

Telegraphing among the ancients, specifically the Greeks, from the earliest mention in Homer through the Peloponnesian war. A pithy account of telegraphing that does not just cover Aeneas Tacticus and Polybius, but the full gamut of Greek literature. Cf J.P. Hershbell, "The Ancient Telegraph."

47. Millar, C. M. H. "Some Escapes and Escapers in the Ancient World," *Greece and Rome* 5 (1958), pp. 57–61.

Since tradecraft techniques are taught to spies, this article on ancient escape techniques has a certain relevance to intelligence field work. Topics include ancient sources on disappearing in crowds, escaping slaves, escaping POWs, and creating disguises. See especially the story on captive men escaping from priestesses holding them captive, and the story of Aristomenes and men who run with the foxes.

48. Minos, Johannes, *Ein neuentdecktes Geheimschriftsystem der Alten.* Mit Proben aus Nikander, Catull, Tibull, Properz, Ovid, Vergil, Horaz, Phaedrus, Val. Flaccus, Martial und andern, und mit einem Nachwort über Akrostichen bei den klassischen Dichtern der Griechen und Römer, Leipzig: Fock, 1901. 64 pp.

Minos is the anagram for Simon. He finds acrostic messages and anagrams hidden in Roman elegaic poems of Ovid, Vergil and Livy. For those who love word games, this will be amusing. Reminiscent of the recently published book by Michael Drosnin, *The Bible Code* (New York: Simon & Shuster, 1997). One can find hidden messages anywhere one wishes to find them.

49. *Old Testament*

Hebrew tradition lists three different word transformations in the Old Testament; none are recorded in the New Testament. The first two are Jeremiah 25:26 and 51:41. The words *Sheshach* and *Leb Kamai* have embarrassed biblical scholars who cannot agree on their use and meaning. See David Kahn, *Codebreakers* (no. **38**), pp. 77–79 for a full explanation of the system. The third example of letter substitution is called "Atbah" and it is based on Hebrew numbers.

There have been many ingenious explanations as to translations and why secrecy would be the goal. Kahn believes, along with other modern authorities, based on examples from other cultures, that scribes have a predilection for amusing themselves with word and alphabet games and that this is the best explanation for these "ciphers."

For the best commentaries on Sheshach see "Sheshach" in *Encyclopedia Biblica*, eds. T.K. Cheyne and J. Sutherland Black, New York: Macmillan Co., 1903, which proposes "editorial manipulation" as a probable answer. A.S. Peake, ed., *Jeremiah and Lamentations*, II, *The New Century Bible*, New York: Henry Frowde, Oxford University Press, 1912, pp. 20–21 with extensive references.

50. Pogge, Adolph, *Die Bedeutung und das Wesen der Antiken Telegraphie*, Frankfurt am Main: 1867.

Not available at press time.

51. Polybius, *The Histories*, translated by W.R. Paton, Loeb Classical Library edition, Cambridge: Harvard University press, 1979, 6 vols.

In book 10.43–47, Polybius has a long passage on fire-signaling. He discusses systems described by previous authors, notably Aeneas Tacticus, Kleoxenos and Demokleitos. For a more detailed description of these systems by modern communications experts, see entries for Aschoff, nos. **13**, **14**, **15**.

52. Poppe, Adolph, *Die Telegraphie von ihrem Ursprunge bis zur neuesten Zeit unter besonderer Beruucksichtigung der ausgeführten telegraphischen Systeme*. Frankfurt am Main: S. Schmerische Buchhandlung, 1848, 75 pp.

A short history of telegraphic communications that begins with the classic texts of the Greeks and Romans: Homer, Pindar, Aeschylus, Sophocles, Herodotus, Thucydides, Polybius, Julius Caesar, Diodorus Siculus, Pliny the Elder, Pausanius, Julius Africanus, Suidas and Vegetius. It then skips ahead to the 18th century.

53. Reinke, E. C. "Classical Cryptography" *Classical Journal* 50 (October 1962–May 1963), pp. 113–121.

The Greeks and Romans possessed a knowledge of cryptography, and they practiced it. Reinke summarizes the various systems for the uninitiated reader. He includes the hidden message in Herodotus 7.239 that warned King Leonidas of the Persian invasion of Greece, and the famous tattooed slave whose head carried the message about the Ionian revolt. He goes into detail about the transpositional cipher of the Spartan *skytale* which has since been refuted (Kelly no. **221**, West no. **231**) and the substitution cipher of Caesar. Finally, he discusses the cryptic memorandum of the Catilinarian conspirator P. Cornelius Lentulus Sura, as quoted verbatim in Cicero's third oration against Catiline.

54. Suess, Wilhelm, "Über Antike Geheimschriftenmethoden und ihr Nachleben," *Philologus*. Zeitschrift für das Klassische Altertum, Leipzig 78 (June, 1922), pp. 142–75.

A survey of ancient methods of secret communication and a good discussion on how this material held interest for Renaissance writers. Among the methods discussed are Caesar's cipher (Reinke, no. **53**), secret writing in Aeneas Tacticus (Sheldon, *Tradecraft* no. **205**), the fire signaling in Polybius, the *scytale* (Leopold no. **223**, Kelly no. **221**, West no. **231**), codes in Cicero's letters to Atticus (Dodge, no. **266**), and secret writing in Ovid (Sheldon, *Tradecraft*, no. **206**).

55. Volts, James D., and Shulman, David, *Bibliography of Cryptography. A Catalogue of Books Pertaining to the Science of Codes and Cyphers*, Cincinnati, 1938. 1941 edition, 93 pp.
A short but useful bibliography of books on cryptography.
Mendelsohn Collection 652M V887

56. Wagner, F., "Studien zu einer Lehre von der Geheimschrift (Chiffernkunde)," *Archivalische Zeitschrift* 13 (1888), pp. 8–44.
A history of early cryptography. Wagner includes a discussion of the ancient sources plus a bibliography of the oldest studies on the Spartan *skytale* on p. 41. His study also covers 15th, 16th, 17th and 18th centuries.

57. Weintraub, Joseph, "Cryptography, an Ancient Art, "*The American Hebrew*, 148, No. 12, (January 31, 1941), pp. 7, 11.
Weintraub describes the Cabalistic cipher systems used by the ancient Jews. He includes the *athbash* cipher that was used in the Bible in the Book of Jeremiah, and the *albam* cipher that appears in the Book of Isaiah (on which, see Kahn, *The Codebreakers* no. **38**).

58. Winter, Werner, "Armenian Cryptography," *The Armenian Review* (Autumn, 1955), pp. 53–56.
Notes on some samples of Armenian cryptography in the collection of H. Kurdian, Witchita, Kansas. They come from three manuscripts—two dating to the sixteenth century and one dating to the seventeenth century. The systems used seem to be simple substitution ciphers, and the first manuscript contains three of them. The author includes an illustration of the seventeenth-century manuscript.

The Ancient Near East

Mesopotamia and Palestine

59. "albam" A cryptographic transformation in the Old Testament (see also Sheshach [no. **80**] and Leb Kamai [no. **71**]) that consisted of a substitution system. It splits the Hebrew alphabet in half and equates the two halves. Thus the first letter of the first half, aleph, substitutes for the first letter of the second half; lamed, and vice versa. The system is explained in David Kahn, *The Codebreakers*, p. 78. According to the Midrash Rabbah (Numbers 18:21), the name Tabeel in Isaiah 7:6 is an albam transformation for Remala or "Remaliah" who figures in verses 1 and 4. Most scholars regard Tabeel as a corruption or some form of contemptuous epithet, and not as albam. See "Tabeel" in *Encyclopedia Biblica*, and George B. Gray and A.S. Peake, *A Critical Commentary on the Book of Isaiah*, International Critical Commentary, New York: Charles Scribner's Sons, p. 118. Isaac Landman (ed.) *Universal Jewish Encyclopedia*, New York: The Universal Jewish Encyclopedia, Inc., Vol. 3.

60. "atbah." Another form of Hebrew letter substitution. Like atbash and albam, its name stems from its system. This is based on Hebrew numbers, which, like Roman numerals, were written with the letters of the Hebrew alphabet. This system is not used in the Old Testament, but there is at least one use in the Babylonian Talmud (*Seder Mo-ed*, Sukkah, 52b), ed. Rabbi I. Epstein, London: Soncino Press, 1938, p. 249 and notes. This example plays on the word "Witness" and its atbah substitution "Master" to make a moral point. See David Kahn, *The Codebreakers* (no. **38**), p. 79; Isaac Landman (ed.) *Universal Jewish Encyclopedia*, New York: The Universal Jewish Encyclopedia, Inc., Vol. 3.

61. "atbash." A form of substitution cipher in which the last letter of the Hebrew alphabet replaces the first, and vice versa; the next to last replaces the second, and vice versa and so on. It is the Hebrew equivalent of a=z, b=y, c=x. The system is described in David Kahn, *The Codebreakers*, p. 77–78. See entries on Leb Kamai (no. **71**) and Sheshach (no. **80**) which are both the products of this system. Isaac Landman (ed.) *Universal Jewish Encyclopedia*, New York: The Universal Jewish Encyclopedia, Inc., Vol. 3.

62. Bauer, J. B., "Aut maleficus aut alieni speculator," *Biblische Zeitschrift* 22 (1978), pp. 109–115.

Bauer's obscure argument focuses on an opening quote taken from an unidentified quotation from the Bible. The quotation says: when one of you is to suffer, be it not because you be a murderer, a thief, or because you do evil or mixes in strange things. He identifies the nature of the first two derelictions, and seeks to explain the nature of the last two.

The term *alieni speculator*, coined by Tertullian, is a construction from an older Latin expression, *curas alienas agens*, and *speculator* that carried the meanings of spy. Bauer concludes the footnote on page 113 with the assertion that Tertullian's phrase *alieni speculator* might refer to members of the Roman intelligence establishment although not exclusively. He tries to cover all bases in an attempt to further explain the derelictions mentioned in the opening quote.

63. Cline, Eric, *The Battles of Armageddon*. Megiddo and the Jezreel Valley from the Bronze Age to the Nuclear Age, Ann Arbor: The University of Michigan Press, 2000, 239 pp.

A discussion of all the major battles fought at Megiddo. The famous battle between Thutmose III and the Canaanites in 1479 BC is treated in chapter one. See entries by Faulkner (no. **100**) and Nelson (no. **112**).

64. Dossin, Georges, "Signaux lumineux au Pays de Mari," *Revue d'Assyriologie et d'archéologie orientale* 35 (1938), pp. 174–185.

The discovery of ostraca (potsherds) in Hebrew dating to the time of the prophet Jeremiah at Lachish confirm that in the 6th century BC, there were fire signals used in Palestine in times of war. Found by J. L. Starkey at Tell ed Douweir, letter IV from Lachish has an exegesis of the text of Jeremiah 6.1 that mentions a signal fire used during the siege of Jerusalem. Judges XX .38 mentions a signal to begin an ambush used while the Israelites were fighting the Benjaminites.

Letters found in the Palace at Mari by André Parrot tell of a communication system that employed fire signals dating back as far as 2,000 BC. A small tablet is of particular interest. Dossin translates it. It is addressed to Zimri Lim, the king, by a servant named Bannum. The Benjaminites are using fire signals to send a message from village to village that there will be hostile action against the king of Mari. A letter from Isme Dagan, Prince of Ekallatum, to his brother Yasmakh-Adad talks of a postal organization and signal fires linking the villages along the Tigris and the Euphrates.

All these pieces of evidence point to a developed system of signal fires in use at Mari around 2,000 BC. No other Akkadian or Sumerian texts seem to provide similar evidence. Dossin concludes that the kings of Mari were, therefore, the inventors of the system.

65. Fish, T., "Letters from the War Front in Ancient Mesopotamia," *Bulletin of the John Rylands Library* 26 (1942), pp. 287–306.

Letters from the library of King Assurbanipal describe the military life of the Assyrian empire, which the author, in his 1942 politically-charged jargon, calls the Assyrian Reich. There was much information gathered by Assyrian military intelligence concerning troops strengths of the enemy, and their locations. Spies operate covertly, scouts do reconnaissance, fifth columnists subvert from within. There seems to be a full range of intelligence activities described showing that the Assyrian kings appreciated accurate intelligence delivered in a timely manner. They needed it to detect revolts, root out disloyal subordinates or allies, and they resorted to deporting entire populations if necessary.

66. Gadd, C.J., and Campbell Thompson, R., "A Middle Babylonian Chemical Text," *Iraq* 3 (1936), pp. 87–96.

The oldest encipherment appears on a tiny cuneiform tablet about 3 × 2 inches dated to the middle of the second millennium BC. It was found at the site of Seleucia on the Tigris and contains the earliest known formula for making pottery glazes. The scribe was jealously guarding his professional secret by writing in cuneiform, but using the least common values for certain signs, creating a form of cryptography. The scribe also truncated sounds by ignoring the final consonant of several syllabic signs and spelled the same word with different signs at different places. As the knowledge of glaze-making spread, the need for secrecy disappeared. Later examples of glaze recipe texts from Nineveh dating to the 7th century are in plaintext. Cf. David Kahn, *The Codebreakers*, p. 75.

67. *Gematria.* A permutation of *atbash.*

See Solomon Gandz, "Hebrew Numerals," *Proceedings of the American Academy for Jewish Research* 4 (1932–1933), pp. 53–112 especially 89, 94.

68. "Handwriting on the Wall." Perhaps the most famous cryptogram in the world that appears in the Bible in Daniel 5. The message appears ominously on the wall at Balthazzar's feast: *Mene mene tekel upharsin.* The real mystery is not what the words mean but why the king's wise men could not read it. The words themselves are ordinary roots in Aramaic, the language in which Daniel is written. They mean "numbered," "weighted" and "divided." When Balthazzar summoned Daniel, the latter had no difficulty in reading the handwriting and interpreting the three words: *Mene*, God hath numbered thy kingdom, and brought it to an end. *Tekel*, thou art weighed in the balances and art found wanting, *Peres*, thy kingdom is divided [*perisa*] and given to the Medes and Persians. There is an extra play on *Peres* which, in Aramaic, would be identical with *upharsin.* The message may also refer to a series of pieces of money whose names stem from the Aramaic roots: a *mina*, a *tekel*, and a *peres* (a half *mina*). Cyrus Gordon came up with an ingenious American equivalent: You will be quartered, halved and cent to perdition. For whatever reason, the Babylonian priests could not read the text, but Daniel did and thus became the first cryptanalyst.

See John D. Prince, *Mene Tekel Upharsin*, Baltimore, 1893, and E.G. Kraeling, "The Handwriting on the Wall," *Journal of Biblical Literature* 63 (1944), pp. 11–18. David Kahn, *The Codebreakers* p. 79 and note p. 988. Solomon Gandz, "Hebrew Numerals," *Proceedings of the American Academy for Jewish Research* 4 (1932–1933), pp. 53–112 especially 89, 94.

69. Harper, R.F., *Assyrian and Babylonian Letters belonging to the Kouyunjik Collections of the British Museum*, in Decennial Publications of the University of Chicago, 2nd series (Chicago, 1902), 14v.

Letters concerning lazy postal officials who impeded the intelligence carried by the royal postal service going to and from Nineveh.

Letter 444 shows reports of spies in Armenia. "With reference to what the king wrote saying 'Send out spies,' I have sent them out twice; some came back and made reports detailed in the letter to the effect that five enemy lieutenants have entered Uesi in Armenia, together with commanders of camel-corps; they are bringing up their forces which are of some strength" (Dvornik translation).

Letter 296 reports finding sympathizers willing to give useful information. Deserters are a useful source on intelligence in Letter 434. And King Esarhaddon himself sends special instructions to his agents on the frontier asking for a written statement of "the tale they [the deserters] have to tell" in Letter 434.

Assyrian intelligence is active in Armenia as we can see from the reports sent to King Sargon (No. 381, 444, 492). They report that the king of Armenia was rewarding Assyrian deserters with fields and plantations (Letter 252). The same offer is made by the Elamites who offered free pasture in the meadow to those providing useful information (Letter 282). King Assurbanapal is warned not to admit certain people into his presence who are suspected of being a fifth column for the Elamites (Letters 277, 736).

The king's agents report any sign of disloyalty among his subjects (No. 774, 1263). The agents study carefully what is said in the streets of the occupied cities and dutifully report to the court any details of anti-Assyrian propaganda. (Letters 1114, 1204).

70. Jones, Tom Bard, and Snyder, John W., *Sumerian Economic Texts from the Third Ur Dynasty,* a catalogue and discussion of documents from various collections. Minneapolis: University of Minnesota Press, 1961, 421 pp.

See pp. 293–302 on the postal system at Lagash. Cf. Casson, *Travels*, London, 1974, p. 147.

71. "Leb Kamai." A word transformation in Jeremiah 51:1 has generated a considerable literature. It substitutes LEB KAMAI ("heart of my enemy") for Kashdim ("Chaldaeans"). The substitution uses a traditional form called "atbash." The system is described in David Kahn, *The Codebreakers*, p. 77–78. This substitution has embarrassed biblical scholars for years because no one really knows why it was done. There have been numerous ingenious explanations for why such an odd result as *leb kamai* would be desired or why secrecy was wanted. Some have suggested Shesach was the name of a Babylonian district. The best explanation remains that scribes liked to play with words and create alphabet games. The earliest traditional reference is Targum Jonathan, Jeremiah 51:1. See *Leb Kamai* in *Encyclopedia Biblica* which suggests the encipherment could be "the trifling of a scribe in *athbash*, but could also be a corruption of other words."

There are numerous examples in other cultures, see Patterson "Jeux des Moines" (no. **588**), and Margoloiuth no. **186** on Greek colophons.

See also "Cryptography" in Isaac Landman (ed.) *Universal Jewish Encyclopedia,* New York: The Universal Jewish Encyclopedia, Inc, Vol. 3, and Solomon Gandz, "Hebrew Numerals," *Proceedings of the American Academy for Jewish Research* 4 (1932–1933), pp. 53–112 especially 89, 94.

72. Leichty, Erle, "The Colphon," in *Studies Presented to A. Leo Oppenheim*, (Chicago: Oriental Institute, 1964), pp. 147–154.

Babylonian and Assyrian scribes sometimes used rare or unusual cuneiform signs in signing and dating their clay tablets. These ending formulas, called colophons, were short and stereotyped. The substitution of different signs were sometimes used, probably not to conceal anything as much as to show off the scribe's knowledge of cuneiform to later copyists. In the final period of cuneiform writing (1st century BC), in colophons written in Uruk under the Seleucid kings, occasionally scribes converted their names into numbers. Because colophons are so stereotyped, and because many use only one or two numbers, scholars have been able to cryptanalze them.

Leichty analyzed the signature at the foot of a large tablet reciting a myth of the goddess Ishtar that might be an indirect source of the biblical story of Esther, whose name might be another version of "Ishtar." The signature reads "tuppi [I]21 35 35 26 44 apil [I]21 11 20 42" or tablet of Mr. 21 35 35 26 44, son of Mr. 21 11 20 42. Leichty suggests that the solution was a "tablet for Mr. Anu-aba-uttirri, son of Mr. Anu-bel.su-nu" whose father-son relationship is well known.

The equivalencies that Leichty used were worked out by Otto Neugebauer (ed.), *Astronomical Cuneiform Texts,* Princeton, NJ: Institute for Advanced Study by Lund Humphries, London, 1955. I, 11, 161–163 for a lunar eclipse tablet.

73. Luckinbill, D.D., *Ancient Records of Assyria and Babylonia*, (Chicago: University of Chicago Press, 1926–27, 2 vols. Reprint edition, New York: Greenwood Press, 1968.

Royal scribes in the Assyrian empire accompanying troops jotted down the distances between important points in the empire through which the troops had passed and the time taken by the army to traverse them. Vol. II, no. 537 records the campaign of Esarhaddon against Bazu in just such notations.

The new communications system established by Assurbanipal worked efficiently. We see revolts being put down efficiently because they were detected early and the intelligence was sent to the king in time to act swiftly. See II, no. 900 and 901 on the invasion of the Ethiopians. II, 989 records signal fires lighted at fixed distances (see C. Fries [no. **119**] on the Babylonian Fire signal system).

Assurnasirapli gets news of a revolt by Suru of Bit-Halupe, *Records* I, 433.

Sargon II gets news of an uprising in Syria II, no, 5, 6. His agents discover a plot in Armenia in the seventh year of his reign, in II.12; See also II.60 where Azuri, King of Ashdod plans to stop paying tribute; Sargon's agents get wind of it before the plot matured. Azuri was replaced by his brother who may have been Sargon's informant (II.62).

Esarhaddon learns of the treachery of the king of Sidon and caught him "like a fish in the sea" in II.511

74. Munn-Rankin, J. M., "Diplomacy in Western Asia," *Iraq* 18 (1956), pp. 68–110.

Studies of the role of the messenger in Mari and the north Mesopotamian city states in relation to their diplomatic function. According to Munn-Rankin, the main function of the Mari messenger-diplomats was to carefully observe the military, economic and diplomatic activities of the countries to which they were sent and to report their findings back to the king; in other words, they were to be spies. See p. 104.

75. Pinches, T. G. "Sumerian or Cryptography," *Journal of the Royal Asiatic Society*, London, (1900), pp. 75–96.

Pinches wrote and presented papers on the non-semitic dialects that appeared in Babylonian and Assyrian inscriptions which he argued were Sumerian loan words. Another Assyriologist, Halévy, however, believed these non-semitic elements were not really languages but a form of cryptography or "allographic systems of writing." Pinches attacks this theory pointing out that this " allography " seems to have had dialects. The "foreign" elements are just Sumerian words that had been adopted as happens whenever two culture comes together or have close communications with each other.

If one reads between the philological arguments, one can see a very clear racial discussion going on here (laughingly illustrated by a discussion over whether short noses or long curved ones were preferable in ancient Mesopotamia). The anti-Akkadists contend there is no non-semitic idiom but only a kind of cryptography that they call a "hieroglyphic system" of writing. The real question is did the civilization of ancient Babylonia originate with the semitic population or with the Sumerian? Pinches favors the latter.

76. Pritchard, James Bennett, (ed.) *Ancient Near Eastern Texts Relating to the Old Testament*, Translators and annotators: W.F. Albright and others. Princeton: Princeton University Press, 1955, 710pp. 3rd edition with Supplement 1969.

See pp. 584–586 in particular 585. The first postal system recorded in history was at Shulgi that dates somewhere around 2100 to 2050 BC. A similar system was established at Lagash, cf. T. Jones-I. Snyder.

77. Saggs, H.W.F., "Assyrian Warfare in the Sargonid Period," *Iraq* 25 (1963), pp. 145–154.

An interesting, if controversial, account of Assyrian psychological warfare. See p. 151 where Sargon II of Assyria leaves a vivid account of what it is like to be in action when all communication has been cut off: "I could not give ease to their weariness, I could not give them water to drink, I could not set up the camp, I could not organize the defense of the headquarters and could not direct my advance guards…"

78. Sasson, J.M., *The Military Establishments at Mari*. Rome: Pontifical Biblical Institute, 1969, 101 pp.

Mari was a city-state prominent in northern Mesopotamia in the second millennium BC until it was destroyed by the army of Hammurabi. As the title implies, Jack Sasson has studied various aspects of the military establishment at Mari including soldiers, weaponry, chariotry, siege devices, etc. Among the most interesting chapters is that on psychological warfare (37ff). It is quite clear that these Mesopotamians understood the importance of timely intelligence and made the connection between having sufficient information on the enemy and winning a war. There was even a special bureau at the palace of Mari dedicated to targeting, collecting, evaluating and disseminating daily intelligence of all kinds. The intelligence cycle was thus alive and well in 1750 BC. For a summary of the intelligence activities at Mari, see Sheldon, "Spying in Mesopotamia" (no. **79**).

79. Sheldon, R.M., "Spying in Mesopotamia: The World's Oldest Classified Documents" *Studies in Intelligence*, 33, 1 (Spring, 1989).

Archaeological excavations at the ancient Mesopotamian city-state of Mari have been going on since the 1930s. It is one of the most important sites in the Habur plains, and the information gathered has been so abundant that there is a journal dedicated to publishing the finds and related topics. The palace at Mari actually had a bureau set up to collect intelligence. One head of this bureau is known to us; his name was, appropriately, "little knat." One can just imagine him buzzing around the palace collecting rumor, gossip or information from visiting dignitaries to report back to the king. There is even one tablet that has survived and has written across it "This is a Secret Tablet," making it perhaps the world's oldest classified document. Not surprisingly, it was an execution order.

80. "Sheshach," in *Encyclopedia Biblica*, T.K.Cheyne and J. Sutherland Black, eds., New York: The Macmillan Company, 1903.

There are three word transformations in the Old Testament (none in the New Testament). In Jeremiah 25:26 and 51:41 the form SHESHACH appears in place of Babel (Babylon). There cannot be a secrecy motive for this since the second reference clearly mentions Sheshach in one line and then Babylon in the next. This particular commentary proposes simply "editorial manipulation" as the answer to its use.

The commentaries on scripture are, of course, endless. For the earliest traditional reference, see Midrash Rabbah, Numbers 18:21, trans. Judah H. Slotki, eds. Rabbi H. Freedman and Maurice Simon, London: Soncino Press, 1939, p. 739. See also A.S. Peake, ed. *Jeremiah and Lamentations*, II, *The New Century Bible*, New York: Henry Frowde, Oxford University Press, 1912, pp. 20–21 which has extensive references. (no. **37**) David Kahn, *The Codebreakers*, (no. **37**), p. 77

81. Yadin, Yigael, *The Art of Warfare in Biblical Lands*, New York: McGraw-Hill, 1963, 2 vols.

Volume I, part 4, pp. 73ff. covers communications and intelligence very briefly. There is not much more discussed than fire signals, and that evidence is from Mari (Sasson, no. **78**). Part V, pp. 99ff talks about the famous siege of Jaffa by Thutmose III and the taking of the city by means of a ruse. Pages 104 ff cover surprise attacks, and pages 110ff have another brief discussion of intelligence. Volume II has a section on "siege, ruse and psychological warfare." Not a very thorough discussion of the subject; most of the book is dedicated to arms and armor. REVIEWED BY: *Library Journal* 89:864 February 15, 1964; *Natural History* 73:8 October 1964; *New Statesman* 67:338 February 28, 1964; *New York Times Book Review* December 22, 1963; *Scientific American* 210: 152 April, 1964; *Times (London) Literary Supplement* p. 176. February 27, 1964.

Egypt

The Egyptians set up the first intelligence networks in the world. Starting with the earliest dynasties, the pharaohs were constantly sending out agents to explore the world of the Nile valley and the deserts that surrounded it. Economic intelligence on the location of gold mines, sources of precious and semi-precious stones, and the location of neighbors who might be useful allies or mercenaries were all high on the list of Egyptian priorities. By the Middle Kingdom, the Egyptians had already established forts in Nubia to protect the land they had conquered and exploit its economic resources. The more territory they conquered, the more intelligence they needed to detect traitors, put down revolts, and keep the provinces secure.

Among the many interesting things the Egyptians developed, was a form of secret writing sometimes referred to as "enigmatic" or "esoteric" writing. As if deciphering Egyptian hieroglyphics was not difficult enough, the ancient Egyptians have made it harder for us by using cryptograms in religious texts to obscure certain information from the casual reader. This type of hieroglyphic writing was especially popular in the Late and Graeco-Roman periods, but it goes back as far as the Old Kingdom.

Enigmatic writings play with the pictorial nature of hieroglyphic writing. Although words are written with groups of pictures, they do not usually mean what the pictures show. That is to say, the sign for "mouth" can mean mouth, but more often it is just the phonetic sound "r" in a word. Most words come to have three of four conventional spellings, although innovative use of signs was never ruled out completely. New writings and even new signs could be invented.

In these enigmatic writings, therefore, the scribe has consciously chosen signs that are non-standard, usually that play on some sort of esoteric associations known only to an educated elite (or in some cases, perhaps only to the scribe himself). So an apparently pictorial representation of a procession of gods can be augmented in inconspicuous places by little hieroglyphs that allow the whole scene to be read as a text.

Professor Ann Macy Roth, of Howard University who supplied the information for several entries, brought to my attention the particularly ludicrous example of two very late hymns to Khnum carved at the entrance to Esna Temple. One was written with row after row of rams, and the other with row after row of crocodiles. In each case, the animal was augmented by some little signs that indicated which word each of the rams/crocodiles was meant to represent. This example illustrates the way that this kind of writing was used: it is obscure and esoteric and hard to understand (like the god himself), and the signs used also have a religious meaning since Khnum was worshipped as a ram and a crocodile at Esna.

82. Breasted, James Henry, *Ancient Records of Egypt. Historical Documents from the earliest times to the Persian conquest, collected, edited and translated.* Chicago: The University of Chicago Press, 1906–1907; New York: Russell & Russell, 1962, 5 vols, and the latest edition with an introduction by Peter A. Piccione, Urbana: University of Illinois Press, 2001.

A superb collection of documents from ancient Egypt that includes many of the primary sources for their intelligence activities. See especially Vol. I. 486 from the Reign of Amenemhet I, the "Tale of Sinuhe." This famous Middle Kingdom texts shows the information lines of information movement between Egypt and Palestine. Vol. II. 408–443 from the reign of Thutmose III contains the evidence for the Battle of Megiddo (on the same battle, Faulkner [no. **100**] and Nelson [no. **112**]). Vol. III. 294–391 from the reign of Ramses II, likewise gives the evidence for the Battle of Kadesh; see Burne (no. **84**), Faulkner (no. **99**), and Kuentz (no. **107**). There are also reports of revolts discovered and put down by the pharaoh's intelligence men. See, for example, Vol. II. 787 from the reign of Amenhotep II, the discovery of the revolt of the Ikathi. Vol. II. 681 from the 18th dynasty comes from the tomb of Rekhmire in the reign of Thutmose III and tells us about the vizier's messengers and their importance.

83. Breasted, James Henry, *The Battle of Kadesh. A Study in the Earliest Known Military Strategy*, Chicago, 1903, 126 pp. and plates.

The Bronze Age battle of Kadesh provides us with the earliest study in military strategy and, not surprisingly, intelligence gathering plays a significant part of the story. Ramses II is fed disinformation by a spy working for the Hittites and is led into a trap. By torturing more accurate intelligence out of local bedouin, he is able to recover somewhat and fight his way out through the surrounding Hittite forces. Breasted uses the reliefs and inscriptions to tell the story, and they are reproduced in the text. These are supplemented with maps and diagrams. This is still a classic work. See also 84, 99, 116.

84. Burne, Major, R.A., "Some Notes on the Battle of Kadesh," *Journal of Egyptian Archaeology* 7 (1921), pp. 191ff.

Burne is critical of Breasted's interpretation. He makes some useful observations about the location of the two armies and about Rameses' intelligence collecting and the Hittite king's generalship. Cf. to Charles Kuentz, 107.

85. *Coptic Egypt*

At the Coptic Monastery of St. Jeremiahs in Saqqara, Egypt, a man enciphered a message perhaps just before the monastery was abandoned in the sixth century of the Common Era. The message is in a monalphabetic substitution and it is scratched on the wall inside the door to a courtyard. In what was perhaps a curious bid for immortality, the inscription reads: "I, Victor, the humble poor man—remember me." Victor's encipherment of his plea gave him his wish (no. **37**). David Kahn, *The Codebreakers*, (no. **38**) p. 86, and p. 989n. J.E. Quibbell, *Excavations at Saqqara*, 1907–1908, Cairo: Service des Antiquités de l'Égypte, 1909. 67. 13. 58. 10. On Coptic cryptography in general see Jean Doresse, "Cryptographie Copte" (no. 88) pp. 215–228.

Coptic Monastery of Epiphanius at Sheikh-abd-el-Gourna in southern Egypt. An unusual object was found here in the cell of a priest named Elias. It was a dried-out piece of wood about a foot long and four inches high, bearing two lines of writing in black ink. The top line is a slightly garbled verse in Greek, notable not for its beauty but because it includes all letters of the Coptic Greek alphabet. It spills over for five letters into the bottom line, that contains 21 letters of that alphabet, divided into four unequal sections that are reversed and shuffled. We do not know how the priest Elias used it. The wooden tablet, now in the Metropolitan Museum of Art in New York, is the oldest surviving cipher key (as distinguished from the code-like cuneiform tablets) in the world. See David Kahn, *The Codebreakers* (no. **38**) p. 865, and p. 990n. The Metropolitan Museum of Art, *Egyptian Expedition: The Monastery of Epiphanius at Thebes*, New York: Metropolitan Museum of Art, 1926. Vol. 2, item 616. The accession number of the object itself is No. 14.1.219. W.E. Crum, *The Monastery of Epiphanius at Thebes* (no. **156**).

86. Darnell, John Coleman, "The Enigmatic Netherworld Books of the Solar-Osirian Unity: Cryptographic Compositions in the Tombs of Tutankhamun, Ramesses VI, and Ramesses IX" (Egypt), University of Chicago Ph.D. Dissertation, 1995.

Some of the most lengthy enigmatic inscriptions of the New Kingdom occur in royal tombs. The three most extensive of these appear on a shrine of Tutankhamun, on a ceiling in the tomb of Ramesses VI and on a wall in the tomb of Ramessees IX. This study is the first detailed examination of these three texts together, and it concludes that these three enigmatic treatises are related in theology, iconography and physical layout. They are based on a common template, incorporating enigmatic texts, Book of the Dead extracts, and a figure of the giant unified Re-Osiris [From *Dissertation Abstracts*, AAI9609965, Vol. 56-12A, p 4744, 00877].

87. Devéria, Théodule, "L'écriture secrète dans les textes hiéroglyphiques des anciens Égyptiens, premier essai," in G. Maspero, *Bibliothèque Égyptologique* contenant les oeuvres des Égyptologues français, Vol. 5, 2 Paris, 1897, pp. 49–80.

One of the first monologues on the subject of Egyptian secret writing. Devéria works from the inscriptions found by Champollion. See also Drioton (no. **91**, **93**), Goodwin (no. **101**) and Darnell (no. **86**).

88. Doresse, Jean, "Cryptographie Copte et Cryptographie Grecque," *Bulletin de l'Institut d'Égypte*, 33, 1 (1950–51) pp. 215–228.

An excellent survey of cryptographic systems from Egypt, beginning with Hatshepsut and the 18th dynasty and running through the Greek and Coptic periods. There are examples of substitution ciphers and cryptographic alphabets used in alchemical, astrological and medical texts to guard trade secrets. Doresse includes charts comparing the various systems used.

89. Drioton, Étienne, "Le cryptogramme de Montou de Médamoud," Paris, *Revue d'Égyptologie*, Vol. 2 (1936), pp. 21–33.

Drioton deciphers a thematic cryptogram found in the excavations near the monumental gateway of Tiberius at Medamut, five miles northeast of Luxor. There is a picture of a procession that seems ordinary on the surface, but it holds a hidden meaning. There are several things that immediately tip us off that this is not an ordinary inscription: 1) the unusual character of certain representations, 2) the presence of signs isolated from the field of characters, 3) bizarre combinations of characters, and 4) the absence of titles near certain individuals.

The scene resembles one on the Naples Stele deciphered by Kurt Sethe, *Hieroglyphische Urkunden der griechisch-römischen Zeit*, p. 1. This type of representation is typical also of the Ptolemaic period.

90. Drioton, Étienne, "Cryptogrammes de la Reine Nefertari," *Annales du Service des Antiquités de l'Égypte, Le Caire*, Vol. 39 (1939), pp. 133–144.

Bernard Bruyère excavated two bas reliefs from the temple at Deir el Medina. They come from a palace of Ramses II next to the Temple of Hathor Drioton decrypts the inscriptions on the reliefs and shows them to be a dedication by a secret admirer of the queen. The rebus hides a message of great personal pain, not unlike the dedications of Senenmout to Hatshepsut. See Drioton (no. **96**), pp. 231–246.

91. Drioton, Étienne, "La cryptographie égyptienne," *Revue Lorraine d'Anthropologie*, Nancy 6 (1933–34), pp. 5–28.

Friedman Collection—866. English translations 866–1, 866–2.

Drioton has published numerous articles on what he refers to as Egyptian cryptography, or examples of secret writing that cover some hidden message in the inscription. He identifies three kinds of cryptography from the pharaonic era: 1) ordinary cryptography which differs from ordinary writing in its choice of symbols or the value given to them; 2) ornamental cryptography, where symbols are selected in such a way and a number of persons place before and after them to produce the picture of a procession decorating a frieze; and 3) thematic cryptography, whereby the artist selected representations in a unique cycle of images and arranges them systematically in such as way as to form a coherent and plausible scene without any connection to the concealed meaning of the inscription.

92. Drioton, Étienne, Deux cryptogrammes de Senenmout," *Annales du Service des Antiquités de l'Égypte*, Cairo, Vol. 37 (1938), pp. 231–246.

The black granite cube statue #42114 in the Museum in Cairo discovered by Legrain at Karnak represents Senenmut, the architect and favorite of the pharaoh, Queen Hatshepsut. On it, there is an inscription that resembles one on a statue in Berlin (published by James Breasted, "Three obscure phrases," *Proceedings of the Society of Biblical Archaeology*, 23 [1901] p. 237.)

Using the techniques that he sets out in a previous article "Essai sur la cryptographie privée..." *Revue Égyptologie* vol. I (no. **93**) he can explain the inscription as a monogram of Hatshepsut's name that represents a rebus of her name.

93. Drioton, Étienne, "Essai sur la cryptographie privée de la fin de la XVIIIe dynastie," *Revue d'Égyptologie*, Paris 1 (1933), pp. 1–50.

Parallel to the official writing style on monuments in ancient Egypt, there existed a tradition of cryptographic writing that hid a secret meaning from the immediate viewer who did not know the system. The oldest known examples were found on the tombs at Beni Hassan. There are two types of cryptographic inscriptions—royal tombs and private tombs of non-royal individuals. These were both collected by Deveria (no. **87**).

Cryptographic writing on private tombs from the 18th dynasty shows a system of phonetic notation. The signs are chosen by acrophony (i.e. using picture symbols to represent the initial sound of the name of an object). Drioton uses four inscriptions: one from Cairo, one from the Metropolitan Museum and two from the Louvre to illustrate his system of decryption. This system was not rigorously codified, but varied from stone to stone and provided a source of commonly used elements of a cryptographic alphabet.

94. Drioton, Étienne, "Une figuration cryptographique sur un stèle du Moyen Empire," *Revue d'Égyptologie*, Paris, Vol I, 1 (1933), pp. 1–50.

Drioton takes the system of deciphering cryptographic writing that he set out in "Essai sur la cryptographie privée de la fin de la XVIII dynastie," *Revue Égyptologie* Vol. I, pp. 1–50 and applies them to various inscriptions from the Middle and New Kingdom (one on the architrave of the first course of the Temple at Luxor, the Temple of Seti I at Abydos, the Naples Stèle, etc.

95. Drioton, Étienne, "Note sur le cryptogramme de Montouemhet." *Annuaire de l'Institut de Philologie et d'Histoire Orientale, Bruxelles*, Vol. 3, 1935, pp. 133–140. (Volume offert à Jean Capart.)

Drioton deciphers an inscription found on a black granite cube statue of Montouemhet, governor-prince of Thebes at the time of the Assyrian conquest. It was excavated by Miss Benson in the ruins of the temple of Mut at Karnak and is now in the Museum at Cairo, no. 646. The inscription shows that the statue was dedicated in the lifetime of the governor in the Temple of Mut where it was found.

96. Drioton, Étienne, "Note sur un cryptogramme récemment découvert à Athribis," *Annales du Service des Antiquités de l'Égypte*, Le Caire, 37 (1938), pp. 109–116.

Alan Rowe of the University of Liverpool dug up at Tell Athrib a stele of Ramses II, reused during the era of Nectanebo. It was of the same genre as the ones already published by Daressy in 1917 from the same site (Daressy, "Bas-reliefs d'Athribis," *Annales du Service des Antiquités de l'Égypte* 17 [1917], pp. 185–193). The bas relief on the new stele is complete and Drioton attempts an interpretation. He believes it is a cryptogram of the type that he has previously published, i.e. there is a message here that goes far beyond the mere phonetic transcription of the words on the stèle.

97. Drioton, Étienne, "A propos du cryptogramme de Montouemhet," *Annales du Service des Antiquités de l'Égypte*, 43 (1943), pp. 177–181.

Drioton deciphered an inscription found on a black granite cube statue of Montouemhet, governor-prince of Thebes at the time of the Assyrian conquest. See Drioton, "Note sur le cryptogramme de Montouemhet" (no. **95**), pp. 133–140.

See pp. 319–349 "Procédé acrophonique ou principe consonantale," and comments of David Kahn, p. 985–86.

98. Drioton, Étienne, "Un rébus de l'Ancien Empire," *Mélanges Maspero*, Vol. 1, (Mémoires publiés par les Membres de l'Institut Français d'Archéologie Orientale du Caire), Vol. 66, pp. 699–704.

Drioton finds a cryptographic puzzle on a monumental inscription from the Old Kingdom. This would make it the oldest example of such a rebus that has ever been found. It is an example of what he calls "thematic cryptography" where the artist carves a frieze of images and arranges them systematically in such as way as to form a coherent and plausible scene (and message) without any connection to the concealed meaning of the inscription. The best examples of this type are the Naples stele and stele C15 at the Louvre.

On this same inscription, see Jean Capart, "Un hiéroglyphe mystérieux, *Kemi II*, p. 1–2.

99. Faulkner, R. O. "The Battle of Kadesh," *Mitteilungen of the Deutsches Archäoligisches Institut*, Abteilung Kairo, 16 (1958), pp. 93–111 (Festschrift H. Junker).

Excellent military analysis of a battle that nearly ended in disaster for the Egyptians because of disinformation planted by the Hittites that led them into a trap. An appendix contains translations of the texts from which a narrative of the battle must be written. Faulkner feels (contra Burne no. **84**) the texts give an accurate account of what happened.

100. Faulkner, R. O. "The Battle of Megiddo" *Journal of Egyptian Archaeology* 22 (1942), pp. 2–15.

The battle of Megiddo is the first military campaign in recorded history of which any kind of detailed account has survived. Egyptian armies of the empire kept detailed accounts of their campaigns, and the chief military scribe would deposit the accounts in archives of the Temple of Amun Re at Thebes. Thutmose III had abstracts from the records of his campaign inscribed on the temple walls. Megiddo was his first victory and it was recorded in more detail than his later campaigns.

The best topographical study of the battle is still Nelson (no. **112**) Faulkner retranslates the hieroglyphic text and comes to some different conclusions on various points of the operations, including his judgment that the Syrian high command was inept.

101. Goodwin, C. W. "On the Enigmatic Writing on the Coffin of Seti I," *Zeitschrift für Aegyptische Sprache* 11 (1873), pp. 138–144.

The enigmatic writing on the coffin of Seti I was first noticed by Champollion. All the writing on the coffin is in the ordinary hieroglyphics of the 19th dynasty except for ten columns (23–32). The enigmatic writing appears in the descriptive text accompanying a picture of Osiris on a throne sitting in judgment over the deceased.

If the business of the text is to give the names and descriptions of all the personnages shown and the words that they are supposed to utter, why, Goodwin asks, would they be veiled in an unusual and difficult style of writing? Especially when all the other inscriptions are plain and legible. The scene was one of great solemnity and the unusual text may have been intended to give dignity and importance to the scene rather than to conceal its meaning from the onlooker.

Goodwin's discussion degenerates at the end into a typical 19th century Orientals condescension to the Egyptians by attributing to them "a childish love of mysticism" that grew up in the Egyptian mind more and more as the nation degenerated." He goes on to say that "traces of this sort of absurdity occur in the writings of the Christian Copts in subsequent times." Perhaps what he calls absurdity is really his frustration in not being able to adequately explain the system. For a more professional, modern discussion see J. C. Darnell, (no. **86**).

102. Griffith, F. L., and Thompson, Herbert, *The Demotic Magical Papyrus of London and Leiden*, London: H. Grevel & Co., 1904, 3 vol.

See especially Section III, "Contents of the Ms.," pp. 105–112.

This papyrus was discovered at Thebes and was written in the Third Century AD in both Greek and a very late form of demotic Egyptian. The scribe used a cipher to conceal the crucial portions of important magical recipes. For Greek content, see no. **169**.

103. Hirschfeld, Otto, "Die aegyptische Polizei der römischen Kaiserzeit nach Papyruskunden," *Könglisch Preussischen Akademie der Wissenschafter, Berlin*. Philosophisch-historische klasse, Sitzungsberichte 1892, pp. 3ff; republished in *Kleine Schriften*, pp. 613–623.

Hirschfeld wrote this article to complement his work on the secret police of imperial Rome (see no. **377**). He discusses two previously unedited papyrus documents that allude to the police organization in ancient Egypt under Roman rule.

The first document discusses five townspeople enlisted to assist local officials in tracking down a criminal. The townspeople, failing to comply, are sent in shackles to the *Praefectus Aegypti*. Hirschfeld cites this threat of imprisonment as evidence that the duty was not a popular one. The second document lists eleven names and positions ("thief catchers") of a well-organized and delineated police force, including the first time the title "keepers of the peace" (*Wächter der Ebene*) appears. The names listed in the document are identifiably Egyptian, and most fall between the ages of 20–35 and they are to be paid either 200, 300 or 400 drachma. The author traces the local police organization in Egypt back to the Ptolomaic period, if nor earlier, and suggests that the later development of Rome's police structure owes much of its design to this earlier Egyptian format.

104. Hohlwein, N., "La police des villages égyptiens à l'époque romaine; *demoösioi tein komein*," *Musée Belge* 9 (1905), pp. 189–195.

Holwein examines the term *demoösios tein komein*, usually translated as "village official" (*dörfbehörde* or *fonctionnaires du village*). Holwein finds this too inexact. He gives several examples from papyrus documents where these officials are all associated with the chief of police of the village. He suggests that they are all part of the policing structure of the village that collects intelligence and enforces laws. In at least one context, *demoösoioi* are the same as *phulakes* (police agents; see Holwein, no. **105**). These *agents de la force publique* or *fonctionnaires de police du village* all cooperated with each other, exchanged intelligence and exercised local control in the name of the Roman administration.

105. Hohlwein, N., "La police des villages égyptiens à l'époque romaine: Ho Phulakes *Musée Belge* 9 (1905), pp. 394–9.

Hohlwein discusses local policing in Egypt during the Roman period. The term *phulax* which, on papyrus, usually appears in conjunction with other words that tells precisely what these particular police were guarding: *desmophulax* = prison guards; *ormophulax*—grain deliverers; *hydrophulax* = river police; *oreophulax* or *ermophulax*—guards of caravan routes; *agrophulax* = guardians of the fields, etc.

106. Holmes, Y., "The Messengers of the Amarna Letters," *Journal of the American Oriental Society* 75 (1975), pp. 376–381.

Holmes writes: "The messenger is a prime key to understanding the trade and diplomacy of the Amarna period, because it was he who controlled both the diplomatic and economic intercourse between the important powers of the time. The messenger served not only as a bearer, reader, interpreter and defender of his master's message, but also as a diplomat, and more importantly, a merchant. Because of his numerous functions, the Amarna messenger usually was a person of importance and had associated with himself many problems that became prime points of discussion in the Amarna letters."

We might also add that he was a spy. Since messengers were wined and dined by foreign kings to leave a good impression, they had the opportunity to interrogate others "in a sly manner" and certainly this worked both ways. On p. 378 Holmes himself notes: "The Amarna messenger always performed the important diplomatic function of spying on the military, economic and political activities of the country to which they were sent."

107. Kuentz, Charles, *La Bataille de Qadech*. Cairo: Imprimerie de l'Institut français d'archéologie orientale, 1929, Mémoires de l'Institut, tome 55, 2e fasc., 398pp.

Beautifully produced folio volume on the battle between Ramses II and the Hittites at Kadesh that almost resulted in a defeat for the great Egyptian pharaoh and general because he was misled by disinformation supplied by Bedouin agents working for the Hittites. One of the two earliest bronze age battles of which we have descriptions. Contains all the original texts and pictures of the bas reliefs.

108. Lauth, Fr. J., "Aenigmatische Schrift," *Zeitschrift für Aegyptische Sprache und Altertumskunde* 4 (1896), pp. 24–26.

Discussion of the enigmatic writing on the tomb of Seti I. See also no. **109**, no. **87**, and no. **94**.

109. Le Page Renouf, P., "The Royal tombs at Biban el Moluk and 'enigmatical' Writing," *Zeitschrift für Äegyptische Sprache und Altertumskunde* (Sept.–Oct., 1874), pp. 101–105.

A transcription, translation and interpretation of the enigmatical writings from the tomb of Ramses VI in the Valley of the Kings. It is a judgment scene similar to the one found on the tomb of Seti I that was commented upon by Goodwin. (no. **101**).

110. Maspero, Jean, *Comptes rendus de L'Académie des Inscriptions et Belles Lettres*, (1871), pp. 189–93.

A Coptic papyrus in Paris contains a secret form of Egyptian writing that one interpreter (M. Pierret) thought was used to write a Nubian dialect. Maspero points out that such hieroglyphs were already known by Champollion and are used for hieroglyphics, hieratic and demotic script. He gives examples such as magical papyri from the 20–26 dynasties. Secret writing was used to list ingredients for medical-magical unguents. The Egyptians did not only invent new signs, they used old signs in different ways. In hieroglyphic script, secret characters were used to write the identity of the scribe in inscriptions on monuments. He gives an example of the Papyrus Leiden A65 for Greek use of substitution ciphers.

111. Mercer, Samuel A.B. (ed.) with the assistance of Frank Hudson Hallock, *The Tell-el-Amarna Tablets*, New York, AMS Press, 1983, 2 vols.

The oldest diplomatic correspondence in human history. The tablets are the letters from the last years of the reign of Amenhotep III and his son Amenhotep IV (Akhenaten) to the princes of their Asiatic possessions. The rising power of the Hittites is chronicled, as they co-opt Egyptian vassals like Aziru of Amor. He worked against the Egyptians while feigning loyalty. Although the pharaoh's intelligence service was working well, the pharaohs were ignoring the bad news being sent to them by Rib Addi, a loyal adherent from Byblos, about the treachery of Aziru. He becomes a tragic figure since he is unable to convince the royal court of his own loyalty, while at the same time trying to convince them of his opponents' treachery

See volume 1, no. 102 ff. the Rib Addi documents. Francis Dvornik, *The Origin of Intelligence Services* (no. **3**), pp. 11–12.

112. Nelson, Harold Hayden, *The Battle of Megiddo.* Chicago: Private Edition distributed by the University of Chicago Libraries, 1913; Chicago, 1921, 63 pp.

A Ph.D. dissertation by a student of Henry Breasted at Chicago on the famous Bronze Age battle between the Egyptians under Thutmose III and the allied forces of the Syrian states. Megiddo was the first battle in history that we can study in any detail, and not surprisingly, it involves the use of spies. Thutmose sent out his reconnaissance people to find out which was the best way to attack the fortress of Megiddo. Thutmose also exercised a common but dangerous practice of ignoring the advice of his intelligence staff once the intelligence had been collected and analyzed.

This text includes translations of the relevant sources, topographical maps, and photos of the relevant sites. Cf. Eric H. Cline, *The Battles of Armegeddon*, Ann Arbor: University of Michigan Press, 200.

113. Preisigke, Fr., "Die ptolemaïsche Staatspost, *Klio* 7 (1907), pp. 241–277.

Preisigke discusses the evidence for a Ptolemaic postal service in Egypt taken from the Hibeh papyrus 110 (see Grenfell and Hunt, *The Hibeh Papyrus*, I, London, 1906). The papyrus contains the fragment of an official day book written by the employee of the Egyptian royal post. It dates to the reign of Ptolemy Philadelpus (285–246 BC) and the daybook itself was probably written around the year 255 BC. It pictures the activity of an important post office somewhere in the center of Egypt from the 16th to the 23rd day of a month that is not marked. Although the document is incomplete it leaves the impression of a very well-organized operation in which each letter received was logged and then re-expedited with the hour of each recorded. This station served the left bank of the Nile but we might assume that there was a corresponding service on the other bank.

114. Smither, Paul, "The Semnah Dispatches" *Journal of Egyptian Archaeology* 31 (1945), pp. 3–10.

A series of intelligence reports from the Middle Kingdom fortress at Semnah, the southern border of Egyptian-held territory in Nubia. These dispatches deal with the comings and goings of the Medjay people. Attempts were being made to keep track of the movements of these people in the desert. They date to the reign of Amenemhet III i.e. about 1844 to 1841 BC making them among the earliest intelligence documents extant.

115. Valloggia, Michel, *Recherches sur les "messagers" (wpwtyw) dans les sources égyptiennes profanes* (II Hautes Études Orientales 6); Genève-Paris: Librairie Droz, 1976, 316 pp.

Valloggia collects references to messengers in ancient Egypt. This includes private messengers (slaves sent with communications for their master), royal messengers carrying diplomatic intelligence, and military messengers carrying everything from information on troop strength to assassination orders. He collects citations from many different sources: literary, funerary, religious and magic texts. The major part of the study is philological—transcribing and translating the documents in question, but his conclusion suggests he sees the full range of information that traveled by these messengers. The New Kingdom especially saw the development of an administrative apparatus for sending state intelligence.

116. Wilson, John A., "The Texts of the Battle of Kadesh," *American Journal of Semitic Languages and Literature* 43 (1927), pp. 266–287.

In the winter of 1925, J.H. Breasted uncovered an inscription on the rear (south side) of the pylon of Ramses II at Luxor, consisting of the Record and the Poem of the Battle of Kadesh. He placed the materials at Wilson's disposal, and Wilson in turn collated all the available copies and photographs of these documents and wrote them up as a doctoral dissertation. This article is an abridgment of that study in which he includes translations of all the texts. Anyone wishing to study the important intelligence aspects of the encounter between the Egyptians and the Hittites must start with these ancient sources. This article should be considered along with Breasted's *The Battle of Kadesh* and *Ancient Records of Egypt*, 3.298ff in any study of the battle.

Assyria and Babylonia

Considering the importance of intelligence gathering to empires, and the fact that Near Eastern empire pioneered these activities, it is surprising how few articles have been written about the Assyrian, Babylonian and Persian intelligence services. Lack of sources is part of the problem. There is a scholarly movement under way to show that the Persian institution described by Xenophon as "The King's Eye" never really existed.

117. Borger, R., "Geheimwissen," *Reallexicon der Assyriologie*, eds. Erich Ebeling and Bruno Meissner, Berlin: Walter de Gruyter & Co., 1964, III 188–191.

Encyclopedic entry on secret knowledge in Assyria and Babylonia and how it was kept secret. Texts with ciphers have been found. The priests who wrote these tablets were familiar with the use of cipher alphabets and numeric codes. The information being disguised was usually astrological or religious—which to the Mesopotamians was the same thing. See also the previous entry in the Reallexicon by Weidner (no. **124**) on secret writing.

Dvornik, Francis, *The Origins of Intelligence Services*. Pp. 15–23 cover communications in Babylonia and the Assyria empire. See entry **3**.

118. Follett, R., "Deuxième Bureau et information diplomatique dans l'Assyrie des Sargonides, quelques notes," *Rivista degli Studi Orientali,* Rome 32 (1957), pp. 68–81.

A study of the intelligence service of the Assyrians during the time between the reigns of Sargon II and Rusa I and how it was used against Urartu. He lists the texts that he uses individually, most of them being royal letters and intelligence reports. A vast range of information is conveyed concerning the geography, people, activities and capabilities of the Kingdom of Urartu. It conveys an impression of a well-organized intelligence service on the part of the Assyrians that knew what to look for and reported back with great frequency and accuracy.

119. Fries, C., "Zur Babylonischen Feuerpost" *Klio* 4 (1904), pp. 117–121.

Fries discusses several magic texts, including a text from the library of Assurbanipal, where a man who wants to protect himself against the malevolence of a witch tells his enemy: "Well my witch, who art kindling fire every 'two hours' journey' ... I know thee and I will post watchmen in order to protect myself." Fries identifies this as an allusion to the Assyrian postal service, the beacons of which were erected at fixed distances of a "double-hour's journey" or a beru along Assyrian roads. When there was an urgent message and the most rapid communication was necessary, the beacons were lit thus announcing the important news. At the same time a fast courier was dispatched to give more details of the intelligence being sent. His arrival would be anticipated at each of the "stations" and he was able to travel quickly without hindrance.

120. Gadd, C.J., and Thompson, R. Campbell, "A Middle-Babylonian Chemical Text," *Iraq* 3 (1936), pp. 87–96.

The oldest encipherment in Mesopotamia appears in a tiny cuneiform tablet only about 3 by 2 inches dating from about 1,500 BC and found on the site of ancient Seleucia on the banks of the Tigris. It contains the earliest known formula for the making of glazes for pottery. The scribe, jealously guarding his professional secret, used cuneiform signs—that could have several different syllabic values—in their least common values. His method resembles George Bernard Shaw's way of using the "fh" sound of GH in "tough," the "I" sound in women and the "sh" sound in nation to write fish as GHOTI. The scribe also truncated sounds by ignoring the final consonant of several syllabic signs, and spelled the same word with different signs at different places. Interestingly, as knowledge of glaze-making spread, the need for secrecy evaporated, and later texts were written in straightforward language.

David Kahn, *The Codebreakers* (no. **37**) p. 75 and 987 note citing personal letters from Dr. Benno Landsberger, January 27, 1964, and Dr. A. Leo Oppenheim, February 21, 1964, both of the Oriental Institute in Chicago.

121. Leichty, Erle, "The Colophon," in *Studies presented to A. Leo Oppenheim*, Chicago: Oriental Institute, 1964, 147–154 at 152–153.

With the help of the equivalencies work out by Neugebauer (no. **122**), Erle Leichty studies the signature at the foot of a large tablet reciting a myth of the goddess Ishtar that might be an indirect source of the biblical story of Esther, whose name might be another version of "Ishtar." The signature reads "*tuppi* [I]21 35 35 26 44 *apil* [I]21 11 20 42" or tablet of Mr. 21 35 35 26 44, son of Mr. 21 11 20 42. Leichty suggested that the solution was "tablet for Mr. Anu-aba-uttirri, son of Mr. Anu-bel.su-nu whose father-son relationship is well known."

Other tablets employ the same numbers with the same values. No simple relationship between the equivalencies appears. "A check of the various lexical series shows that the numbers are not based on a counting of signs either forward from the beginning of the series, nor backward from the end," wrote Leichty. "It is of course possible that a tablet of equations between numbers and signs existed." He suggested that two little tablet-fragments from Susa might comprise such a codebook, but added that they were too short to be certain. The broken pieces of clay list cuneiform numbers in order in a vertical column; opposite them stand cuneiform signs. Unfortunately, none of the numbers used in the cryptograms occurs on these fragments (except for 35, whose cuneiform sign is blurred in illegibility), and so it is not possible to determine whether these tablets served as the codebook for the colophon cryptography. But if they are indeed codebooks, then they are the oldest in the world.

For more on colophons in Assyrian texts, see: R. Borger, no. **117**, and E. Weidner no. **124**. On the Ishtar tablet, see: France. Ministère de l'Éducation Nationale des Beaux Arts, *Textes Scolaires de Suse*, ed. P.E. v.d. Meer, Memoires de la Mission Archéologique de Perse, XXVII, Paris: Librairie Ernest Leroux, 1935, no. 233 and 234 for possible code lists. But the texts cited by de Meer do not shed any light on the problem.

122. Neugebauer, Otto (ed.), *Astronomical Cuneiform Texts*, Princeton, NJ: Institute for Advanced Study by Lund Humphries, London, 1955. I, 11, 161–163 for lunar eclipse tablet.

Babylonian and Assyrian scribes sometimes used rare or unusual cuneiform signs in signing and dating their clay tablets. These ending formulas called "colophons" were short and stereotyped, and the substitution of the unusual signs for the usual were not intended to conceal but simply to show off the scribe's knowledge of cuneiform to later copyists. Nothing precisely like this exists in the modern world, because literacy is so widespread and spelling so standardized.

In the final period of cuneiform writing, in colophons written at Uruk under the Seleucid kings in the last few score years before the Christian era, occasional scribes converted their names into numbers. The encipherment, if this is what it was meant to be, may have only been for amusement or to show off. Because colophons are so stereotyped and because several of the enciphered ones have only one or two number signs among many plaintext, Assyriologists have been able to "cryptanalyze" them.

A tablet giving lunar eclipses from 130 to 113 BC includes in its colophon "palih 21 50 10 40 1a… "Comparing this with the identical formula in plaintext in another tablet, Otto Neugebauer figured out that 21 = Anu, 50 = u. 10 40 = An-tu. The formula reads: "He who worships Anu and Antu shall not remove it (the tablet).

For the original text of the Ishtar tablet, see F. Thureau-Dangin (ed.), *Tablettes d'Uruk*, Textes cunéiformes, Musée du Louvre, Département des Antiquités Orientales, Vol. 6, Paris: Librairie Orientaliste Paul Geuthner, 1922, no. **51**, and F. Thureau-Dangin, "L'exaltation d'Istar," *Revue d'Assyriologie* 9 (1914), pp. 141–158.

123. Oppenheim, A. L., "The Eyes of the Lord" *Journal of the American Oriental Society* 88, 1 (Jan.–March, 1968), pp. 173–180.

Oppenheim discusses several literary expressions used widely in the ancient Near East including "the Eyes of the King" and "the Ears of the King." He then investigates the concepts behind them as well as their basis in actual practice. The earliest references to such officials come from Egyptian sources datable to the second half of the second millennium B.C.E. There are similar references in Assyria, Persia, India (2nd century AD) and China (7th century AD). The activities of informers, accusers, internal spies, censors, and secret agents are then transferred in some sources to a supernatural level where they become either evil demons or "Eyes of the Lord."

Riepl, Wolfgang, *Das Nachrichtenwesen des Altertums*. Discusses state postal systems including the *Assyrian*-Babylonian, Persian, and Hellenistic systems. See entry **3**.

124. Weidner, E., "Geheimschrift," *Reallexicon der Assyriologie*, eds. Erich Ebeling and Bruno Meissner, Berlin: Walter de Gruyter & Co., 1964, Vol. III, pp. 185–188.

An encyclopedia entry on secret writing in Babylonia and Assyria. Weidner lists both the original texts and secondary literature on writing systems. Some of the texts used alternative alphabets and other numeric codes. They are sometimes religious texts, sometimes astrological information which was meant to be kept secret from the general reader. There is an entry following this one in the *Reallexicon* by Borger (no. **117**) on "Geheimwissen."

Persia

125. Aristotle, *De Mundo*, in *The Complete Works of Aristotle*, Revised Oxford Translation, edited by Jonathan Barnes, Princeton University Press, 1984, 2 volumes. See volume one, pp. 626–640.

A short work falsely attributed to Aristotle, but written most likely in the second half of the first century AD. It has an interesting description of the means by which the Persians tried to obtain rapid intelligence. The system included "couriers, watchmen and messengers and superintendents of signal fires." According to this passage, the King "received on the same day news of all that was happening in Asia."

126. Aschoff, Volker, "Die Rufposten im alten Persien. Historische Wirklichschaft oder nachrichtentechnische Legende?," *NTZ* (Nachrichtentechnische Zeitschrift) 30 (1977), pp. 451–455.

For the last two hundred years, scholars of communications techniques have been reporting that the ancient Persians had a postal system and relay stations for long distance communications across their empire. Aschoff does a technical feasibility study that leads him to conclude that the existence of such a pre-electric, long distance communications network by the Persian Empire is very unlikely. But he concedes it is likely that at the height of its empire, the Persians could call together their troops by some sort of oral communications system.

127. Brisson, Barnabé, *de regio Persarum*, Paris, 1590. Can be found in his collected works: *Barnabae Brissonij Regii Consistorij consiliarij* ... Opera varia ... multo quamantehac emendatiora & tertia amplius parte auctiora, quorum catalogum sequens pagina indicat, cum locupletissimis insicibus. Paris: Apud Bartholomaeum Macaeum, 1607.

Brisson was the first author to collect all of the classical references to the Achaemenid office called the "King's Eye," which is traditionally interpreted as the head of the Persian secret service. In recent years, a debate has broken out over whether this office actually existed. See, for example, Dvornik (no. 3) who accepts the classical texts and Hirsch (no. **133**) who does not. Then compare Shahbazi (no. **138**) on the Iranian sources.

128. Cryptography. Persia in the first five hundred years of the Common Era apparently made use of cryptography for political purposes. A chronicler mentions "a script called *shah-dabiriya* and the kings of the Persians used to speak it among themselves to the exclusion of commoners and prevent the rest of the people of the kingdom from learning it for fear that one who was not a king should discover the secrets of the kings." He also referred to "another script called *razsahriya*, in which the kings used to write secrets [in correspondence] with those of other nations that they wished and the number of its consonants and vowels is forty, and each of the consonants and vowels has a known form, and there is no trace of it in the Nabataean language." Though the historian gives no examples, a 10th century compiler of a handbook for secretaries, in setting down two nonalphabetic substitutions, said that they were of Persian origin. One substituted the names of birds for the letters of the alphabet. The other equated the letters of the alphabet with the names of the 28 astronomical lunar mansions: the horns on the ram, the ram's belly, the Pleiades, and so on. See David Kahn, *The Codebreakers* (no. **38**), p. 86.

See also: Ibn al-Nadim, Muhammed ibn Ishaq *The Fihrist of al-Nadim*; a tenth century survey of Muslim culture, Bayard Dodge, editor and translator, New York: Columbia University Press, 1970, 2 volumes. Volume I 22–27, Persian scripts, Volume II, pp. 863–864 for *shah-dabiriya* and *raz-sahriya*.

Abu Bakr Muhammad b. Yahya as-Suli, *Adab al-kuttab*, ed. Muh. Bahjat al-Athari, Cairo, 1341/1922–3,) 186–87 for birds and lunar mansions.

129. Diodorus Siculus, *Diodorus of Sicily*, translated by C.H. Oldfather, Cambridge: Harvard University Press, 1989, 12 volumes.

19.17 reports on the Persians being able to muster troops by voice signal; 19.37 tells how, in the Persian Empire, urgent messages were carried by fast dromedaries that could "travel continuously for almost 1,500 stades," or about 170 miles.

Dvornik, Francis, *The Origins of Intelligence Services*. Chapter one covers the ancient Near East including a large section on Persia. See entry **3**.

130. Hennig, Richard, *Die älteste Entwicklung der Telegraphie und Telephonie*, Leipzig: J.A. Barth, 1908.

Not available at press time.

131. Herodotus, *The Histories, A.D.* Godley translation, Loeb Classical Library edition, Cambridge: Harvard University Press, 1996, 4 volumes.

Book 5.52 tells of the great royal road of Persia with great detail about its length and resting stages. According to Herodotus, the journey from the Greek city of Ephesus on the coast to Sardis and from there to Susa, the Persian capital, lasted three months and three days. For greater detail on this road and its route and remains, see W.M. Ramsay, *Historical Geography of Asia Minor*.

In Book 8.98, Herodotus goes on to describe the messengers who travel over the royal road carrying dispatches for the king. He claims that there is nothing mortal that accomplishes a course more swiftly than do these messengers. There is a new man and a new horse for every day in the journal. He then delivers the immortal line: "these are stayed neither by snow nor rain nor heat nor darkness from accomplishing their appointed course with all speed." (*Pace*, the U.S. Postal Service). The service is called the *angareion*—a word with Babylonian origins.

Book 9.3 tells of the fire beacons used by the Persians to signal during the invasion of Greece by Xerxes.

132. Hinz, Walther, *Neue Wege im Altpersischen*, Wiesbaden: Otto Harrassowitz, 1973, 174 pp.

On pp. 98–101 he proposes that the title given by Greek sources, "The Eye of the King," has an actual equivalent in Persia. The name for the position is reconstructed from the Elamite and Akkadian. In this he is following Eilers, *Iranische Beamtennamen in der keilschriftlichen Überlieferung*, Leipzig, 1940, p. 119.

133. Hirsch, Steven W., *The Friendship of the Barbarians*, Hanover and London: University Press of New England, 1985, 216 pp.

Chapter five covers the subject of the position of the King's Eye. Hirsch believes no such post is attested. Orientalists were disturbed by the absence of all mention of a King's Eye in the Oriental sources for any period, including the Achaemenid, and have developed elaborate theories to account for the state of the evidence. Hirsch believes these theories, predicated on unattested offices and alleged false etymologies, are all ultimately unsatisfactory. The available evidence provides no corroboration, not even well-attested analogies, for the Achaemenid King's Eye. For other authors who believe such sources have been found, see Shabazi (no. **138**). And reviewers were quick to pick up on the fact that suggesting there was no intelligence service at all is extreme. (See, for example, W. E. Higgins, *American Historical Review* 92, 1 [February, 1987], p. 105.)

134. Karras, Theodor, *Geschichte der Telegraphie*, Braunschweig: Friedrich Viehweg und Sohn, 1909.

Not available at press time.

135. Meyer, Eduard, *Geschichte des Altertums*, Stuttgart: J.G. Cotta'sche Buchhandlung, 1953–58, 5 vols.

In IV.1. pp. 39–45 Meyer discusses the institution of the King's Eye and the King's Ears. He does not believe the classical evidence supports the existence of such an institution. Hirsch (no. **133**) makes the same argument that is countered by Shahbazi (no. **138**).

136. Niz-am al-Mulk, *The Book of Government or Rules for Kings*, translated by Hubert Darke, London, Boston: Routledge & Kegan Paul, 1978, 2nd edition, pp. 63–64

The fullest discussion of the nature and the function of organized intelligence gathering in post-Sasanian Iran given by Khwaja Nizam al-Mulk, the grand minister of the first Seljukid emperors. His book sums up two thousand years of Iranian experience in statecraft.

Riepl, Wolfgang, *Das Nachrichtenwesen des Altertums, mit besonderer Rücksicht auf die Römer*. Part 2, section 9 discusses fire signaling in the Persian empire.

Part 4, section 1 discusses state postal systems including the Assyrian-Babylonian, Persian, and Hellenistic systems. See entry **9**.

137. Schaeder, Hans H., "Das Auge des Königs," *Abhandlung der Gesellshaft der Wissenschaften zu Göttingen*, phil.-hist. Klasse, Ser. 3, Folge Nr. 10, Berlin, 1934, pp. 3–19.

The term "the King's Ears," mentioned in classical sources, has an equivalent in Persian texts, *gausaka* and it refers to the king's spies. The term "The King's Eye" however, does not have any obvious correspondence in Iran outside of the Greek references. He tries to trace such a term from old Iranian word that was related to a Scythian word for "eye" and meant supervisor. The term is attested in Manichaean texts in a middle Iranian form. An ingenious argument, but not universally accepted.

Against Schaeder's view, see A. Pagliaro, *Rivista degli Studi Orientali* 1929, pp. 129ff, and O. Szemerenyi, *Monumentum H.S. Nyberg* (*Acta Iranica*) vol. 2, Leiden-Teheran, 1975, 354ff. A development of Schaeder's suggestion is offered by H. Lommel, "die Späher des Varuna und Mitra und das Auge des Königs," *Oriens* 6 (1953), pp. 323 ff.

138. Shahbazi, A. Sh., "The 'King's Eyes' in Classical and Iranian Literature," *American Journal of Ancient History* 13, 2 (1988), pp. 170–189.

Shahbazi takes on the critics who believe there was no such institution as the King's Eye and King's Ear in ancient Persia (Hirsch no. **133**; Meyer no. **135**). His evidence indicates that in post-Sasanian Iran, the spies and informers were, as in the days of old, designated "the Eyes and Ears" of the King. He also produced sources that established a link between The Achaeminid and Sasanian institutions. He concludes that the existence of the Persian "King's Eye and King's Ears" is established by classical and Aramaic sources, by the continued use of it in the Parthian and Sasanian periods and by the parallel Cypriot institution of the *Kolakes*. There is no reason to deny its existence simply because we have not yet found an Old Persian equivalent for it.

139. Shaked, Shaul, "Two Judaeo-Iranian Contributions," *Irano-Judaica*. Studies Relating to Jewish Contacts with Persian Culture Throughout the Ages, Jerusalem: Ben Zvi Institute for the Study of Jewish Communities in the East, 1982 (1990), pp. 292–322.

On pages 301–303 Shaked discusses the Persian *title wenen-pad-tan sabistan* that indicates a position of great proximity to the king and is attested in both Achaemenid and Sasanian nomenclature. The question is whether or not this is the equivalent of the "the Eye of the King" (referring to the study by Schaeder, no. **137**). He believes it possible to suppose that the Greek title "the King's Eye" is rendering, although a somewhat inadequate one, of an original Persian title encountered in Esther and in Sasanian nomenclature.

140. Sheldon, R. M. "Spies and Mailmen and the Royal Road to Persia," *American Intelligence Journal,* (Autumn/Winter 1992/3) pp. 37–40.

A short description of the Persian secret service, and a commentary on the relationship between intelligence, communications, and national security.

141. Westberg, F., "Zur Topographie des Herodot, die Persische Königstrasse," *Klio* 4 (1906), pp. 259–268.

Using the Greek text of Herodotus that he reproduces in great length, Westberg tries to reconstruct the topography of the Persian royal road. No illustrations.

142. Xenophon, *Cyropaedia*, Carlton L. Brownson trans. Loeb Classical Library Edition. Cambridge: Harvard University Press, 1968–1971.

8.2.10 is the famous passage about "The King's Eyes" and "the King's Ears" which relates, no doubt, to a type of secret service or intelligence collection system; 8.6.16 describes the overseer who keeps an eye on the satraps (governors) of Persian provinces and reports back to the King; 8.6.17–18 describes the postal system with fixed stations and a pony-express type messenger that traveled "faster than the cranes." Xenophon describes the system as "the fastest overland traveling on earth; and it is a fine thing to have immediate intelligence of everything in order to attend to it as quickly as possible."

Greece

The ancient Greeks knew a great deal about the ins and outs of spying, but they did not make the distinctions implied by modern nomenclature e.g. intelligence collection, security, counterintelligence, and covert operations. If the Greeks did have a word for it, the word was *stratagemata*, the single heading under which they grouped all stratagems of war. We are able to study these stratagems today thanks to the survival of several Greek military handbooks called *strategika biblia*. The chapters on intelligence gathering instruct a commander in what would today be called tradecraft: the finer arts of running agents, sending secret messages, using codes and ciphers, donning disguises and conducting surveillance.

Of all the surviving military treatises, by far the best guide is the book written around 357 BC by Aeneas Tacticus, thought to be Aeneas of Stymphalos, a general of the Arcadian Confederacy. He describes in detail eighteen different methods for sending secret messages, some of them in cipher. But intelligence activities are not limited to military writers alone. Almost any history containing information about wars or diplomatic history will contain hints about how Greeks gathered information, analyzed it and acted upon it. Nor should we generalize about Greek attitudes toward intelligence. The Spartans had a controlled state with a completely different attitude toward internal security than say the Athenians whose democratic society prided itself on its openness. Yet both sides needed information to conduct their wars and their foreign policy.

The literature below shows that although the Greeks did not have a centralized intelligence service, they appreciated the importance of having timely and accurate intelligence, and they brought to intelligence gathering the same cleverness and ingenuity they brought to many other fields in which they excelled. Their tricks for collecting information and concealing messages may seem amusing to us because of their quaintness and simplicity by our modern technological standards. Their cryptogams would hardly deceive a modern military censor, but could well have fooled a simple-minded gatekeeper of a barbarian policeman in an age when reading and writing were uncommon. Like other elements of great inventions now part of our thought and action, the ideas behind these ancient practices still apply.

Two separate sections are added here on topics which are germane to the subject of intelligence, and that have generated books and articles for some time; both are Spartan. The first is on the Spartan *krypteia*, portrayed by some as a secret service organization and others as a rite of passage in the life of young Spartan citizens. The second is the Spartan *skytale*, long believed to be a method of encryption for Spartan military intelligence; in recent years this view has been seriously challenged. A number of recent books have surveyed Greek intelligence activities, and they show a strong interest in Greek spying. The academic controversy surrounding this subject will, I hope, generate scholarship that contributes to our knowledge of how the Greeks conducted the "shadow trade."

General

143. Adcock, Frank, and Mosley, D. J., *Diplomacy in Ancient Greece*, London: Thames and Hudson, 1975, 287 pp.

Mosley took up the labor of editing Sir Frank Adcock's notes after he died and added to them a second part of this manuscript on ancient Greek diplomacy. Mosley actually believes Greek diplomacy never depended "upon indirect methods of communication ... or by means of third parties." This certainly was not true of the *proxenoi*, on which see Gerolymatos, André, *Espionage and Treason* (no. **166**). Why then were heralds among the first to be arrested and detained in times of hostilities? Aeneas the Tactician (no. **144**) talks about measures used to deal with envoys and strangers who might come on missions of espionage or sabotage. Philip of Macedon was reputed to have a good system of intelligence that enabled him to find out within hours what his arch-opponent Demosthenes had said in his speeches in Athens. In fact, intercepting envoys was a form of intelligence gathering in an of itself as the Athenians found when they intercepted Spartan envoys to Persia on their way through Thrace in 430/29. (Thucydides 2.67.1). REVIEWED IN: *Times Literary Supplement* 74 (1975) 1348 Cartledge; *American Historical Review* 81 (1976) 828 Roebuck; *Journal of Hellenic Studies* 106 (1976) 223 Seager; *Greece and Rome* 23 (1976) 90 Percival; *Classical Review* 27 (1977) 134 Lewis; *Annali della Scuola Normale Superiore di Pisa* 5 (1975) 1576–1577 Piccirilli.

144. Aeneas Tacticus, *On the Defense of Fortified Positions*, Illinois Greek Club trans. Loeb Classical Library, 1948, 527 pp. and index.

The author of this work on fortified positions is probably Aeneas of Stymphalos, general of the Arcadian League in 367 BC. Polybius tells us he is the author of several treatises on the art of war; this is the only one that has survived. Chapter 31 gives eighteen methods of cipherment and interesting descriptions of stratagems employed to send secret messages. The latest translation is by David Whitehead who makes no comment on the author's contribution to the history of intelligence. See David Kahn, *The Codebreakers* (no. **38**), p. 82–83.

145. Anderson, J. K., *Military Theory and Practice in the Age of Xenophon*, Berkeley, 1970, 419 pp.

Excellent study of the Greek hoplite army, and a comparison of hoplites and the lightly-armed peltasts of the fourth century. Passing references to dispatch riders, messengers, and visual signalling. Discussion of the *skytale* on p. 68. REVIEWED IN: *Choice* 7:1114 October 1970 190W; *Library Journal* 95: 1363 April 1, 1970 100W; *Classical Philology* 66 (1971) p. 74 Starr; *Greece and Rome* 18 (1971) p. 106 Sewter; *Révue Archéologique* 1971 pp. 133–134; *Hermathena* 113 (1972) p. 69 Parke; *Classical Review* 22 (1972) pp. 194–196 Snodgrass; *Gnomon* 44 (1972) 362–366 Westlake; *Classical Journal* 68 (1972) pp. 187–198 Buck.

146. Andrewes, A., "Lysias and the Theramenes Papyrus," *Zeitschrift für Papyrologie und Epigraphik* 6,1 (1970), p. 35.

A discussion of the famous Michigan papyrus 5982 originally published by Youtie and Merkelbach in *ZPE* 2 (1968) 161–169 (no. **213**) that discusses the secret mission of Theramenes to Lysander at the end of the Peloponnesian War in 404 BC. Cf. Breitenbach (no. **152**), Heinrichs, (no. **173**).

147. Baillie Reynolds, P.K., "The Shield Signal at the Battle of Marathon" *Journal of Hellenic Studies* 49 (1929), pp. 100–105.

One of the great open questions in the field of ancient communications is whether Herodotus' account of the shield signal at Marathon is either historical or accurate. Did it really happen? What message was being sent? By whom to whom? Baillie Reynolds follows the reconstruction of events set down by J.A.R. Munro (*Journal of Hellenic Studies* 19, p. 185) and Grundy (*The Great Persian War*). After the Athenians won the battle of Marathon, the Persians took their ships and attempted to make a dash on Phaleron. They expected to be let into Athens by the Alcmeonidae, a pro-Persian faction. A signal was given by means of a shield reflecting in the sunlight from the top of Mount Pentelicus to Datis in his ship five miles away. Macan (*Commentary on Herodotus*) suggests that they were made by means anticipating modern heliotelegraphy. This would have required a prearranged code known to both parties.

Munro in the *Cambridge Ancient History* has drawn attention to the difficulty of signalling by such a means. The distance would be too great for an accurate reading. And if the pro-Pisistratid party could communicate by clandestine means, then why use an elaborate signalling system? Why privilege visual over verbal communications? Herodotus says the signal was given when the Persians were already on their ships. The traitors in Athens knew of the Persian intention to embark and sail around to Phaleron with the major part of their force, and the shield was the only means of communication they had with Datis while he was at sea.

The only message that could have been communicated is "Now's the time" or a yes or no to an agreed upon question. If the signal was "the plot has failed" then this would explain why Datis never made his run on Phaleron.

148. Balcer, J. M., "The Athenian Episkopos and the Achaemenid 'King's Eye,'" *American Journal of Philology* 98, no. 3 (1977), pp. 252–263.

The Greeks borrowed the imperial Achaemenid office of "The King's Eye" and its functions for the Episkopos—one of several imperial officers who governed the fifth century Athenian Empire. Their function was to supervise the imperial territories, to prevent rebellion and to supervise the local governments. They were overseers and legal advisors who supervised the foundation of new cities. As itinerant imperial officers they could call on the *proxenoi* (see Gerolymatos, no. **167**) and other imperial magistrates. The Episkopos had no military duties, but relied upon the garrison commanders (*phrouarchoi*) and the imperial navy and its Athenian generals. The difference between the two institutions was that The King's Eye was appointed by the king whereas the Episkopos was governed by the democratic Boule and Demos. The Episkopos was responsible to the Athenian people.

149. Balogh, Elemer, *Political Refugees in Ancient Greece*, Johannesburg: Witwatersrand University Press, 1943, 133 pp.

A detailed study of political refugees in Greece. Refugees were caused when citizens were banished from Greek poleis. Cohesion and survival of the polis was maintained by ejecting malcontents, traitors, and those committing political offenses. Balogh focuses on the legal aspects of the status of refugees, but misses a big opportunity to investigate how they were used for intelligence on foreign states. His discussion of the *proxenoi* briefly discusses their diplomatic role in handling sensitive intelligence matters. Cf. Walbank, (no. **208**), Gerolymatos, *Espionage and Treason* (no. **167**). REVIEWED IN: *Journal of Hellenic Studies* 1943 pp. 132–133 Treves; *Classical Review* 1945 pp. 23–24 Charlesworth; *American Journal of Archaeology* 1944 pp. 110–111 Murphy; *American Journal of Philology* 1945 pp. 203–206 Wolff; *Classical Weekly* 38 (1944–45) pp. 45–46 Shero.

150. Bauman, R. A., "A Message for Amphipolis," *Acta Classica* 11 (1968), pp. 170–181.

The fall of Amphipolis in the winter of 424/423 during the Peloponnesian War has raised many questions. One of those questions is why the city capitulated when help was on the way. The Spartan general Brasidas had taken the Strymon bridge, camped outside the city, and was waiting for his partisans to open the gates, saving him the trouble of a siege. The pro-Athenian party within the city sent a message for help, and the general (and later historian) Thucydides received it. He was on Thasos with a squadron of seven triremes. He reached Eion on the mouth of the Strymon, three miles from Amphipolis, only to learn that the city had already surrendered. He secured Eion, but then went into exile as a result of the disgrace connected with losing Amphipolis. (Thucydides 4.103–107; 5.26.5).

Bauman suggests that the communications between Thucydides and the beleaguered partisans in Amphipolis was carried out by smoke or fire signalling. He guesses that whatever Thucydides said to them, it made them believe there was little hope and thus the local governor lost control of the situation. Speculative, but an interesting discussion on the timing of the signals and the importance of such diplomatic communications.

151. Bradford, Alfred S., "Plataea and the Soothsayer," *The Ancient World* 23, No. 1 (1992), pp. 27–33.

The ancients were superstitious, although they would call it pious. Their minds were not modern, nor their way of thinking always rational in our terms. They often sought military intelligence from the gods even when more objective information could be collected by more scientific means. One of the most enigmatic events is reported in Herodotus 9.46 about the Battle of Plataea in 479 BC. Both the Greeks and the Persians took the appropriate sacrifices but the signs were not good for an offensive campaign. Only eleven days later did the soothsayers report favorable signs and only then did the Greeks commit to battle.

In a second unexplainable move, the Greek commander Pausanias decides to switch the places of the Athenians and the Spartans so that the Athenians would face the Persians and the Spartans would face the Boeotians. When the Persians found out, they switched their positions too and so the Spartans were back facing the Persians. Throughout the battle, decisions are made based on the soothsayers assessment of the situation and the signs from the gods. This has lead many historians to reject Herodotus's account and to try and reconstruct "what really happened." Bradford finds the Herodotean account consistent and reasonable.

152. Breitenbach, Hans Rudolph, "Der Michigan-Papyrus 5982 Über Theramenes. Historische Probleme und Autorschaft," *Historia* 60 (1989), pp. 121–135.

Breitenbach discusses the composition and authorship of the Theramenes papyrus that describes a secret mission of Thermenes to Lysander in last years of the Peloponnesian War. The text is provided in full, with Germany translation and commentary. Compare Andrewes, (no. **146**) Heinrichs (no. **173**) and Youtie & Merkelbach (no. **213**).

153. Brown, Truesdell S., "Aeneas Tacticus, Herodotus and the Ionian Revolt" *Historia* 30, 4 (1981), pp. 385–393.

Brown researches the sources for stories on tradecraft in Greek authors. For example, the story from Aeneas Tacticus 31.9-9a of a messenger delivering a letter to a traitor who is about to betray a city under siege resembles a story in Xenophon's *Anabasis* I.6.3 on the betrayal of Otanes to Cyrus. Each version of the story varies in detail; who borrowed from whom? There are at least four instances where scholars agree that Aeneas borrowed from Herodotus and three of these come from the chapter on secret messages.

154. Bugh, Glenn Richard, *The Horsemen of Athens*, Princeton: Princeton University Press, 1988, 271 pp.

A history of the Athenian cavalry from the Archaic period throughout the Hellenistic age. The book contains a detailed administrative and prosopographical analysis of a military and social organization whose members came predominantly from the upper classes of Athens, and whose loyalty to the Athenian democracy could and did fluctuate. He discusses Athenian horsemen as messengers on pages 11–12, 99 and 99n and whether they were regular cavalry men or just mounted heralds. He also discusses their use as scouts. REVIEWED IN: *Greece and Rome* 36 (1989), p. 243 Rhodes; *Antiquité Classique* 59 (1990) pp. 483–485 Viviers; *Gnomon* 62 (1990) pp. 420–423 Spence; *Museum Helveticum* 47 91990) p. 262 Knoepfler; *Journal of Hellenic Studies* 110 (1990) p. 251 Anderson; *American Historical Review* 95 (1990) 463–464 Ober; *American Journal of Philology* 111 (1990) pp. 274–277 Clemons; *Annales* (ESC) 45 (1990) pp. 890–891 Schmitt-Pantel; *Classical Review* 40 (1990) pp. 98–100 Lazenby; *Classical Journal* 86 (1990–91) pp. 277–278 Remer; *Historische Zeitschrift* 255 (1992) pp. 152–154 K.W. Welwei.

155. Chroust, A. H., "Treason and Patriotism in Ancient Greece," *Journal of the History of Ideas* 15 (1954), pp. 280–288.

Much of Greek history is littered with stories of political plottings, banishments, defections and massacres. Political parties within the city of Athens divided their population. Oligarchs desperately changing the old order fiercely resisted the new "democrats" who demanded political recognition and social reforms.

One's city state was neither the first nor the only institution that made demands on the allegiance or loyalty of the Athenian. He was a member of a kinship organization (phratry, genos, phyle, oikos) or of any one of many religious confraternities or professional associations. Then there were business associations. Philosophers or rhetoricians formed "schools" of disciples who preferred private meetings to the agora, the palaestra, or the shop. Membership in such associations or clubs was often prized above citizenship. A man's attachment to his city was fundamentally conditioned by his belonging to one or several of these lesser groups. At times such groups expected a loyalty from their members that was incompatible with a citizen's allegiance to his city. Intense party loyalty became incompatible with "patriotism" as we understand it. Chroust discusses the specific examples of Alcibiades, Xenophon and Cleisthenes and their relationship to their polis.

What Chroust does not discuss, but which would make an interesting study, was how factions spied on one another, moved intelligence, or how defections were accomplished.

156. Crum, W. E., *The Monastery of Epiphanius at Thebes,* New York: The Metropolitan Museum of Art Egyptian Expedition, 1926. part 1: Archaeological Material by H. G.E. Winlock. Literary Material by W. E. Crum. Part 2. Coptic Ostraca and Papyri. Edited with Translations and Commentaries by W. E. Crum. Greek Ostraca and Papyri, H. G. Evelyn White.

Vol. II.616. A cipher alphabet found in the Cell of "Priest Elias" on Wood. (*Anthologia Palatina* IX 538 (ed. Stadtmüller)

It is a verse that contains every letter of the Greek alphabet. The cipher is formed by breaking the alphabet into four unequal parts which are shuffled and then inverted. A fragmentary copy of the same line is painted in red ochre in the doorway of the vestibule leading to the Hall of the Altar in the XVIII Dynasty Temple at Deir el Bahri.

A short text enciphered this way was also found at the Monastery of Jeremias at Saqqara (see Thompson, Coptic Inscriptions, no. **104**, ap. Quibell, *Excavations at Saqqara*, t. ii) and the section "Coptic Egypt."

157. Darmstaedter, Ernst, "Feuer-Telegraphie im Altertum," *Die Umschau* (1924), pp. 505–507.

Darmstaedter begins with a quotation of the famous passage from Aeschylus's *Agagmemnon*, 284–315 in which Clytemnestra describes how the intelligence about the fall of Troy has arrived in Athens. The passage contains a list of points over which a signal flame traveled until it arrived at her palace. Taking this as his starting point, the author draws out a map of the area between Troy and Athens, shows where the signal flames would have been and then calculates the amount of light needed to cross such distances, and feasibility of such long-distance communications in the fifth century BC or earlier.

158. David, E., "The Conspiracy of Cinadon," *Athenaeum* 67 (1979), pp. 239–59.

At the beginning of the fourth century B.C. an extremely dangerous revolutionary attempt against the government of Sparta took place. David presents a detailed analysis of the conspiracy, its background, roots, leadership, extent, aims and character and general significance. Not surprising, the plot was detected by a nameless spy whose name and status are not known to us. What we know of the rebels' plan comes from Xenophon's report of the conversation between Cinadon and a new fellow conspirator who is actually the informer (Xenophon, *Hellenica* 3.3.4–5. We do not know why he was trusted in the first place, but he did not have the full information. He knew none of the other conspirators save Cinadon, nor did he know the date at which the movement was time to take place. Still word leaked out, and when Agesilaus was conducting one of his regular sacrifices, he was told by the officiating seer that the gods had revealed a conspiracy of the most terrible sort.

159. Diels, Hermann, *Antike Technik*, Leipzig and Berlin : B. G. Teubner Verlag, 1914, 140 pp. New editions in 1920 and 1965.

Chapter four covers ancient telegraphy, and discusses the *skytale*.

160. Dorjohn, Alfred P., "Smoke-Screens in Ancient Warfare," *Classical Bulletin* 35 (1959), p. 33.

Several examples of the use of smokescreens taken from the handbook of stratagems written by Polyaenus, the second century Macedonian rhetorician. Smoke was used as a cover, for creating deceptive signals, or for diversions when planning a surprise attack.

161. Dorjohn, Alfred P., "Some Ancient Military Stratagems," *Classical Bulletin* 36, 6 (April, 960), pp. 61–63.

Polyaenus, the Macedonian rhetorician, compiled eight books of stratagems to serve as a guidebook for military leaders. He dedicated the book to the emperors Marcus Aurelius and Lucius Verus as they set out for their Parthian campaign in AD 163. Dorjohn highlights a few of the 833 extant examples from Greek contexts.

162. Fichtner, D.P., "Intelligence Assessment in the Peloponnesian War," *Studies in Intelligence* 38, 3 (Fall, 1994), pp. 59–64.

Fichtner examines the Peloponnesian War for the relationship between intelligence assessment and the formulation of policy. Like Kagan, he studies the circumstances surrounding the key political decisions and challenges the conventional wisdom that the war was inevitable. He suggests alternative courses of action that could have been pursued if the available information had only been seen a bit differently. He uses Kagan as his only source; there is not a single reference to Thucydides.

163. Fischl, Hans, "Die Optische Telegraphie der alten Griechen," *Weltverkehrund Weltwirtschaft*. Zeitschrift für Weltverkehrswissenschaft und Weltverkehrspolitik, Berlin 2 (1912), pp. 173–179.

A well-documented account of telegraphing among the ancient Greeks. Fischl begins with the Trojan War and takes his summary through the Persian Wars, the Peloponnesian Wars, the fourth century writers like Aeneas Tacticus, the descriptions in Polybius and Polyaenus, and the Alexander historians Arrian and Q. Curtius Rufus. Texts of the ancient authors are given in the original Greek.

164. Foucault, J.A. de, "Histée de Milet et l'esclave tatoué," *Revue des Études grecques* 80 (1967), pp. 181–86.

The article discusses one of the most famous secret message in ancient history. The incident is from Herodotus 5.35 in which Histiaeus, a Greek residing at the Persian court, wanted to communicate with his son-in-law Aristagoras, the tyrant of Miletus. Since the roads were guarded, he shaved the head of a trusted slave, tattooed the message on the slave's head, and let the slave's hair grow back. The slave was sent to Aristagoras with verbal instructions to shave his head. Aristagoras complied, read the message, and began the Ionian revolt against Persia.

Foucault provides three parallel columns with the Greek texts of this story from three different ancient historians: Herodotus 5.35, Aeneas Tacticus 31.28–29, and the Byzantine historian Nicephorus. He points out that tattooing the message would eliminate the step of trusting the slave with the contents of the message since the slave would not have seen it. Nor could he have confessed to its contents under torture.

165. Gardthausen, Viktor Emil, *Griechische Palaeographie*, Leipzig: B. Teubner, 1879, 472 pp.

Book II, Chapter 5 pp. 231–242 discusses cryptography among the Greeks, secret writing, the *skytale*, cryptography in the Bible, Caesar's cipher. With numerous bibliographical references.

166. Gerolymatos, André, "Ekphantos of Thasos: An Example of Political Use of the Athenian Proxenia," *The Ancient World* 15 (1987), No. 1 & 2 45–48.

A *proxenos* was a citizen of a Greek city state who represented his fellow citizens in a foreign city state. (See Gerolymatos, André, *Espionage and Treason* [no. **167**]. Ekphantos of Thasos, for example, was one of the pro-Athenian democratic leaders of Thasos who was exiled when the Spartans took over the island at the end of the Peloponnesian War (404–403 BC). He was welcomed at Athens and given the *proxenia* by Athens for his part in the capture of Thasos by Thrasyboulos in 407 BC. While in exile, he could serve as an intelligence liaison between the Athenians and their supporters back in Thasos. When a new generation of democratic leaders arose, Ekphantos could advise Athens on whom to trust. Some of the supporters of Ekphantos were even exiled by the Spartans (Demosthenes XX. 59–60).

In 390–389 BC Thrasyboulos once again captured Thasos and the Spartan garrison was expelled. Ekphantos may have returned to Thasos as an Athenian *proxenos*, still acting as a conduit for intelligence between the Athenians and the democratic faction in Thasos. Unfortunately for Ekphantos, the oligarchic faction regained power in 385 BC and banished everyone with close ties to the Athenians (*Inscriptiones Graecae* XII P. 79). Thus Ekphantos was expelled a second time, went to Athens as an exile, and took with him his supporters who had expelled the Spartan garrison in 390–389 BC.

167. Gerolymatos, André, *Espionage and Treason. A Study of the Proxenia in Political and Military Intelligence.* Amsterdam: Gieben, 1986, 140 pp.

Gerolymatos studies the Greek institution of *proxenia*, a term that has no modern equivalent. A *proxenos* was literally a "guest-friend" of a city-state. Since Greek states did not have permanent representatives abroad, local citizens served as *proxenoi* and looked after the interests of other states in their own communities. Unlike an ambassador, a *proxenos* had to be a citizen of the state in which he served, not of the state he represented.

Gerolymatos points out that *proxenoi* were in an excellent position to collect and transmit both political and military intelligence. They could also be involved in covert activities such as assassination, sabotage, subversion and the instigation of political disruption and revolution.

The politicization of the *proxenoi* in the fourth century eroded their prestige and loss of trust in them made them ineffective as intelligence agents. REVIEWED BY: Jack Cargill, *American Historical Review* 92, 1 (February, 1987), pp. 105–106; R.M. Sheldon in *Intelligence and National Security*, Vol. 3, No. 1, January 1988, pp. 220–223; J. F. Lazenby, *Journal of Hellenic Studies* 107 (1987), p. 223; C. Marek, *Gnomon* 60 (1988) Heft 7, p. 594.

168. Gerolymatos, André, "The Proxenia and Foreign Politics of Ancient Sparta at the Beginning of the Fourth Century B.C.," *Acts of the 3rd International Congress of Peloponnesian Studies*, Kalamata 8–15 September 1985, Vol. II, pp. 208–212. *Peloponnesiaka* Suppl. No. 13 (Athens, 1987–88), 3 vols.

Not available at press time.

169. Griffith, F. L. and Thompson, Herbert, *The Demotic Magical Papyrus of London and Leiden*, London: H. Grevel & Co., 1904.

See especially Section III, "Contents of the Ms.," pp. 105–112.

This papyrus was discovered at Thebes and was written in the Third Century AD in both Greek and a very late form of demotic Egyptian. The scribe used a cipher to conceal the crucial portions of important magical recipes. In the section telling how to give a man an incurable skin disease, for example, the papyrus uses secret signs to encipher the words for "skin disease" and the names of lizards. It reads [if you] "wish to produce a *skin disease* on a man and that it shall not be healed, a *hantous* lizard and a *hafleele*-lizard, you cook them with oil, you wash the man with them." There is also a section telling how to make a woman desire a man. The original love potion number 9.

The plain text in most of the cipher sections is in Greek, and the cipher alphabet consists basically of Greek letter signs.

170. Grmek, M., "Les ruses de guerres biologiques," *Revue des Études grecques* 92 (1979), pp. 141–63.

Among the many *ruses de guerres* one could chose from in antiquity, biological warfare was a possibility. Under this heading Grmek discusses poisoned arrows, poisoning wells, and using venomous serpents or insects. He then discusses disease and epidemics and has a long excursus on the battle between the Athenians and the Syracusans in the Peloponnesian War during which malaria became a big problem. He suggests the ancients were very aware of fighting wars in the right location and the right season because of contracting plagues of various kinds.

For more on poisoned arrows, see M.A.J. Reinach, "La fleche en Gaule. Ses poisons et ses contre-poison," *Anthropologie* 20 (1909), pp. 51–80, and E. Pichon-Vendeuil, *Sur les Pharmaques et Venins de l'Antiquité*. Poisons de guerre, de chasse, de justice et de suicide des anciens peuples de l'Europe (Scythes, Hellènes, Italiotes, Celtes, Germains et Ibères), Bordeaux, Gounouilou, Imprimeur de la Faculté de Médecine, 1914.

171. Harmand, J., *La guerre antique de Sumer à Rome*, Collection SUP Ser. l'historien XVI Paris: Presses universitaires, 1973 208 pp.

REVIEWED IN: *Revue des Études Latines* 51 (1973) 432–33 Chevallier; *Syria* 51 (1974) p. 199, Parrot; *Latomus* 34 (1975) pp. 520–521 Brisson; *Rivista Storica Italiana* 86 (1974) pp. 750–754 Liberani; *Revue Historique* 99 no. **254** (1975) pp. 230–234 Will.

172. Harvey, D., "The sykophant and sykophancy: vexatious redefinition?" in P. Cartledge, P. Millett and S. Todd (eds.) *Nomos. Essays in Athenian Law, Politics and Society.* Cambridge, 1990, pp. 103–21.

Harvey refutes Robin Osborne's (no. **188**) attempt to redefine the term sycophant that refers to private informers in Athens. There is no easy definition, but some characteristics remain clear. Sycophancy is a crime. To call someone a sycophant is a pejorative term. Harvey lists as the six characteristics: 1) someone with a monetary motivation, 2) someone who levels false charges, 3) someone who uses sophistical quibbling, 4) someone who makes slanderous attack, 5) someone who frequently takes people to court, 6) someone who acts after the event and rakes up old charges.

Osborne believes there are no professional sycophants; Harvey believes there are. Since they attacked men who were politically active as well as those who were not, Harvey believes sycophancy ultimately hurt the democracy. Reference to them is included here because informers are a means of maintaining internal security. Paid or unpaid, professional or unprofessional, sycophants were a means to gather information on possible threats to the democracy. For a Roman example, see the entries on the *delatores*.

173. Henrichs, A., "Zur Interpretation des Michigan Papyrus über Theramenes," *Zeitschrift für Papyrologie und Epigraphik* 3 (1968), pp. 101–108.

Excursus on Papyrus Michigan 5982 found in Karanis in 1930 that discusses the two missions of Theramenes to Lysander at the end of the Peloponnesian War in 404 BC. Since our only two sources—Xenophon and Plutarch disagree in their accounts, this is an important document. Henrichs believes the author was a lesser historian at Athens, or a partisan with literary ambitions who wrote in the fourth century and was more concerned with the role of Theramenes than with historical facts. He depended heavily on Lysias. Cf. Breitenbach (no. **152**), Heinrichs (no. **173**), A. Andrewes (no. **146**).

174. Herodotus, (c. 484–425 BC) *Histories*, translated by A.D. Godley, Cambridge, MA: Harvard University Press, 1996. 4 volumes. Loeb Classical Library edition.

References to early methods of cryptography and to ingenius stratagems employed to conceal communications in:

In I.123, Herodotus tells the story of a Median noble named Harpagus who wanted to avenge himself on the king of the Medes, who years before had tricked him into eating his own son. He hid a message in the belly of a hare and sent a messenger disguised as a hunter to Cyrus, king of Persia. The hunter was able to travel undetected and arrived at Cyrus's palace with an oral message to "open the hare himself." Cyrus found the message and realized Harpagus would work on the inside to aid him in a revolt against the Medes. Cyrus led the Persians to victory, defeated the Medes and captured the king. This is an example of steganography, not cryptogrphy. See David Kahn, *The Codebreakers*, (no. **38**), p. 81.

In Herodotus 7.239 we read of Demaratus, a Greek exiled in Persia. When news reached him at Susa that Xerxes had decided to invade Greece, he felt he must pass the information on to Sparta. He scraped the wax off a regular writing tablet and wrote a secret message on the wood. He then reapplied wax. Any guard along the road finding the wax tablet would not be suspicious of so common an item. When the tablet arrived in Sparta, no one was able to guess the secret except Gorgo, the daughter of King Cleomenes. Gorgo thus becomes the first female cryptanalyst in history. It is ironic that in the ensuing war, it was her own husband, Leonidas, who died with the 300 Spartans defending the pass at Thermopylae. See David Kahn, *The Codebreakers*, (no. **38**), p. 81.

In Herodotus 5.35 we hear of Histiaeus, who wants to send word from the Persian court to his son-in-law, the tyrant Aristagoras at Miletus. He shaved the head of a trusted slave, tattooed the secret message on his head, and waited for his hair to grow. He sent the slave off to his son-in-law with the verbal instruction to shave the slave's head. The message urged Aristagoras to revolt against Persia. See David Kahn, *The Codebreakers*, (no. **38**), p. 81.

175. Homer, *The Iliad*, 6/168ff.

Queen Anteia, Proteus's wife, falls in love with the handsome youth Bellerophon, and wants him to satisfy her passion in secret. So Homer begins the story that contains the first conscious reference to, as opposed to use of, secret writing. Bellerophon refuses so Anteia goes to King Proteus with the lie that Bellerophon had tried to rape her. The King dares not kill Bellerophon outright, so instead he sends him to Lycia carrying tablets purported to be credentials, with the instruction to hand them over to the Lycian king. The Lycian king tries many ways of killing Bellerophon indirectly, such as commanding him to kill the Chimera (the fire-breathing monster with the head). In the end, he realizes Bellerophon stands under the protection of the gods and gives him his daughter and half his kingdom.

This is the only mention of writing in the *Iliad.* Homer does not tell us what the markings on the tablet were. David Kahn believes they were simple letters and that actual substitution of symbols for letters would have been too sophisticated for the era of the Trojan War. But the mystery that Homer throws around the tablets does suggest that some rudimentary form of concealment was used. An allusion, perhaps. Such as: Treat this man as you did Glaucus, naming someone else the king had assassinated. The tone of the passage makes it certain that here, in the first great literary work of European culture, appears the first faint glimmerings of secrecy in communication for the Greeks. See David Kahn, *The Codebreakers*, (no. **38**), p. 81. The oldest Greek cryptographic text is that on the Acropolis Stone, fourth century BC. See Herbert Boge, *Griechische Tachygraphie und Tironische Noten* (no. **233**).

176. Hunt, Arthur Surridge, "A Greek Cryptogram," *Proceedings of the British Academy*, 15 (1929), pp. 127–34.

A papyrus purchased in Egypt by the late Professor F. W. Kelsey for The University of Michigan. It has, on one side, a document in cursive Greek dating to the time of the Roman emperor Hadrian. The writing on the recto did not seem to be Greek. Rather there is a Greek text in substitution cipher. This type of cryptography in Egypt was no novelty.

The reason for this papyrus being in code is that it contains a magical treatise containing the directions and formulae for the production of certain effects. This particular spell was concerned with the production of comeliness.

The method of writing adopted in this treatise illustrates a characteristic feature of the theory and practice of magic. Magic was an occult science, whose mysteries were revealed to a select few, and needed to be guarded jealously. Often they were handed on from father to son. (See Pap. Berlin 5025 (Preisendanz, i). Caution and secrecy are repeatedly insisted upon. Several of the instances of Egyptian cryptography mentioned below are associated with magic. The writer of this papyrus, therefore, took a further precaution of endeavoring to secure that, if his book fell into profane hands, the spells should remain unread.

The text includes a photograph of the Michigan Cryptographic Papyrus.

Cf. Coptic Papyrus in Paris, Maspero, *Comptes Rendus de l'Academie des Inscriptions et Belles Lettres* 1871 pp. 189–93; pp. 185–87.

Papyrus Leiden A 65 verso.

Adaptations of ordinary letters in Greek cryptographic alphabets occur in Medieval manuscripts:

Gardhausen, *Griechische Palaeographie,* Vol. II, p. 306

The simpler device of giving normal letters abnormal values was used in Egypt in the Coptic period, see W.E. Crum, *The Monastery of Epiphanius* ii, 616. (no. **157**).

177. Hunter, V.J., *Policing Athens. Social Control in the Attic lawsuits 420–320 B.C.*, Princeton: Princeton University Press, 1994.

Ancient Athens had no police force other than a relatively small number of publicly owned slaves (300 Scythians) at the disposal of different magistrates., Furthermore, the city of Athens did not have an army available for large-scale police duties. Hunter studies what she calls a "...continuum extending from the self-regulation of kin and neighbors, or the community in general to the punitive sanctions of the state..." (p. 4). In a society where slaves played a role in the social control of their masters and Athenian citizens were encouraged to spy on each other, one wonders how long treason would have escaped notice. The atmosphere reminds one of the saying that espionage is done occasionally by spies and all the time by neighbors, relatives and colleagues. REVIEWED IN: *L'Antiquité Classique* 64 (1995) 452–453 S. Gotteland; *American Historical Review* 100,5 (1995) p. 1540 R.S.J. Garland; *American Journal of Philology* 116,4 (1995) pp. 659–662 J.P. Sickinger; *Classical Review* 45,1 (1995) pp. 89–91 S.C. Todd; *Greece and Rome* 42,1 (1995) pp. 92–93 H. Van Wees *Prudentia* 27,2 (1995) pp. 77–81 Gilmour.

178. Kroll, W., "Kolax," in Pauly-Wissowa, *Real-Encyclopaedie d. klassischen Altertumswissenschaft* XI.1 (1921), col. 1069–1070.

Kolax (pl. *kolakes*) According to Plutarch, *De curiositate* 522f–523a, informers and parasites surrounding the monarchs of Cyprus. One type in Salamis are called *Gerginoi* and hold the position of spies. They supposedly eavesdropped while mixing with people throughout the city, in workshops and markets and reported back what they found out to the masters called *Anaktes*. Another type of informer, the *Promalanges*, are investigators who conduct inquiries into whatever is reported by the *Gerginoi*. Russell p. 109 believes the four passages in Plutarch point to the existence of "organized, permanent, and perhaps professional intelligence networks in the fifth and fourth centuries." See Frank S. Russell, *Information Gathering in Classical Greece* (no. **201**), pp. 108–114.

179. Lammert, "*kataskopos*," Pauly-Wissowa, *Real-Encyclopaedie d. klassischen Altertumswissenschaft* 10, 2 (1919), col. 2485.

Short encyclopedia entry on the word for "spy" in the Greek world. See Russell (no. **201**).

180. Lewis, Sian, *News and Society in the Greek Polis*, Chapel Hill: University of North Carolina Press, 1996, 206 pp.

Although news about events and individuals, public and private, flowed ceaselessly into the ancient *polis*, the Greeks did not have a word for "news." Lewis studies the role that news played in Greek society, and how spoken and written information were transmitted. What was the relationship of news to information and dissemination, to affirmation and propaganda, to an individual's status and role in the community, to a government's control over its citizens and to the maintenance of cultural values? Lewis sees her book as a corrective to studies that she believes have overemphasized the role of military intelligence and certain forms of ancient technology. She is more interested in social interaction than the mechanics of information-gathering. She relies on a construct of the ancient world built by Starr and Adcock: that the Greeks neglected intelligence and bumbled their way through diplomacy and wars. For a corrective, see Frank Russell's review in *Bryn Mawr Classical Review* 98.3.9, and his book *Information Gathering in Classical Greece* (no. **201**). REVIEWED IN: *Classical Review* n.s. 48, 2 1998, pp, 393–395 C. Taplin; *Revue des Études Grecques* 1998, pp. 347–349 P. Payen.

181. Lofberg, J. O., *Sycophancy in Athens*, University of Chicago dissertation, 1917, 104 pp.

A detailed and important study of the role of the sycophants in Athens. His material is drawn almost entirely from Aristophanes and the orators. No attempt is made to carry the study beyond the period of Demosthenes. For that see his article in *Classical Philology*, 1920.

Wealthy and non-litigious Athenians were at the mercy of these private informers and shrewd legal tricksters. Payment of blackmail was safer for combating their threats than an actual appearance in court. The popular courts were not well-disposed toward the rich and in this lay the advantage of the sycophant. As informers they terrified both the guilty and the innocent. Through club organizations they strengthened their power, and often served as the hired agents of others.

182. Lofberg, J. O., "The sycophant-parasite," *Classical Philology* 15 (1920), pp. 61–72.

A continuation of his study on the sycophants of Athens, carrying it beyond the time of Demosthenes and examining what later writers had to say, especially those writers of New Comedy, Plautus and Terence. *Sycophanta impudens* was a stock character in New Comedy suggesting that sycophants were still active and well-known members of Athenian society. With the take-over of Greece by Philip and Alexander there were fewer opportunities to attack men in high political office or sell their services to revolutionary parties. The term eventually becomes synonymous with parasite and loses its technical meaning.

183. Losada, Luis, *The Fifth Column in the Peloponnesian War*, Mnemosyne Supplement 21, Leiden: Brill, 1972, 156 pp.

Losada has made an interesting study of what we today call a "fifth column" in the Peloponnesian War. This included Athenians working for the Spartans, Thebans working for the Athenians, Spartan helots working for the Athenians. These men would be called "traitors" by their own *poleis*, because they betrayed their home state and helped a foreign government in times of war. For obvious reasons, much of this work had to be clandestine, including the movement of intelligence. This study covers both the methods used by fifth columnists and the ideologies that caused them to work for the enemy.

184. Margoliouth, David Samuel, *The colophons of the Iliad and the Odyssey, deciphered by D.S. Margoliouth with a reply to some criticism of Herr v. Wilamovitz Möllendorf*, Oxford: B. Blackwell, 1925, 21 pp.

Professor Margoliuth deciphers the colophons of the *Iliad* and the *Odyssey* using the same method he applied to the prologues. (See Margoliuth, *The Homer of Aristotle* [no. **185**].) His earlier book was criticized by Wilamowitz-Mollendorff; this volume contains Professor Margoliouth's defense against the charge of knowing Greek improperly. Friedman Collection 98. REVIEWED IN: *Times Literary Supplement* 5 November 1925.

185. Margoliouth, David Samuel, *The Homer of Aristotle*, Oxford: Blackwell, 1923, 245 pp.

Professor Margoliouth continues his investigations into the anagrams which he claims to have discovered to lurk hidden in the opening lines of certain Greek authors. Chapter one discusses the cipher of Attic tragedy that contains messages from the three great Attic tragedians. He then proceeds on to the Homeric cipher that he claims to have found in the opening lines of the *Iliad* and the *Odyssey*. These concealed messages are written in iambics, and tell us that Homer wrote both the *Iliad* and the *Odyssey*, that he came from Kos, and that the number of books of each poem was 24. Clever, but ultimately unconvincing. REVIEWED BY: J.R. in *Baconiana*, London, 17 (September, 1924), pp. 305–309; *Saturday Review*, London, 12 (1924), p. 418; *Times Literary Supplement*, Thursday April 17, 1924; *Journal of Hellenic Studies* 1925, p. 185 V.S; *Literarische Zentralblatt* 1925, p. 518 Arnim; *Philologische Wochenschrift* 1925, pp. 97–108 Wallies; *Deutsche Literatur Zeitung* 1924, p. 1108w Wilamowitz-Moellendorff; *Revue des Études Anciennes* 1924, p. 365 Boulanger.

186. Margoliouth, David Samuel, "The Use of Cypher in Greek Antiquity," *Baconiana*, London, Jan. 1938, Vol. 23, pp. 1–12.

Margoliouth gives examples of Greek dramatists introducing cryptic signatures into their work. He also believes the prologues and the colophons to the *Iliad* and the *Odyssey* contain such signatures.

187. Montfaucon, Bernard de, *Palaeographia graeca sive de Ortu et progressu literarum graecarum, et de variis omnium saeculorum scriptionis graecae generibus ... opera et studio D. Bernardi de Montfaucon* ... Parisiis: L. Guérin, J. Boudot et C. Robustel, 1708 xxix–574 pp. In-fol.

Chapter 5, pp. 285–290 discuss cryptography among the Greeks.

188. Osborne, R., "Vexatious Litigation in Classical Athens: Sykophancy and the Sykophant," in *Nomos*. Essays in Athenian Law, Politics and Society, ed. Paul Cartledge, Paul Millett, and Stephen Todd, pp. 83–102 (see Harvey no. **172**).

Osborne tries to reinterpret the meaning of the term sycophant, which is usually defined as a private informer who turns people in for money. He argues instead that sycophancy was a vitally important part of the nature and running of the Athenian democracy. In his view, sycophants prosecuted aristocrats who refused to do their full share politically and financially to support the governmental structure. Private litigation took from these rich men what they should have voluntarily given to the state and thus spread the money around. For a contrary interpretation, see Lofberg no. **182**.

189. Parke, H.W., "Polyaenus VI,18," *Classical Review* 42 (1928), pp. 120–121.

Parke analyzes the story reported by Polyaenus 6.18, Pausanias 10.1.2 and Herodotus 8.27 concerning a route of the Thessalians by the Phocians. The stratagem is a rather clever one. The Phocians assembled a small advanced force and covered them with chalk and had them deliver a night attack. Pausanias and Polyaenus (but not Herodotus) tell us the moon was full; the sight of these phantom troops in the moonlight must indeed have been ghostly. Parke points out the corruptions in the text of Polyaenus and suggests a proper emendation.

190. Pekáry, Thomas, "Nachrichtenwesen," *Lexicon der alten Welt*, Stuttgart, 1965.

Short encyclopedia entry on the movement of intelligence in the ancient world. For a full treatment, see W. Riepl, *Das Nachrichtenwesen des Altertums* (no. **9**).

191. Pekáry, Thomas, "Spionage," *Lexicon der alten Welt*, Stuttgart, 1965.
Short encyclopedia entry on espionage in the ancient world.

192. Plutarch, *Lysander*, Bernadotte Perrin translation, Loeb Classical Library edition, Cambridge: Harvard University Press, 1916.

Passage 26.2: "Sundry very ancient oracles were kept in secret writings by the priests there [at Delphi], and that it was not possible to get these, nor even lawful to read them, unless someone born of Apollo should come after a long lapse of time, give the keepers an intelligible token of his birth, and obtain the tablets containing the oracles."

David Kahn, *The Codebreakers*, (no. **38**), p. 91.

193. Polyaenus, *Stratagems of War*, R. Shepherd Trans. Ares Press 1974. Peter Krentz and Everett L. Wheeler translation, Ares Publishers, Inc., 1994, 2 vols.

The latter translation is a more readable and accurate version of the work of Polyaenus, a Macedonian rhetorician of the 2nd century AD who dedicated a collection of stratagems to the Emperors Marcus Aurelius and Lucius Verus on the occasion of their Parthian War of 161–166. The word stratagem captures the very essence of the doctrine of ancient military theory—resourcefulness, innovation, cleverness, deceit, trickery, seizing the proper moment for action, and an efficient use of intelligence. There are only two surviving examples of the genre of stratagem collections from the ancient world. This is one of them, Frontinus (no. **360**) provides the other. The examples are amusing, although historical accuracy was not his goal. For his sources and methods, see R.J. Phillips, *The Sources and Methods of Polyaenus*, Ph.D. Dissertation, Harvard University, 1970. Summary in *Harvard Studies in Classical Philology* 76 (1972) 297–98.

194. Polybius (c. 204–122 BC) *The Histories*. Translated by W. R. Paton, London: Heinemann, 1922, 6 vols.

General account of the affairs of Greece and Rome from 220 to 146 BC. Only five of the original forty books are extant. References to early methods of cryptography are found in Vol. IV, Book 10, ch. 43–48, pp. 207–219. 10.43 describes a signalling system that is a combination of fire signals and a water clock. He mentions the fact that two other Greeks, Kleoxenos and Demokleitos, tried to improve this system.

195. Preisendanz , Karl, *Papyri Graecae Magicae* (*Greek Magical Papyr*), Leipzig and Berlin, 1928; Stuttgart: Teubner, 1973, 2 vols.

Greek cryptographic alphabets preserved in medieval manuscripts: Bibl. Nat. suppl. Gr. 574; Preisendanz IV, 2518.

196. Pritchett, W. K., *The Greek State at War*, Berkeley: University of California Press, 1971–1991, 5 vols.

An invaluable multi-volume work on warfare in the Greek world. See especially: Volume 1: Chapter X, p 127–133 on Scouts; Volume 2: Chapter VIII on

Surprise Attacks, pp. 156–176; Chapter IX, Ambuscades pp. 177–189; Volume 5: Chapter III, section 4F on the fate of *proxenoi* when captured. REVIEWED: *American Historical Review* (February, 1987), p. 105, Ober.

197. Richmond, J.A., "Spies in Ancient Greece," *Greece and Rome* 45 (1998), pp. 1–18.

A brief overview of the use of spies in ancient Greece. Richmond discusses security measures taken against enemy spies, and clandestine communications. This latter discussion is taken mostly from Aeneas Tacticus, on which see Sheldon, "Tradecraft in Ancient Greece" (no. **206**), Richmond's statement that the Roman Empire "carefully organized its intelligence service" should be taken in the context of his comparison to the Greeks who were certainly less bureaucratized.

198. Roisman, Joseph, *The General Demosthenes and his Use of Military Surprise*, Stuttgart: Franz Steiner Verlag, 1993, 84 pp.

A discussion of the career of the Greek general Demosthenes whose use of surprise by infantry is rare in classical Greece. The usual reasons given for its neglect are deficient intelligence and cultural inhibitions. But Demosthenes seemed to have overcome both and scholars now recognize him as one of the best Greek generals for his pioneering use of military intelligence. REVIEWED IN: *Gnomon* 67,4 (1995) p. 367 K. Welwei; *Klio* 1996, p. 257 J. Seibert.

199. Ruelle, Charles Emile, *La cryptographie grecque; simples notes, suivies d'un tableau général des alphabets secrets,* Paris, D. Morgand, E. Rahit successeur, 1913. (Mémoires lu à l'Academie des Inscriptions et Belles-Lettres, le 22 septembre, 1911.) Reprinted in: *Mélanges Picot*, 1913 (Slatkine Reprints: Geneva, 1969), Vol. I, pp. 289–306.

A series of 42 Greek alphabets listed with the manuscripts in which they appear. Some are used for cryptographic purposes. A large section at the end treats cryptographic signs that were non-identifiable.

See also Lange et Soudart, *Traité de cryptographie,* X, 84 (no. **41**); Locard, *Bibliographie cryptologique*, p. 918.

200. Ruelle, Charles Emile, "Note relative à la cryptographie grecque," *Bulletin de la Société Nationale des Antiquaires de France*, Paris, 1894, 2e Trim, pp. 119–121.

Ruelle discusses a cryptographic system discussed by both Montfaucon (no. **187**) and Gardthausen (no. **165**) that was used by copyists when they wanted to conceal their signatures. The evidence is cited in Garthausen, *Griechische Palaeographie*, (no. **165**), p. 235, and appears also in a 9th century Arab manuscript in the Vatican (no. 1085). Such systems continued in use until the 16th century. Ruelle adds to these examples a new papyrus published by Carl Wessely (no. **242**) dating to the fourth century. He also reports that Hebrew scholars have discovered an analogous cryptological system.

201. Russell, Frank Santi, *Information Gathering in Classical Greece*, Ann Arbor: University of Michigan Press, 1999, 300 pp.

Derived from his doctoral dissertation on the subject, Frank Russell has published the first systematic study of intelligence gathering in Classical Greece since Chester G. *Starr's Political Intelligence in Classical Greece* (see no. **207**). The different between the two books is that Russell deals mostly with military intelligence and Starr with political.

The book is divided into chapters on Tactical Assets, Strategic Assets, Spies, Conveying Messages, and Counterintelligence. A solid work with a truly professional understanding of the Greek sources. REVIEWED BY: R.M. Sheldon in *International Journal of Intelligence and Counterintelligence*, 14, 2 (Summer 2001), pp. 289–296. V. Erhart, *Journal of Military History* 65, 2 April 2001, pp. 476–477.

202. Russell, Frank Santi, "A Note on the Athenian Defeat at Notium," *Ancient History Bulletin* 8.2 (1994), pp. 35–37.

A short but perceptive article on the use of reconnaissance in force by Antiochus in 407/6 BC to test the mettle of Lysander's fleet. This may have caused the battle of Notium unintentionally.

203. Schuller, Wolfgang, "Grenzen des Spätrömischen Staates: Staatspolizei und Korruption," *Zeitschrift für Papyrologie und Epigraphik* 16 (1975), pp. 1–21.

Schuller believes the *agentes in rebus* were not a secret service who oppressed civilians. He, like A.H.M. Jones before him, believes they were harmless bureaucrats. He does admit, however, that they functioned as state police, and had the job of supervising the state apparatus and those sections of society from which the highest officials were recruited. He believes abuse arose because Roman officials were corrupt, accepted bribes and used strong-arm tactics to line their pockets.

204. Semmet, R., *Intelligence Activity in the Classical World*, M.A. thesis (Humanities), Wright State University, 1984.

A general survey of intelligence activities in the Greco-Roman world. It is done from English translations of the ancient sources and secondary works. Semmet relies heavily on Dvornik and seems to accept his conclusions without much critical analysis. Chapters cover communications, sources (state and private), deception and counterintelligence. She covers both intelligence successes and failures.

205. Sheldon, R. M., "The Ill-fated Trojan Spy," *Studies in Intelligence* Vol. 31, No. 1 (1987), pp. 35–39. Reprinted in *American Intelligence Journal,* 9, 3, Fall (1988), pp. 18–22.

The tenth book of Homer's *Iliad* tells the story of the Trojan spy Dolon who was captured by Diomedes and Odysseus in one of the most famous intelligence operations in Greek literature. A couple of scouts pull off what a brigade of cavalry might have attempted in vain. Dolon, brash but not careful, loses his own life and provides intelligence that results in the deaths of almost an entire contingent of allied soldiers. Short bibliography on the *Doloneia* included.

206. Sheldon, R. M., "Tradecraft in Ancient Greece," *Studies in Intelligence* 30, 1 (1986), pp. 39–47.

A discussion of Greek tradecraft, i.e. the running of agents, sending secret messages, using codes and ciphers, disguises and surveillance. Taken from the works of Aeneas Tacticus, Polyaenus, Pausanias, Xenophon, Herodotus, Ovid, Pliny, Onasander, Polybius and Frontinus.

207. Starr, Chester G., *Political Intelligence in Classical Greece*, Mnemosyne Supplement 31, Leiden, 1974, 48 pp.

The first and still best discussion on the role of political intelligence in classical Greece. After defining the nature of the problem, Starr begins by surveying the intelligence gotten from spies, deserters and traitors. Then he moves on to open sources such as intelligence retrieved by ambassadors, merchants and aristocrats. He ends with a perceptive section on the limits and misuse of intelligence. REVIEWED IN: *Classical World* 69 (1976) pp. 479–480 Connor; *Annali della Sculo Normale Superiore di Pisa* 5 (1975) pp. 1611–1612 Piccirilli.

208. Walbank, Michael B., *Athenian Proxenies of the Fifth Century B.C.* Toronto, 1978, 552 pp.

Athens issued a series of decrees to honor foreigners who served the city's commercial and political interests. These *proxenoi* could also be conduits of sensitive political intelligence (Gerolymatos, no. **167**). These decrees date to the fifth century BC when Athens was leading the Delian Confederacy and becoming an imperial power in the Aegean. Walbank collects the sixty-eight inscriptions that record the grants of proxeny, plus those known from literary sources and fourth century documents recording children or grandchildren trying to revive a proxeny held by an ancestor. Walbank believes there was a *proxenos* for every state that constituted Athens' empire, so this is just a small fraction of the men she could call on to collect information.

This book should be used in conjunction with the work of Gerolymatos who is more convinced of the espionage capabilities of these political appointees.

209. Wernicke, K., "Die Polizeiwache auf der Burg von Athen," *Hermes* 26 (1891) pp. 51–75.

Increased thieving activity in Athens during the refurbishment of the Acropolis included the loss of clothing, and ivory and gold from nearby workshops during the construction of the Parthenon. During its construction, a provisional police force was created enabling three policemen to be on duty right inside the entrance. They were given a provisional base that also served as a temporary holding cell for thieves who were caught. Kallikrates was entrusted with the planning of this "as-cheap-as-possible" structure. The completed structure would also house a police force. Scythian slaves were used as the public police.

210. Whitehead, David, "The Laconian Key," *Classical Quarterly* 40 (1990), pp. 267–268.

There is an enigmatic reference in Aristophanes (*Thesmophoriazeusae* 423) to something called "The Laconian Key." Paul Cartledge ("Spartan Wives: Liberation of Licence?," *CQ* 31 [1981], 84–105) suggested it was used to keep Spartan women under control or confinement. Whitehead suggests that since the Spartans were known for their brutal monitoring and winnowing out of foreigners, the Laconian key may have taken its name from a security device that was used to lock doors from the outside, and may have been used for forms of nocturnal house arrest not just for women but also for aliens.

For other ancient references to the key, see Aristophon, *Peirithous*, fr. 7 Kassel-Austin; Menander, *Misoumenos*, fr. 8 Sandbach (10 Koerte); Plautus, *Mostellaria* 404–5, cf. 419–26. Cf. I. M. Barton, "Tranio's Laconian Key," *Greece and Rome* 19 (1972), pp. 25–31. Barton does not explain the use of the key.

211. Williams, Mary Frances, "Crossing the Enemy Lines: Military Intelligence in the *Iliad* 10 and 24," *Electronic Antiquity* 5, 3 (November 2000), pp. 1–57.

An excellent article that covers reconnaissance, religious sources of information (taken quite seriously in antiquity), the story of Dolon, and combat intelligence in Homer's *Iliad*, chapters 10 and 24. The author finds many parallels between the two chapters.

212. Xenophon, *Anabasis*, Carleton L. Brownson translation, Loeb Classical Library edition, Cambridge: Harvard University Press, 1961, 2 vols.

The "Up-Country March" as it is called relates the story of 10,000 Greek mercenaries stranded in Asia Minor after supporting an abortive coup led by Cyrus against his brother Artaxerxes II, King of Persia. Unlike the normal Greek hoplite phalanx battles conducted on familiar Greek territory, Xenophon had to establish special military detachments whose unique purpose was to reconnoiter unfamiliar terrain, to discover the position and strength of enemy forces, and to ascertain the sentiments of the natives towards the Greeks. The officers used this intelligence to plan their course of march, to avoid ambushes, and to get their troops back to the Black Sea and eventually Byzantium.

213. Youtie, H.C and Merkelbach, R., "Ein Michigan-papyrus über Theramenes," in *Zeitschrift für Papyrologie und Epigraphik* 2 (1968), pp. 161–169.

Discussion of Papyrus Michigan 5982 found in Karanis in 1930 that discusses the first mission of Theramenes to Lysander on Samos at the end of the Peloponnesian War in 404 BC. Since our only two sources—Xenophon and Plutarch—disagree in their accounts, this is an important document, especially on the subject of diplomatic missions. Cf. Breitenbach (no. **152**), Heinrichs (no. **173**), A. Andrewes (no. **146**).

The Skytale

No other cryptological method from the ancient world has been more discussed or more misunderstood. Traditionally described as a method of encrypting messages used by the Spartans, in the standard interpretation it consisted of a stick of known diameter around which a piece of leather or paper was wound. A message was written along the length of the stick. When the leather or paper was unwound, the message became unreadable until it was wound around an identical stick kept by the recipient. There is debate as to whether it was meant to conceal the content of a message that fell into enemy hands or prove the authenticity of the delivered message. Many later authors used the term to describe any secret or hidden message, even without the use of sticks.

It has been suggested that that *skytale* was originally a simple token—a broken staff of which the commander took one half and the government kept the other. When it was time to send a message, the messenger was given one half so that it would establish his identity when he arrived at the other point. An obvious disadvantage is that this would make the method usable only once. More recently, scholars have suggested that the *skytale* never existed but was a concept made up by a Hellenistic librarian to define an unknown term he had stumbled across in manuscripts.

In any event, there have been many ingenious explanations for this so-called cryptological tool. Almost every book or article on cryptography mentions it (see above, section IX). Herewith are a few of the more creative and lengthy discussions.

214. Anderson, J.K., *Military Theory and Practice in the Age of Xenophon*, Berkeley: University of California Press, 1970, 419 pp.

Pages 67–68 contain a brief but sensible discussion of the *skytale.*

215. Aulus Gellius, *Attic Nights*, 17.9. John C. Rolfe Translation, Loeb Classical Library edition, Cambridge: Harvard University Press, 1984, 3 vols.

The first part of the passage is about the substitution ciphers found in the letters of Julius Caesar. These include letters addressed to Gaius Oppius, Cornelius Balbus. Gellius mentions a commentary by the grammarian Probus called *On the Secret meaning of the Letters appearing in the Epistles of Gaius Caesar.* Cf. Leighton, (no. **42**).

The second part of the passage concerns other secret forms of writing taken from ancient history. These include the Spartan *skytale*, Hasdrubal Barca's disguising letters written on wax tablets, and Histaeus and the tattooed slave (cf. Foucault, J.A. de, "Histée de Milet et l'esclave tatoué" no. **164**).

216. Birt, Theodor, *Die Buchrolle in der Kunst. Archaeologisch-Antiquarische Untersuchungen zum antiken Buchwesen,* Leipzig: B. G. Teubner, 1907, 352 pp.; New edition Hildesheim, New York: Olms, 1976, 352 pp.

A discussion of the *scytale* on pp. 274–275 with a line drawing that makes it look suspiciously like a candy cane wrapped in leather.

217. Crell, Ludwig Christian, *Dissertatio de scytala laconica … d. 13 martii 1697, secundum disputabit M. Ludovicus Christianus Crellius,* … Lipsiae, literis Fleischerianus (n.d.) In-4°

Deals with the Spartan *skytale.* Cf. Kelly (no. **221**), West (no. **231**) For information on Crell and his works, see Carmona, *Tratado de criptografia*, p. 176; Lange et Soudart, *Traité de cryptographie*, XIII (no. **42**); Locard, *Bibliographie cryptographique*," p. 924; J.S. Galland, *Bibliography of the literature of Cryptography*, (no. **29**), p. 49.

218. Diels, Hermann, *Antike Technik*, B. G. Teubner Verlag: Leipzig and Berlin, 1914, 140 pp.

Chapter four covers ancient telegraphy, and discusses the *skytale*.

219. Diodorus Siculus, *Library of History*, translation by C.H. Oldfather, Loeb Classical Library edition, Cambridge: Harvard University Press, 1989, 12 volumes.

14.11.1-3 on the *skytale* citing Ephorus (in Jacoby, *Fragmente der griechischen Historiker* 1841–70, Frag. 70).

220. Forelius, Hemming, *Dissertatio de modis occulte scribendi et praecipue de scytala Laconica,* Holmiae, 1697.

The second oldest study of the *scytale* after Klauer (no. **222**).

See J.S. Galland, *Bibliography of the Literature of Cryptography* (no. **29**) p. 65. Mentioned also by Carrmona, *Tratado de criptografia,* p. 176; Lange et Soudart, *Traité de cryptographie*, XIII (no. **42**); Locard, *Bibliographie cryptographique*," p. 924, and F. Wagner, "Studien zu einer Lehre von der Geheimschrift (Chiffernkunde)," *Archivalische Zeitschrift* 13 (1888), p. 41.

See above no. **165**. Gardthausen, V., *Griechische Palaeographie* II, 2 (1913) p. 300.

221. Kelly, Thomas, "The Spartan Skytale" in J. Ober & J. Eadie (edd.) *The Craft of the Ancient Historian: Essays in Honor of Chester G. Starr*, Lanham, Md. 1985, 141–169.

The *skytale* is described by the *Oxford Classical Dictionary* as a secret method of communication used by Spartan magistracies during wartime, especially between ephors and king or general. Each of them had a stick of equal size so that the message written on a strip of leather wound round the stick of the sender, and then detached, became illegible until the strip was rewound on the stick of the recipient.

L. Jeffrey, *The Local Scripts of Archaic Greece* (Oxford, 1961), pp. 57–58 and Terrence A. Boring, *Literacy in Ancient Sparta*, Mnemosyne Suppl. 54 (Leiden, 1979), pp. 39–41, Pritchett, *Greek States at War*, pp. 45–46 each recognizes to some degree the discrepancy between the use of the word by early and late authors, but all accept the later tradition.

Kelly takes the argument one step farther and shows that the evidence from the classical sources suggests this was simply a method of conducting open communications. The misconception of the *skytale* as a cryptograph was introduced by Apollonius Rhodius during the Hellenistic period. He was then followed by later authors. Stephanie West (no. **231**) comes to the same conclusion.

222. Klauer, Georg Caspar, *Disputatio historico-philologica de Scytala Lacedaemoniorum, quam ... sub praesidio ...* Dan. Guil. Molleri ... d. [ ] junii 1695 ... erudityotrum examini exponet Georgius Casparus Klauer ... Altdorfi, literis kohlesiainis (s.d. 1695?) 36-ivp In-4°.

Listed by J.S. Galland, *Bibliography of the literature of Cryptography* pp. 103–104; Locard, *Bibliographie cryptologique*, p. 923 and F. Wagner, "Studien zu einer Lehre von der Geheimschrift (Chiffernkunde)." *Archivalische Zeitschrift*, Munich 1886–1888 Vol. XIII, p. 41. It is the earliest study of the *scytale*.

223. Leopold, J. H., "De Scytala Laconica," *Mnemosyne* 28 (1900), pp. 365–91.
Leopold cites all of the ancient sources in the original, making this a useful early reference, although few authors refer to it. Exceptions are W. Suess *Philologus* 78 (1922), (no. **230**), pp. 158–162, Kelly p. 162, n. **221**.
For other useful discussions of the *scytale*, see K. Dziatzko, *Zwei Beiträge zur Kenntniss des antiken Buchwesens* (Göttingen, 1892), pp. 5–8; W. Riepl, *Das Nachrichtenwesen des Altertums*, (no. **9**), pp. 313–315, and Reincke, "Classical Cryptography" (no. **53**) Kelly (no. **221**) and West (no. **231**).

224. Martin, Albert, "Scytale," in Daremberg-Saglio, *Dictionnaire des antiquités grecques et romaines* (Paris, 1877–1919), col. 1161ff.
Martin gives the once standard, but possibly now defunct, definition of the Spartan *scytale*. The scytale consisted of a tapered baton, around which was spirally wrapped a strip of parchment or leather on which the message was written. When unwrapped, the letters were scrambled in order and formed the cipher. However, when the strip was wrapped around another baton of identical proportions to the original, the plain text reappeared. (See *Encyclopædia Brittanica*, Cryptology—History). Were this truly the origin of the word *scytale*, it would make the Greeks the inventors of the first transpositional cipher. Martin discusses all the literary evidence beginning with Plutarch, *Lysander* 19 and Aulus Gellius, *Attic Nights* 17.9. For a more recent critical treatment see Kelly (no. **221**) or West (no. **231**).

225. Moller, Daniel-Guillaume, *Dissertatio de scytala lacedaemoniorum*. Altdorfi, 1695.
Listed by J.S. Galland, *Bibliography of the Literature of Cryptography*, (no. **29**), p. 127; Locard, *Bibliographie Cryptologique*, p. 923.

226. Nepos, Cornelius, *Cornelius Nepos*, J.C. Rolfe translation, Loeb Classical Library edition, Cambridge: Harvard University Press, 1984, 348 pp.
Alcibiades 9–10 on the *skytale*.

227. Oehler, J., "Scytale," Pauly-Wissowa, *Real-Encyclopaedie d. klassischen Altertumswissenschaft* (1927).
Encyclopedia entry on the *scytale*. He uses a fragment of Aristotle to prove that the *scytale* was used as a cryptograph at Ithaca. The argument is rejected by Kelly (no. **221**) p. 166, n. 44.

228. Opperman, S., "Skytale" *Der Kleine Pauly, Lexicon der Antike* (Munich, 1975), col. 241.
Short dictionary entry defining the *skytale*, the supposedly Spartan method of encryption.

229. Plutarch, *Lysander*, 19. in *Plutarch's Lives*, translated by Bernadotte Perrin, Loeb Classical Library edition, Cambridge: Harvard University Press, 1982, 11 volumes.
When Thorax, one of Lysander's friends and fellow generals, is put to death, a dispatch scroll (*scytale*) is sent to Lysander ordering him back to Sparta. There seems to be nothing secret about this method. Kelly (no. **221**), West (no. **231**).

230. Suess, Wilhelm, "Über antike Geheimschriftmethoden und ihr Nachleben," *Philologus* 78 (June, 1922), pp. 142–75.

Survey of ancient methods of secret communication and a good discussion on how this material held interest for Renaissance writers. Among the methods discussed are Caesar's cipher (Reinke, no. **53**), secret writing in Aeneas Tacticus (Sheldon, *Tradecraft*, no. **206**, the fire signalling in Polybius, the *scytale* (cf. Leopold, Kelly no. **221**, West no. **231**), codes in Cicero's letters to Atticus (Cf. Dodge no. **266**), and secret writing in Ovid (Cf. Sheldon, *Tradecraft*, no. **206**).

231. West, Stephanie, "Archilochus' Message Stick" *Classical Quarterly* 38, 1 (1988), pp. 42–48.

One of two articles (see Kelly no. **221**) debunking the traditional definition of the *skytale* as a scrambling device. A strip of leather would be wound slant wise onto the stick and the message written lengthwise. When the strip was unwound, the message would become unintelligible until rewound by the recipient onto a stick of equal thickness. West shows how the Spartans came to use the term to designate any official written communication.

Tachygraphy

Another method of disguising messages might be the use of shorthand. Although such systems were used by civilians for reasons (i.e. taking down speeches verbatim), the effect of writing something in shorthand would be that the text would become unreadable to one who did not know the system. The origins of Greek shorthand are, and are likely to remain, obscure. There is no clear evidence for the existence of a Greek system of shorthand until the Roman period (see *Oxford Classical Dictionary*, 3rd edition, p. 1468). Two inscriptions were originally thought to have represented a system of shorthand, but these are now interpreted as proposals for a system of abbreviations (brachygraphy) rather than as a method of taking dictation. (See *IG* 2/3^2 2783, 4th century BC; and one from Delphi J. Bousquet *Bulletin de Correspondence Hellénique* (1956) 20–32, 3rd century BC).

Evidence for Greek shorthand comes mostly from papyri and wax tablets found in Egypt like the Papyrus Oxyrrhynchus 4.724 (AD 155) that is, appropriately, an apprenticeship contract with a shorthand teacher. After the second century AD, however, specimens of Greek shorthand and portions of manuals become much more common and show a fully organized system. Some appear on stone inscriptions. The following works provide full descriptions of the system and show possible influence on Tironian notes used by Cicero's secretary, Tiro, and named for him. I have not gone into the details of the systems. Most of the systems were used for reasons of speed (shorthand) or space (abbreviation), but many authors note their possible use for secret writing. Considering their obscurity, Tironian notes could probably be used today as a cryptographic system. Very few specialists could break the code. Another category of documents that use secret writing is magical papyri. Professional magicians (i.e. priests who practiced magic) attempted to keep their technical secrets to themselves, and when they wrote down spells and formulas for their sons or protégés, they did so in a manner that could not be read by a casual reader. There are too many magical papyri to list here, but I have included some of the collections that discuss their shorthand systems. Interested readers should certainly start with Gardthausen, Viktor Emil, *Griechische Palaeographie*, Leipzig: B. Teubner, 1879. Since many of these authors write about both the Greeks and Romans, readers should refer to the section on The Roman Republic, "Tironian Notes" for more bibliography.

232. Birt, Theodor, "Zur Tachygraphie der Griechen," *Rheinisches Museum für Philologie* 79 (1930), pp. 1–6.

Did Greeks invent tachygraphy before the time of Tiro, the slave of Cicero, who is generally attributed with its invention? Birt believes they did.

233. Boge, Herbert, *Griechische Tachygraphie und Tironische Noten*. Ein handbuch der Schnellschrift der Antike und des Mittelalters, Berlin: Akademie-Verlag, 1973, 280 pp. with bibliography.

A handbook on ancient and medieval shorthand that discusses alphabets, ancient writing, and how words are shortened. Contains a good bibliography on stenography, abbreviations, and Greek and Roman tachygraphy. There is a useful chronological chart comparing known examples of Greek inscriptions containing shorthand and Latin manuscripts with Tironian notes.

234. Foat, F.W.G., "On Old Greek Tachygraphy," *Journal of Hellenic Studies* 21 (1901), pp. 238ff.

Scholars have detected at least three systems of shorthand writing in Greek antiquity. Foat investigates whether they were used as cryptographic systems or just speed writing. What is the relationship of these systems to the Latin Tironian notes? Was the system syllabic, alphabetic or phraseographic? Was it purely arbitrary or related to the ordinary forms of writing? These systems can be traced in various phases from the Ptolemaic period down to the fifteenth century. Foat surveys these questions and provides a detailed bibliography on the subject.

235. Gardthausen, Viktor Emil, "Geschichte der griechischen Tachygraphie," *Archiv für Stenographie*, Berlin, Teil 1, N.F. ii, (1906), pp. 1–10.

A survey of Greek shorthand writing systems by Viktor Emil Gardthausen, who has written extensively on Greek palaeography and Greek cryptography.

236. Gitlbauer, Michael, Die drei Systeme der Griechischen Tachygraphie," *Wochenschrift für klassische Philologie* 12 (1895), p. 206.

237. Gitlbauer, Michael, "Die Drei Systeme Griechischer Tachygraphie," Akademie der Wissenschaften, Wien, *Denkschriften* 44 (1896), II, pp. 1–50 with tables.

Compares three systems of Greek shorthand writing, one called the Xenophon system. Compares them with Tironian notes. Examples of both inscriptional and cursive writing illustrated on the plates. Similar to the systems discussed in Wessely (no. **243**).

238. Johnen, Christian, *Geschichte der Stenographie im Zusammenhang mit der allgemeinen Entwicklung der Schrift and der Schriftkürzung*, Berlin: F. Schrey, 1911, 295 pp.

A history of shorthand and the creation of symbols for speedwriting. He covers the Greeks, the Romans, the Byzantine world and the Middle Ages.

239. Mentz, Arthur, *Geschichte und Systeme der griechischen Tachygraphie*, Berlin: Gerdes & Hödel, 1907, 55 pp.

A short work on Greek shorthand, beginning with a discussion of the famous Acropolis stone, one of the earliest examples of Greek abbreviated script. On the stone, see also Gardthausen, "Tachygraphie oder Brachygraphie des Akropolissteines," *Archiv für Stenographie* 1906. pp. 81ff. Mentz includes an excellent bibliography.

240. Mentz, Arthur, "Die hellenistische Tachygraphie," *Archiv für Papyrusforschung*, 8 (1927), pp. 34–59

Publishes syllabaries contained in wax tablets at Halle and in Papyrus 5464 at Berlin.

241. Milne, Herbert John Mansfield, *Greek Shorthand Manuals. Syllabary and Commentary*, London and Antrim: N.H. Egypt Exploration Society, 1934, 77 pp.

In his introduction, Milne argues that the basic principles of the Greek and Roman systems are identical and the formal coincidences too frequent and too striking to ignore. A good introduction to the problem.

242. Wessely, Carl, "Neue griechische Zauberpapyri," *Denkschriften der kaiserlichen Akademie der Wissenschaften in Wien, philos.—hist. Classe* (memoires de l'Academie imperiale de Vienne) 42 (1893) II, pp. 1ff.

Magical papyri are a good place to look for encoded writing because magicians attempted to keep their technical secrets to themselves when they wrote down spells and formulas for their sons or protégés. Pp. 53–54 gives such a papyrus with a tachygraphic system used for this purpose.

243. Wessely, Carl, "Ein neues System griechischer Geheimschrift," *Wiener Studien* 26 (1904), pp. 185–189.

The first example of this secret writing system comes from Papyrus CXXI in the British Museum dating to the 3rd century BC that he published in his "Neuen griechischen Zauberpapyri (no. **242**). It is a type of numerical shorthand that

Wessely works out and charts on page 188.See also Gardthausen, *Griechische Palaeographie*, (no. **169**) p. 235ff, Gitlbauer (no. **237**), Wessely, "Ein System Altgrieschischer Tachygraphie" (no. **244**).

244. Wessely, Carl, "Ein System Altgriechischer Tachygraphie," *Denkschriften der kaiserlichen Akademie der Wissenschaften in Wien, philos.—hist. Classe,* 43 (1894) IV, p. 1–44, with plates.

Discusses three handwritten manuscripts that contain Greek shorthand. Paris Nr. II 599–3032 from the 10th century AD, on which see Gitlbauer, Codex Vaticanus Graecus 1809, and one from the British Museum, Additional Ms. 18231. But he also discusses earlier examples and then pulls them altogether into a developing system and puts them into the context of the history of speed writing, condensed writing and secret writing.

245. Wessely, Carl, "Ein System Altgriechischer Tachygraphie," *Denkschriften der kaiserlichen Akademie der Wissenschaften in Wien, philos.—hist. Classe*, Band 44, Abhandl. iv, 1895.

Edits fragments of syllabaries from papyri and waxed tablets in the Rainier collection dating chiefly to the 4th–6th century AD. This forms the basis of all subsequent study.

The Spartan Krypteia

The four principal sources on the so-called Spartan secret service, or the *krypteia*, are:

1) Plato, *Laws*, I.633 b–c.

2) the scholia on the same passage. See W.C. Greene, *Scholia Platonica*, Haverford, Pa.: Philological Society of America, 1938.

3) Plutarch, *Life of Lycurgus* 28 1–7.

4) pseudo-Heraclitus of Pontus in C. Müller, *Fragmenta Historicortum Graecorum*, 2, p. 210 = Aristotle frag. 538 Rosë.

Two allusions:

5) Plato, *Laws* 6, 763b.

6) Plutarch, *Life of Cleomenes* 28,4.

Other commentators

7) a papyrus fragment in the British Museum no. **187**.

8) Justin 3,3.

246. Girard, P., "*Krypteia*," *Daremberg-Saglio Dictionnaire des Antiquités grecques et romaines* 3, 1 (1900) pp. 871–873.

A short encyclopedia entry on the *krypteia* listing the ancient and some secondary sources.

247. Girard, Paul, "Un texte unédit sur la cryptie de Lacedémonienne," *Revue des Études Grecques* 11 (1898), pp. 31–38.

Girard comments on a text first published by Kenyon in the *Revue de Philologie* in 1897. It is a fragment of a papyrus in the British Museum, no. **187**. He compares it to Plato's *Laws* VI.761 that has an allusion to the Spartan *krypteia.* He believes it was a two year stint served by young Spartans who hunted down helots. For alternative interpretations, see Jeanmaire (no. **249**), Vidal-Naquet (no. **252**) and Wallon (no. **253**).

248. Jeanmaire, H., *Couroi et courètes, Essai sur l'éducation spartiate et les rites d'adolescence dans l'antiquité hellénique*, Travaux et Memoires de l'Université de Lille, Lille: Bibliothèque universitaire, 1939.

See especially pp. 550–554 where he discusses the sources upon which our knowledge of the *krypteia* is based and reiterates his interpretation first paid out in the article from *Revue des Études grecques*, 1913 cited above.

249. Jeanmaire, Henri, "La cryptie Lacedémonienne" *Revue des Etudes Grecques* 26 (1913), pp. 121–150.

A review of the sparse evidence on the Spartan secret service or *Krypteia.* We have short descriptions in Plutarch, *Lycurgus* 28, a passage attributed to Heraclitus of Pontus (Müller, *Fragmenta Historicorum Graecorum* II, 210), Justin III.3, and some allusions in the Laws of Plato (*Ad Plat.* Leg I .633 B).

Jeanmaire sees the *krypteia* not as an anomaly, but as an integral part of Spartan institutions. He makes sociological comparisons with groups in North and South Africa to show the initiation rites into male institutions. He concludes that the *krypteia* was the last stage of an initiation rite into the *ephebeia*; a period of retreat where the initiate had to go into the countryside and not return until he had killed a helot. Cf. Pierre Vidal-Naquet, *The Black Hunter,* ch. 5. (no. **252**).

250. Koechly, Hermann, *De Lacedaemoniorum cryptia commentatio*, in *Hermann Köchlys Gesammelte Kleine Philologische Schriften,* Leipzig: B.G. Teubner, 1881, Vol. 1, no XXIX.

Koechly sees the Sparta *krypteia* not as a standing institution but as a stage in the preparation of a Spartan soldier for military life.

251. Levy, Edmond, "La kryptie et ses contradictions," *Ktema* (1988), pp. 245–52.

Reproduces the texts upon which our knowledge of the *krypteia* is based. He points out that in some the *krypteia* seems to be some sort of endurance test imposed on young Spartans. In others, its function is repressive and seems to be part of the internal security system that kept helots in place. Ethnographers have recognized in the initiation rituals some parallels with other more modern societies.

252. Vidal-Naquet, P., *The Black Hunter*, Baltimore: Johns Hopkins University Press, 1986, 367 pp.

Chapter five "The Black Hunter and the Origin of the Athenian Ephebeia," discusses initiation rites of young Greek men (ephebes) into full citizenship and as members of the hoplite phalanx. He makes some very good observations about the tactics used by ephebes such as night ambushes, surprise, stealth and *ruses de guerre* that trained them to guard the wild areas beyond the border of the city. This model of behavior was contrary to what they would swear in their oath as hoplites, and the author carefully maps out this logical inversion. REVIEWED IN: *Greece and Rome* 34 (1987) p. 106 Walcott; *Classical Bulletin* 63 (1987), pp. 126–127 Papalas; *American Journal of Philology* 109 (1998), pp. 282–285 Robertson; *Classical Weekly* 82 (1988–89) pp. 211–212 Sinos.

253. Wallon, Henri, "Explication d'un passage de Plutarque sur la loi de Lycurgue nommé la cryptie," *Journal général de l'instruction publique* (1850), pp. 470–473.

A study that reduces the *krypteia* to a simple curfew law.

Alexander the Great and The Hellenistic Age

It is ironic, perhaps, that classic works like J.F.C. Fuller's, *The Generalship of Alexander the Great* (London, 1958) do not mention the use of intelligence by a general as great as Alexander. Such a great military figure as Alexander found intelligence gathering useful. To be sure, the sources are meager for many parts of Alexander's life and accomplishments, as they are for Hellenistic history in general. But this has been remedied recently by other studies that have mined the ancient sources for evidence showing a great deal of intelligence gathering occurred in the Hellenistic age, not only by Alexander and his armies but by the generals of the successor states. If the ancient sources were better, if Ptolemy's history had survived, and if Hieronymus of Cardia's work had survived, modern historians would have more to say about the intelligence activities from the death of Alexander to the death of Cleopatra.

254. Aristotle, *De Mundo* 398 b 30–35. In *The Complete Works of Aristotle*, Revised Oxford Translation, edited by Jonathan Barnes, Princeton University Press, 1984, 2 volumes. See volume one, pp. 626–640.

On the Persian postal system. We have no sources to inform us if the system existed in Alexander's time or if he ever used it.

255. Borza, Eugene N., "Alexander's Communications," *Ancient Macedonia 2* (1977), 295–303. Reprinted in Makedonica, Regina Books, Claremont, CA, 1996.

Conventional wisdom dictates that a great commander needs good communications and intelligence. There is unanimous agreement that Alexander was a great commander and yet no serious study has been done on his use of communications. W.W. Tarn's biography (*Alexander the Great*) devoted only 9 pages to it. The texts of Arrian, Q. Curtius Rufus, Diodorus, Justin and Plutarch offer no precise description of the procedures by which Alexander established and maintained a communications system. Yet there is abundant evidence of intelligence activity at Alexander's headquarters.

Badian characterized Alexander's army as a "moving isle in a hostile sea." Borza rejects this image and maintains Alexander was in constant contact with Macedonia and Greece. One new study (see Rossi, no. **259**) examines nearly 300 references in sources that deal with Alexander's communications. Therefore, we know some system existed even if we lack the details to describe it. Some general patterns emerge. Messages appeared to have been written and the delivery system was flexible enough to permit a variety of types of transport. Even in the remote areas of central Asia Alexander maintained contact with the heart of the empire. Troop replacements arrived, reports from Greece were received and numerous administrative measures were implemented. Even difficulties of weather never completely cut off Alexander's ability to communicate. He was never incommunicado. Borza summarizes the findings of Engels on logistics that were later published (see Engels, no. **257**). This was not a few hundred hoplites but a huge army. Only logistical organization could guarantee their survival. One needed to know about intended routes, advance parties needed to secure alliances or make other arrangements with local people to provide supplies along the line of march.

Borza mentions but does not elaborate on the human "filters" that may have acted as deterrents to the full flow of information. This is a political problem associated with Alexander's court which was notorious for its intrigues.

Diodorus Siculus, *Diodorus of Sicily*, translated by C.H. Oldfather. Book 19.57 Tells how the old Persian post service in Asia Minor was re-established and kept working in order by Antigonus, founder of the Seleucid dynasty. He established at intervals throughout all of Asia which he controlled, a system of fire-signals and dispatch carriers, by means of which he expected to have news of his realm. See entry **219**.

256. Engels, Donald, *Alexander the Great and the Logistics of the Macedonian Army*. Berkeley, 1978, 194 pp.

More than twenty references in the text to Alexander's need for advance intelligence and his internal security methods. Engels' article in *CQ* 1980 (no. **257**) treats the subject in more detail, but this book puts the material into the narrative of Alexander's campaigns and the general overall logistical problems.

257. Engels, Donald, "Alexander's Intelligence System" *Classical Quarterly* N.S. 30 (1980), pp. 327–340.

The collection and use of accurate military intelligence was of fundamental importance for the success of Alexander's campaigns. This was the first study to analyze the procedures Alexander used to obtain and evaluate intelligence.

The sources are silent on the institutional organization and administrative procedures, but Engels does a good job of piecing together the references we do possess showing coherent patterns of intelligence gathering, analysis, dissemination and counterintelligence. He also goes into two of Alexander's major intelligence failures, a topic rarely touched on by authors who only wish to praise the successful general.

This material was later incorporated into Engels' book length study on *Alexander the Great and the Logistics of the Macedonian Army*. (no. 256)

258. Fournie, Daniel A., "Intrigue. The supposed rescue of a beleaguered rebel king in 214 BC turned out to be an elaborate double cross," *Military History* (March 1997), p. 28, 78.

A retelling of Polybius 8.15–21. Two Cretans, Sosibius and Bolis, betray Achaeus, governor of Asia Minor and rebellious cousin of Antiochus III. Treachery, coded messages, secret rendezvous, disguises, torture, decapitation, crucifixion—this story has it all.

Polybius, *The Histories*, translated by W.R. Paton. Book 10.42.7ff tells how Philip II, King of Macedonia, organized throughout his state a signalling system to enable him to receive as fast as possible any information about any kind of danger. He was especially interested in enemy invasions. This is the first evidence of a fire-signalling system being used on Greek soil. See entry **194.**

259. Rossi, Gwen H., *The Communications of Alexander the Great*, Ph.D. Dissertation, The Pennsylvania State University, University Park, Pa. 1973, 102 pp.

An important study on a sadly neglected aspect of Alexander's career, his communications system, without which intelligence could not have been transmitted. The historian Ernst Badian in his article "Agis III" (*Hermes* 95 [1967] p. 189), characterized Alexander's army as "a moving island in a hostile sea." The military importance of such a communications system cannot be stressed enough. Alexander needed to have a good communications network to provide supplies, reinforcements and intelligence reports. Rossi concludes that without such a network, Alexander could not have achieved such outstanding success.

The Roman Republic

Standard studies of the Roman military during the Republic do not often contain information on how the army might have collected intelligence, or analyzed and transmitted it. Nor do they discuss whether the early Romans used clandestine means to communicate or staged covert actions.

Works like Frank Adcock's *The Roman Art of War Under the Republic* (New York, 1940) or W. V. Harris's *War and Imperialism in the Roman Republic* (Oxford, 1979) would lead us to believe the Romans did none of these things. The ancient sources indicate otherwise. That is not to say all modern authors accept what ancient writers had to say. Austin and Rankov in their book *Exploratio*, for example, give little credence to the sources on the early Republic. There is no lack of ancient or modern authors who have written about intelligence activities from the regal period to the fall of the Republic. Readers may choose from among these and decide whom to believe.

Republican Rome was at war a great deal of the time, especially during the years of the middle republic (roughly the fourth to second centuries BC). And where there is war, there is intelligence gathering. Messages needed to be transferred from headquarters to the field and back. Commanders needed to scout battlefields or put spies among the enemy. As Rome's overseas possessions became more numerous, the Senate needed information on its own provinces and the enemies who might threaten them. Information on the battlefield would become particularly important during the war with Hannibal, who had a formidable spy network to use against the Romans. Although much of Roman intelligence gathering was done on an ad hoc basis, by the end of the Republic many of the institutions which would appear full-blown in the empire had already made their appearance. The legionary scouts or exploratores are in evidence by the time of Caesar, as are the speculatores who were used to carry messages to and from headquarters.

Communication in the capital and across Rome's overseas provinces became problematic as Rome's empire grew. Although some scholars have suggested the Republic had a postal service, the evidence remains unconvincing. Nevertheless, messengers called *tabellarii* were used to keep information flowing. Slaves played no small part in the movement of information during the Republic. They not only acted as intelligence carriers for their masters, they also used the shorthand system invented by a freed slave of Cicero's, Tiro, to record messages, speeches and take notes. The system survived until the Middle Ages. Although it did not have a specific military application as far as we know, any message written in Tironian notes would be unintelligible to a reader unfamiliar with the system.

Finally, the subject of internal security is an important one. Keeping public order in an age of urban unrest and eventually civil war cannot have been an easy task for the Roman government. The Spartacus revolt shows how easily the Roman government could be brought to a halt by even a handful of revolting slaves who used intelligence as a force multiplier against the Roman legions. One of the contributing factors in the fall of the Republic was the government's inability to keep the peace in Rome and Italy which gave rise to generalissimos like Pompey, Caesar and Crassus rising to power. The *Commentaries* of Caesar give us an inside view of the late Republic, and show us the full scope of Roman intelligence capabilities in both the Gallic and Civil Wars.

General

260. Amiotti, Gabriella, "I Greci ed il massacro degli Italici nell'88 A.C." *Aevum* 54 (1980), pp. 132–139.

Amiotti studies the sources relative to the massacre of the negotiatores or Roman and Italian businessmen living in Asia Minor when Mithridates VI, King of Pontus, decided to declare war on Rome in 88 BC.

As an intelligence coup, this is an interesting case study. Mithridates sent out the message that on a given day, all Romans and Italians should be killed. It was carried out mostly in the Greek cities and islands. There does not seem to be much evidence for the participation of the indigenous population of the client states in the interior of Anatolia. Amiotti finds traces of factions that fought for the Roman side. The lower classes who had nothing to lose went with Mithridates. Those of the ruling classes sided with the greatest commercial power at the time—Rome. Some people were killed because they were commercial rivals, others for political reasons. We do not know, to this day, how Mithridates coordinated this feat, how he communicated with his agents, or how he kept such a deadly plan secret.

261. Brizzi, Giovanni, *I sistemi informativi dei Romani. Principi e realtà nell' età delle conquista oltremare (218–168 AC.)*, Wiesbaden: Steiner, 1982, 282 pp. (Historia Einzelschriften no. 39).

The title of this book is misleading. Very little of it is about the methods used by the Romans for acquiring information. The bulk of the book is a study of Roman military and diplomatic policy. Brizzi argues that before the Hannibalic War, the close links between the senate and the upper classes in the cities of Italy provided the senate's main source of information. After 200 BC individual Greek states were added as additional sources. But when their information proved untrustworthy, the Romans then sent out missions of their own *legati*. The most controversial part of the book is Brizzi's idea that in the first part of the Second Punic War Roman commanders, loyal to the idea of *fides*, were averse to the use of any kind of underhanded method. It was Scipio who realized that such attitudes were an obstacle to victory, and he deliberately abandoned fides as a determinant of his policy. In total contradiction to this thesis see Everett L. Wheeler, *Stratagem and the Vocabulary of Military Trickery* (no. 11).

See also reviews of Brizzi's book: John Briscoe, *Journal of Roman Studies* 205–206; Andrew Lintott, *Gnomon* 56 (1984) 555–556; Richard, *Revue des Études Latines* 61 (1983) 404; Vidman, *Listy Fololologicke* 107 (1984) 55; Bollini, *Rivista storica dell'Antichità* 12 (1982) 286–292; Wankenne, *L'Antiquité Classique* 53 (1984) 503–504; Botteri, *Latomus* LI (1992) 213–214.

262. Caesar, Gaius Julius, *The Battle for Gaul*, A newly illustrated translation by Anne & Peter Wiseman, London: Chatto and Windus, 1980, 208 pp.

Caesar's commentaries on the Gallic wars give us the best first hand account we have of a Roman commander at war. Not surprisingly, Caesar's works show a great sensitivity to the intelligence needs of the Roman army. He was a master at surprise and speed, managed to choose a favorable battlefield against the enemy, and except for the last incident in 44 BC, always kept himself informed about his enemy's intentions.

Reference to Caesar's use of cipher in Suetonius, Deified Julius 56.6. See also, David Kahn, *The Codebreakers*, (no. **38**), p. 83–84.

263. Culham, Phyllis, "Archives and Alternatives in Republican Rome," *Classical Philology* 84, no. 2 (1989), pp. 100–115.

It has been a highly debated question whether or not Republican Rome kept government archives. Did historians like Livy and Polybius have access to public documentary sources? (Or for our purposes, could there have been intelligence files for use by consuls?) Ancient historians have commonly assumed that state documents were filed originally in the *aerarium* and later in the *tabularium* (constructed in 78 BC). Culham does not discuss intelligence matters. She is concerned with reference to these documents for legal purposes (checking for forgeries, settling legal disputes). After a review of the evidence, Culham concludes that neither the *aerarium* nor the *tabularium* in Rome successfully functioned as a public archive during the Republic, and that they were not originally intended to serve that purpose. We know of only one man who tried to consult documents in the aerarium. Cicero's attempt demonstrates that it was next to impossible to use documents in the aerarium. Cicero claimed that consulting such documents was impossible and that the permanent staff was worse than no help at all (De Legibus 3.20.46).

The usual assumptions about the archival function of the aerarium are therefore incompatible with the Romans' own accounts of conditions in the Republic and with the mass of evidence for the actual disposition of documents. Culham proposes an alternative explanation of why and how Romans handled documents as they did. Posting instead of deposition in an archive was the standard means of making information publicly available.

264. Dawson, A., "Hannibal and Chemical Warfare," *Classical Journal* 63 (1967), pp. 117–125.

Dawson discusses a number of clever stratagems described by Livy as being used by Hannibal in the Second Punic War. At first, he seems to debunk Hannibal's cattle stratagem in Livy 22.17 and Silius Italicus 7.3111ff, the story of Hannibal blasting a pass through the Alps using vinegar (in Livy 21.37 and repeated by Florus, Eutropius and Orosius), and he doubts the report that Hannibal plowed the battlefield at Cannae in advance to create a dust storm against the Romans. But then he provides a chemical explanation for all these curious incidents. It shows a great deal of technical skill and advance intelligence on the part of the Carthaginians to pull these tricks off.

265. Desjardins, M., *Les tabellarii, porteurs des depèches chez les Romains*, Bibliotheque de l'École des Hautes Études vol. 35 (1878), pp. 51–81.

The magistrates in Rome used *tabellarii*, who were freedmen or slaves employed as couriers. These should not be confused with the tabellarii employed by the publicani whose letter-bearers also exercised the function of modern tax collectors. These latter tabellarii often carried private mail for important men, and, to reduce costs, friends often shared the services of a courier. For a study on Roman civilian and military transport, for example, see also Giuseppina Pisani Sartorio, *Messi di trasporto e traffico*, published by the Museo della Civilta Romana (Rome: Edizioni Quasar, 1988).

266. Dodge, Louise, "Cipher in Cicero's Letters to Atticus," *American Journal of Philology* 22 (1901), pp. 439–41.

Roman letter writers resorted to all manner of devices to render their private correspondence unintelligible to private eyes. Examples abound in Cicero who, during his exile, no doubt wished to protect himself and his brother Atticus. Dodge points out that when code was used there is always a tell-tale absence of Greek words. In the encoded portion of the message, letters were moved a certain number of places forward or back. Greek words could not have been left intact on such a page; their significance would have been too suggestive to the suspicious reader. If they had been transposed also, according to the same system (but in their own alphabet), the small, isolated groups of foreign characters would have given the clue to the cipher. Nor could the letters of the Greek words have been transposed and then written in Latin characters because of the different order in which the letters occur in the two alphabets, not to mention the presence in the Greek of the double-consonant symbols. The only feasible way would have been to "keep to the vernacular," which is exactly what Cicero did.

267. Ezov, Amiram, "The 'Missing Dimension' of C. Julius Caesar," *Historia* 45 (1996), pp. 64–94.

A fine analysis of Julius Caesar's use of *exploratores* and *speculatores* in both the *Gallic Wars* and the *Civil War*. A good companion to R.M. Sheldon, *Tinker, Tailor*, 94ff (no. **456**), and Richardson, (no. **272**).

268. Kübler, "Statores," *Pauly-Wissowa Real-encyclopedie der classischen Altertumswissenschaft*, Vol. 3, A, 2. Stuttgart, 1929.

Provincial magistrates retained special messengers called *statores* for the transport of official letters containing information for the Senate and the magistrates in republican Rome. We know very little about their precise function or how they discharged their duties, but Cicero, in his letters from Cilicia, speaks of them in a manner that suggests they had been around for quite some time. A governor might have several *statores* at his disposal. In the absence of a state-sponsored postal and transport system they were obliged, when traveling long distances, to wait for suitable means of conveyance or requisition alternative transportation as best they could. Even governors faced such difficulties with transport arrangements when journeying to or from their provinces. Kübler lists the inscription and literary evidence for these runners.

269. Nippel, Wilfried, *Aufruhr und "Polizei" in der römischen Republic*, Stuttgart, 1988, 334 pp.

A revised version of his *habilitationsschrift* presented in 1982/3 that deals with various aspects of the maintenance of public order in the city of Rome under the Republic. Two chapters deal with the growing violence of the last century of the Republic and the ways in which the senatorial government responded to it. The final chapter deals with order in the city under the Principate.

Nippel rejects the common view that lack of a police force was a serious weakness in the Roman Republic and helped to account for its downfall. For Nippel, the essential guarantors of order were social and political stability and consensus and respect for legitimate authority. REVIEWED BY: J.W. Rich *Journal of Roman Studies* 81 (1991), pp. 193–5.

270. Nippel, Wilfried, *Public Order in Ancient Rome*, Cambridge: Cambridge University Press, 1995, 163 pp.

The absence of a professional police force in the city of Rome has often been identified as one of the reasons for the collapse of the Republic. Yet Augustus did nothing to remedy this "structural weakness." Nippel shows that a specialized police force is a modern invention. There were, however, mechanisms of "self-regulation" that operated as a stabilizing force in Roman society and Nippel studies this system of law and order.

271. Ramsay, A. M., "A Roman Postal Service Under the Republic," *Journal of Roman Studies* 10 (1920), pp. 79–86.

According to most modern scholars, there was no postal service during the Roman Republic. Suetonius, in his account of the institution of the imperial post by Augustus (*Deified Augustus* 49), speaks of this system as if it were a new departure in history of Roman administration. Ramsay suggests that courier relays already existed and that Augustus simply made more efficient this old Roman method of communication. The major innovation was to replace courier relays with postal carriages that carried the same messenger from the sources of the intelligence to the emperor himself.

272. Richardson, M.A., *Julius Caesar's Use of Intelligence*, M.A. Thesis, Defense Intelligence College, 1984.

A detailed study of Julius Caesar's use of intelligence in both the Gallic Wars and the Civil War. Not strong on analysis, and written by a non-classicist who has no profound knowledge of the original texts, but Richardson has a good grip on what intelligence activities look like and finds much evidence for them in Caesar's writings. He is especially helpful in breaking down intelligence activities into their component parts, i.e. counterintelligence, installation security, scouting and reconnaissance, etc. A much neglected work that should be used in conjunction with Ezov (no. **267**) and Sheldon, *Tinker* (no. **456**).

273. Ruess, Ferdinand, *Über die Tachygraphie der Römer*, Munich: Ernst Stahl, 1879, 30 pp.

This is a treatise on Tironian shorthand. Not used for military purposes, but nonetheless a type of "secret writing" if one did not know the system. Tiro was the slave and after 53 BC freedman of Cicero. He was Cicero's lifelong companion and close friend. Tiro took down Cicero's speeches in a shorthand system that he invented. His system survives in an extant collection of ancient abbreviations.

Tiro was also distinguished as a librarian, and after Cicero was murdered, he piously devoted himself to the publication of Cicero's complete works and compiled a catalogue of them. He wrote an unflattering biography of Cicero that has not survived. Ruess gives a good account of the publication history of Tironian notes from 1603–1879 then explains and illustrates the system.

274. Ruess, Ferdinand, *Über griechische Tachygraphie.* Festgabe der Königlischen Studienanstalt. Neuberg A.D. zur dreihundertjährigen Jubelfeier der K. Julius-Maximilians-Universität, Würzburg, Griessmayersche Buchdruckerei, 1882, 56 pp.

A study of Greek shorthand systems from 400 BC to AD 1,000 including Greek writing in the Roman period and Tironian notes.

Cf. Meister, *Die Anfänge der modernernen diplomatischen Geheimschrift.* p 10.

275. Russell, Frank, "The Battle of Notium," *Ancient History Bulletin*, Vol. 8, No. 2 (1994), pp. 35–37.

A short but perceptive article on the use of reconnaissance in force by Antiochus in 407/6 BC to test the mettle of Lysander's fleet that may have caused the battle of Notium unintentionally.

276. Sheldon, Rose Mary, "Hannibal's Spies," *International Journal of Intelligence and Counterintelligence* 1, 3 (1987), pp. 53–70.

The only full treatment of Hannibal's use of intelligence assets against the Romans in the Second Punic War. Although his clever stratagems and advance planning kept him successful on the battlefield in Italy for thirteen years, Hannibal eventually lost the war because Rome had control of the seas, Rome's allies remained loyal, and the offensive strategy of Scipio was successful.

277. Sheldon, Rose Mary, "The Spartacus Rebellion: A Roman Intelligence Failure?" *International Journal of Intelligence and Counterintelligence*, vol. 6, no. 1 (1993), pp. 69–84.

The escaped slave Spartacus organized and trained an army that numbered in the tens of thousands. He kept Roman forces at bay for two years, scored nine resounding victories and defeated six Roman legions. Sheldon examines the intelligence techniques Spartacus used to defeat the Romans, and what intelligence failures on the part of the Romans contributed to Spartacus' success.

278. Wheeler, Everett, "Sapiens and Stratagems: The Neglected Meaning of a Cognomen" *Historia* 37 (1988), pp. 166–195.

Wheeler discusses the cognomen Sapiens. It is an unusual nickname in Latin and does not seem to refer to legal expertise, to domestic political skills, nor to old Roman virtues. Wheeler argues that the cognomen was used in a military context, denoting in particular the skill and ingenuity of a general seen in his use of stratagems. The subsequent "demilitarization" of its use resulted from the image of crafty, sly Romans giving way to the emphasis on *fides Romana* in the second century.

This study goes contrary to those like Giovanni Brizzi (no. **261**) who think such stratagems were foreign to the Roman mentality and that the Romans only resorted to them after being victimized by Hannibal. This view is discussed in more detail in Wheeler's book, *Stratagem and the Vocabulary of Military Trickery* (no. **11**).

Tironian Notes

Marcus Tullius Tiro, the faithful slave and later freedman of Marcus Tullius Cicero, was Cicero's confidential secretary and literary adviser. After Cicero's death he published some of his speeches and letters. Tiro is most famous, however, for having invented a system of shorthand known as *notae Tironianae* or Tironian notes. Cicero had scribes especially trained in the system. Tironian notes used signs for prepositions and other short words. Then signs were invented for endings (*declinationes*). Tironian notes were used in the imperial administration of Rome and later by the Christian Church. In the third and fourth centuries, they were modified into a system of syllabic shorthand.

Some scholars have suggested that Romans like Cicero or Tiro, may have copied this technical invention from the Greeks. There is a good discussion of that possibility in Milne's introduction to *Greek Shorthand Manuals*. He argues that the basic principles are identical and the formal coincidences too frequent and too striking to ignore. I have listed the main works, but I have not commented on all of them since many of them simply describe the same system. Readers interested in the technical aspects of how the system worked can find more than enough information in these sources to satisfy their curiosity. Since many of these writers have described both the Greek and Roman systems, see the section on "tachygraphy," in the previous chapter on Greece.

Boge, Herbert, *Griechische Tachygraphie und Tironische Noten: Ein Handbuch der antiken und mittelalterlichen Schnellschrift*. Boge begins with definitions of Tachygraphy (stenography) then goes on to discuss the examples found in the Greek world from the fourth century bc including the Acropolis system, the consonant tables from Delphi, and examples from the second and first century BC. He then goes on to discuss Tironian notes and Roman shorthand writing. He includes an excellent bibliography. See entry **233**.

279. Boge, Herbert, "Die Tachygraphie, eine Erfindung römischer Sklaven," *Festschrift Hartke* (Altertumswissenschaft mit Zukunft. Dem Wirken Werner Hartkes gewidmet, hrsg von Scheel, H.; Sitzungsberichte des Plenums der Klassen der Akademie der Wissenschaften der DDR, 1973, Berlin: Akademie Verlag, 1973, 141 pp.), pp. 52–68.

A short history of the development of Greek and Roman shorthand writing. He has separate sections on the application of Roman tachygraphy, its history, its external development and its internal structure. He believes that the Roman slaves developed it and then the system was copied by the Greeks.

280. Carpentier, Dom Pierre, *L'Alphabetum Tironianum*, Lutetiae Parisiorum, apud Hippolytum-Ludovicum Guerin & Jacobum Gerin, 1747.

Beautifully produced, mid-eighteenth century folio volume on the Tironian notes, mostly on its ecclesiastical uses. Magnificently drawn charts illustrating the notes. Worth a trip to the rare book room.

281. Chatelain, Emile Louise Marie, *Introduction à la lecture des notes tironiennes*, New York: B. Franklin, 1964. Originally published privately by the author in Paris, 1900.

282. Costamagna, Giorgio, Baroni, M.F., Zagni, L., *Notae Tironianae quae in lexicis et in chartis reperiunt*, Roma: Centro di ricerca, 1983, 171 pp.

283. Dewischeit, Curt, *Goethes beziehungen zu den tironischen noten*, Berlin: Verband Stolzescher stenographenvereine, H. Schumann, 1896, 21 pp.

284. Ganz, Peter, *Tironischen Noten*, Wiesbaden: O. Harrassowitz, 1990, 97 pp.

285. Giry, A., *Manuel de diplomatique*, Paris 1894. See p. 931 (index) under *Notes brèves de notaires* and *Notes tironiennes.*

286. Gregg, John Robert, "Julius Caesar's Stenographer," *Century Magazine*, N.Y. Vol. 102, N.S. Vol. 80–88, (May, 1921), pp. 80–88.

Stenography, or the art of abbreviated writing, has been know since classical times. The first mention of it among the Romans was by the poet Q. Ennius c. 200 BC. A method of shorthand was invented by Tiro, the freedman and secretary to Marcus Tullius Cicero. References to shorthand are found in the works of Cicero, Horace, Livy, Ovid, Martial, Pliny, Tacitus and Suetonius.

Knowledge of shorthand could have both political and military applications. Julius Caesar wrote in shorthand, and the poet Ovid, when referring to this, said: "By these marks, secrets were borne over land and sea." It was a way of keeping communications secret in an age when literacy was not common.

Sometimes the obscuring of the meaning was unintentional. Cicero used shorthand, but was not very good at it. He wrote to his brother Atticus: "You did not understand what I wrote you concerning the ten deputies; I suppose because I wrote you in shorthand."

Accuracy was highly valued. When a shorthand writer in the third century made a mistake in reporting a case, the emperor Severus had him banished and had the nerves in his fingers cut so that he could never write again.

287. Gruterus, Janus, *Inscriptiones antiquae totius orbis Romani in absolutissimum corpus redactae olim auspiciis Iosephi Scaligeri et Marci Velseri, industria autem et diligentia Iani Gruteri: nunc curis secundis eiusdem Gruteri et notis Mar-*

quardi Gudii emendatae et tabulis aeneis a Boissardo confectis illustratae; denuo cura viri summi Ioannis Georgii Graevii recensitae. Accedunt adnotationum appendix et indices xxv emendati et locupletati. Ut et Tironis Ciceronia lib. et Senecae notae. Amstelaedami: F. Halma, 1707.

Collection of Latin inscriptions that also lists the Tironian note system.

288. Guénin, Louis Proper and Guénin, Eugene, *Histoire de la sténographie dans l'antiquité et au moyen-âge*; Les notes tironiennes, Paris: Hachette, 1908, 416 pp.

An extensive history of stenography in antiquity and the middle ages with special reference to Tironian notes. Part one discusses Marcus Tullius Tiro and the creation of his eponymous notes. He includes several letters addressed to Tiro by his master. Guénin adds side discussions on paper, parchment and wax tablets. The eighth book discusses the disappearance of the notes.

The same author has written as small pamphlet entitled: "Recherches sur la nature et l'origine des notes Tironiennes."

289. Havet, Julien Pierre Eugène, *L'écriture secret de Gerbert*, Paris: Imprimerie nationale, 1887.

See: *CRAI* 4th series XV (1887), pp. 94–112.

Gerbert of Aurillac's tachygraphy was a system which diverted from Tironian notes. In this article Havet explains the system.

See, by the same author, "La Tachygraphie Italienne du Xe siècle," *Comptes Rendues, Académie des Inscriptions et Belles Lettres*, 4th series XV (1887), pp. 351–374. that discusses 10th century documents that use Gerbert's system. These include three bulls written by Gerbert when he became Pope Sylvestre II. They date from 999, 1001 and 1002. Some of the symbols are taken from Tironian notes.

290. Johnen, Christian, *Geschichte der Stenographie im Zusammenhang mit der allgemeinen Entwicklung der Schrift and der Schriftkürzung*, Berlin: F. Schrey, 1911, 295 pp.

A history of shorthand and the creation of symbols for speedwriting. He covers the Greeks, the Romans, the Byzantine world and the Middle Ages.

291. Kopp, Ulrich Friedrich, *Lexicon Tironianum.* Nachdruck aus Kopp's Palaeographia critica von 1817 mit Nachwort und einem Alphabetum Tironianum von Bernhard Bischoff. Osnabrueck: Zeller, 1965, 664 pp.

292. Kopp, Ulrich Friedrich, *Palaeographic critica, aut tachygraphia veterum exposita et illustrata.* Mannheimii sumtibus auctoris, 1817–1829. 5 vols.

Vol. I—II: *Tachygraphia veterum.*

Kopp's work on deciphering Tironian notes became the basis for subsequent studies in the field.

293. Legendre, Paul, *Études Tironiennes*, Paris: Honoré Champion, 1907, 88 pp.

Essay on Tironian notes with chapters on Virgil's 6th Ecologue, the sermons of Saint Methodius, Remarks on the use of Tironian notes in the 13th ms.

at Chartres and ms. 611 in Berne. Includes a very complete list of Tironian manuscripts and their location, and a full bibliography of secondary works on the subject.

294. Lehmann, Oscar, *Quaestiones de notis Tironis et Senecae*, Lipsiae: typis Naumannianis, 1869, 32 pp.
An excellent review of the entire question.

295. Mentz, Arthur, "Die Entstehungsgeschichte der römischen Stenographie," in *Hermes* 66 (1931), pp. 369–86.
He breaks new ground in the Roman study of the Roman system, with special reference to the Madrid notae.

296. Mentz, Arthur, *Die Tironischen Noten, eine Geschichte der römischen Kurzschrift*, Berlin: W. de Gruyter, 1944, 256 pp.

297. Mentz, Arthur, "Die tironischen Noten" in *Archiv für Papyrusforschung*, 8 (1927), pp. 34–59.
He carries the study of shorthand a long step forward by publishing the syllabaries contained in waxed tablets at Halle and in papyrus 5464 in Berlin.

298. Milne, H.J.M., *Greek Shorthand Manuals. Syllabary and Commentary*, London and Antrim: N.H. Egypt Exploration Society, 1934, 77 pp.

299. Mitzschke, Paul Gottfried, *Quaestiones Tironianae*, Berolini, In Weraria E.S. Mittlin eiusque filii, 1875, 46 pp.

300. Perugi, Giuseppe Ludovico, *Le note tironiae*, Roma: Società editrice "Athenaeum," 1911, 199 pp.

301. Ruess, Ferdinand, *Die Kasseler Handschrift der Tironischen Noten*, Leipzig: B.G. Teubner, 1914.
Mendelsohn Collection 652M T735.2

302. Schmitz, Wilhelm. *Beitrage zur lateinschen sprach-und literaturkunde*, Leipzig: B.G. Teubner, 1877, 330 pp.

303. Schmitz, Wilhelm, *Commentarii Notarum Tironianarum cum prologomenis*, Lipsiae: B.G. Teubner, 1893.
The standard edition of the Roman shorthand system.

304. Schmitz, Wilhelm, *Commentarii notarum Tironianarum. Cum prologomenis ad notationibus criticis et exegeticis notarumque indice alphabetico.* Osnabrück: Zeller, 1968, 117 pp.
Reprint of 1893 edition that is the standard edition of the Roman shorthand system.

305. Tardiff, Jules, "Mémoire sur notae tironiennes," *Académie des Inscriptions et Belles Lettres*, Séries 2, Vol. iii, 1852.

306. Tardiff, Jules, *Une minute de notaire du IXe siècle en notes tironiennes, d'après la lecture donnée en 1849*. Paris: A. Picard, 1888, 15 pp.

307. Verrua, Pietro, *Tra pergamene e palinsesti can note tironiane nello Scrittorio di Bobbio*, Padova: Tipografia e libreria Antoniana, 1935.

Roman Empire

Of all the civilizations of the ancient world, the Roman Empire has inspired the greatest number of books and articles on intelligence matters. This is no coincidence. The Roman empire, like the Persian and Assyrian empires before it, had a centralized government that established a postal and communications system to unite its many provinces. Rome had a highly successful, well-organized army that certainly needed accurate, up-to-date intelligence to perform well. Spies both public and private have left their traces. Unlike other Near Eastern empires, however, narrative histories of Rome supplement the official records, public and private inscriptions, papyrus documents and the literary output of poets and playwrights. Thus we know so much more about the inner workings of the Roman empire than we do about any of its predecessors. This does not mean that all secondary works exploit this wealth of information. Many standard books on the Roman army simply ignore the intelligence function. H.M.D. Parker's *The Roman Legions* (Oxford, 1928), Chester Starr's *Roman Imperial Navy* (Ithaca, NY, 1959), Michael Simkins' *Warriors of Rome* (Blandford, 1988), and many similar books contain no listings for intelligence, signalling, espionage, or spies. Edward Luttwak's *The Grand Strategy of the Roman Empire* (Baltimore, 1976) purports to outline the Roman imperial system without a single reference to how the Romans might have collected the intelligence to build and maintain such a system. More recent books like Lawrence Keppie's *The Making of the Roman Army; From Republic to Empire* (Barnes & Noble, 1984), and Yann Le Bohec's *The Imperial Roman Army* (New York: Hippocrene Books, 1994) at least make passing reference to scouts and messengers.

The sheer diversity of the Roman material gives scholars much to ponder. While classicists continue the never-ending task of locating, translating and interpreting ancient authors, historians refine our understanding of the mechanisms of the Roman government, locating institutions and individuals who most likely would have been involved in intelligence activity. The *frumentarii* of the early empire, and the *agentes in rebus* of the post-Diocletianic world not only provided political and military intelligence but were also involved in covert operations, arrests and sometimes even political executions. The only thing that scholars seem to agree upon is that both these groups had varied tasks and only some of them were intelligence related. Yet there is no doubt that as the major users of the state postal/communications system, the *cursus publicus*, the *agentes in rebus* were at the nerve center of a large information network that kept the emperor informed of developments throughout his empire. Added to these were the many other military functionaries like *the beneficiarii consularis*, and civilian groups like the *delatores* who became involved in observing and reporting on matters of interest to the emperor.

A prominent trend in the literature on signalling is that twenty years ago many scholars argued for the exisstence of organized and rapid-functioning signalling systems on the borders of the Roman empire. Further archaeological excavation and a reinterpretation of the evidence suggests, however, that these systems were neither extensive nor set up for long-distance communication. Some installations formerly thought to have been signal stations have been reidentified, and many date later than the Roman period. Also, several do not work together as a system.

The Romans dabbled in code and ciphers and even invented their own form of shorthand. They wrote in invisible ink and hid uncoded messages in an amazing array of ingenious locations. Secret information was always at a premium, especially during wartime. How did Hannibal's spies operate in Rome at the height of the Second Punic War? How did Arminius ambush three legions in the Teutoburg Forest? Did the Jews ever have a chance of beating the Romans in AD 66? These questions and many others have been posed and grappled with by scholars.

Two non-Latin scripts of Europe, Teutonic runes and Celtic ohgams, were occasionally enciphered to keep their contents secret. Runes flourished in Scandinavia and in Anglo-Saxon Britain during the seventh, eighth and ninth centuries. They were nearly always used for religious purposes.

As the head of a large empire made up of diverse and sometimes hostile peoples, Roman emperors had to worry about internal security. This could entail discovering nascent revolts by means of agents in place, identifying traitors within their midst, and of course, detecting any plans to assassinate the emperor. One group which Roman authorities investigated thoroughly was the Christians, an ever-growing community within the empire. First perceiving them as a security threat, the Romans began with individual prosecutions and later progressed to blanket persecutions of the ever-growing sect.

The nature of many Roman institutions is ambiguous. Some were organized ostensibly for spying, but performed many other duties as well, e.g. tax collecting, policing, record keeping, soldiering, fire fighting, or maintaining public order. These people have left inscriptions, tombstones, even pictures of themselves (carved in stone, of course), and their adventures are described by Roman historians. Herewith is a guide to their activities.

General

308. Amiotti, Gabriella, "I Greci ed il Massacro degli Italici nell'88 A.C.," *Aevum* 59 (1980), pp. 132–139.

Amiotti studies the sources relative to the massacre of the *negotiatores* or Roman and Italian businessmen living in Asia Minor when Mithridates VI, King of Pontus, decided to declare war in 88 BC.

As an intelligence coup, this is an interesting case study. Mithridates sent out the message that on a given day, all Romans and Italians should be killed. It was carried out mostly in the Greek cities and islands; there does not seem to be much evidence for the participation of the indigenous population of the client states in the interior of Anatolia. Amiotti finds traces of factions that fought for the Roman side. The lower classes who had nothing to lose went with Mithridates. Those of the ruling classes sided with the greatest commercial power at the time, i.e. Rome. Some people were killed because they were commercial rivals, others for political reasons.

We do not, to this day, know how Mithridates coordinated this feat, how he communicated with his agents, or how he kept the secret.

309. Ammianus Marcellinus, *Res Gestae,* Trans. J. C. Rolfe, Cambridge: Loeb Classical Library, 1956, 3 vols.

Ammianus is our best source for military history in the late empire. As *protector domesticus,* he was in a post admirably suited to observing military developments and intelligence operations. To give just one example, Amm. Marc. 28.3.8. speaks of the Arcani [corruption of Areani] as "a class of men established in early times who were clearly convicted of having been led by the receipt, or the promise, of great booty at various times to betray to the savages what was going on among us. For it was their duty to hasten about hither and thither over long spaces, to give information about our generals of the clashes of rebellion among neighboring peoples." He supposedly described them in more detail in his section on the emperor Constans which is, unfortunately, not extant.

For Ammianus on intelligence, see N.J.E. Austin, *Ammianus on Warfare,* (no. **313**).

310. Arias Bonet, J. A., "Los agentes in rebus. Contribucion al estudio de la policia en al Bajo Imperio Romano" *Anuario Hist. Derecho Espan.* 27–28 (1957–58), pp. 197–219.

The author examines the police system of the late Roman empire from the point of view of public law. He starts from the earliest legal mention of the *agentes in rebus*—a constitution of Constantine (Codex Theodosianus VI.35.3) dating to the year AD 319. A passage in Aurelius Victor suggests that it was Diocletian who founded the service to replace the notorious *frumentarii* who had been disbanded because of their abuses of power. The *agentes* took over the job as overseers of the *cursus publicus*, and as secret agents of the central government. Arias Bonet traces the abuses of the new corps and the laws passed to ameliorate them. He also traces how they were put under the direction of the *magister officiorum* rather than the *magister militum* to keep too much power from accruing to the latter. See also Sinnigen, "Two Branches of the Late Roman Secret Service" (no. **466**).

311. Ashby, T. and P. K. Baillie Reynolds, "The Castra Peregrinorum," *Journal of Roman Studies* 13 (1923), pp. 152–167.

Excavation report on the site that housed the headquarters of the *frumentarii*, the so-called Roman Secret Service. Sinnigen, no. **463**.

312. Aulus Gellius, *Attic Nights*, trans. John C. Rolfe, Loeb Classical Library edition, London: W. Heinemann, 1927–28 3 vols.

Grammarian of the second century AD who jotted down notes on grammar, archaeology, ethics, philosophy and physics. Book 17, ch. 9 contains references to early methods of cryptography including the substitution cipher of Caesar, and the Spartan *scytale*. For commentary see Lange et Soudart, *Traité de cryptographie*, (no. **42**) pp. 18–19.

See also 15.7.3. on the *cursus publicus.*

313. Austin, N.J.E., *Ammianus on Warfare*, Brussels: Collection Latomus, Vol. 165, 1975.

Ammianus Marcellinus was the last great Latin historian of the Roman empire. He was a soldier himself, admitted to the elite corps of *protectores domestici*. As a member of the personal staff of general Ursicinus, he saw action in north Italy, Gaul, Germany, Illyricum and Mesopotamia. He thus had an inside view of the campaigns and a soldier's eye for military detail. Austin's study includes chapters on the collection of strategic and tactical intelligence. Austin later collaborated with Boris Rankov to produce a full-length study of Roman intelligence gathering called *Exploratio* (see no. **315**.). REVIEWED BY: J. M. Alonso-Nunez in *Classical Review* 31 (1981), p. 123.

314. Austin, N.J.E., "What Happened to Intelligence Information from the Frontiers?," *Prudentia* 19, 2 (1987), 28–33.

This article attempts to answer the question "what evidence is there for the existence of a filing cabinet containing intelligence briefing material in a provincial governor's office?" Austin discusses the ad hoc nature of Roman intelligence gathering, their sources and means of collection. Contemporary with the growth of reconnaissance units on the border is the growth of a branch of the provincial governor's staff called the *beneficiarii consularis*. When you superimpose a map of the *stationes* of the *beneficiarii consularis* on a map of the known stations of the *exploratores* ones sees: 1) there's an exact overlap on the line of the frontiers, 2) They are stationed on main roads leading back from the frontiers to the provincial capitals at intervals of 20 and 40 kms.

Much of this work is based on the research of Boris Rankov who concluded that the *beneficiarii* were a sort of super messenger corps beefed up in response to the great military crises of the 160s onward faced by Marcus Aurelius. The new policies and intelligence network were successful until the later third century when even greater pressures on the frontiers weakened by administrative chaos and civil war required new defense strategies and a new reliance on effective intelligence work. The former were successful; the latter failed to develop.

These conclusions were later expanded into a book by Austin and Rankov. *Exploratio*, no. **315**.

315. Austin, N. J. E. and N. B. Rankov, *Exploratio. Military and Political Intelligence in the Roman World from the Second Punic War to the Battle of Adrianople*. New York: Routledge, 1995, 292 pp.

The history of Roman intelligence activities from the Second Punic War to the late empire. The authors do not believe the sources are reliable enough to comment on intelligence activities in the early Roman Republic. For coverage of that period, see R.M. Sheldon, *Tinker, Tailor, Caesar, Spy* (no. **456**).

Tough reading for non-classicists but thorough and accurate. For differing opinions on the *agentes in rebus* see Sinnigen (no. **466**), Frank (no. **357**), Seeck, (no. **444**), Clauss (no. **335**), and Hirschfeld, nos. **375**). REVIEWED BY: A.D. Lee, *Classical Review* 47, 1 (1997), pp. 121–122; V. Erhart, *Journal of Military History* 61, 3 (July. 1997) 605–607; R.M. Sheldon, *International Journal of Intelligence and Counterintelligence*. Vol. 11, No. 1 (Spring. 1998), pp. 104–115; F. S. Russell, *Bryn Mawr Classical Review*, 96.3.14; B. Isaac, *Journal of Roman Studies* 88 (1998), p. 179.

316. Bagnall, Roger S., "The Army and Police in Roman Upper Egypt," *Journal of the American Research Center in Cairo*, 14 (1977), pp. 67–86.

As one moved away from centers of population in the ancient world, one's chances of being robbed assaulted or killed rose greatly. Bagnall points out that "Roman Egypt had a large measure of both violence and the means to control it." The principal external threat were various groups of non-Egyptian nomads in the deserts to the east and west of the Nile Valley. The main internal threat came from ordinary criminals. Unlike most areas of the Roman Empire, Egypt had a tradition of professional police to guard the deserts and keep peace in the valley. The police, called the "Medjay" in the New Kingdom, were organized and dressed like the army but formed a distinct organization.

Bagnall examines evidence from *ostraka* (potsherds) in the collections of Florida State University and the University of Amsterdam. He discusses the implications of this evidence for the system of policing in use in the Thebaid, the area least Hellenized in the Ptolemaic period and one that was particularly plagued by revolts. He gives particular attention to the *stationes* (military posts with an officer of centurion rank or lower in charge) and the *skopeloi* (watch-tower guards) and their occupants.

317. Baillie Reynolds, P. K. "Troops Quartered in the Castra Peregrinorum" *Journal of Roman Studies* 13 (1923), pp. 168–189.

Milites Peregrini (foreign soldiers) was the official collective name for soldiers in the capital detached for special duty from the provincial armies. They were stationed at the *Castra Peregrinorum* (camp of the foreigners). Among these soldiers were the *frumentarii*, Rome's so-called Secret Service (Sinnigen, no. **463**), and the *speculatores* whose duties also included spying.

The permanent staff of the barracks consisted of the Camp-Commandant (the *Princeps*), an Adjutant (the *Subprinceps*) and a Sergeant Major (the *Optio*). In the camp under their command were the detached men from the legions, who were collectively called *peregrini*, but individually retained their regimental rank and appellation of *frumentarius*, *speculator*, etc.

All legions provided *frumentarii*. These men were detached and formed a *numerus* in Rome and were stationed in the *Castra Peregrinorum* under the orders of the *Princeps Peregrinorum* . Each legion had a certain number of *frumentarii* but how many is not clear. There was at least one *Centurio Frumentarius* to a legion, but this does not prove that there was a century of these men under his command. There are a number of inscriptions of centurions of the *frumentarii* in which the number of the legion was not given. This suggests that some of them formed part of the "Q" branch of the General Staff.

The *speculatores* were also housed in this camp. Although we know there were ten *speculatores* per legion, we do not know how many of them were detached to Rome. But they seem to have formed the second largest group in the camp.

Reynolds agrees with Mommsen that the whole system of the *frumentarii* and of the camp in Rome for men from the provincial armies was an integral part of the original organization of the Imperial Army by Augustus.

318. Baillie Reynolds, P. K. *The Vigiles of Imperial Rome*. Oxford, 1926, 133 pp. Reprint edition, Ares Publishers, 1996.

No fully developed fire or police force existed in Rome until the time of Augustus. The first emperor established the *Vigiles* who performed both duties until the end of the empire. Its corps consisted of seven cohorts recruited from freedmen (later anyone of free birth). This work was the only comprehensive work on the subject until the publication of Rainbird's article and book (nos. **427**, **428**). The *frumentarii* in Rome seem to have worked closely with the *Vigiles*. Their headquarters on the Caelian was across the street from the station of the *vigiles*. See Sinnigen, (no. **463**), p. 72 n. 37. REVIEWED BY: von Premerstein in *Gnomon* 3 (1927), p. 248ff; E.T.M. in *Classical Journal* (1927), p. 700; J. Hammer, in *Classical Weekly* 22,1 (Oct. 1928), p. 7–8; M. Cary in *Classical Review* (1927), p. 44.

319. Bauman, Richard A., *Crime and Punishment in Ancient Rome*, London and New York: Routledge, 1996, 228 pp.

A study of Roman criminal law. There are sections on treason, and Cicero and the uncovering of the Catilinarian conspiracy, but as the title suggests, more about crime and punishment than the arresting agents or investigating agencies that uncovered these crimes.

320. Bauman, Richard A., *The Crimen Maiestas in the Roman Republic and Augustan Principate,* Johannesburg, Witwatersrand University Press, 1967, 336 pp.

Bauman studies the process whereby the public criminal law of Rome evolved rules for the protection of the sovereignty of the state during the Republic and the early empire. This is a discussion of the laws of treason (*crimen maiestatis* or *maiestas*). Bauman does not discuss how the law was enforced, who was prosecuted under it or how the evidence against them was collected.

321. Bauman, Richard A., *Impietas in Principem. A Study of Treason Against the Roman Emperor with Special Reference to the First Century A.D.* Mun. Beitrage zur Papyrus Forschungen & Antike Rechtsgeschichte 67, Munich: C.H. Beck'sche Verlagsbuchhandlung, 1974, p. 243.

Legal study of Roman treason laws under Augustus and the Julio-Claudians.

322. "Beneficiarius" in *Dizionario Epigrafico di Antichità Romane*, I, (1895), pp. 992–996.

Beneficiarii is a term used originally by Caesar for soldiers specifically attached to a particular commander and so freed from ordinary duties by his *beneficium* (*BC* 1,75,2; 3.88.5). Under the Principate the term was used for a specific grade of staff officer within each military office in the provinces. When the Roman government began to create a series of posts, or *stationes*, at key points along major roads in the provinces of the empire in the early second century AD, they were manned by these *beneficiarii* attached to the governors' staffs. We know about these men because of their habit of erecting votive altars at the *stationes* where they served. They were a key element in the apparatus of administration and communication (thus intelligence gathering) of the empire. Their number multiplied dramatically in the early third century. Cf Schallmyer and Ott (no. **439**), Dise (nos. **342–347**), Rankov (no. **431**), Mirkovic (nos. **406**, **407**), Domazewski (**349**), Herz (no. **374**), and Lopuszanski (no. **399**).

323. Blockley, R.C. "The Coded Message in Ammianus Marcellinus 18.6.17–19" *Classical Views* 30 n.s. 5, 1 (1968), pp. 63–65.

Discusses a message smuggled by a Roman envoy, Procopius, out of Persia. The message was in cipher and hidden in a scabbard, both well-known methods of concealing information (see Frontinus, *Stratagems* 3.13.5). The message it conveys seems to be nonsense since it incorporates data both from the present and from two different historical circumstances.

Blockley "decodes" the message and shows that it contains precise and vital information that the Persians wished to conceal: that in AD 359 their plan was not to fight in Mesopotamia as before, but to strike straight at Syria.

If the message is genuine it is an interesting example both of a three-stage method of concealing intelligence (hiding place, cipher, code). It is also possible that the entire story is fabricated, just another example of Ammianus using historical material to give excitement to his narrative and connect it with the famous past.

324. Blockley, R.C., "Internal Self-Policing in the Late Roman Administration. Some Evidence from Ammianus Marcellinus," *Classica et Medievalia* 30 (1969), pp. 403–419.

In the office of the late Roman civil and military administration the office staffs were used as a check upon their chief. This sort of police duty was forced on them as a result of the Emperor's attempt to halt corruption, and was also necessitated by the complete lack of a regular police force.

Notarii (the imperial secretaries) performed this duty on specific assignments, usually in high level political cases. Elements of the *agentes in rebus* (not considered secret police by the author) sometimes performed similar duties of investigation in political cases. But there was at this time no one organization whose sole or major function was to act as police, political or otherwise.

Many of the cases reported by Ammianus Marcellinus have political overtones and some concern treasonable activities. Laws in the Theodosian Code cast responsibility for the behavior of the chief of an *officium* upon his officials and created the atmosphere in which information about misdemeanors would be passed along. By rewarding those who successfully exposed a high official in wrong doing, the emperors added a carrot to the stick. One purpose of this approach was to weaken the loyalty of the *officiales* to their department and to their chief and render them less likely to conceal wrongdoing. On the other hand, excessive and at times undeserved rewards would certainly encourage informers to make a career of informing on people.

This system could also be used by ambitious men against their rivals out of sheer jealousy. It became a means of checking the growing power of individuals, thus providing a balance between the chiefs of the various branches of the bureaucracy. Administrative efficiency could be badly impaired by such infighting. Emperors using this system to gain intelligence might remain uninformed or badly informed. The author gives illustrations of how the flow of intelligence to the Emperor could be controlled and his actions thereby influenced.

325. Blum, Wilhelm, *Curiosi und Regendarii.* Munich: Uni Druck, 1969, 116 pp.

The author re-examines the internal organization and function of the *agentes in rebus.* He concludes that the primary function of the so-called *curiosi* (those sent to the provinces in connection with the *cursus publicus*) was detective work. More controversially, he believes that the office of the praetorian prefect was supervised not just by the princeps derived from the *agentes in rebus* but by three people—the *princeps*, a *regendarius* and a *chartularius*. Finally, he believes that the *regendarii* of the *Notitia Dignitatum* were all control officers drawn from the *agentes in rebus.*

Reviewed by Liebschuetz in *Journal of Roman Studies* 1970 229–30 who believes Blum's arguments are based on peculiar interpretations of inscriptional evidence and that Blum has been led astray by "the analogy of secret police forces of modern Europe." OTHER REVIEWS: Lippold, *Gnomon* 44 (1972), pp. 95–96; Clauss, *Bonner Jahrbucher* 62 (1971), pp. 750–752; Simon, *Zeitschrift für Savigny Stiftung für Rechtsgeschichte* 88 (1971), pp. 545–546.

326. Boak, Arthur Edward Romilly, *The Master of Offices in the Later Roman and Byzantine Empires*, New York: Macmillan, 1919, 1924, New York: Johnson Reprint Corp. 1972.

Part one of Boak's *Two Studies in Later Roman and Byzantine Adminstration.* No modern parallel for this office exists; the Master of Offices' sphere of activities was made up of an aggregation of various powers that brought him into touch with many branches of government. Of great importance to intelligence gathering was his overseeing of the *agentes in rebus* (see part III pp. 68–74), the *cursus publicus* (pp. 74–82), and the *scrinia* or the three secretarial bureaux responsible for imperial correspondence (pp. 82ff.) In many ways his job resembled a Minister of Information.

Boak avoided translating the term *agentes in rebus*, but at one point calls the organization the imperial intelligence office. Compare Ernst Stein, *Geschichte des spätrömischen Reiches* (Vienna, 1928) Vol. 1, p. 173 who refers to it as "a corps of militarily organized police officials and mounted dispatch carriers"; Clyde Pharr, *The Theodosian Code* (Princeton, 1962) calls them the "secret service" as does J. Rolfe, *Ammianus Marcellinus* (Cambridge, Mass., 1935–1939), 3 vols., passim.

327. Boissier, Gaston, "Les Délateurs," *Revue des Deux Mondes*, 72, (1867), *Paris: Bureau de la Revue des Deux Mondes*, pp. 305–340.

Under the reign of Augustus, a group of informers arose named *delatores* who turned in influential men on treason charges. They were notorious for making false accusations in the hope of enriching themselves. Boissier believes, however, that such men did not crop up only under the empire, but that there was a republican tradition of informing. Boissier compares the treason trials under Tiberius to the Terror in revolutionary France. Bloodletting in the name of justice and freedom, a flood of people ready to turn in their neighbors. A bit over done. For a more detailed study of their activities, see Gustav Boissière's *L'accusation publique* (no. **328**), Froment (no. **359**), Dumeril (no. **351**), Gaudemet (no. **361**), Zijlstra (no. **477**), Giovannini (no. **364**) and O'Neal, (no. **417**).

328. Boissière, Gustave, *L'accusation publique et les delateurs chez les Romains*. Niort, 1911, pp. 375.

The most complete study of informers and the social role of the *delatores*. The *delatores* were citizens who traded information about supposed treasonable plots against the emperor in return for a portion of the estate of the accused if he were convicted. They were somewhat analogous to the sycophants of ancient Athens (Loftberg, no. **181**, **182**). Boissière studies their role in the Roman legal system, their appearance in literary works, and their social function. Gaudemet (no. **361**.) writes on their repression in the late empire.

Cf. Froment (no. **359**), Boissier (no. **327**), Dumeril (no. **351**), Zijlstra (no. **477**) and Johnson (no. **384**).

329. Brizzi, G. "Cursus Publicus e transmissione della notizia: l'esempio di Augusto," in *Studi Militari Romani,* Bologna, CLUEB, 1983, pp. 31–48.

Brizzi starts with a discussion of the governmental messenger services dating back to the third millennium BC in Mespotamia. He then moves on to a comparison of the *cursus publicus* as established by Augustus. He concludes that the *cursus publicus* was fundamentally a support system for the *frumentarii* and the successive offices of Roman state security.

330. Brunt, P.A. "Did Emperors Ever Suspend the Law of Maiestas?," *Sodalitas*. Scritti in Onore de Antonio Guarino, Naples, 1984, pp. 469–480.

The Julian law of *Maiestas* penalized any one assisting Rome's enemies, bearing arms against the state, inciting soldiers to sedition, or seeking to procure the death of any person with *imperium* or *potestas*. The law was couched in terms of offenses against the Roman people, but since the emperor Augustus was the representative of the people, he expanded the law to include anything that impinged upon his dignity or criticized or threatened his autocratic regime.

Under certain emperors, the law could become quite odious because of the way it was enforced. Brunt believes that it was never suspended entirely (as suggested by R.S. Bauman, *Impietas in Principem*, Ch. 8, no. **320**). No country or government would announce that treason would go unpunished. Rather it was narrowly construed under some emperors, and more liberally under others. The infamous *delatores* were the most likely ones to turn in people who had broken the law. The would have more latitude for accusation if the law of *maiestas* was interpreted as it was under the reign of Tiberius for example.

331. Brunt, P. A. "Evidence Given Under Torture in the Principate," *Zeitschrift für Savigny Stiftung für Rechtsgeschichte* 97, 1 (1980), pp. 256–265.

When one was discovered in the act of treason by the secret service and tried, how was one convicted? Sometimes by evidence extracted under torture. Although in the Roman Republic, citizens were legally immune from torture, slaves and foreigners were not. Scholars have argued over when the practice of torturing free citizens simply for the evidence they might provide began. By the fourth century, only soldiers and persons of rank were exempt.

332. Cagnat, René, "Frumentarius" in Daremberg-Saglio, *Dictionnaire des antiquités grecques et romaines* (Paris, 1877–1919), p. 1348.

Traces the origins of the *frumentarii* from their beginnings as soldiers charged with supplying grain to the troops to their development into a Roman secret service. He believed they were recruited from the legions in Germany and the Danube where other security police were recruited. This has since proven to be wrong; they were not a Roman SS. They were taken from all legions. Compare Sinnigen "Origins" (no. **466**), Paribeni (no. **420**), Purpura (no. **426**), Clauss (no. **335**), Fiebiger (no. **357**), Henzen (no. **372, 373**), Paschoud (no. **421**), Austin & Rankov (no. **315**).

333. Campbell, Brian, "Teach Yourself How to Be a General," *Journal of Roman Studies* 65 (1975), pp. 13–29.

This is one of the few works to deal with the question of how a Roman general learned his craft. From an intelligence point of view, this also meant tradecraft. Military manuals of the imperial period are not considered great literature, but they can give us an insight into what the Romans considered "professional advice." Campbell discusses Onasander, Frontinus, Polyaenus, Vegetius, Hyginus, Aelian, and Arrian.

The Romans had no formal training for their commanders, and many of them lacked experience in the field. A handbook would be useful for reading about famous exploits of the past. They were not textbooks in the modern sense; they were sometimes intended to entertain. Those written by experienced commanders tended to be more useful than those compiled by rhetoricians. The fact that these books discuss intelligence operations certainly shows that the Romans considered these activities important, and that fact should not be ignored or undervalued (Campbell does not discuss intelligence separately).

334. Clauss, Manfred, "Frumentarius Augusti," *Epigraphica* 42 (1980), pp. 131–134.

The title *frumentarius Augusti* is clearly different from the title "*frumentarius legionis*." Clauss discusses several examples from Greek and Latin inscriptions of *frumentarii Augusti*. He makes the parallel between *speculator Augusti* and *frumentarius Augusti*—i.e. special intelligence officers detailed to the emperor.

335. Clauss, Manfred, *Der Magister Officiorum in der Spätantike*, Munich: Beck, 1980, 252 pp.

Described by one reviewer as "the Pooh-Bah" of the late Roman court, the *Magister Officiorum* had a hand in almost every area of the Roman government. Among the most important vis à vis information gathering was his control over the imperial secretaries, command of the palatine guards, control of the ubiquitous *agentes in rebus*, and management of the *cursus publicus*. This gave him virtual oversight of communication between the provinces and the emperor and vice versa. He was responsible for the reception of foreign embassies at the imperial court, and his corps of *agentes* furnished the chiefs of staff for the praetorian prefects, the urban prefects, the proconsuls and the vicars. By the end of the fourth century, he had taken over from the praetorian prefects the supervision of the imperial arms factories. He was, in short, one of the most powerful men of his time.

Clauss's volume is the first study of the *Magister Officiorum* since that of A.E.R. Boak (no. **325**) which appeared in 1918. Clauss uses a wider range of historical sources and gives a much better picture of the historical evolution of the office and its accumulation of power as "the eyes and ears of the emperor." REVIEWED BY: R.I. Frank in *Gnomon* 54, 8 (1982), pp. 755–63; Frank in *American Historical Review* 87 (1982), pp. 1062–1063; Demougeot in *Latomus* 41 (1982), pp. 387–391; Foiller in *Revue des Études Byzantines* 40 (1982), p. 249; Burian in *Byzantinoslav ica* 43 (1982) 223–224; Klein in *Zeitschrift für Kirschen Geschichte* 94 (1983), pp. 129–132; Lippold in *Historische Zeitschrift* 236 (1983), pp. 653–654; Chastagnol in *Revue des Études Latines* 60 (1982), pp. 451–453; Hunt in *Classical Revue* 33 (1983), pp. 86–87; Horst Kotte in *Bonner Jahrbucher* 75 (1985), pp. 628–630; Giardina in *Revista di Filologia e de Istruzione Classica* 112 (1984), pp. 233–238; Kuhoff in *Historisches Jahrbuch* 104 (1984) 180–182; Schuller in *Zeitschrift-der Savigny-Stiftung für Rechtsgeschichte* 100 (1983), pp. 708–711; Karayannopoulos *Byzantinische Zeitschrift* 76 (1983), pp. 359–360; Vera in *Athenaeum* 62 (1984), pp. 378–380.

336. Clauss, Manfred, "Ein tödlisches Scherz," *Rheinisches Museum* 128 (1985), pp. 97–98.

The security climate in the late empire often left no room for humor—in this case, a deadly joke reported in the 30th book of Ammianus Marcellinus, dated to the year AD 375. Faustinus, the nephew of the Praetorian Prefect Viventius, was executed on two charges. The first accused him of killing a donkey in cahoots with a secret sorcerer. Faustinus pleaded innocent to this charge and claimed that all he was seeking was a remedy against hair loss. The second charge was the joke that ultimately led to his demise. A certain Nigrinus (about which nothing else is known) asked in jest to be made a *notarius*. Faustinus laughed and replied: "make me Emperor, and I'll make you a *notarius*." That statement was taken as a threat to the emperor and led to the execution of Faustinus, Nigrinus and others.

On the *notarii* and their connection to the Roman secret service, see W.G. Sinnigen, "Two Branches of the Late Roman Secret Service" *American Journal of Philology* 80 (1959), pp. 238–254. (no. **466**).

337. Clauss, Manfred, *Untersuchungen zu den principales des römischen Heeres von Augustus bis Diocletian. Cornicularii, speculatores, frumentarii* (Bochum, 1973), 204 pp.

Inaugural dissertation. A particularly good discussion of the praetorian *speculatores* on pp. 46–58, the legionary *speculatores* pp. 59, the *frumentarii* pp. 82–115. REVIEWED BY: J. Harmand, *Latomus* 35 (1976), p. 186.

338. *Codex Theodosianus*, *The Theodosian Code and novels*, and the Sirmondian constitutions; a translation with commentary, glossary, and bibliography by Clyde Pharr, in collaboration with Theresa Sherrer Davidson and Mary Brown Pharr. With an introduction by C. Dickerman Williams. Princeton: Princeton University Press, 1952, 643 pp.

Laws applying to the *cursus publicus*, the Roman postal system use for carrying political and military intelligence: "de cursu publico" VII.5–6; VIII 1, 5, 7, 16, 16 , 26, 28, 30, 47, 48, 364.

339. Davies, R. W., "Augustus Caesar. A Police System in the Ancient World," in P. J. Stead, *Pioneers in Policing*, Maidenhead, 1977, pp. 12–32.

Augustus walked a fine line between keeping order while not appearing to turn Rome over to anyone with *imperium*. Augustus also wished to avoid the centralization of power establishing a police force would create. Davies traces the use of the *Vigiles*, the Urban Cohorts, the Praetorians (and in the provinces) the army to keep an eye on unruly elements, investigate crimes, and maintain order.

340. Davies, R. W., "The Investigation of Some Crimes in Roman Egypt," *Ancient Society* 4 (1973), pp. 199–212.

During the Principate, the Roman authorities made use of the army on a wide range of police duties. These included controlling the capital of Alexandria, road patrols, plain clothes police work, guarding the mint, policing the harbor and patrolling the Nile, securing work gangs, guarding grain ships, safeguarding merchants, caravans and border crossings, arresting smugglers and confiscating contraband, and suppressing brigandage. *Beneficiarii* and *stationarii* were used. Egyptians often appealed to these men for justice because they felt a Roman officer might be more effective than a village policemen. This put officers in a position to collect a wide range of intelligence on the populace and on crime.

341. Davies, R. W., "Police Work in Roman Times," *History Today* 18, no. 10 (October 1968), pp. 700–707.

Davies explains how the legions and their auxiliaries were employed by Roman governors to maintain law and order in their provinces. In the cities, small forces of gendarmes were recruited from slaves and acted under the direction of civilian magistrates.

The provincials were especially grateful to the army for ridding the countryside of bandits. An inscription dated October 28th, AD 144 was put up by the town council of Sala in Mauretania Tingitana (Morocco) publicly thanking M. Sulpicius Felix, the commanding officer of the Second Cavalry Regiment of Syrians, for one of his many acts of kindness toward the town, namely provide soldiers to protect their fields, flocks and forests against brigandage.

We have evidence for the investigation of criminal cases involving assault and battery, blackmail, robbery, breaking and entry, missing persons, arson, trespassing, and attempted murder. Davies ends with a brief discussion of the duties of the *frumentarii* and the *benficiarii consularis*.

342. Dio Cassius (Cassius Dio Cocceianus), *Roman History*, Ernest Cary translation, Loeb Classical Library edition London: W. Heinemann, 1914–1927, 9 vols.

One of the most important authorities for the history of the last years of the Republic and the early empire. References to ancient methods of cryptography in Bk. 40.9 and 41.3. See also the commentaries in Lange 4 Soudart, *Traité de cryptographie*, p. 18 (no. **42**).

343. Dise, Robert L., Jr., "The *Beneficiarii Procuratoris* of Celeia and the Development of the *Statio* Network," *Zeitschrift für Papyrologie und Epigraphik* 113 (1996), pp. 286–292.

Early in the second century, the Roman government began to create a series of posts, or *stationes*, at key points along major roads in the provinces of the empire. They were a key element in the apparatus of administration and communication (thus intelligence gathering) of the empire. Their number multiplied dramatically in the early third century. They were manned by *beneficiarii* attached to the governors' staffs. We know about these men because of their habit of erecting votive altars at the *stationes* where they served.

Dise studies twenty of these altars found at Celeia in the province of Noricum (in the eastern Alps, south of the Danube). They are important because they shed light on the early history of the *statio* network (before the Marcommanic wars). He concludes that from the beginning the network was conceived on a scale that transcended provincial boundaries. He notes the *stationes* were not heavily manned, but had a strong relationship, especially in the Danubian provinces, with roads and towns.

344. Dise, Robert L., Jr., "Beneficiarius Eius," *Electronic Antiquity*, 4, 1 (1997), pp. 1–10.

A continuation of Dise's discussion of the change in titulature of the *beneficiarii consularis*, and the use of associative titulature. One form of this title linked the *beneficiarius* directly with a particular governor. The other, *beneficiarius eius*, did the same thing but in a different form.

For his earlier discussion, see Dise (no. **345**).

345. Dise, Robert L., Jr., "A Reassessment of the Functions of *beneficiarii consularis*," *Ancient History Bulletin* 9.2 (1995), pp. 72–85.

No scholar has successfully defined a single or primary function or pattern of functions for the *beneficarii consularis*. Although they were from time to time connected with internal security activities, this was not their primary use. Evidence for their participation in intelligence collecting comes from several inscriptions that show *beneficiarii* with previous service as *frumentarii*. Cf. Sinnigen, "The Roman Secret Service" (no. **463**).

346. Dise, Robert L., Jr., "Recruitment and Assignment of *Beneficarii Consularis* in the Danube Provinces," *The Ancient World* 28.2 (1997), pp. 149–161.

A study of the recruitment of the *beneficiarii consularis* that illuminates the way in which the imperial government managed its administrative manpower resources during the second and third centuries. Dise concludes that the management of those resources was dictated by expediency rather than by system. "The central government concerned itself with broad personnel issues, and left the determination of how best to utilize manpower to the governors themselves." Personnel assignment at the clerical level presents a picture of "improvisation that defies systematization." Dise wisely warns not to read the modern experience of complex and intricately regulated bureaucracy into the Principate, or even to read the intricate system of the fourth and fifth centuries back into the second and third.

347. Dise, Robert L., Jr., "Trajan, the Antonines, and the Governor's Staff," *Zeitschrift für Papyrologie und Epigraphik* 116 (1997), pp. 273–283.

Dise contributes to the study of the elaborately-structured third-century Roman governor's staff, the *officium consularis*. Dise believes Trajan devised a new role for the *beneficiarii* by using them to man his *stationes*. That an imperial directive led to the creation of these *stationes* rather than the spontaneous initiative of individual provincial governors suggests a need on the part of the imperial government to have useful generalists in position around the empire to collect intelligence or do whatever tasks the central government found necessary. Marcus Aurelius especially faced chronic and severe military crises through most of his principate. Both Antoninus Pius and Marcus Aurelius altered the connection between the governors and their *beneficiarii*, making the later attached to the governorship itself and not to individual governors. This Antonine reform represents a shift away from the informal Republican past of the governor's office, and a move toward its institutional imperial form. The Antonine revival of the *statio* network inaugurated a century during which these posts, manned by one or two *beneficiarii consularis*, proliferated rapidly until they became a frequent presence in the towns and along the roads of the empire. They thus strengthened the institutional structure of the imperial administrative apparatus

348. Dise, Robert L., Jr., "Variation in Roman Administrative Practice: the Assignments of *Beneficiarii Consularis*," *Zeitschrift für Papyrologie und Epigraphik* 116 (1997), pp. 284–299.

Variation rather than standardization characterized the functions of the gubernatorial *beneficarii* who played such a large part in the administration of the Roman Empire during the Principate. The Antonines revived and expanded the *statio* network created by Trajan, creating many new *stationes* and using gubernatorial *beneficiarii*, which they renamed *beneficiarii consularis*, to man them. By examining and assignment and rotation of these *beneficiarii*, Dise shows the extent and character of the variation in administrative practice. There was no standard term of assignment to a *statio*. It is also not immediately clear why the transfer of *beneficiarii* from one post to another was confined to the European frontier. There seem to be some strong regional peculiarities in their use, and the Rhine and Danube provinces contained more than four times the number of *stationes* found in the northern African provinces and the East.

349. Domaszewski, A von, "Die Beneficiarierposten und die römischen Strassennetze," *Westdeutsche Zeitschrift für Geschichte und Kunst* 21 (1902), pp. 158–211.

Domaszewski was the first to conceive of the idea of *stationes* with *beneficiarii* stationed along the main roads for the purpose of traffic control. However, he does not specify what he understands by the terms road and traffic control. His ideas emerged from his study of the road network of the Roman empire, which is still of great value in the study of *beneficiarii*. Cf R. Dise.

350. Drinkwater, J. F. "The Pagan Underground: Constantine II's Secret Service and the Survival and Usurpation of Julian the Apostate." *Studies in Latin Literature and Roman History.* Collection Latomus 180, Brussels 1983 pp. 348–387.

Scholars have suggested that from the date of the emperor Julian's formal conversion to paganism in 351 and his accession to the throne in 360 he was the center of a pagan "resistance movement," a type of fifth column plotting to replace the ruling emperor and restore the "old worship." Drinkwater questions whether such a movement existed. He also questions whether the *agentes in rebus* were really the "secret service" of the emperor Constantius. Based on their performance in not uncovering this "conspiracy" the author concludes that the *agentes* were not hard-bitten members of a super-efficient service dedicated single-mindedly to the safety of the emperor or his empire. They were minor aristocrats of the decrial class who more than likely worked for their own profit by terrorizing those who had no means of resisting them, i.e. their social inferiors. Their activities had really very little to do with espionage as we would understand it, or the genuine maintenance of the security of the regime that they served. In fact, Drinkwater believes that the *agentes* almost completely betrayed what trust Constantius put in them. There were only two real and potentially dangerous plots against Constantius during his period of office and neither attracted the attention of the so-called secret police.

351. Dumeril, A., " Origine des Délateurs et Précis de leur histoire pendant la durée de l'empire romain," *Annales de la Faculté des Lettres, Bordeaux*, Paris, 3(1881), pp. 262–281.

Unlike Froment's study in an earlier issue of this journal, Dumeril treats the more historical aspects of the development of the informers. He begins with Caepio Crispinus who is described by Tacitus (Annals 1.74) as "the pioneer in a walk of life which the miseries of the age and the effronteries of men soon rendered popular" (C.H. Moore and J. Jackson translation, Loeb Classical Library). Dumeril takes the history through to the end of the empire to the time of the emperors Arcadius and Honorius.

352. Echols, Edward, "The Roman City Police: Origin and Development," *Classical Journal* 53 (1957–58), pp. 377–385.

Traces the development of urban policing procedure in Rome. During the Republic there were a number of officials assigned to supervise police duties. Augustus recognized the need for a permanent force of reserve police in Rome. The post-Augustan history of the Roman city police is basically the history of the urban cohorts. Aurelian established a *castra urbana* for the city police on the Campus Martius. When the emperor moved permanently to the East, the urban prefect assumed the role of Rome's governor and turned policing over to the urban tribune with a police force reduced to three cohorts. The urban cohorts were thus reduced to the status of municipal policemen.

353. Eliot, C. W. J. "New Evidence for the Speed of the Roman Imperial Post," *Phoenix* 9 (1955), pp. 76–80.

Both W. M. Ramsay ("Roads and Travel") and A.M. Ramsay ("The Speed of the Roman Imperial Post") argue persuasively from available evidence that 50 Roman miles a day was the *average* rate of Roman imperial couriers. Eliot accepts the Ramsays' findings, but discusses another piece of evidence that was not available to the earlier writers which suggests that speeds higher than 50 miles a day were even more extraordinary than A.M. Ramsay considered them to be.

The proclamation of Septimius Severus at Carnuntum in AD 193 offers evidence for the speed of Roman communications because we know (more or less) when the message left Rome and when it arrived at Carnuntum. The calculations show that the average of 5 mph or 50 Roman miles a day was about the *best* speed the couriers could achieve. If they could have gone faster, this is certainly one of the important occasions when they would have been expected to do so.

354. Erhart, Victoria, "The Information Age: Spies in Late Antiquity," *Military and Naval History Journal*, 5 (March 1997), pp. 19–25.

Since the Byzantine and Sasanian empires were the continuators respectively of the Roman and Persian empires, Erhart looks into the question of whether the function of acquiring and distributing information was the same in each of these successor empires. In other words, who were the spies of late antiquity? In addition to discussing the official network of internal and foreign-based spies, she examines the numerous informal networks of people whose primary function was not spying, but who acquired information for their governments, i.e. diplomats, merchants and bishops. She argues well that intelligence gathering was important to internal security and the conduct of foreign relations in late antiquity.

355. Ferrill, Arther, "Roman Military Intelligence," in *Go Spy the Land. Military Intelligence in History*, Westport, CT.: Praeger, 1992, pp. 17–29.

One article from an anthology on historical intelligence. Ferrill surveys Roman military intelligence in the empire. His conclusion that the Romans "had an intelligence network in the first century AD" remains unsubstantiated. As evidence, he cites a work that comes to the opposite conclusion, and two articles that concern material dating from two centuries later. REVIEWED IN: *Journal of Military History* 58,1 (1994), pp. 139–140 Sheldon.

356. Fiebiger, H. O., "Exploratores," *RE* 4 (1909), col. 122–5.

Exploratores were scouts who were formally part of the Roman cavalry but were attached from their units to go on missions. Their primary job was to locate the enemy. First attested in Caesar, we do not know how many scouts made up a scouting party, but there were usually at least two but not more than ten. Caesar always speaks of them in the plural.

Under the empire there were ten attached in each legion. Fiebiger lists the literary and inscriptional evidence for their use and for the location of the units of *exploratores* on the borders of the empire. (See also Michael Speidel, (no. **467**) on the use of *exploratores* units, especially in Germany).

357. Fiebiger, H. O., "Frumentarii" *RE* 7 (1912), vol. 1690–3.

Extremely useful encyclopedic article on the *frumentarii*, the a class of military bureaucrats who have been called by some "The Roman Secret Service." They were supply sergeants detached for special duty in the capital or in the *officium* of provincial governors. Fiebiger lists much of the inscriptional and literary evidence for *frumentarii* and also lists some important 19th and early 20th century bibliography.

There is still debate over their origins and use. See Rankov (no. **431**), Sinnigen, "The Origins of the Frumentarii" (no. **462**) and J.C. Mann (no. **401**).

358. Frank, R. I., *Scholae Palatinae.* Papers and Monographs of the American Academy in Rome, Volume 23, 1969.

The *scholae palatinae* or Palace Guards in the later Roman empire played a significant role in internal security. Their primary mission was to serve the emperor personally, to guard him and to assist him in court ceremonies. They also served as agents of imperial control in the provinces and in army headquarters. Their role changed considerably in the third and fourth centuries. While the emperor's bodyguards had occupied a relatively undistinguished place in the military hierarchy of the early empire, their successors under Aurelian, Constantine and Theodosius enjoyed high position and came to play leading roles in military affairs and politics as well. They were in a position to see much of interest to the emperor and to enforce his will.

359. Froment, Théodore, "L'éloquence des délateurs," *Annales de la Faculté des Lettres de Bordeaux*, Paris, 1 (1880), pp. 35–57.

Although snitches both public and private existed, no doubt, throughout Roman history, the professional informers known as *delatores* appear only after the empire is established. The word itself dates to the reign of Tiberius and is attested under his successors. One encounters the word for the first time in Quintilian and Martial. Their arguments convincing the emperor of someone else's treason introduced a new genre that Froment calls the "eloquence de lucre et de sang." This eloquence was surpassed evidently only by their venality. This study predates Gaston Boissiere's *L'accusation publique et les délateurs chez les Romains* (Niort, 1911, pp. 375) which is a more complete study of all the activities of the *delatores.* This is primarily a literary study. See in the same journal the work of Dumeril (no. **351**).

360. Frontinus, Julius, *Strategems*, trans. Charles E. Bennett, Cambridge: Loeb Classical Library, 1925.

Julius Frontinus was a three-time consul of Rome, a governor of the province of Britain, and author of two books on the Roman military. He wrote a treatise on the *Art of War* which has not survived, but we have this work on stratagems. As the book has come down to us, three of the books were written by Frontinus, and a fourth was done by an unknown author. The volume is replete with clever stratagems, means of clandestine communication, ways to spring traps, almost all of it based on gathering accurate intelligence on the enemy.

See especially III. 13 on sending and receiving messages that contains the only Roman reference to the use of carrier pigeons, or I.2.2 on Fabius Caeso as an undercover agent in the Ciminian Forest.

361. Gaudemet, J., "La répression de la délation au bas-empire," in *Philias charin.* Miscellanea di Studi Classici in onore di Eugenio Manni, vol. III, Rome: Bretschneider, 1980, pp. 1065–83.

In the absence of a minister publicly charged in the name of the republic with tracking down enemies of the state and threats to public order, it was the duty of each citizen to denounce those breaking the law. Rome, therefore, raised delation (private informing) to a public institution. Public denunciation could often be motivated by envy, vengeance or ambition, especially when large profits were at stake.

Gaudemet discusses examples from the late empire where delation was frequently used by high-ranking members of society to attack each other while jockeying for social position. Citing evidence from the Theodosian Code, Gaudemet demonstrates that the frequency of such denunciations caused emperors to try and curb the excesses of these informers. They became menacing figures and a dreaded presence to the population. Yet no emperor could afford to do away entirely with a source of intelligence on threats against his regime. The balancing act became how to control the excesses of the *delatores* legally while continuing to use them as a means of maintaining internal security.

362. Gauld, W. W., "Vegetius on Roman scout-boats," *Antiquity* 64 (1990), pp. 402–6.

Vegetius, the 4th century Roman author, wrote the *Epitoma Rei Militaris* (Digest of Military Affairs) which he addressed to the Emperor Theodosius (AD 383–95) . In the section on naval warfare, chapter 37 discusses scout craft (*speculatoria navigia*). According to Vegetius, attached to the larger Liburnian warships were smaller scout boats that had 20 oarsmen in single oar rooms. They were called *picatos* by the Britains. These craft were used for reconnaissance, and intercepting supplies heading for enemy ships. To remain unseen, the sails and ropes and the dressing on the hulls were colored *venetus* (Adriatic blue). The crews wore similarly colored uniforms as camouflage. Gauld discusses the correct translation and interpretation of this passage.

363. Gichon, Mordechai, "Military Intelligence in the Roman Army," in H. E. Herzig and E. Frei-Stolba (eds.) *Labor Omnibus Unus. Festschrift Walser*, Historia Einzelschriften 60, (Stuttgart, 1989), pp. 154–170.

A good summary of Roman military intelligence gathering by an ancient historian with twenty years of regular service in military intelligence with the Israeli Defense Forces. Gichon recognizes that the gathering of information has been one of the first staff functions of any army since the beginning of time. The Roman army developed its own complex system of intelligence gathering. There were special forces (*exploratores* and *speculatores*) assigned the duties of reconnaissance and scouting throughout the imperial period. Special outfits were raised and developed into mobile units designed to operate in border areas. Speidel, (no. **467**) and Austin & Rankov (no. **315**).

Not a comprehensive treatment, but extremely sensitive to intelligence issues.

364. Giovannini, A., "Pline et les délateurs de Domitien," in *Opposition et résistances à l'Empire d'Auguste à Trajan.* Geneva (*Entretiens sur l'Antiquité classique* 33 (1986), pp. 219–48.

Domitian was an emperor who made good use of the *delatores*, or private informers against his political enemies. Giovannini argues convincingly that the historian Pliny, who later tried to distance himself from this emperor and his activities, actually collaborated with Domitian.

365. Girardon, Pierre, *Droit Romaine. De l'Accusation publique*, thèse de doctorat, Paris: A. Derenne, 1876.

Criminal procedures begin with an accusation. Girardon discusses public accusation in both Roman law and nineteenth-century French law. The first seventy pages cover both the Roman Republic and Empire. He discusses the laws covering public accusation, the magistrates who administered those laws, the punishments and how the laws affected different social classes. This includes the treason laws and those used against people denounced by private informers, the *delatores*, on which see Johnson (no. **384**), O'Neal (no. **417**), and Zijlstra (no. **477**), Froment (no. **359**), Boissier (no. **327**), Boissière (no. **328**), Dumeril (no. **351**), and Gaudemet (no. **361**).

366. Graves, Charles (Bishop of Limerick), "The Ogham Alphabet," *Hermathena*, Dublin 2 (1876), pp. 443–472.

In this first article in a series of three, the author lays out his theory that the Beithluinin was a cipher founded on the Roman alphabet and closely related to the Tree Runes.

367. Graves, Charles (Bishop of Limerick), "On Ogam Inscriptions," *Hermathena*, Dublin, Vol. 6, No. 13, (1887), pp. 241–268.

Third article in a series. This one shows that Ogam inscriptions found on grave markers were Latinized. That bolsters his argument that the Ogam alphabet was based on the Roman alphabet. This goes against scholars who believe Ogham was invented long before the arrival of the Romans and that it survived and kept its ground long after the introduction of Latin and Christianity into Celtic lands.

368. Graves, Charles (Bishop of Limerick), "On the Ogam Beithluisnin," Dublin, *Hermathena*, Vol. 3, No. 5 (1877), pp. 208–244.

In this second article in the series, the Bishop of Limerick has collected references to the use of Ogam characters, and shows that Irish native authors unanimously agreed in regarding it as a cryptic mode of writing, intended to be understood only by the initiated.

369. Habicht, Christian, *Die Inschriften des Aesklepions*, Berlin: Walter de Gruyter, 1969. In DAI *Altertümer von Pergamon*, Band VIII, 3.

Number 106, p. 125 is a dedicatory inscription to the god Aesklepios by a *frumentarius* of the Legio VI Ferrata dating to the second century AD.

370. Hartmann, Eugen, *Entwicklungsgeschichte der Posten von den ältesten Zeiten bis zur Gegenwart mit besonderer Beziehung auf Deutschland*, Leipzig: Franz Wagner Verlag, 1868. 400 pp.

Only the first and second chapters of this work cover antiquity. From chapter three on it discusses postal communications in Germany beginning with

Ludwig XI. The ancient sections begin with a discussion of the Babylonians and Persians, then proceed to the Greeks and Romans. Hartmann includes some useful ancient citations. More useful, however, are his many citations to eighteenth and nineteenth century secondary books on the history of postal systems. For a more updated description of the Roman *cursus publicus*, see Pflaum (no. **425**), Holmberg (no. **378**), Brizzi (no. **329**), Hudeman (no. **380**), Humbert (no. **381**), and Seeck (no. **447**).

371. Helm, R., "Untersuchungen über den Auswärtigen diplomatischen Verkehr des römischen Reiches im Zeitalter der Spätantike," *Archiv für Urkundenforschungen* 12 (1932), pp. 375–436.

Helm's article discusses Rome's shifting diplomatic policy toward the end of the third century AD and the importance of written documentation in the process. The strengthening of Persia by the Sassanids, the Huns under Attila, and the emergence of the Avars presented a challenge to Rome that had to be dealt with not only through military means but through diplomacy.

Section thirteen deals with "Scheingesandschaften" that implies false front diplomacy. Helms discusses buying time for war preparations, surprise attack, espionage and extortion. Examples are listed on page 396, note 3: Justinian sending Amalaswintha to make observations about the entrances to Ravenna in AD 359, Totila to Belisarius on troop strength AD 544, Chosroes I to Belisarius on a covert mission to check him out personally in AD 542. Section three discusses the selection and qualifications of emissaries, and under the section on dependability and discretion he lists further examples of covert operations. A list of emissaries on both sides with their titles and ranks is included at the end.

372. Henzen, Guglielmo, "Le castra peregrinorum ed i frumentarii," in *Bulletino dell' Instituto di Corrispondenza Archeologica* (1884), pp. 21–29.

There was much discussion in the 19th century among archaeologists over who the *frumentarii* were, whether they were all stationed in the *castra peregrinorum*, which legions they were attached to and what their duties were. Henzen lists the inscriptional and literary evidence for them and distinguishes between the secret service agents and those soldiers merely involved in provisioning duties.

373. Henzen, Guglielmo, "Sui militi peregrini e frumentarii," *Bulletino dell' Instituto di Corrispondenza Archeologica* (1851), pp. 113–121.

Discusses who the foreign soldiers (*milites peregrini*) were who were stationed in the *Castra Peregrinorum* (Foreigners Camp) on the Caelian Hill. Shows through inscriptional evidence that they are *frumentarii*, those officers seconded to the staffs of provincial governors. They carried military intelligence and acted as internal security officers. Their detached status made them "foreigners" in Rome. See also W.G. Sinnigen (nos. **462, 463**), Otto Hirschfeld (no. **377**), Krenkel (no. **391**), de Laet (no. **395**), Mann (no. **401**), Martini (no. **402**), and Austin & Rankov, *Exploratio* (no. **315**).

374. Herz, P., "Neue Benefiziarier Altäre aus Mainz," *Zeitschrift für Papyrologie und Epigraphik* 22 (1976), pp. 191–9.

Three new altars found near Mainz dedicated by *beneficarii consularis*. They were manning *stationes* in the provinces. Herz discusses their function and dates inscriptions for such *stationes* in the region.

375. Hirschfeld, Otto, *Die agentes in rebus*. Könglisch Preussischen Akademie der Wissenschaften, Berlin, Philosophisch-historische klasse, Sitzungsberichte (1893), pp. 421–441.

Hirschfeld believes the *agentes in rebus* were formed by Diocletian to employ the "indispensable, but unused police force" that had been created when the *frumentarii* were disbanded. He believes they were first and foremost a police force, but their role changed over time. Their duties were based around two areas of responsibility: the imperial post and overseeing the implementation or execution of imperial commands. A lot of the "enforcer" role was taken over from the *frumentarii*. He cites examples of them squelching uprisings in the provinces, and investigating real and presumed cases of anti-imperial dissenters. Due to increased incidents of blackmail, bribery and insurrection involving members of the *agentes*, in AD 395, the Emperors Arcadius and Honorius confined the *agentes* to customs duties along coasts and in harbors.

For later discussions of the *agentes*, see Sinnigen (no. **466**), Jones (no. **385**), Paschoud (no. **421**), Clauss (nos. **335**, **337**), Purpura (no. **426**), Seeck (no. **444**), Blum (no. **325**), Arias Bonet (no. **310**), Austin & Rankov (no. **315**), and Krenkel (no. **389**).

376. Hirschfeld, Otto, "Die ägyptische Polizei der römischen Kaiserzeit nach Papyrusurkunden," (*Könglich Preussische Akademie der Wissenschaften*, Berlin, Philosophisch-historische klasse, Sitzungsberichte, 1892); republished in: *Kleine Schriften*, pp. 613–623.

Hirschfeld wrote this to complement his article on the secret police of imperial Rome. He discusses two previously unedited papyrus documents that allude to the police organization in ancient Egypt under Roman rule. The first document discusses five townspeople enlisted to assist local officials in tracking down a criminal. The townspeople failing to comply are sent in shackles to the Praefectus Aegypti. Hirschfeld cites this threat of imprisonment as evidence that the duty was not a popular one. The second document lists eleven names and positions of a well-organized and delineated police force, including for the first time the title "keepers of the peace" (*Wächter der Ebene*). The names listed in the document are identifiably Egyptian, most fall between the ages of 20 and 35 and they are to be paid either 200, 300 or 400 drachma.

377. Hirschfeld, Otto, *Die Sicherheitspolizei im römischen Kaiserreich*. Sitzungsberichte der könglischen Preussischen Akademie der Wissenschaften in Berlin, (1891) 845–877; *Kleine Schriften* Berlin (1913), pp. 576–612.

A long and very detailed article on the organization of the various police institutions in the first three centuries of the Roman empire. Hirschfeld concentrates on describing the organization with little attention paid to specific actions of the police or secret police. He begins with a description of the street and market police in Athens who fell under the control of the aediles. The secret police and foreign police (*fremdenpolizei*) were under the control of the consul. The consuls were ultimately responsible for peace in the city and this capacity had a jurisdiction that overrode local police.

The first truly professional police organization came into existence after AD 6 when Augustus created the vigiles, seven cohorts of at least 1,000 men. Hirschfeld then goes on to discuss the police duties of the *beneficiarii*, *speculatores*, *curiosi*,

as absurd, were it not for Jones' authority." The same view has been stated in even more uncompromising terms by a student of Jones' in reviewing Blum (no. **325**). "The author ... has been led astray by the analogy of the secret police forces of modern Europe" (W. Liebschuetz, *JRS* 60 [1970], 229–230). The same view has been endorsed by W. Schuller, "Grenzen des spätromischen Staates," *Zeitschrift für Papyrologie und Epigraphik* 16 (1975), pp. 1–21, and Andrea Giardina, *Aspetti della Burocrazia nel Basso Impero* (Rome, 1977), p. 72.

386. Julius Africanus, Sextus, *Kestoi*. Two annotated editions to consult are Giacomo Leopardi, *Giulio Africano: introduzione, edizione critica e note*, a cura di Claudio Moreschini, Bologna: Il Mulino, 1997, 319 pp.; and Jean-René Viellefond, *Les "Cestes" de Julius Africanus. Études sur l'ensemble des fragments avec Édition, Traduction et Commentaires*, Edizioni Sansoni Antiquariato, Firenze, Librarie Marcel Didier, Paris, 1970.

Christian philosopher from Aelia Capitolina (Jerusalem) who established a library in the Pantheon in Rome. His Greek work *Kestoi* or "Charmed Girdles" was a compilation of 24 books on miscellaneous topics including magic, medicine and military tactics. Cf. Lange et Soudart, *Traité de cryptographie*, III, 17. Of particular interest is the section on signalling systems. [No. 42]

387. Kaegi, Walter E., "Constantine's and Julian's Strategies of Strategic Surprise Against the Persians," *Athenaeum* n.s. 59 (1981), pp. 209–213.

Kaegi discusses the source for Julian's idea to surprise the Persians. Did he get it from Constantine? What documents did he have at his disposal that might have given him the blueprints for such a campaign? Much on the decision-making process but nothing on how the intelligence for this expedition was gathered. Cf. A.D. Lee, *Information and Frontiers*, pp. 87–88 (no. **397**).

388. Kneppe, A. "Die Gefährdung der Securitas. Angst vor Angehörigen sozialer Randgruppen der römischen Kaiserzeit am Beispiel von Philosophen. Astrologen, Magieren, Schauspiel und Räubern," in Weiler, (ed.) *Soziale Randgruppen und Aussenseiter im Altertum*, Graz: Leykam, 1988, pp. 165–76.

Kneppe discusses perceived threats to the *securitas* of Imperial Rome caused by fear of outsiders as represented by philosophers, astrologists, magi, actors and thieves. Any group with the ability to instill fear or uneasiness in the general public was considered a threat to security. Members of these groups were treated with both awe and contempt, and were often subject to humiliation, banishment or death. Unfortunately, Kneppe does not discuss who was used to investigate, arrest, harass or execute them.

389. Krenkel, W. "Agentes in rebus," *Lexicon der Alten Welt*, Zurich and Munich: Artemis Verlag, 1990, p. 66.

Short encyclopedia entry on the infamous Roman secret service agents. Gives literary references, inscriptions and law code citations. See also Sinnigen (no. **459**), Paschoud (no. **421**), Purpura (no. **426**), Blum (no. **325**), Clauss (nos. **335**, **337**), Jones (no. **385**), Lopuszanski (no. **398**), Arias Bonet (no. **310**), Austin & Rankov, *Exploratio* (no. **315**), and Seeck (no. **444**).

390. Krenkel, W. "Curiosi," *Lexicon der Alten Welt*, Zurich and Munich: Artemis Verlag, 1990, p. 677.

Short encyclopedia entry on the high level *agentes in rebus* who were used as postal inspectors in the Roman empire. See also Sinnigen (no. **459**), Paschoud (no. **421**), Purpura (no. **426**), Blum (no. **325**), Clauss (nos. **335**, **337**), Jones (no. **385**), and Lopuszanski (no. **398**).

391. Krenkel, W. "Frumentarii," *Lexicon der Alten Welt*, Zurich and Munich: Artemis Verlag, 1990, p. 1009.

Short encyclopedia entry on the Roman supply sergeants who were detailed to act as couriers for the Roman government from the time of the emperor Domitian to the time of Diocletian. They eventually took over much of the policing duties of the *speculatores*. Disbanded by Diocletian and their duties were taken over by the *agentes in rebus*. See also Sinnigen (no. **463**), Paschoud (no. **421**), Purpura (no. **426**), Blum (no. **325**), Clauss (nos. **335**, **337**), Jones (no. **385**), and Lopuszanski (no. **398**).

392. Krenkel, W. "Speculatores," *Lexicon der Alten Welt*, Zurich and Munich: Artemis Verlag, 1990, p. 2855.

Short encyclopedia entry on the military intelligence officers of the Roman army. They were also used as assassins, arresting officers and spies. In Mark 6.27 it is a *speculator* who accompanies Saint Paul to Rome. Lists literary and inscriptional evidence.

393. Kübler, B., "Beneficiarus," in Ruggiero (ed.) *Dizionario Epigrafico di Antichità Romane*, (1895) Vol 1, pp. 992–6.

Beneficiarii is a term used originally by Caesar for soldiers specifically attached to a particular commander and so freed from ordinary duties by his *beneficium* (*BC* 1.75.2; 3.88.5). Under the Principate the term was used for a specific grade of staff officer within each military office in the provinces. When the Roman government began to create a series of posts or *stationes* at key points along major roads in the provinces of the empire in the early second century AD, they were manned by these *beneficiarii* attached to the governors' staffs. We know about these men because of their habit of erecting votive altars at the *stationes* where they served. They were a key element in the apparatus of administration and communication (thus intelligence gathering) of the empire. Their number multiplied dramatically in the early third century. Cf. Schallmeyer and Ott, (no. **439**), Dise (nos. **342–347**), Rankov (no. **430**), Mirkovic (nos. **406**, **407**), Domazewski (no. **349**), Pekary (no. **422**) and Lopuszanski (no. **398**).

394. Kübler, Bernhard, "Statores." *Pauly-Wissowa, Real-encyclopaedie der classischen Altertumswissenschaft*, vol. III, A. col. 2228–2229.

Provincial magistrates retained special messengers called *statores* for the transport of official letters containing information from the Senate and the magistrates in republican Rome. We know very little about their precise function or how they discharged their duties, but Cicero in his letters from Cilicia speaks of them in a manner that suggests they had been around for quite some time. A governor might have several *statores* at his disposal. In the absence of a state-sponsored postal and transport system, officials were obliged, when traveling long distances, to wait for suitable means of conveyance or requisition alternative transportation as best they could. Even governors faced such difficulties with transport arrangements when journeying to or from their provinces. Kübler lists the inscriptional and literary evidence for these runners.

395. Laet, S. J. de, "Les pouvoirs militaires des préfets du prétoire et leur dévelopment progressif," *Revue Belge de Philologie et d'Histoire* 25 (1946–47), pp. 509–554.

On the *frumentarii* within the chain of command of the praetorian prefecture, pp. 533–536.

396. Lammert, F., "Speculatores," Pauly Wissowa, *Real-encyclopaedie der classischen Altertumswissenschaft*, 3A (1929), pp. 1583–6.

Speculatores were military troops used as spies and scouts. Their primary role was to deliver dispatches (*litterae*) both between camps and from camps to Rome. Each of Caesar's legions had ten *speculatores* under the general staff. Under Augustus, they were used as couriers on the *cursus publicus*. At least one sculpted relief shows such a courier performing his duties. See M. Rostovtzeff, *Röm. Mitt* (1911). According to the Gospel of Mark, Herod sent a *speculator* to the prison with the order to execute John the Baptist.

Speculatores could also be used for police functions. A special corps of *speculatores*, called "*speculatores* of Caesar" belonged to the praetorian guard. They were sometimes used for arrests, espionage, guarding suspects and detainees, or the execution of condemned men.

Lammert lists the literary and inscriptional evidence from which we gain our knowledge and some 19th century secondary literature.

397. Lee, A. D., *Information and Frontiers*. (Roman Foreign Relations in Late Antiquity.) Cambridge: Cambridge University Press, 1993, 213 pp.

Lee attacks the question of how and to what extent the Romans gained political and strategic information about the peoples living beyond their own directly-administered territories. He restricts himself to two regions—the eastern frontier and the German frontier. He dispels the mistaken belief that borders were somehow impermeable to intelligence. REVIEWED BY: Boris Rankov, *Classical Review* 45, 1 (1995), pp. 113–114; John W. Eadie, *American Historical Review* (June 1995), pp. 883–884; A. Marcone, *Athenaeum* 83 (1995), pp. 560–561; R. Delmaire, *Latomus* 54,4 (1995), pp. 912–913; David Potter, *Journal of Roman Archaeology* 9 (1996).

398. Lopuszanski, A., "La police romaine et les chrétiens," *Antiquité Classique* 20 (1951), pp. 5–46.

Lopuszanski mines the hagiographic literature and the early Church fathers for evidence on the organization of police organizations used to hunt down Christians. The Roman government used a great variety of institutions to maintain state security, and although their primary jobs may not have been intelligence or police functions, they were used often enough in those capacities to show up in the literary and inscriptional evidence. Among the people being used to persecute

Christians were *beneficiarii,* (Dise, nos. **342–347**, Rankov, no. **430**), *curiosi,* (Blum, no. **325**), *delatores,* (O'Neal, no. **417**), *agentes in rebus* (Sinnigen, no. **466**), *frumentarii,* (Sinnigen, nos. **462–463**), *stationarii, vigiles*, (Baillie Reynolds, no. **317**), and in Egypt a variety of *Phulakes* (Hohlwein, nos. **104–105**). The corruptibility of all Roman officials made them open to bribes and they often extorted money from Christians in return for not turning them in.

Even the Romans themselves did not distinguish clearly between the army and the police or between the functions of a soldier and a cop. Thus we see many ad hoc situations where one or the other might be used as the occasion arose. They might participate in the detection of Christians, their arrest, incarceration or execution. These Christians became martyrs to their faith and the accounts of their lives became a source for us on policing in the later Roman empire.

Lopuszanski ends with a discussion of Christians in the army and how their martyrdom often informed the soldiers around them of what Christians believed, how they led their lives, and the strength their faith gave them.

399. Macmullen, Ramsay, *Enemies of Roman Order. Treason, Unrest and Alienation in the Empire*, London and New York: Routledge 1992 (new edition), 370 pp.

An important study about the people who might have been hunted down had there been a Roman equivalent of the House Un-American Activities Committee. He discusses philosophers, magicians, astrologers, diviners, prophets, and all sorts of outsiders and their connection to urban unrest. How did the "non-conformists" within the empire protest? What made a person Roman or un-Roman?

Not a lot of information of who might have hunted these people down or how they were watched, but they would have been sure targets of government surveillance.

400. Madvig, Johan Nikolai, *Verfassung und Verwaltung des Römischen Staates* Leipzig: B.G. Teubner, 1881, Vol. 2, p. 738–745, "Wege-und Befördungswesen, sowie der spätere Kourierdienst."

Madvig studies the traffic along Roman imperial roads. He begins with an overview of the three main roadways from Rome through Italy then shows how this network expanded into the provinces, financed first by rich senators and eventually by public funds. The development of a public transportation was followed by the development of a courier service. In the first century this was made up of the *speculatores* who were later replaced by the *frumentarii.* The *frumentarii* were not only couriers but spies and informers. Madvig comments on how they were named to hide their sinister activities. Although the *frumentarii* were disbanded by Diocletian, the *agentes in rebus* soon appeared in a similar role. They had both the job of delivering and enforcing imperial commands plus gathering information that would have been useful to the Roman government.

401. Mann, J. C., "The Organization of the Frumentarii," *Zeitschrift für Papyrologie und Epigraphik* 74 (1988), pp. 149–50.

There is agreement that the *frumentarii* were, in origin, connected to the distribution of grain (*frumentum*) for the army (not Rome itself; this was the preserve of the *praefectus annonae*). This was merely a cover, however, for their operations in intelligence gathering and secret police work. Mann outlines their organization and functions. He does not believe that they served in the *officia* of provincial governors (as do Domaszewski, *Rangordnung*, 34; W.G. Sinnigen, no. **463**), pp. 213–224, and N. B. Rankov, *Britannia* XVIII (1987), p. 244.

A *frumentarius* often served in provinces far removed from that in which his legion was stationed. His enrollment in a legion was a mere formality, and according to Mann, there is no evidence that he served at his legion's headquarters or had any formal duties with his legion. *Frumentarii* were thus distinct from the ordinary enlisted man. Operating under the immediate orders of a *centurio frumentarius*, he would have served the emperor not the governor. He could be ordered to both arrest or assassinate people. (*Acta Martyrorum* [p. 52 Ruinart]; Eusebius, *Ecclesiastical History* 6. 40.; St. Cyprian, *Letters,* 81.) Even when promoted to *centurio frumentarius* he would continue to work directly for the emperor and therefore can be "clearly distinguished from all other men in the public service of Rome during the principate."

402. Martini, G., "I milites frumentarii," *Atti del Istituto Veneto di Scienza, Lettere ed Arti, Classe di Scienze morali e Lettere, Venezia* 139 (1980–81), pp. 143–151.

The *frumentarii* were soldiers detached from their legions to act as messengers between Rome and the provinces. From the time of Hadrian, they were used for more delicate intelligence missions to spy on relatives, citizens and friends. As political assassins they were active under Caracalla. In the provinces they were used for police work and to maintain public order. This position allowed them to abuse the public who came to hate them as the corrupt minions of a police state. They were suppressed under Diocletian.

Martini traces the recruitment of some *frumentarii* and sees that they originated from the eastern legions as well as the west. Their recruitment resembled that of the *speculatores* and the *equites singularis legionis.*

403. Massmann, H. F., "Runen aus Rom und Wien," *Germania*, Leipzig, (1871), pp. 252–258.

Article on the decipherment of runes. See Locard, *Bibliographie cryptologique*, p. 927.

See below "Runes" under Medieval section.

404. Matthews, John F., "Hostages, Philosophers, Pilgrims, and the Diffusion of Ideas in the Late Roman Mediterranean and Near East," ch. 3 in F.M. Clover and R.S. Humphreys, *Tradition and Innovation in Late Antiquity*, University of Wisconsin Press, 1989, 343 pp.

Matthews discusses the role of certain travelers in carrying information of use to the late Roman government in the formation of its diplomatic policy. He feels the information acquired in this way about foreign lands and peoples was considerable and can be easily documented. He also wisely notes that the absence of formal intelligence-gathering institutions in no way implies the absence of functions, or of the forms of imperial policy-making that these made possible: "The relative deficiency of the Roman imperial government in sponsoring foreign exploration and in organizing the collection of information about foreign peoples should not be taken to imply that this information was not collected, or that it was not available for the use of the government" (p. 40).

405. Millar, F., "Condemnation to Hard Labour in the Roman Empire, from the Julio-Claudians to Constantine," *Papers of the British Scxhool at Rome* 52 (1984), pp. 128–47.

From the second century AD onwards, condemnation to hard labor in mines and quarries was a familiar fate for lower-class criminals and Christians. Some scholars have suggested there was an extension of the police functions of the Roman army during the Imperial period, and along with this military prisons or city prisons run by soldiers. Prisons were not intended for long-term sentences, but only as places for short-term detention for defendants or persons waiting execution. The real punishment was being condemned *ad metallum*—to the metal mines. There are a variety of agencies who might keep a man under arrest—the *statores*, the *frumentarii*, regular legionaries. *CIL* 11.1322 = Dessau 2371; *L'Année Épigraphique* (1936), no. 61 shows *frumentarii* supervising public mines and quarries, *CIL* 3.433 shows them supervising or prisons.

406. Mirkovic, Miroslava, "*Beneficiarii Consularis* and the new Outpost in Sirmium," *Roman Frontier Studies* 1989 (Exeter, 1990), pp. 252–256.

In 1988, a *statio* of *beneficiarii* was discovered near the western wall of Sirmium in Pannonia Inferior. In a pillared courtyard were found 84 altars, 80 of which bore inscriptions of *beneficiarii consularis*. From the dated inscriptions Mirkovic deduces that there was no fixed duration of a *statio*. Until Severan times there was one *beneficiarius consularis* in one station. As of AD 221 the altars mention two in each. In other words, the number of *beneficiarii consularis* serving simultaneously in any one province was rather small.

These *beneficiarii* were posted to stations along main roads and junctions. They supervised traffic acted as a police force, collected intelligence, levied customs duties and controlled local markets. They also performed courier services between the *territorium legionis* and the *territorium coloniae*. Indeed, their link with the *cursus publicus* was their principal duty in the Late Empire. During the early empire the *beneficiarii* were often elected from among the *frumentarii* and no doubt collected intelligence as the *frumentarii* used to do.

407. Mirkovic, Miroslava, "Der Benefiziarierposten bei Novi Pazar," *Ziva Antika* 21 (1971), pp. 263–71.

Stations of the *beneficiarii* in Serbia. Article in Serbian with German summary.

408. Mitchell, Stephen, "Requisitioned Transport in the Roman Empire: A New Inscription from Pisidia," *Journal of Roman Studies* 65, 1 (1975), pp. 106–131.

Mitchell's discussion of a new inscription from Turkey can be added to a long series of imperial documents referring directly or indirectly to the requisitioning of transport in the Roman empire and its associated liturgies (civic obligations). He concludes that requisitions for the imperial post only comprised a small fraction of the total amount of transport regularly commandeered under the empire. Augustus's need to maintain large armies on a pemanent basis created a major supply problem. It was necessary to devise a method of requisitioning that could supply the legions in an organized way. The *annona militaris* thus provided the greatest usage.

One can see how burdensome maintaining a road system with an intelligence service transport capabilities became. It is accompanied by an extensive bibliography.

409. Mommsen, Theodor, "Das römische Militärwesen seit Diocletian," *Hermes* 24 (1889), pp. 195–279.

A long and authoritative essay on the Roman army in the time of the emperor Diocletian. See especially pages 221 and following on the *protectores*, and later in the third century, the *protectores domestici*. These troops formed a type of staff college in the late empire and protected the emperor, especially against usurpers. Diocletian himself was a member of the *protectores domestici*. So was Ammianus Marcellinus (no. **309**). Men passing through the service as *protectores* had no statutory term to complete, but would be promoted according to personal merit. This flexibility disappeared in the fifth century when men were appointed for almost life-long terms. This, in effect, ended the use of the *protectores* as a staff college.

410. Moynihan, R., "Geographical Mythology and Roman Imperial Ideology," in R. Winkes (ed.) *The Age of Augustus*, Providence, RI, 1985, pp. 149–157.

The Romans had to form a mental image of the world before they could formulate grand strategy or send intelligence gatherers into it. Can it be that the men who planned the Roman empire's imperial strategy did so partly on the basis of faulty geographical information, i.e. on a "geographical mythology" that encouraged them to believe effective control of the whole earth was written within their reach? Those who study Roman frontiers (Luttwak, *The Grand Strategy of the Roman Empire*) have failed to show how the Romans' knowledge or lack of knowledge of geography may have affected their formulation of political and military strategy and their conduct of empire. Nor do they explain how Rome collected the level of geographical intelligence necessary to formulate an effective grand strategy. Appendices include maps of the world according to Hecataeus, Eratosthenes, Strabo, Ptolemy and Agrippa.

411. Naudet, M., "Analyse d'un Mémoire sur la Police des Romains sous les Empereurs" *Académie des sciences morales et politiques*, Séances et travaux Ser 2:6 (1849) p. 183–188.

Naudet believes that whatever policing was done in Rome was necessary to keep law and order in the empire. The blessings of civilization only come with security. This is the second part of a two-part article (Part one in Volume IV, p. 796) that gives the full literary treatment of policing in Rome as it appears in the evidence of historians, poets, and orators.

412. Naudet, M., "Sur la signification du mot *frumentarius*, à propos de la communication de M. E. Desjardins," *Comptes Rendus de l'Académie des Inscriptions et Belles-Lettres* (1875), pp. 144–151

A number of graffiti of the 7th cohort of Vigiles was commented upon by M. Desjardins in *CRAI*. One of them, a man named Harius, is called "*frumentarius cohortis*." Desjardins believes he had served his triennial service and was awarded with a ration of grain for life, thus the title *frumentarius*, i.e. one receiving *frumentum*, or grain. Naudet disagrees. He identifies Harius as a *frumentarius*, i.e. an intelligence officer detached for spying. He is also the first to connect the *frumentarii* with the distribution of grain to the royal court. Paribeni (no. **419**) agrees. Sinnigen "Origins" (no. **463**) does not.

413. Nicolet, Claude, *Space, Geography and Politics in the Early Roman Empire*, Ann Arbor: University of Michigan, 1991, 230 pp.

Rev. by Nicholas Purcell in *Journal of Roman Studies* 1990 "Maps, Lists, Money, Order and Power," pp. 178–182.

Nicolet, unlike most Roman historians, tries to come to grips with the conceptual geography of the Roman empire and the sociocultural nature of administrative structures. How did the Romans see the world which they conquered? When a conqueror conquers, *what* does he conquer? What is the relationship between place and power? How can we conceive of space that we cannot comprehend with our vision?

Nicolet believes that the Augustan Age was pivotal in the history of these subjects. Critics, like Purcell, believe he has created an exaggerated picture of the complexity and sophistication of both ancient geography and thinking about space. One thing is clear: the communications routes established by Augustus were central to his geography and its administrative use. The *cursus publicus* was the heart of the Augustan empire—giving it shape and carrying the intelligence that was marshaled to display shape and, above all, the collecting resources (money, goods and people) which it was the function of empire in antiquity to deploy.

Discovery, exploration and new knowledge provided the progressive extension of the ease of movement. New territories were not revealed by scientific inquiry but by conquest and the inevitable expansion of unrestricted travel.

414. Nippel, Wilfried, *Aufruhr und "Polizei" in der römischen Republik*, Stuttgart: Klett-Cotta, 1988, 334 pp.

A revised version of his *habilitationsschrift* presented in 1982/3 that deals with various aspects of the maintenance of public order in the city of Rome under the Republic. Two chapters deal with the growing violence of the last century of the Republic and the ways in which the senatorial government responded to it. The final chapter deals with order in the city under the Principate.

Nippel rejects the common view that lack of a police force was a serious weakness in the Roman Republic and helped to account for its downfall. For Nippel, the essential guarantors of order were social and political stability and consensus and respect for legitimate authority. REVIEWED BY: J. Rich *Journal of Roman Studies* 81 (1991), pp. 193–5.

415. Nippel, Wilfried, "Policing Rome," *Journal of Roman Studies* 74 (1984), pp. 20–29.

Rome never had a specialized law-enforcement apparatus. This is a modern invention. The Romans had several different organizations used to secure public order in Republican times. (aediles, *tresviri capitales*, etc.) This gave the upper classes great flexibility in dealing with matters of public order. Nippel outlines the special instruments of enforcement that a magistrate had at hand. Defense meant primarily self-organization of the upper classes and the mobilization of the "reliable parts" of the citizenry. Consensus within the citizenry was a necessary precondition for the implementation of emergency measures with respect to the physical means of power as well as to the legitimacy of armed repression.

He concludes that when discussing the policing of Rome we have to avoid a fixation on agencies of enforcement. The problems of maintaining law and order during the Republic have to be seen within the broader framework of the aristocracy being able to integrate all parts of the urban population socially and politically. When they lost that consensus in the late 50s they lost public order with it.

The new institutions of the Principate (the urban cohorts and the praetorian guard) are fundamental elements of a new, comprehensive attempt at regaining stability by intensifying welfare as well as control.

416. Nippel, Wilfried, *Public Order in Ancient Rome*, Cambridge: Cambridge University Press, 1995, 163 pp.

A discussion of public order in the cities and provinces of the Roman Empire which suggests that, in general, governmental intervention was limited. Protection of property and personal security were the responsibilities of the citizens themselves. One had to rely on relatives and neighbors or influential patrons. Even in the later empire under Christian emperors, there was no comprehensive policy for disciplining the lower orders of society. State intervention was most interested in cases that were a direct threat to the Roman government—treason and sedition, counterfeiting, smuggling and brigandage. The majority of everyday crimes were left to be settled through private initiative and communal arbitration. Professional police forces, as distinct from ordinary citizens and amateur magistrates or the military with their distinctive uniforms, did not appear in most European states until the 18th and 19th centuries.

That the Romans understood how to collect intelligence to prevent conspiracies can be seen in the section on "conspiracies and illegal associations."

417. O'Neal, William J., "Delation in the Early Empire," *Classical Bulletin* 55 (1978), pp. 24–28.

The *custodes legum* or *delatores* were private informers who pressed cases against those who broke the laws of *maiestas*. This treason law included abuse of the divinity of Gaius Caesar, verbal abuse and slander of the Princeps, and even slander of the members of the Princeps' family as well as high treason. Delators were encouraged by hopes of rewards established by Augustus. The amount of reward stipulated by the law was one-fourth of the convicted's estate, but the amounts could vary. Additions in the form of political offices were not uncommon. Thus delators could amass an enormous fortune and honors in a very short time.

The laws of Augustus for the restoration of social morality gave the first impulse to professional delation. Tiberius brought this profession to maturity. According to Seneca, *De Beneficiis* 3.26. "In the reign of Tiberius Caesar, there was a common and universal frenzy for informing, which was more ruinous to the citizens of Rome than the whole civil war."

The Lex de Maiestate gave certain individuals the opportunity to exploit their fellow citizens and in the early empire, this exploitation took place to the degree permitted by the Princeps. Under Claudius the number of informers increased and the profits of their profession increased even more. Claudius limited the fee that might be taken to 10,000 sesterces. Any person exceeding the limit was liable to prosecution for extortion (Tacitus, *Annals* 13.23.) The legal basis for the prosecution of the Christians under Nero was failure to worship the gods of the State (treason). This provided a rich field for delation.

The *delatores* came from every section of society but the most prominent seem to have come from the upper ranks. What motivated them? Hope of wealth, gaining political favor by prosecuting the enemies of the emperor, and patriotism. It was the one forum where a Roman well trained in rhetoric could practice his skills to a lucrative end. Though despised by their fellow citizens they continued to be a part of Roman society until the fall of the empire.

One reason not mentioned by the author is their intelligence value. Whatever *their* motivations, the emperors would use anyone at all to collect intelligence on possible threats to his position or attempts on his life. No emperor, no matter how securely he thought he sat on his throne, could ignore information about a possible coup, and he would take that information from any source available.

418. Ott, Joachim, *Der Beneficiarier. Untersuchungen zu ihrer Stellung innerhalb der Rangordnung des römischen Heeres und zu ihrer Funktion.* (Historia Einzelschriften, 92) 246 pp., 15 maps, 5 pls. Stuttgart: Franz Steiner, 1995, 245 pp.

A study of the Roman army officers who bore the rank of *beneficiarius.* This work developed out of Ott's Frankfurt dissertation submitted in 1993. This work appeared after the publication of E. Schallmayer et al. (edd.) *Der römische Weihebezirk von Osterburken* I (no. **440**) yet does not make any direct use of its contents. These *beneficiarii* varied enormously in rank and function depending on the senior officer to whom they were attached. See the comments of Boris Rankov in his review in *Classical Review* n.s. 49, 1 (1999), 182–183.

419. Ovadiah, A., "The Relief of the Spies from Carthage," *Israel Exploration Journal* 24 (1974), pp. 210–213.

Spies show up in ancient art as well as ancient literature. Ovadiah, in this article, publishes for the first time a relief from a private collection in Paris depicting the episode described in Numbers 13:1–25 in which Moses sent men to spy out the land of Canaan. They return carrying grapes (i.e. the fruit of the land). Such subjects appear frequently on Christian sarcophagi, particularly on examples dating to the fourth and fifth centuries AD. This relief appears to be a panel broken from the upper part of the side wall of such a sarcophagus and Oviadiah dates it to that period.

420. Paribeni, R. "Dei milites frumentarii e del'approvigionamento della corte imperiale," Deutsches Archaeologisches Institut, *Römische Mitteilungen* 20 (1905), pp. 310–320.

All legions provided men for the *frumentarii* and the men so detached formed a *numerus* in Rome and were stationed in the Castra Peregrinorum under the orders of the *Princeps peregrinorum.*

Paribeni picks up on the two articles of Henzen (no. **372, 373**) and continues the discussion of whether these *frumentarii* were involved in supplying grain to the court at Rome. He suggests Hadrian set up a system of *frumentarii* to unify the service of provisioning the Roman imperial court with grain. His argument rests essentially on the late and untrustworthy testimony of John Lydus, *De Mag.* 3–7. His argument is rejected by Fiebiger, *RE* 7, 122, Rostovtzeff, "frumentum" *RE* 7 (1910) 181, Baillie Reynolds, *Journal of Roman Studies* 123 (1923), p. 184 and Sinnigen, "Origins" (no. **462**). Such a connection existed, at least in the urban grain administration, but the surviving evidence indicates that they were so employed at a rather late date, perhaps no earlier than the reign of Septimius Severus.

Sinnigen (no. **463**) argues that the functions of the *frumentarii* were more probably related to the military grain administration, the *annona militaris*, and their origin should be sought in their relationship as *officiales* to the grain administration as a part of the general military supply organization.

421. Paschoud, F., "Frumentarii, agentes in rebus, magistriani, curiosi, veredarii; problèmes de terminologie," *Bonner Historia-Augusta Colloquium* 1979/81 (Bonn, 1983), pp. 215–243.

Paschoud examines five different agencies in the Roman empire that were used at one time or another for policing duties. His task is not easy since the Romans never relied on one single institution, and the ones they used were constantly evolving. Plus the documentation is not abundant. Paschoud seems to privilege the inscriptional evidence over the literary, especially where the *frumentarii* are concerned. He does not see them as a detective force (on this, compare Clauss, no. **337**). They were not as clearly defined nor well-organized as the *agentes in rebus*. On the subject of the *agentes*, he does not consider the term a synonym of *curiosi* (Cf. Sinnigen, no. **466**).

422. Pekáry, T., "Seditio. Unruhen und Revolten im römischen Reich von Augustus bis Commodus," *Ancient Society* 18 (1987), pp. 133–50.

Although the Augustan peace is often presented as a golden age, when looked at from the point of view of revolts and uprisings against it, we see that there were many unhappy campers in the empire. Pékary has painstakingly listed these revolts in chronological order and shows that not a single decade went by without some unrest occurring. Between Actium and AD 190 there were over 200 disturbances. The cost to the empire in money and manpower in putting down such revolts could not have been insignificant. The deaths alone would have been in the tens if not hundreds of thousands.

Keeping informed of possible uprisings and controlling their outbreak was the job of all officials charged with internal security duties—*speculatores, beneficiarii, and frumentarii* (see p. 146).

423. Pekáry, T., "Spionage," *Lexicon der Alten Welt*, Zurich and Munich: Artemis Verlag, 1990, p. 2862–3.

Short encyclopedia entry on the history of espionage in the ancient world.

424. Pekáry, T., *Untersuchungen zu den römischen Reichstrassen*, Bonn: Rudolf Habelt Verlag, 1968, 195 pp.

A study of the Roman imperial road system, including military roads, the people who presided over their building, administration and upkeep. Provides important bibliography on the *cursus publicus* published since 1940 that was not included in Holmberg and Pflaum in their histories of the Roman postal system.

425. Pflaum, Hans Georg, "Essai sur le cursus publicus sous le haut-empire romain," *Mémoires de l'Académie des Inscriptions et Belles Lettres* 14 (1940), pp. 189–390.

The *cursus publicus* was one of the emperor Augustus' great gifts to the Roman Empire. The public road system with the accompanying postal service acted as the arteries of a vast intelligence network that kept the emperor informed of events throughout his domain. Pflaum surveys the pre-Roman systems of the Persians, the Greeks, and Ptolemaic Egypt. He discusses most of the inscriptions found before 1940. He makes the unfortunate assumption that all the evidence relates to the imperial post, whereas much of it is more relevant to transport in a wider context. (Mitchell, no. **408**, p. 112.)

Whether Augustus got his model of empire (including the communications system) from the East or not is an ongoing discussion. See for example A. von Premerstein, *Vom Werden und Wesen des Prinzipats*, Abhandlung der Bayerischen Akademie der Wissenschaft, phil.-hist. Abteilung, n.F. Heft 15 (Munich 1937) who discounts the influence of Greek thought on Augustus. Then compare Mason Hammond, "Hellenistic Influences on the Structure of the Augustan Principate," *Memoires of the American Academy in Rome* 17 (1940) and his review of von Premerstein in *American Journal of Philology* 59 (1938), 481–487.

426. Purpura, G., "I curiosi e la schola agentum in rebus," *Annali del Seminario Giuridico dell' università di Palermo* 34 (1973), pp. 165–275.

Purpura analyzes the term "*curiosi*" as it is applied to certain members of the *agentes in rebus*. He determines that they are a sub-group of the *agentes* given the responsibility of overseeing the *cursus publicus*. He does not agree with Blum (no. **325**) or Sinnigen (no. **463**, **466**) that they constitute part of the Roman Secret Service. He also discusses the *regendarii* and *chartularii*.

427. Rainbird, J. S., "The fire stations of Imperial Rome," *Papers of the British School at Rome* 54 (1986), pp. 147–69.

The *vigiles*, the fire brigade of Imperial Rome, functioned for more than 300 years. The evidence for them is sparse and scattered. The standard work on the *vigiles* is Baillie Reynolds (no. **318**). There is no published work on what these men actually did. Many believe they spent their time doing more than putting out fires. (Sinnigen, no. **463**.) Even Rainbird notices, as others have, that their method of patrolling appear police-like. One of the main stations was at Ostia, for example, where the grain sheds were. Any threat to the food supply of Rome presented a threat to the emperor and was thus a security issue.

Rainbird reviews the antiquarian evidence for the fire stations, and the archaeological evidence for the fire stations in Rome and Portus, and new epigraphic evidence from Ostia. This article updates Baillie Reynolds' work on the layout of the barracks and the number of *vigiles* they accommodated. Rainbird says nothing new about the function of the *vigiles* themselves.

428. Rainbird, J. S., *The Vigiles of Rome*, Ph.D. Thesis, University of Durham, 1976.

Dissertation on the fire brigade of imperial Rome. An update of Baillie Reynolds' pioneering 1926 study. See his condensation in the *Papers of the British School at Rome*. (no. **427**.)

429. Ramsay, A.M., "The Speed of the Roman Imperial Post," *Journal of Roman Studies* 15 (1925), pp. 60–74.

The postal system of the Roman empire was established by Augustus as a means of centralizing the administration of the empire. Ramsay does not look to eastern empires for Augustus' inspiration for this system nor to Republican precedents, but to the circumstances of his own time. Among the reasons for the failure and eventual downfall of the Republic were lack of centralization, the consequent absence of co-ordinated action, continuity in policy and control of ambitious officials in the outlying provinces.

The Roman system consisted of relays of couriers and post-horses stationed at regular intervals along main roads and the message was transmitted from hand to hand. Experience soon showed, however, that if a single messenger made the journal he might be able, if required, to supplement verbally the written dispatches he brought. For this reason, Augustus altered the system so that there would be relays of couriers and carriages. The Roman imperial post did not aim at speed, but rather certainty of arrival within a reasonable and calculable time.

Ramsay asserts that the journeys along the imperial post for which we have times and distances are usually exceptional cases, and therefore modern writers have miscalculated the speed of the imperial post, erring on the side of quickness. He carefully discusses each author and his calculations, then by using what he considers certain characteristic, long-distance journeys concludes that the average rate of the post carriers was fifty Roman miles per day. This rate, of about five Roman miles per hour, is what could be reasonably maintained, unvaryingly, in all seasons without lessening the efficiency of either the couriers or the animals. Even this modest rate of speed was an enormous improvement over the Republican system when communications with the provinces was always uncertain and dependent upon private enterprise.

430. Rankov, B., "Die Beneficiarier in den literarischen und papyrologischen Texten," in *Der römische Weihebezirk von Osterburken* II. Kolloquium 1990 und paläobotanische-osteologische Untersuchungen, Forschungen und Berichte zur Vor-und Frügeschichte in Baden-Württemberg, Bd. 49 (Stuttgart, 1994), pp. 219–232.

Introductory essay to the collection of *beneficiarii* references collected by Schallmeyer and Ott (no. **439**). Rankov discusses inscriptions on stone, literary references and papyrus texts that are evidence for the policing and other administrative duties of the *beneficiarii consularis*.

431. Rankov, B., "Frumentarii, the Castra Peregrina and the Provincial Officia," *Zeitschrift für Papyrologie und Epigraphik* 80 (1990), pp. 176–82.

A response to J.C. Mann's article (no. **401**) asserting that the *frumentarii* owed their loyalty to the emperor and not to the provincial governors in charge of the legions. Mann sees them as the emperor's eyes and ears in the provinces. Rankov believes that attachment to the emperor for special projects does not necessarily preclude an attachment to the *officium* of a provincial governor. He argues that local recruitment would have eliminated any mechanism by which the emperor could have controlled who was taken and used as a spy. Rankov plays down the role of the *frumentarii* in espionage and sees their primary role as simply carrying messages. As couriers, they served the provincial governors as much as the emperors. They were members of both the *officium consularis* and the Castra Peregrina in Rome. These roles were complementary. They shuttled between the two carrying messages—when in the provinces they did the bidding of the governors, and when in Rome, the emperor could use them for spying or even murder.

Cf. Sinnigen (no. **463**), Clauss (nos. **335**, **337**), Fiebiger (no. **357**) and Paschoud (no. **421**).

432. Rankov, N. B., "M. Oclatinius Adventus in Britain," *Brittania* 18 (1987), pp. 243–9.

M. Oclatinius Adventus, a former *speculator* and head of the *frumentarii*, was sent to Britain to help prepare for the emperor Septimius Severus' projected invasion of Scotland. Rankov points out the coincidence that this procurator, who had specialist intelligence experience, arrived at the same time and place as the raising of Britain's first known unit of *exploratores*. This makes it seem likely that Adventus was sent to Britain partly with this task in mind. Why was an intelligence specialist chosen?

The raising of units in AD 205–7 would involve recruiting personnel to collect information about local conditions and the strength and state of the peoples in the lowlands of Scotland. The acquisition of such information required more than simple scouting. It necessitated making contact and questioning natives—perhaps in plain clothes under the guise of trade. New *numeri* were recruited from among the natives who lived around Hadrian's wall and who spoke the local dialects. As a trained spy master, Adventus came to the northern border already skilled at the organization of men to collect political and perhaps military intelligence in secret. Rankov poses the question: did this sort of specialist intelligence gathering operations precede all Roman campaigns?

433. Reinke, G., "Nachrichtenwesen," *Pauly-Wissowa, Real-encyclopaedie der classischen Altertumswissenschaft* 16 (1935), col. 1496–1541.

A general overview of communications systems, both civilian and military, in the ancient world. He begins by noting the differences between ancient and modern communications and the terms used for them. He then covers scouting and reconnaissance, signalling and telegraphy, official announcements both oral and in writing, and publication. This is followed by the postal systems of Persia, the Ptolemies and the *cursus publicus* of Rome. He finishes with business and commercial communications. This is an excellent summary, but for a more detailed treatment, see Wolfgang Riepl, *Das Nachrichtenwesen des Altertums* (no. **9**).

Riepl, Wolfgang, *Das Nachrichtenwesen des Altertums*, mit besonderer Rücksicht auf die Römer. See entry **9**.

434. Ritterling, E., "Ein Amtsabzeichen der beneficiarii consularis im Museum zu Wiesbaden," *Bonner Jahrbücher* 125 (1919), pp. 23–25.

In each province there was an out posting of governor's staff officers sent out from the provincial capital. Their position was symbolized by special spear standards, known in the modern literature as *Beneficiarierlanzen*, that were carried by these officers. They are depicted on many inscriptions and tombstones. Such lances are only shown on inscriptions concerned with men attached to the provincial headquarters staffs, and more specifically with the three grades whom we know from epigraphic and literary evidence to have carried out duties away from the capital, especially as intelligence carriers, namely the *frumentarii*, *beneficiarii consularis* and *speculatores*. These spears marked these men out as officials of the governor, operating on his behalf and independently of any other military commander in the province. They would be carried by men doing their duties overtly. Ritterling discusses an example of one such bronze lance decoration in the Museum at Wiesbaden and compares it to other examples from European museums. See also, N.J.E. Austin and N.B. Rankov, *Exploratio* (no. **315**), p. 200–201.

435. Rostovtzeff, M. I., "Die Domänenpolizei in dem römischen Kaiserreiche," *Philologus* 64 (1905), pp. 297–307.

Rostovtzeff does not refute Hirschfeld's work (see O. Hirschfeld), "Die Sicherheitspolizei im römischen Kaiserreich" (no. **377**), but rather seeks to complement it by addressing the organization of the security forces in large Roman agricultural estates in the empire, specifically North Africa. He identifies the forces as *saluarii* and discusses their main function as guards (Wächter). Primarily slaves, *saluarii* were guards and border police of the farms and woodlands (*fundus* or *saltus*), and were also used to oversee field production. He cites the inscriptional and papyrological evidence for information about these forces and includes a hierarchy used in Africa to delineate ranks of the *saluarii* that suggests a faint military connection.

436. Rostovtzeff, M. I., "Ein Speculator auf der Reise," *Römisches Mitteillungen* 26 (1911), pp. 267–283.

Rostovtzeff comments on two gravestones in the museum at Belgrad. One shows a *speculator* traveling in a wagon along the *cursus publicus*, i.e. using the Roman imperial postal system. If the identification is correct, then this is one of the few surviving pictures of a Roman intelligence officer that has survived.

See the same figure in Casson, *Travel*, fig. 13; and A.M. Ramsay, "Speed of the Roman Imperial Post" (no. **429**), p. 61, fig. 58.

437. Rostowzew (*sic.* alternative spelling for Rostovtzeff), M., "Angariae" *Klio* 6 (1906), pp. 249–258.

Early article by Michael Rostovtzeff while he was still in St. Petersburg. It concerns the word *angariae*. The word *angaros* was taken from the Babylonian into Persian and was the name of the messengers of the Royal Persian postal system. A riding post along the route was an *angareion*. The word was adopted into Greek and was used for the courier flame that brought the news of the fall of Troy in Aeschylus' *Agamemnon* (281–315). The same word was then absorbed into Latin and used in the Roman imperial postal system. The obligation to contribute to the maintenance of the imperial post was the *praestatio angariorum*. Communications system throughout the Middle East adapted the word.

438. Rutledge, Steven, *Imperial Inquisitions. Prosecutors and Informants from Tiberius to Domitian*, New York: Routledge, 2001, 416 pp.

"*Delatores* (political informants) and *accusatores* (malicious presecutors) were a major part of life in imperial Rome and part of the emperor's internal security system. Contemporary sources depict them as cruel and heartless mercenaries, who bore the main responsibility for institutionalizing and enforcing the tyranny of the infamous rulers of the early empire, such as Nero, Caligula, and Domitian. Rutledge's study examines the evidence and asks if this is a fair portrait and puts them in their political and social context. See also nos. 327–328, 351, 359, 361, 364, 384, 398, 417, 477.

439. Schallmayer, Egon, et. al., *Der Römischen Weihebezirk von Osterburken* I. Corpus der griechischen und lateinischen Beneficiarier-Inschriften des römischen Reiches, Forschungen und Berichte zur Vor- und Frügeschichte in Baden-Würtemberg, Bd 40, Stuttgart: Landesdenmalamt Baden-Württemberg, Archäologische Denkmalplege: Kommissionsverlag K. Theiss, 1990–1994, 2 vols.

A collection of the inscriptions recording *beneficiarii* of all kinds. See introductory essay by Rankov.

440. Schallmayer, Egon, "Zur Herkunft und Funktion der Beneficiarier," in V.A. Maxfield and M. J. Dobson (edd.) *Roman Frontier Studies* 1989. Proceedings of the XVth International Congress of Roman Frontier Studies, University of Exeter Press, 1991, pp. 400–406.

Schallmayer traces the inscriptional evidence for the presence of *beneficiarii consularis* in three Roman provinces: Britain, Germania, and Dalmatia. Maps chart out the locations. He goes on to discuss the military, political, and social role of these government officials in the life of the empire. As representatives of the central government, they were in a position to collect intelligence and expedite its transmission to provincial governors or Rome. He believes their main function was first and foremost financial and economic in nature, and that their military function really lay in the background. He takes his argument from gravestone depictions with the *beneficiarii* shown in the dress and accoutrements of bookkeepers. Yet their social prestige depended almost exclusively on their military associations. Upon retirement, they were afforded a certain respect, often becoming decurions and patrons of their cities.

441. Schmid, W., "Die Römische Poststation in Noreia," *Jahreshefte des Österreichischen Archäologischen Institutes in Wien*, 27,2 (1932), col. 193–222.

The Roman postal system, known as the *cursus publicus*, covered the empire and allowed the Roman emperor to receive intelligence from his provinces. Post stations existed along the route to give fresh horses and carriages to the dispatch riders. Here Schmid describes the discovery of just such a post station in the Roman province of Noreia, present day Austria. He includes a map of the village where it was found (Einod), and a sketch and detailed description of the station itself. He includes illustrations of the pottery finds used to date the site to the first century AD, and the metal objects found.

442. Schroff, "Tabellarii," *Pauly-Wissowa, Real-encyclopaedie der classischen Altertumswissenschaft* Vol. III, A. (1932), col. 1844–1848.

As the pivotal role of communications became more apparent to the Romans, so was the status of a peculiar class of Roman civil servant called *tabellarii* who became the messengers of Rome. It was realized slowly that responsible errands could not be entrusted to people who were hostile or stupid. A good *tabellarius* needed not only physical stamina, but certain moral and intellectual qualities as well. The slaves or freedmen of races considered intelligent by the Romans—Phoenicians, Greeks, Illyrians, and Gauls—were eventually assigned to this function. The Romans came to recognize that the outcome of crucial political and military ventures often hinged on the intelligent fulfillment of a courier's mission. Their professionalism had evolved to the point that we think they adopted a uniform. This inference is based on a letter from Cicero (*Letters to His Friends,* 15.17.1) that refers to the couriers as *petaseti,* the Latin equivalent of the Greek term *pterophoroi* or feather bearers, which might indicate that the messengers wore feathers in their caps and identified themselves with Hermes, the divine messenger. See also Plutarch, *Otho* 4: swift couriers (*pterophoroi*) were continually coming with accounts. Schroff lists a great deal of the inscriptional and literary evidence for these couriers in the republic and empire.

443. Schuller, Wolfgang, "Grenzen des Spätrömischen Staates: Staatspolizei und Korruption," *Zeitschrift für Papyrologie und Epigraphik* 16 (1975), pp. 1–21.

A detailed discussion of the administrative realities of the late Roman empire, the role of the *agentes in rebus* in state security. Schuller believes their sinister reputation comes from third century activities under Constantius. He acknowledges their role in supervising the state postal system, their supervisory role over the state bureaucracy, and their security duties, but he does not see them as a secret police. Part of their sinister reputation was due to their corruption, and Schuller spends the last section of the article discussion corruption in the late Roman empire. He concludes that the picture of an all-embracing coercive state in late antiquity needs a correction.

444. Seeck, Otto, "Agentes in Rebus," *Pauly-Wissowa, Real-encyclopaedie der classischen Altertumswissenschaft* I (1894), cols. 776–779.

A detailed overview of the establishment of the *agentes in rebus*, their recruitment, their membership, their promotion patterns, their overseeing of the *cursus publicus*, and most importantly their function as spies. All this is accompanied by the line references to classical sources.

445. Seeck, Otto, "Angareia," *Pauly-Wissowa, Real-encyclopaedie der classischen Altertumswissenschaft* I, 2 col. 2185–6.

Brief encyclopedic entry on the *Angarium* (Gr., *Angareion*), the Persian postal service that ran along the Royal Road. It later lent its name to the postal service established on the *cursus publicus* by Augustus.

446. Seeck, Otto, "Angaria," *Pauly-Wissowa, Real-encyclopaedie der classischen Altertumswissenschaft* I, 2 col. 2184–5.

Name for the *cursus clabularius* or the slower postal service for the transport of heavier items run along the *cursus publicus* in the later Roman Empire. Seeck provides references to the relevant law codes that regulated its use.

447. Seeck, Otto, "Cursus Publicus," *Pauly-Wissowa, Real-encyclopaedie der classischen Altertumswissenschaft* IV (1901), Col. 1849.

Encyclopedia entry on the *cursus publicus*, the Roman road system and postal service.

448. Sheldon, Rose Mary, "Clandestine Operations and Covert Action: The Ancient Imperative," *Proceedings of the Military and Naval History Forum*, (3–4 March 1995), Lancaster, Pa., 1995.

The debate over whether covert action and clandestine operations should be a function of the intelligence community or not continues to rage. This article attempts to dispel the myth that such activities are a modern invention. Activities carried out under the reigns of the Roman emperors Augustus and Tiberius show the Roman government relying on covert operations when full-scale military activities were not feasible. Evidence exists for activities such as influencing political factions, propaganda, paramilitary operations, assassinations and seeding.

449. Sheldon, Rose Mary, "The Great Jewish War and Rome," *Proceedings of the Military and Naval History Forum*, 8–9 March 1996, Lancaster, Pa.

Abbreviated version of article in *Small Wars and Insurgencies* above.

450. Sheldon, Rose Mary, "Jesus, The Security Risk: Intelligence and Security in First Century Palestine," *Small Wars and Insurgencies*, Vol. 9, No. 2 (Autumn, 1998), pp. 1–37.

The story of passion week as told through the eyes of Pontius' Pilate's chief of station in Jerusalem. The Roman point of view of security matters surrounding the arrest and execution of Jesus of Nazareth. Not a matter on which definitive answers are possible, but the footnotes cover the sources and the controversies over them.

451. Sheldon, Rose Mary, "L'Occhio di Roma," *Storia e Dossier*, January 1989, n. 25, pp. 46–49.

A brief history of Roman intelligence gathering.

452. Sheldon, Rose Mary, "The Polygraph, Adultery and the Romans, or Fluttering in Antiquity," *Foreign Intelligence Literary Scene* 5, 2. March/April (1986), p. 2.

There is ancient evidence for the use of a type of polygraph in Roman times. Macrobius, a Latin writer c. AD 400, told a tale that was later picked up by the *Gesta Romanorum*, a medieval source dating to the fourteenth century. It tells of a man who suspects his wife of adultery and tests her honesty by getting someone to check her pulse. This is one of the same physiological changes measured by our more technologically advanced fluttering machines. One might argue that modern testing has not produced better results.

453. Sheldon, Rose Mary, "The Roman Secret Service" *Intelligence Quarterly* 1, 2 (July 1985), pp. 7–8.

A brief account of the role of the *frumentarii* and the *agentes in rebus* in Roman intelligence gathering. For a more detailed treatment, see W.G. Sinnigen, "The Roman Secret Service" (no. **463**).

454. Sheldon, Rose Mary, "Slaughter in the Forest," *Small Wars and Insurgencies*, 12, 3 (Autumn, 2001), pp. 1–38.

One of Rome's biggest intelligence failures surely must be allowing three of its best legions to be ambushed and wiped out in the Teutoburg Forest in AD 9.

And it was planned and executed by one of their own German auxiliaries, Arminius. This article helps make clear how the Romans were duped. It includes a discussion of a new archaeological site which may be the location of the battle.

455. Sheldon, Rose Mary, "Taking on Goliath: Low Intensity Conflict in the Great Jewish War," *Small Wars and Insurgencies*, 5/1 (Spring, 1994), pp. 1–28.

The war of liberation fought by the Jews against Rome shows the strengths and weaknesses of guerrilla warfare, terrorism, insurgency and intelligence activities when used by a small country waging war against a much larger occupation force.

Once one separates the various Jewish groups at work and untangles the chronology of events, one discovers that there were two wars being waged simultaneously—a civil war and a revolt against Rome. The civil war prevented the Jews from presenting a united front toward the Romans. Thus, in spite of the superb use of intelligence, surprise operations, ambushes and terrorist tactics, the Jews lost what one might suggest what was, for them, an unwinnable war.

456. Sheldon, Rose Mary, *Tinker, Tailor, Caesar, Spy. Espionage in Ancient Rome* Dissertation, University of Michigan, Ann Arbor, 1987. University Microfilms International No. 8720338.

The first systematic study of Roman intelligence from the founding of the city through the reign of Diocletian. Begins with the founding of the city and Livy's accounts of the early Republic, through the high empire. The chapter on Varus and the slaughter in the Teutoburg Forest has been updated by no. **454**.

The study concludes that there were many different organizations collecting intelligence for the Romans throughout their history. Some were ad hoc creations; others were tasked with other duties which were not intelligence related. When the system failed, the costs were enormous.

457. Sheldon, Rose Mary, "Caesar, Intelligence and Ancient Britain," *International Journal of Intelligence and Counterintelligence*, 15, 1 (Spring, 2002), 77–100.

458. Sheldon, Rose Mary, "Toga and Dagger: Espionage in Ancient Rome," *Quarterly Journal of Military History*, Autumn 2000, pp. 28–33.

A brief history of the intelligence profession in the ancient Roman Republic and Empire. Nicely illustrated.

459. Sinnigen, William G., "Administrative Shifts of Competence Under Theodoric," *Traditio* 21 (1965), pp. 456–467.

The Roman Empire in the West did not come to an end administratively when Romulus Augustulus was deposed in AD 476. The Gothic kingdoms of Odoacer and Theodoric were administered by the same agencies that had managed the empire since the reforms of Diocletian and Constantine. This bureaucratic apparatus helped control the senatorial order by giving them offices that would gratify their traditional ambitions. On the other hand, force of circumstance demanded flexibility, the creation of new offices, and the transfer of competence within the government. The *scholae palatinae*, for example, was disbanded under Theodoric. He kept the *agentes in rebus* but added two new corps of officials who took over many of their duties. The first was the *comitiaci* who were drawn from the Italian population and who functioned in a ministry called the *officium nostrum* by Cassiodorus. The second group were Gothic officials called *saiones.* (s.v. Morosi). Sinnigen investigates the identity of these two new groups and concludes that they were replacing the *agentes in rebus* and interfering in their areas of competence.

Kings like Odoacer and Theodoric were conscious of where their power originated. As non-Romans, they were grafting a new power structure on to an older one. They respected the old Roman aristocracy and gave them the semblance of governmental authority, but many offices were being denatured by the interference of agencies dependent more directly on the new kings. Theodoric did much to encourage this tendency.

The wars of Justinian for the reconquest of Italy destroyed much of the traditional governing structure and its administrative offices along with the senatorial elite.

460. Sinnigen, William G., "Two Branches of the Late Roman Secret Service," *American Journal of Philology* 80 (1959), pp. 238–254.

According to Sinnigen, there were two branches of the late Roman secret service. One was the *agentes in rebus*, a group that has attracted much scholarly attention. Less noticed by scholars has been the espionage activities of the *schola notariorum*, or corps of imperial secretaries. Both corps were involved with the corruption and intrigue of the late Empire. The highly organized and authoritarian state of the fourth century had institutionalized its information services and espionage agencies to an extent unknown during the Principate and used them to spy on other government agencies.

461. Sinnigen, William G., *The Officium of the Urban Prefecture in the Later Roman Empire.* Rome: American Academy in Rome, Papers and Monographs, 17 (1957) 123 pp.

See especially, chapter 10, on "The Urban Officium and the Policing of Rome and Constantinople" where Sinnigen discusses the evidence for policing in 4th-6th century Rome. Previous studies have done little more than project into the Later Roman Empire the well-known institutions of the first, second and third centuries. There seem to be marked changes involving the participation of the urban *officium* in the maintenance of public order; indeed it becomes an integral, permanent part of the police force of the city.

The Praetorian Guard, the *vigiles*, and the Urban Cohorts disappeared during the reign of Constantine. In Rome (and later Constantinople) the fire and night watch were entrusted to the guilds and to the *curatores regionum.* The Urban Officium was responsible for keeping peace in the city when mass violence threatened.

462. Sinnigen, William G., "The Origins of the Frumentarii," *Memoirs of the American Academy in Rome* 27 (1962), pp. 211–224.

Sinnigen traces the origins of the *frumentarii*, a class of military bureaucrats who have been called by some "The Roman Secret Service." Like other *officiales*, they were at the disposal of the provincial governors, but they differed in two important ways: 1) they had a special headquarters in Rome, the *castra peregrinorum*, to which they might be summoned by the central government for periods of service; 2) they were called upon to perform a wide range of missions, some of them intelligence related.

While detached for service at headquarters they came under the direction of its commandant, the *princeps peregrinorum,* who was probably responsible to the praetorian prefecture. (See S. J. de Laet, "Les pouvoirs militaires des préfets dur prétoire" [no. **394**], pp. 509–554.) The earliest literary references to them date to Trajan or Hadrian. Sinnigen believes that their existence predated the beginning of the second century. He argues that had the *frumentarii* functioned under the Julio-Claudians, had they spied on friends of the emperor, been commissioned to assassinate prominent generals in the provinces, then Tacitus would most likely have mentioned them. He does not.

Sinnigen concludes that there are good reasons for relating the centralization of the *frumentarii* in Rome to major changes in both the supply organization and the communications network datable to the reign of Domitian.

463. Sinnigen, W. G., "The Roman Secret Service," *Classical Journal* (1965), pp. 65–72.

The most comprehensive work in English on the *frumentarii*, Roman military bureaucrats often dubbed (by Sinnigen and others) as the Roman Secret Service. Sinnigen believes the Roman Secret Service was developed out of a basic reform instituted by Domitian (see Sinnigen, "Origins" no. **462**) in the G-4 or supply section of the imperial general staff—the praetorium. The reforms involved the use of non-commissioned officers and sometimes centurions. Stated simply, the Roman Secret Service was staffed by supply sergeants whose original function had been the purchase and distribution of grain (*frumentum*), thus their name—*frumentarii.*

Sinnigen traces the typical recruitment and career path. He also has a detailed description of the different types of intelligence-related duties in which they were involved. These duties included acting as intelligence couriers, spying, detective work and political assassinations. Because of their unpopularity and propensity for exploiting the public, the emperor Diocletian disbanded the *frumentarii* and replaced them with a civilian organization staffed by the *agentes in rebus.*

464. Sinnigen, William G., "Three Administrative Changes Ascribed to Constantius II" *American Journal of Philology* 83 (1962), pp. 369–382.

Three reforms previously dated to the years AD 341 or 346 and to the administrative initiative of Constantius II are reconsidered. The reforms include:

1) The seconding from the imperial court of former spies (*ex agentes in rebus)* to serve as chiefs of staff (*principes officii*) in the praetorian and urban prefectures.

2) The appointment of high ranking spies on active duty (*agentes in rebus*) to function as superintendents of the state postal system in the provinces (*praepositi cursus publici*).

3) The creation of a special college of thirty bureaucrats (*Augustales*) in the praetorian prefecture.

The reforms more likely originated in the reign of Constantine the Great.

465. Sinnigen, William G., "Tirones and Supernumerarii," *Classical Philology* 62 (1967), pp. 108–112.

A constitution in the Codex Theodosianus 6.27.4 issued March 382 by Theodosius I lays down the rules to be followed while recruiting potential *agentes*. An aspiring *agens* had his qualifications examined first by the corps itself, a favorable vote of the majority earning him a *probatoria* in the name of the emperor from one of the central ministries, followed by the *sacramentum* (military oath). This first "honor" did not make newcomers full-fledged *agentes*. The edict refers to them as *novi*. These new recruits were entered on a list in which they advanced according to seniority, until they took the final step that made them full-fledged bureaucrats with official status, matriculation on the rolls of the *schola agentium in rebus*. The remainder of the edict guarantees that such matriculated *agentes* would be advanced according to the rules of the corps.

The characteristics of these *novi* in this edict correspond exactly to the *tirones* in the military establishment. In both cases personnel were regarded as recruits in the period between their probation and their matriculation in some ministry or military unit. In both cases they could be called upon to serve during that period even though they were not, respectively, full-fledged officials or soldiers. Evidently, the state found it convenient to classify supernumeraries as recruits since such a status provided a pool of manpower from which service could be extracted on terms advantageous to the government. In this manner the late imperial government tried to save money in the face of a greatly expanded and hence more expensive governmental apparatus.

466. Sinnigen, William G., "Two Branches of the Late Roman Secret Service," *American Journal of Philology* 80 (1959), pp. 238–254.

According to Sinnigen, there were two branches of the late Roman secret service. One was the *agentes in rebus*, a group that has attracted much scholarly attention. Less noticed by scholars has been the espionage activities of the *schola notariorum*, or corps of imperial secretaries. Both corps were involved with the corruption and intrigue of the late Empire. The highly organized and authoritarian state of the fourth century had institutionalized its information services and espionage agencies to an extent unknown during the Principate and used them to spy on other government agencies.

467. Speidel, Michael P., "Exploratores. Mobile Elite Units of Roman Germany," *Epigraphische Studien* 13 (1983), pp. 63–78.

The reconnaissance details known as *exploratores* existed in every Roman army. At times large numbers of them were brought together to serve an entire provincial or field army and in those cases they became independent, mobile units. Evidence for highly mobile *exploratores* units have only been found so far in Rome's German armies. The large, mobile elite units differed from the lower-ranking *exploratores* units that garrisoned some of the forts along the Upper German *limes*. The emergence of large mobile *exploratores* units as an elite cavalry strike force is a noteworthy strategic development in the defense of Roman Germany. According to Speidel, they became part of the emerging imperial field army that saved the empire during the great crisis of the third century AD.

468. Starr, Chester G. *Civilization and the Caesars*, Ithaca: Cornell University Press, 1954, 413 pp.

On of the best accounts of the loss of liberty under the early empire. Covers the uses of private informers, secret police and the Roman security apparatus in general.

469. Stein, E., *Die kaiserlichen Beamten und Truppenkörper im römischen Deutschland unter dem Prinzipat*, Vienna: L.W. Seidel & Sohn, 1932, 301 pp.

Good source on the use of *exploratores* in Germany.

470. Suetonius Tranquillus, Gaius (AD 75–160). *Lives of the Twelve Caesars.* Loeb Classical Library edition, J. C. Rolfe translation, 1979, 2 vols.

In Suetonius's Life of *The Deified Julius* 56 he describes the substitution cipher used by Julius Caesar in his private correspondence when he had something confidential to report. The key is to substitute the fourth letter of the alphabet, namely D, for A, and so forth with the others. Compare this to the description in Aulus Gellius 17.9. In speaking of their technical importance, Mendelsohn says: "Of the cipher of Caesar mentioned by Aulus Gellius 17.9 and said to have received treatment by Probus, nothing is known. If Aulus Gellius is right, the cipher must have been something more than a simple one mentioned by Suetonius and Dio Cassius." See also Lange et Soudart, *Traité de cryptographie* (no. **42**), pp. 18, 19; Meister, *Die Anfänge der modernen diplomatischen Geheimschirft*, (no. **583**), p. 3.

471. Syme, Sir Ronald, "Military Geography at Rome," *Classical Antiquity* Vol. 7, No. 2 (October, 1988) 227–251.

The author concludes that "whereas the Greeks created a science of geography, with the Romans the description of lands and peoples became a branch of literature." These works of literature incorporate traditional lore or fables about remote nations along and beyond the northern fringe of the known world. Digressions about far countries and exotic peoples supplied variety and adornment. Roman maps had nothing to do with cartography. They were itineraries: registering the stages and distances along known roads. Maps of countries were mainly for show, i.e. decorative purposes.

The question of how good the Romans were at geography relates to the larger issue of how one builds an empire, and can one do it without proper geographical intelligence? Syme sees the Romans as an imperial people with little use for geography. (Cf. Nicolet, no. **413**) Others would question whether this is even possible. Can you conquer what you cannot locate? What losses might have been attributed to bad geographical intelligence? (Sheldon, no. **454**, on the Teutoburgerwald).

Difficult terrain was sometimes the reason for defeat as was native treachery. It was not ignorance of geography that caused this, however, but overconfidence, obstinacy, errors of judgment (ex. Flaminius at Lake Trasimene, who knows the terrain but blunders strategically). Generals often lacked experience in high commands.

One often finds a great difference between the written sources (literature) and the information really available to generals and governments. Their policies were sometimes cautious (and rightfully so) where poets would have them march into glory.

472. Teitler, Hans C., *Notarii und exceptores.* An inquiry into the Role and Significance of Shorthand Writers in the Imperial and Ecclesiastical Bureaucracy of the Roman Empire (from the Early Principate to c. 450 AD) Amsterdam: J.C. Gieben, 1985, 380 pp. (Dutch Monographs on Ancient History and Archaeology 1).

A lightly revised version of his doctoral thesis, and translated from the Dutch. This is a study of the role of the *notarii* and *exceptores* in the imperial and ecclesiastical bureaucracies of the late empire. On the surface they are imperial stenographers and secretaries. Being privy to imperial correspondence, however, put them in the position to handle a great deal of intelligence. Sinnigen (no. **466**) referred to them as one of the two branches of the late imperial secret service. Compare Austin & Rankov, *Exploratio* 19, 49, 54–55, 58, 151, 221–6.

Reviewed in *Antiquité Classique* 60 (1991), pp. 594–595 Sansterre.

473. *Thesaurus Linguae Latinae*, Vol. V,2 Fasc XIII Leipzig: Teubner, 1953.
See entries for *explorator*, col. 1742–1744; *frumentarius* col. 1407–8

474. Vaglieri, D., "Frumentarii," *Dizionario Epigrafico di Antichità Romane* 3 (1922), pp. 221–224.

A detailed article on the *frumentarii* of the legions of Rome, among the most important carriers of intelligence in the empire. Particularly useful is the long list of inscriptions mentioning these soldiers, and identifying them by region and legion.

475. Vegetius Renatus, Flavius, *Military Institutions of Vegetius.* trans. John Clarke, edited by T.R. Phillips, Harrisburg, Pa., 1944. Newer edition, Vegetius: Epitome of Military Science, translated with notes and introduction by N.P. Milner, Liverpool: Liverpool University Press, 1993.

A military handbook from late antiquity that became one of the most popular Latin technical works read in the Middle Ages and the Renaissance. Vegetius was the most widely read military theorist before Clausewitz. See especially Book 3, chapter 5 on military signalling, 3.6 on moving an army in the vicinity of an enemy, and 3.9 on staging raids and ambushes. Book 4.26 tells of precautions to be taken to prevent the enemy from taking a position by stratagem, 4.27 on surprise attacks made by the besieged, 4.28 on how to avoid surprise attacks from the besieged and 4.45 on how ambushes are set in naval warfare.

See a review of the Milner translation by Everett Wheeler in *Journal of Military History* 58,1 (January, 1994), pp. 136–138.

476. Youtie, H.C. and J.G., Winter, *Papyri and Ostraca from Karanis* (Michigan Papyri, 8), Ann Arbor, 1951, pp. 472, 16 (p. 41).

A document dated to the period AD 100–125 shows a *frumentarius* probably serving in the *officium* of the *praefectus Aegypti* who worked closely with a *speculator.*

477. Zijlstra, J.S.A., *De delatores te Rome tot aan Tiberius' regering*, Alberts' Drukkerijen Sittard, 1967.

Tacitus in his *Annals* is concerned with how a republic developed into a monarchy, and, depending on the behavior of the ruler, could also develop into a tyranny. Among the objectionable practices that had arisen under the reigns of Augustus and Tiberius was the use of private informers or *delatores*. An example is Caepio Crispinus who successfully raises the suspicions of Tiberius and thus receives a fixed income by reporting all kinds of violations of the laws, especially the *Lex Julia de Maiestate* (see Bauman, R.A., *The Crimen Maiestas* [no. **319**]. The law could be interpreted in many different ways and thus provided many opportunities for profitable accusations. They become an unofficial intelligence gathering arm of the emperor. For Tacitus, they are the willing tools in the hands of a monarch who has "no respect for anything or anybody." They become one of the more contemptuous features of the tyrannical government in Rome.

Did they exist before Tiberius? Zijlstra believes that although the word "*delator*" only appears for the first time in the writings of Livy (59 BC–AD 17) the word was already used in vulgar Latin long before (he cites examples from Cicero and Plautus). It developed from a legal practice used especially by the *tresviri capitales* who had the principal duty to prevent and to police criminal activity in the rapidly growing city of Rome. It may have then developed that any citizen or third person could appear before them with an accusation. The *tresviri* did not have professional investigators to draw on and were therefore not prepared to collect proof of guilt or innocence before a trial. The accusor himself was responsible for this and thus the function of a formal "accusator" arose. It is from this practice that Zijlstra believes the *delatores* arose.

Signalling

478. Bell, T.W., "A Roman Signal Station at Whitby," *Archaeological Journal* 155 (1998), pp. 303–322.

Bell argues for the possible existence of a Roman signal station at Whitby, even though there is no absolute archaeological evidence for one. The toponym suggests there was one, plus the author discusses the results of a GIS application which addresses the feasibility of such a station's intervisibility from its neighboring station to the south. A station would close the gap that exists between Goldsborough and Ravenscar (see no. **480**). Good bibliography on signalling and Roman occupation in general along the Yorkshire coast.

479. Clark, Vincent A. and Parker, S. Thomas, "The Late Roman Observation and Signaling System," in Chapter 5 of *The Roman Frontier in Central Jordan* (Oxford: BAR, 1987), p. 165–181.

Relay systems of signalling posts in the Near East served as an early warning system that could send intelligence of enemy movements to major troop concentrations farther west. Many individual posts for observation and communication have been identified. Yet it is difficult, given the imperfect state of preservation along imperial frontiers, to identify and analyze regional systems. The excellent preservation of the sites of the Roman frontier east of the Dead Sea offered the chance for just such a study. The authors discovered major gaps in this alleged communications network and there is no evidence all of them were occupied at the same time. Further survey and excavation are needed before anything conclusive can be stated with confidence.

480. Collingwood, R. G., "The Roman Signal Station," in A. Rowntree (ed.) *The History of Scarborough*, London: J. M. Dent & Sons, 1931, pp. 40–50.

There are remains of five signal stations on the Yorkshire coast: Huntcliff, Goldsborough, Ravenscar, Scarborough and Filey. The southern half of the system was lost through erosion since antiquity. Collingwood dates the station at Scarborough to the time of Theodosius because of similarities of these forts to another ascribed to the same emperor in Cumberland and another on the southern shore of the Bristol Channel. The pottery evidence dates them to the second half of the fourth century AD. The coin evidence (of which 300 have been found in the four excavated sites) also suggest Theodosius.

The system relied on the rapid transmission of signals and consequent operations carried out with concentrated and mobile forces, both naval and military. Towers were provided for fire and smoke signals. Uniformity of design suggests they were built at the same time. The motive for this new system is not difficult to discern. The dispersion of troops in small garrisons that was the key to the frontier strategy of the early empire, was successful only as long as the work to be done was mainly police work, and no very powerful concentration of hostile troops were to be feared. But a sudden attack by a large enemy force would shatter the network of forts and destroy the Roman army details. To guard against dangers of this kind, it was necessary to provide a large and mobile striking force. In order to make such a force effective, a system had to be created by which enemy concentrations could be detected as rapidly as possible. That such a threat actually did arrive can be seen in the archaeological evidence. The forts show similar signs of a final overtaking—bodies throw down wells, skeletons with sword wounds in the skull.

481. Donaldson, G.H., "Roman Military Signalling on the North British Frontiers," *Archaeologia Aeliana* 13 (1985), pp. 19–24.

For many years it was accepted uncritically that the Romans had a complex signalling network along and behind the frontiers of northern Britain. Sheppard Frere, *Britannia* (2nd ed., London, 1974), p. 170 postulates a long distance signalling by beacon from Croy Hill, and Sir Ian Richmond, *History of Northumberland* (Newcastle, 1940), vol. 15, pp. 101–102 postulated a system of seven bright lights transmitting complicated codes from Four Laws. Donaldson brings some much-needed scepticism. He points out that to operate visual communications systems on a scale visualized by modern historians, the Romans would have had to be able to deploy large numbers of highly trained personnel. The critical question is not whether such positions could be set up and manned, but whether visual networks were superior in terms of reliability, speed and accuracy to a system of fast-riding couriers.

For other criticisms of the traditional view, see Malcolm Todd, *Roman Britain 55 B.C.–A.D. 400* (Glasgow, 1981), 142 who has commented on the difficulties of lateral signalling along Hadrian's Wall. R.A.H. Farrar, "Roman Signal Stations over Stainmore and Beyond," *Roman Frontier Studies* 1979 (Oxford, 1980), pp. 211–231 raised the problem of the intervisibility and the spacing of optical relay posts in an article on Stainmore pass.

482. Donaldson, G.H., "Signalling, Communications and the Roman Imperial Army," *Britannia* 19 (1988), pp. 349–56.

Donaldson feels that the subject of Roman military signalling installations has generated an excess of enthusiastic, but misguided speculation. In order to prove a building was used in signalling, archaeologists must establish requirement, feasibility and capability. He distinguishes between strategic, long distance command communications involving the transmission of high-grade, complicated and enciphered messages, and tactical communications, i.e. short-range, combat/contact signalling of simple information. The fact that there is no Latin word for signaler suggests that signalling was not a Roman military specialization. A much-needed corrective to the overly optimistic systems envisioned by G. Webster, *The Roman Imperial Army*, (London, 1969), 135–136, M. Grant, *The Army of the Caesars* (London, 1974), 299 and P. Salway, *Roman Britain* (Oxford, 1981), 570–571.

483. Farrar, R.A.H., "Roman Signal Stations over Stainmore and Beyond," *Roman Frontier Studies* 1979 (Oxford, 1980), pp. 211–231.

Farrar revisits the Roman signalling stations in the Stainmore pass originally examined by Sir Ian Richmond (no. **492**). Farrar does not believe any of the stations in the Stainmore Pass can be dated even broadly within the Roman period. They are too far apart and not particularly visible to each other. Only Roper Castle is in a skyline position from both directions. Therefore Richmond's theory collapses. Farrar recommends more practical experimentation to test the system than has been attempted so far.

484. Haverfield, F., "Notes on the Roman Coast Defences of Britain, Especially in Yorkshire," *Journal of Roman Studies* 2 (1912), pp. 201–214.

The Roman government made a change in the system of British coast defense in the late empire. Diocletian established an officer with the title "Count of the Saxon Shore" and put under him nine forts that stood at close intervals from Wash to Portsmouth. At the same time, all reference to the British fleet disappears. The garrisons of these forts kept in touch by means of signal stations, strong enough to be held against small raiding parties, but meant primarily for scouts whose beacons would flash back to the interior and to their fellow-stations along the coast the approach of any large fleet of pirates. Haverfield discusses these forts, the archaeological remains found in them, their dates and fates.

485. Hornsby, W. & Laverick, J.D. "The Roman Signal Station at Goldsborough, near Whitby," *Archaeological Journal* 89 (1932), pp. 203–19.

The Roman signal station at Goldsborough near Whitby has escaped the erosion damage that destroyed other signal stations in this late Roman system because it is farther inland than the sites at Huntcliff, Scarborough and Filey. This is one of the surviving links in a chain of signal stations that guarded the Yorkshire coast and are thought to date to the time of Theodosius. Coin evidence suggests occupation until the last 30 years of the 4th century AD. The article includes a sketch of the berm and ditch, the fort and its tower. A gruesome clue to the end of occupation there is the skeleton of a man with the skeleton of a large dog at his throat—the dog being the defender against the intruders.

See also *Journal of Roman Studies* Vol. 2, 209ff.

486. Hornsby, W. and Stanton, R., "The Roman Fort at Huntcliff, Near Saltburn," *Journal of Roman Studies* 2 (1912), pp. 215–232.

The remain of a Roman signalling station found at Huntcliff was excavated before those at Goldsborough, Scarborough and Filey. They make a chain of signal stations on the Yorkshire coast. The ramparts, ditch and bastion are similar to the others in this series. The station was burnt in late antiquity, and all the human remains were found down in the well including men, women and children. The coins date no earlier than Constantius II and no later than Arcadius leading the authors to conclude the station was built a little after the middle of the fourth century AD and destroyed before or just possibly a little after 400. The pottery evidence is both numerous and datable and illustrates one of the lesser known periods of Romano-British pottery.

487. Hull, M. R., "The Pottery from the Roman Signal-Stations on the Yorkshire Coast," *Archaeological Journal* 89 (1932), pp. 220–53. With an appendix: H.H.E. Craster, "The Coin Evidence from the Signal Stations," pp. 251–53.

The dating of the Yorkshire signal stations and the pottery from them is dependent upon the evidence of the coins. Scarborough has produced a more plentiful supply of coins than any other Roman signal station on the Yorkshire coast. Theodosius created the Yorkshire signal stations to close the gap in the defenses of Britain between Hadrian's Wall and the Isle of Wight.

488. Johnson, Stephen, *The Roman Forts of the Saxon Shore*, New York: St. Martin's Press, 1976, 172 pp.

The final link in the defensive chain of forts on the Saxon shore was the signal stations. The Saxon Shore forts had three tactical purposes: 1) they were strongholds and naval bases for sailors of individual flotillas whose duty was to control pirate raids; 2) they were garrisoned and defended bases where a body of mobile troops could be ready to combat pirate landings; and 3) they were an active discouragement to pirates from sailing up the major river estuaries and into the inland areas of both Gaul and Britain. When linked by signal stations, they could control shipping. Johnson describes how the tactics of this scheme worked.

489. Leiner, Wolfgang, *Die Signaltechnik der Antike*, Stuttgart: W. Leiner, 1982. 147 pp.

A self-published summary of the signalling techniques of antiquity. Leiner starts with the Greeks and discusses the systems described by Aeneas Tacticus, Polybius and Julius Africanus; he then goes on to the Carthaginians. There is a short section on Mesopotamia, and then he ends with the Romans. The bibliography includes only German works, none of them recent.

490. Ottoway, P., "Filey Roman Signal Station." *Transactions of the Scarborough Archaeological Historical Society* 30 (1993) pp. 8–10.

Excavations by the York Archaeological Trust and friends of Scarborough Archaeological and Historical Society took place at Filey between 21 September and 1 November 1993. They examined the site of the late Roman signal station that is threatened by erosion of the cliff sides. The Filey station is the southernmost of a group of five located on high headlands on the Yorkshire coast. The stations are thought to date to the last decades of the fourth century and to have been part of an attempt to strength the defenses of Britain against sea-borne raiders.

The stations all have a standard plan consisting of a tower in the center and a walled courtyard that was surrounded by a ditch.

The site had been partially excavated twice before. No certain trace of human activity pre-dating the signal station was found in 1993. The latest excavation confirmed the plan produced by the second excavator F.G. Simpson. Pottery found confirmed the date to the last decades of the fourth century.

491. Ottoway, P., "Filey Roman Signal Station," *Transactions of the Scarborough Archaeological Historical Society* 31 (1995), pp. 8–10.

A second season of excavation took place in 1994 at the late Roman signal station at Filey in Yorkshire. The Romans chose to locate this signal station on the highest point of the headland overlooking Filey Bay to the south. Large deposits of animal bones provided some information on the diet of the inhabitants. The most exciting find was a substantial earthwork on the east side of the site that is likely to be post-Roman. It pre-dates the final demolition of the Roman courtyard wall which probably took place during the medieval period. The abandoned signal station may have been incorporated into an earthwork fortification at some stage in the Anglo-Saxon period, perhaps at the time of the Viking raids of the late 8th or early 9th century.

See also P. Ottoway, *Romans on the Yorkshire Coast,* York: York Archaeological Trust, 1995.

492. Richmond, I. A., "A Roman Arterial Signalling System in the Stainmore Pass" in W.F. Grimes (ed) *Aspects of Archaeology in Britain and Beyond. Essays Presented to O.G.S. Crawford.* London: H. W. Edwards, 1951, pp. 293–302.

A survey of the Roman signaling system in the Stainmore Pass, between Yorkshire and Westmorland. This area has always been one of the major traffic routes of Northern Britain. In Roman times it was the main line of penetration into Cumberland for the great base fortress and legionary headquarters at York. Later, it became the main road to the western end of Hadrian's wall. Signalling posts identified in the Stainmore Pass cannot have stood alone. They are comprehensible only as part of a major installation. Through surveys, enough installments have been found to suggest that the trunk road between Hadrian's Wall and York was supplied with a military telegraph intended to afford rapid, two-way communication between base and frontier. This telegraphic system represented a heavy commitment in manpower and specialist staff. This system, along with three outpost forts beyond the wall and elaborate coastal defenses show clearly that this western flank was the most vulnerable and considered likely to be the principal theater of action by contemporary strategists.

493. Rivet, A.L.F., "Gask Signal-Stations," *Archaeological Journal* 121 (1965), pp. 196–198.

The Gask Signal Stations, Perthshire are a chain of small posts strung along the road between Parkneuk and Dupplin. We currently know of ten stations, but Rivet believes there are certainly more to be found, especially at the eastern end of the series where the exact path of the road is lost.

Each station consists of a circular platform from 35 to 50 feet in diameter surrounded by a ditch and a wall with an outer bank. The plan is a well-known

Roman design that had a two-story tower. Both floors were enclosed, and the upper floor, reached by a ladder, had a balcony equipped for signalling. The type can be seen clearly on Trajan's Column. The excavation of five of these towers in 1900 provided no direct evidence of date, but the small size of the towers and the use of timber rather than stone suggests the Flavian rather than the Antonine period.

The signal stations are not the only Roman works along the ridge. Two camps have been located by aerial photography to the west and south of Parkneuk.

Rivet includes a short bibliography.

494. Sockett, E.W., "A Note on Major Donaldson's Article on Military Signalling," *Archaeologia Aeliana* 14 (1986), pp. 187ff.

A panel from Trajan's column shows what look like two straw ricks. Some have identified these as hay bales ignited to send signals (P. Southern no. **495**). Sockett believes these were outdoor granaries used to store produce above ground as it is done on modern Italian farms.

495. Southern, P., "Signals Versus Illumination on Roman Frontiers," *Britannia* 21 (1990), pp. 233–242.

Recent work by Donaldson (*Britannia* 19) (1988) has suggested that long-distance communication by fires or torches would not have been feasible during the Roman empire. There is no evidence as yet for military bases acting in conjunction with the watchtowers. This leaves the question of what these towers were used for, what was the purpose of the platforms piled with hay bales (presumably ignited) or the torches protruding from the towers depicted on Trajan's column. Southern attempts to answer these questions.

1) On some Roman frontiers warning fires may have been used to alert an area to low-intensity threat. Signals from one of the towers could result in the assembly of its own local militia at specific muster points. The use of bonfires as an early warning system was not capable of great sophistication. They served to alert troops and bring them out to an agreed muster point. Some indication might be made (by prearranged signal) of the method of approach (One if by land …) or the strength of the enemy force.

2) Warning fires could be used to control the movement of unauthorized persons abroad at night. They simply lit up the area around the fort making it easier to see night attackers. Concerning the bales on Trajan's column, fires may have been lit along the Danube to guide shipping.

3) Signal systems could be set up between groups of watchtowers. Regular spacing and neat straight lines do not play a part in this system because the object was not long-distance linear communication by a chain of successive relays between two points. Sight lines need only be straight between adjacent posts. If they were close enough, communication could have been effected by audible signals (trumpets). The systems in the cases that we know in Britain were nuclear rather than linear.

496. Wilson, P.R., "Aspects of the Yorkshire Signal Stations," in V.A. Maxfield & M.J. Dobson (eds.) *Roman Frontier Studies 1989*. Proceedings of the XVth International Congress of Roman Frontier Studies, Exeter: Exeter University Press, 1991, pp. 142–147.

Wilson discusses the signalling stations at Huntcliff, Goldsborough, Ravenscar, Scarborough and Filey along the Yorkshire Coast. He reviews the plans of the signalling stations and the earlier archaeological evidence from the 1930s. He finds many problems with the traditional interpretation of the sites as a signalling system along the coast or one used to constant the fleet at sea. First, there are many gaps in the system. Secondly, we have no evidence of a fleet operating off the north-east coast of England in the late Roman period. The received tradition is of sites signalling back to some form of late Roman "rapid-deployment force" based at Malton. For this to work, the intelligence would have to be transmitted to cavalry that could be dispatched to aid the threatened area. But the response time would be relatively slow and any raiders could easily get away. If the raiding party penetrated inland, the system would need to have the ability to follow and report on them if they were to be intercepted.

If the sites did form a signalling system, the purpose may have been to alert troops in the more populous regions of the Vale of Pickering and perhaps the Tees Valley to warn them of the approach of raiders and give them time to deploy troops to protect the area. Since all the sites lie in an area where Roman remains have been found, there were probably civilian settlements here and the fortresses might have been *burgi*—refuges where groups of the population could go when attacked by sea-borne raiders. Their prominent locations could provide a vantage point from which a signalling function would have warned the local population of the approach of unwelcome visitors.

He concludes that these "signal stations" were therefore small forts, designed to be defended, at least in part, by artillery, and manned by regular troops, and that they were probably introduced as a response to a particular problem, that of coastal raiding against relatively isolated communities.

497. Wooliscroft, David, "Das Signalsystem an der Hadriansmauer und seine Auswirkungen auf dessen Aufbau," *Roman Frontier Studies*, 1989, XV International Congress, Exeter, 1991, pp. 148–152.

Wooliscroft seeks to explain several irregularities in the construction of Hadrian's Wall and their relevance to its signalling system. The Roman mile towers are not exactly one mile apart and are often not visible to each other. Additionally, the mile-towers would have lacked qualified signalmen and the miserable weather conditions would have made optical signals more often than not impossible. What probably happened instead was that in case of a threat along the wall, a messenger was dispatched. Concurrently, a simple signal fire would alert the next tower of the nature and location of a threat so that the messenger would arrive at an already alerted outpost or meet the troops en route. Wooliscroft attributes the variation in distances and often strange and tactically inferior lie of the wall to a southern-oriented signalling system oriented on Stanegate. Outposts without direct contact to this outpost would receive information relayed through the others.

The Byzantine Empire

Although long neglected as a field of inquiry, the Byzantine military has been, in recent years, the target of some excellent researchers. Not all of them touch on the intelligence aspect of either the Byzantine military or their political operatives. A work like Mark C. Bartusis, *The Late Byzantine Army: Arms and Society 1204–1453* (Philadelphia: University of Pennsylvania Press, 1992) limits its reference to spies to footnote 36 on page 250. Several excellent works have been turned out by J.F. Haldon, including "Some Aspects of Byzantine Military Technology from the Sixth to the Tenth Centuries," *Byzantine and Modern Greek Studies* 1 (1975), pp. 11–47, and *Recruitment and Conscription in the Byzantine Army* (Vienna, 1979), but they do not touch upon the intelligence aspect of the military. Other excellent military studies are J.D. Howard-Johnston, *Studies in the Organization of the Byzantine Army in the Tenth and Eleventh Centuries* (D.Phil. dissertation, Oxford University, 1971); Jean Maspero, *Organisation militaire de l'Égypte byzantine*, (Paris: H. Campaion, 1912); H. Glyzkatzi-Ahrweiler, "Recherches sur l'administration de l'empire byzantin aux IX-XIe siècles," *Bulletin de Correspondence Héllenique* 84 (1960), pp. 1–109; Walter E. Kaegi, *Byzantine Military Unrest 471-843. An Interpretation* (Amsterdam: Hakkert, 1981); Giorgio Ravegnani, *Soldati di Bisanzio in Età Giustinianea* (Rome: Jouvence, 1988); and two works by T.S. Brown, *Social Structure and the Hierarchy of Offical-dom in Byzantine Italy, 554-800 A.D.* (Ph.D. thesis, University of Nottingham, 1976), and *Gentlemen and Officers. Imperial Administration and Aristocratic Power in Byzantine Italy A.D. 554-800* (Rome, 1984).

The existence of a Byzantine internal security service is certain (see Miller, p. 468, no. **528** below) and the involvement of the Logothete of the Drome is also certain. The old Roman secret service, the *agentes in rebus*, exercised its duties in association with the imperial post and fell under the command of the Master of Offices. What happened to them is not known. (See under "Roman Empire," A.E.R. Boak, *Master of Offices*, no. **326**, p. 74.) The need for such a body of confidential agents did not die with the Roman empire in the West. The Eastern Empire continued the pattern of the Western empire by attaching such functions to the Imperial Post. In Byzantium, the necessity for maintaining an internal intelligence service actually grew in proportion to the waxing powers of the provincial aristocracy in the 9th and 10th centuries. Whatever information came to the Logothete from abroad or through channels of the Post was probably made available to whichever of the Emperor's intimates had the responsibility for the "operational" aspects of internal security and counterespionage. Miller suggests it was to the emperor's advantage and interest not to establish his secret service as the province of one official, but to divide responsibility between different confidants.

General

498. Antonucci, Michael, "Barbarians Sought Out. Byzantium's systematic intelligence bureau lasted for 800 years." *Military History*, October 1992, pp. 12ff.

A popular article about the Byzantine Bureau of Barbarians. Unfortunately, the spy stories related in the article do not always involve members of this bureau which makes the thesis that this was an effective, centralized intelligence service that lasted 800 years hard to establish. With no notes or suggestions for further reading, the reader is left at the mercy of the author's conclusions.

499. Aschoff, Volker, *Über den byzantinischen Feuertelegraphen und Leon den Mathematiker*, Münschen: R. Oldenbourg, Düsseldorf: VDI-Verlag, 1980, 41 pp.

During the reign of Theophilus (AD 829–842), Leo the Mathematician was supposed to have invented a telegraphic system based on fire signals. There have been many interpretations of how this system actually worked; Aschoff's is one of the most detailed. He lists the ancient sources and discusses them each in detail. Aschoff also provides maps and topographical charts of the areas where this system was to have operated, and graphs plotting the strength of the light used and the distance it could cover. See also Dvornik (no. **3**) pp. 142–3.

For the primary sources on Byzantine signalling systems, see: Theophanes Continuatus (ed. I. Bekker, *Corpus Scriptorum Historiae Byzantinae*, Bonn, 1838, pp. 197–8=*PG*, 109, col. 211 C-D); Constantine Porphyrogenitus, *De ceremoniis* (ed. J.J. Reiske, *Corpus Scriptorum Historiae Byzantinae*, Bonn, 1829, I, pp. 492–3 = *PG* 112, col. 932C-933B); John Scylitzes, *Synopsis Historiarum*, ed. J. Thurn (Berlin, New York, 1973), pp. 107–8; George Cedrenus (ed. I. Bekker, *Corpus Scriptorum Historiae Byzantinae*, Bonn, 1839, II, pp. 174–5 = *PG* 121, col 1060 A-C); Zonaras, ed. L. Dindorf (Teubner, Leipzig) IV 1871, p. 16 (=M. Pinder, *Corpus Scriptorum Historiae Byzantinae*, Bonn) III (1897) pp. 404–406 = *PG* 135, 28B-29A; Pseudo-Symeon, *Symeon Magister et Logotheta* (ed. I. Bekker, *Corpus Scriptorum Historiae Byzantinae*, Bonn 1838, pp. 681–2 = *PG* 109, col. 743 B-D).

500. Audollent, Aug., "Les Veredarii émissaires impériaux sous le Bas Empire," *Mélanges d'archéologie et d'histoire* 9 (1889), pp. 249–278.

Audollent describes the duties of the *veredarii*—imperial couriers of the late empire. He compares them, in turn, to the *speculatores*, the *agentes in rebus* and notes that they had duties as both couriers and certain police functions.

501. Aussaresses, F., *L'Armée byzantine à la fin du VIe siècle d'après le Strategicon de l'empereur Maurice* (Bibliothèque des Universités du Midi 14), Bordeaux: Feret & Fils, 1909, 115 pp.

A study of the Byzantine army from the 6th century AD based on the Strategicon of Maurice.

502. Bury, John Bagnall, *The Imperial Administrative System in the Ninth Century*, New York: B. Franklin, 1958, 179 pp.

Discusses the Byzantine Postal System and its inspectors.

503. Canard, M., "Deux épisodes des relations diplomatiques arabo-byzantines au Xe siècle," *Bulletin d'Études orientales de l'Institut Français de Damas*, 13 (1949–50), p. 55.

Discusses the flight of Samonas and dates it to 907.

504. Cecaumenos, *Strategicon*, ed. H.G. Beck, Graz, 1956.

The last in a series of Byzantine manuals on strategy. It is a curious compilation of advice addresses to a Byzantine general (*strategus*). He gives interesting narratives on the failures of Byzantine armies in cases where their generals ignored intelligence. He also deals with rebellions and usurpations and how to prevent them.

505. *Codex Theodosianus, The Theodosian Code and Novels*, and the Sirmondian constitutions; a translation with commentary, glossary, and bibliography by Clyde Pharr, in collaboration with Theresa Sherrer Davidson and Mary Brown Pharr. With an introduction by C. Dickerman Williams. Princeton: Princeton University Press, 1952, 643 pp.

Laws applying to the *cursus publicus*, the Roman postal system use for carrying political and military intelligence: "de cursu publico" VII. 5-6-; VIII 1, 5, 7, 16, 16, 26, 28, 30, 47, 48, 364.

506. Constantine Porphyrogenitus, *De Administrando Imperio*. Greek text ed. Gy. Moravcsik, English translation by R.J.H. Jenkins. New Revised edition (CFHB 1) (Dumbarton Oaks Texts I). Washington, 1967; II Commentary, ed. R.J.H. Jenkins, London, 1962.

Chapter 42 describes the re-opening of the *cursus publicus* from Constantinople to Thessalonika and Belgrad after the defeat of the Bulgar Tsar Symeon in 927.

An excellent source that shows the importance the Byzantines attached to the collection of intelligence on foreign peoples.

507. *Corpus Iuris Civilis*, (*Codex Justinianus*) edd. Theodor Mommsen—P. Kruger, R. Schoell, Berlin : W. Kroll, 1892–1895, 3 vols. (Reprint 1945–1963, and Weidemann 1967–68.)

See XXII (XXIII) *De curiosis* on the laws relating to the inspectors of the imperial post and the *agentes in rebus*.

508. Dain, A and Foucault, J.A., "Les stratégistes byzantins, *Trauvaux et mémoires* 2 (1967), pp. 317–92.

Treastise on Byzantine strategic writers. See nos. **504**, **509**, **524**, **526**.

509. Dennis, George T. , translator, *Three Byzantine Military Treatises*, Corpus Fontium Historiae Byzantinae 25: Washington, D.C.: Dumbarton Oaks, 1985, 380 pp.

These three treatises reflect the practical concerns of soldiers entrusted with the tasks of going on campaign and defending the frontiers. Gathering intelligence played a large part of this.

The first treatise is *An Anonymous Byzantine Military Treatise on Strategy* that seems to have been composed by a retired army engineer about the middle of the sixth century, a period of success for the Byzantines on the battlefield. It is more systematically organized and more theoretical than the other two. The author is familiar with the writings of the military historians of classical antiquity. He has also obviously been in combat himself.

The second treatise was composed toward the end of the tenth century, also a period of success and prosperity. This second collection contains little in the way of theory; it deals with skirmishing, and has details about border warfare in the mountains of eastern Anatolia. It was obviously written by a man with much experience in this type of fighting.

The third treatise was also composed toward the end of the tenth century and is titled *Campaign Organization and Tactics*. It concentrates on the progress of an army with the emperor himself in command and its setting up camp on hostile territory, namely, Bulgaria. The author provides details, numbers, and precise measurements suggesting that the author had participated in such expeditions.

Index is in Greek. See especially entries under *kataskopos*. For references to spies, scouts see 153, 293, 303.

510. Diesner, H. J., "Zum vandalischen Post- und Verkehrswesen," *Philologus* 112 (1968), pp. 282–287.

Diesner discusses Vandal postal and communications service, pointing out the resemblances to the Byzantine *veredarii*, the late Roman *cursus publicus*, and the Ostrogoth *saiones* (see Sinnigen, *Traditio* 21 [1965] no. **459**).

511. *Digenes Akritas,* Edited with introduction and English translation by John Mavrogordato, Oxford: Clarendon press, 1956, 273 pp.

Other translations available in French, Russian and Armenian.

The surveillance of the border lands in Asia Minor was entrusted to a special guard corps called *akritai* chosen from among the finest soldiers. They were the successors to the *limitanei* of the Roman Empire. Their duty was to be on alert for trouble and to prevent the penetration of enemy spies and secret agents into Byzantine territory They were extremely mobile and posted at fixed places along the frontier. The men responsible for signalling intelligence were changed every two weeks. Information obtained by them was quickly transmitted by messenger along the imperial post to the capital.

Their hazardous and adventurous life is portrayed in this epic poem that inspired young men in Byzantium and also obtained enthusiastic reception in old Russian literature. The hero of the story actually existed. His name was Basil

Pantherios from the aristocratic house of Ducas and he was in command (a *klisurarch*) of the passes of the Taurus Mountains.

Akritai were posted not only on the Arab frontier but also along the Bulgarian frontier and their property was exempt from taxation. This privilege was rescinded in the thirteenth century by the Emperor Michael Palaeologus causing the *akritai* to revolt. They were defeated and liquidated as a military class.

512. Gardthausen, Viktor Emil, "*Zur byzantinischen Kryptographie*," *Byzatinische Zeitschrift* 14 (1905), pp. 616–619.

Gardthausen compares cryptographic systems from three twelfth-century Byzantine manuscripts containing a "doppelstelligen Zahlenkryptographie."

513. Grosse, R., *Römische Militärgeschichte von Gallienus bis zum Beginn der byzantinischen Themenverfassung*, Berlin: Weidemann, 1920, 346 pp.

Chapter A, VI discusses the *protectores domestici*. From AD 354 they were a separate corps based at the imperia l court and charged with protecting the emperor. See also J.F. Haldon no. **515**. Chapter B, III on the *scholae palatini*, and the *agentes in rebus*., IV on the *domestici* and *protectores*.

514. Guilland, R.J., "Les Logothetes. Etudes sur l'histoire administrative de l'Empire byzantin," *Revue des Études Byzantines* 29 (1971), pp. 6–115.

The "Logothete of the Drome" was responsible for supervising the inspectors (*curiosi*) of the postal route who carried military intelligence between the emperor and his provincial governors. In the eight century, this official became director of the Post itself. This work should be used in conjunction with the earlier one by Miller "The Logothete of the Drome in the Middle Byzantine Period," *Byzantion* 36 (1966). See no. **528**.

515. Haldon, John F., *Byzantine Praetorians: An Administrative, Institutional and Social Survey of the Opsikion and Tagmata c. 580–900,* Bonn: R. Habelt, 1984, 669 pp.

See especially the chapters on *the protectores domestici*. From AD 354 they were established as a separate corps under its own *comes* based at the imperial court and charged with protecting the emperor. By 362 there were more than two units of *domestici*, identified by the early part of the fifth century as the *domestici equites* and *pedites*. This corps was replaced by the *excubitores*, a small unit of 300 men enrolled by the emperor Leo I. Haldon discusses the structure and duties of these corps in great detail.

Hirschfeld, Otto, *Die agentes in rebus*. For their use in the eastern empire, see Francis Dvornik, *Origins of Intelligence Services* (no. **3**), pp. 129–140).

For other discussions of the *agentes*, see Sinnigen (no. **466**), Jones (no. **385**), Paschoud (no. **421**), Clauss (nos. **335**, **337**), Purpura (no. **426**), Seeck (no. **444**) and Blum (no. **325**). See entry **377**.

Hirschfeld, Otto, *Die Sicherheitspolizei im römischen Kaiserreich*.

Full entry for this article under "The Roman Empire." The institution of the *agentes in rebus* continued in the eastern empire. (See Francis Dvornik, *Origins of*

Intelligence Services, [no. **3**] pp. 129–140). Intelligence services are one example of institutions that survived from late antiquity rather than disappeared after the fall of the West in AD 476. See entry **375**.

516. Jenkins, R.J. H., "The 'Flight' of Samonas," *Speculum* 24 (1948), pp. 217–235.

The author himself describes the Byzantine court as a "diplomatic world where spying and treason were the order of the day." The "flight" of the title refers to the defection of the Arab eunuch Samonas, who was *cubicularius* and confidential agent of the Emperor Leo VI. He supposedly deserted to the Saracen enemy in the spring of 904; or did he? This is a tale of intrigue in which the emperor and his spy master Samonas foil a plot against the throne by the powerful eastern aristocrats. Secret messages, double agents, secret police ... they're all here.

Byzantine writers George Monachus, the *Continuator* of Theophanes, Symeon Magister, and the biographer of Euthymius all report the plot.

517. Johnen, Christian, *Geschichte der Stenographie im Zusammenhang mit der allgemeinen Entwicklung der Schrift and der Schriftkürzung*, Berlin: F. Schrey, 1911, 295 pp.

A history of shorthand and the creation of symbols for speedwriting. He covers the Greeks, the Romans, the Byzantine world and the Middle Ages.

For other examples of shorthand writing in antiquity, see chapters on Greece, The Roman Republic, and The Middle Ages.

518. John Skylitzes, Skylitzes Matritensis, *Sinopsis de historias*, por Sebastián Cirac Estopañan, Barcelona, 1965, Vol. 1.

The Master of Office controlled the use of the state post until the eighth century. However, the head of the *curiosi* gradually became the most important agent in the surveillance of the use of the state post, overshadowing the post of the Master himself. In the eighth century, the direction of the post ceased to be a part of the Master's duties. A new office arose from that of the first *curiosus*, and its head was called Logothete of the Post (*logothetes tou dromou*).

In a fourteenth century illuminated manuscript of this work kept in Madrid, an artist depicts two spies, sent by the Emperor Leo VI, eavesdropping on the conversation of two people suspected of plotting against the emperor.

519. Jones, A.H.M., *The Later Roman Empire 284-602. A Social, Economic and Administrative Survey,* Norman, Oklahoma: University of Oklahomas Press, 1964, 2 vols.

Superb work on the administrative structures of the late Roman empire, many of which continue in the eastern half of the empire after the fall of Rome in AD 476. See Jones (no. **385**) on the *agentes in rebus* 128–9; 578–82; 547–9; 579–81, *speculatores, stationarii, beneficiarii, curiosi, curagendarii, cursus publicus, regendarii, protectores domestici, Magister Officiorum*, and *notarii*. Jones disagrees with Sinnigen (no. **466**) on the intelligence responsibilities of the *agentes in rebus*. See entry on Jones (no. **385**) above.

520. Kaegi, Walter E., *Some Thoughts on Byzantine Military Strategy*. Brookline, MA: Hellenic College Press, 1983, 18 pp.

Nineteenth century military writers warn against excessive confidence in one's ability to predict, to control, or to direct the course of a war once full-scale hostilities had commenced. They stressed the imponderables in war. They assumed that decision-makers should try to know the political and military situation as fully and as accurately as possible (i.e. intelligence, although Kaegi does not say this). The absence of modern means of surveillance and rapid communications contributed much to this confusion in war. All the more so in Byzantium.

Strategy and stratagems are indissolubly linked with Byzantium. Byzantine military manuals discuss stratagems that rely on surprise as a force multiplier, and on deception, craftiness, and cunning as opposed to open battles. The critical element was a readiness to exploit uncertainties while minimizing one's own casualties. This can only be done with good intelligence. Kaegi quotes the terms artifices, diplomacy, delay, dissimulation, sowing dissension, corruption, ruses etc. but never discusses the role of intelligence in effecting them. He warns that this mindset of using stratagems to wage war effectively and cheaply created a dangerous, even disastrous, overconfidence in the ability of the strategist to offset, through cleverness, superior forces. As Clausewitz pointed out, the principles of war are simple; what is difficult is their implementation. Kaegi notes that because of the slowness of communications and other logistical difficulties, the military texts and narratives do not justify any effort to impute a "grand strategy" or rigorous, comprehensive or total strategy for all frontiers of the empire. The lack of anything resembling a Joint Chiefs of Staff or General Staff reinforced that absence.

521. Koutrakou, N., "Diplomacy and Espionage: Their Role in the Byzantine Foreign Relations," *Graeco-Arabica* 6 (1995), pp. 125–144.

Although the Byzantine era lacked the modern concept of resident ambassadors, diplomatic contacts were made by embassies and missions exchanged on an *ad hoc* basis. Even the lack of sufficient documentation cannot cover up the fact that special agents were sent to collect intelligence. Clandestine means were used to pursue foreign policy objectives. Holy men, official envoys, or traveling merchants could all be used as agents, and many times innocent bystanders were accused of espionage. In short, there was a constant supply of "unofficial contacts" used to gather information for the Byzantine empire.

522. Lee, A.D., "Embassies as Evidence for Movement of Military Intelligence Between the Roman and Sassanian Empires," in P. Freeman and D. Kennedy, *The Defense of the Roman and Byzantine East*, Proceedings of a colloquium held at the University of Sheffield in April 1986, *British Archaeological Reports International Series* 297, 1986, pp. 455–461.

523. Lee, A.D., "Procopius, Justinian and the kataskopoi," *Classical Quarterly* 83 (1989), pp. 569–572.

The Byzantine historian Procopius makes two different claims about why Rome lost the province of Lazica to the Persians. In the *Secret History* Justinian is responsible by virtue of having abolished the *kataskopoi* (spies) as a result of which the Romans had no forewarning of Persian moves. According to his account in the Wars, it was not the absence of *kataskopoi* but rather being misled by deliberate Persian disinformation.

Procopius is unreliable. He was prejudiced against the emperor Justinian and accuses him in various places of disbanding the *kataskopoi*, the *limitanei* and the *cursus publicus*. We know from other sources that this is not true. We should also consider the probability of any government doing away with the intelligence gathering facilities at its disposal. It may be that the *kataskopoi* were not, in fact, disbanded completely but rather their numbers were reduced—as part of the cost-cutting measures of the 530s by John the Cappadocian. This reduction would be reflected in less thorough cross checking and confrontation of intelligence reports that could account for the ease with which the Romans were misled. This is the interpretation the author uses to marry the divergent accounts by Procopius.

524. Leo, *Tactica*, Leonis Imperatoris Tactica, in *PG* 107, cols. 672–1120; ed. R, Vari, Leonis Imperatoris Tactica I (proem. const. I-XI). II (const. XII-XIII, XIV/1-38) *Sylloge Tacticorum Graecorum* III). Budpest 1917–1922.

At the beginning of the tenth century, Maurice's *Tactica* was revised and reissued under the name of the Emperor Leo VI (886–912). This new edition added new intelligence on the Turks (the name they use to describe the Magyars and tribes dwelling north of the Euxine). This is one of the best descriptions we have of these people, and how they fought. Their security was so good it was almost impossible to surprise them.

525. McGeer, Eric, *Sowing the Dragon's Teeth: Byzantine Warfare in the Tenth Century*, Washington, D.C.: Dumbarton Oaks Research Library and Collection, 1995, 405 pp.

The theory and conduct of Byzantine warfare during the age of the soldier-emperors Nikephoros II Phokas (963–969), John I Tzimiskes (969–976) and Basil II (976–1025) as taken from the *Praecepta militaria* (ca. 965) attributed to Nikeophoros Phokas and the revised, expanded version of the treatise written by Nikephoros Ouranos as chapters 56–65 of his Taktika (ca. 1000). McGeer translates the texts of both.

Numerous references to spies, their detection and counterintelligence techniques.

526. Maurice, *Strategicon*, trans. George Dennis, Philadelphia, 1984.

The treatise ascribed to the Emperor Maurice (582–602) was based not only on military science inherited from the Romans (especially Arrian) but also includes his own and contemporary experiences. It was revised many times and appeared again in a longer form at the beginning of the tenth century under the name of Emperor Leo VI (Leo, *Tactica*, no. **524**). It summarizes the results of military intelligence when describing how the army should fight new nations that appeared in the neighborhood of Byzantium and whose tactics were, up to that point, unknown.

527. Menander Protector, *Menandri Protectoris Fragmenta*, in *HGM* II 1–131; Exc. de Leg. I 170–221. II 442–477.

Records relations between Sassanid Persia and Byzantium. The description of the Byzantine embassy of 561, for example, is particularly important for the history of international diplomatic relations. It contains important intelligence on the situation in Persia at that time and on the character of Chosroes I. (Dvornik, no. **3**, p. 168.)

528. Miller, D.A., "The Logothete of the Drome in the Middle Byzantine Period," *Byzantion* 36 (1966), pp. 438–468.

The office of "Logothete of the Drome" evolved out of the *Curiosus cursus publici praesentalis* in the office of the Master of Offices in the late Roman empire. In other words, he was responsible for supervising the inspectors (*curiosi*) of the postal route that carried military intelligence between the emperor and his provincial governors. In the eight century, this official became director of the Post itself, and through this office began to direct the administrative detail involved in sending envoys abroad and in receiving foreign embassies (another area where espionage was carried out). Through these duties and his supervision of the corps of interpreters, the Logothete was able to bring under his control most of the diplomatic functions exercised by the Master of Offices, and in effect became the Byzantine "Minister of Information" and intelligence specialist.

529. Mudd, Mary, "Upward Mobility Among *Notarii* Under Constantius II," *Seventh Annual Byzantine Studies Conference*, Abstract 1981, pp. 23–24.

The palatine civil servants known as *notarii* had three functions. They served as the secretaries who recorded the minutes of the consistory (the emperor's council of state), as envoys who carried the resolutions of the emperor and the consistory to the appropriate recipients, and as investigators of potential cases of treason or other internal security matters that might threaten the emperor. Especially remarkable is the advancement these made men under the reign of Constantius II. Former *notarii* were made provincial governors, praetorian prefect, consul, patrician and count.

Notarii were not the only functionaries who served as envoys and investigators. The corps of *agentes in rebus* performed similar investigations. while both the *agentes in rebus* and *palatini* acted as envoys. What sets the *notarii* apart from their fellow palatine civil servants was their unusual social mobility, and their high qualifications for office.

On the *agentes in rebus*, see W.G. Sinnigen, "Two Branches of the Late Roman Secret Service" (no. **463**), 238–254, Blockeley (no. **324**), Blum (no. **325**), Clauss (nos. **335**, **337**), Hirschfeld (no. **375**), Paschoud (no. **421**), and Purpura (no. **426**), Krenkel (no. **389**), Austin& Rankov (no. **315**).

530. Nicephorus II, *Historia syntomos* (*On Skirmishing*) Teubner: Leipzig, 1880; and George Dennis, (ed. and trans.) *Three Military Treatises* (no. **509**), pp. 137–139.

This work on hit-and-run warfare or skirmishing has been falsely attributed to Nicephorus Phocas, but the preface makes clear he is not the author. He did, however, give orders that such a work should be composed. He entrusts the task to another author, who writes in the first person, and mentions in the preface that he had commanded troops in the West. He also claims to have received much of his training from Bardas Phocas which would make him a contemporary of Nicephorus. George Dennis believes he was an officer of high rank, perhaps a *strategos*, for he gives instructions to the general as if he were a colleague. He was either a member of the Phocas family or someone quite close to them. Dennis suggests Leo Phocas, but under the reign of John Tzimisces (969–76) who had Nicephorus murdered, or perhaps that of Basil II (976–1025) it may not have been prudent to attribute anything to Leo Phocas.

531. Pattenden, T., "The Byzantine Early Warning System," *Byzantion* 53 (1983), pp. 258–299.

Several Byzantine chronicles and the history of Constantine VII Porphyrogenitus censure the Emperor Michael III (AD 842–867) for dismantling the beacon system that gave warning in the capital of hostile Arab movements on the eastern frontier in Cilicia. Pattenden dissects the system technologically to see how it might have worked and then discusses whether the accounts are accurate. He doubts very much that the system was used, and if so, it may not have carried the message attributed to it in the time of Michael III.

532. Procopius, *Procopius*, H.B. Dewing Translation, Loeb Classical Library Edition, Cambridge: Harvard University Press, 1943–54, 7 vols. Includes The Secret War, The Persian Wars, The Gothic Wars, The Vandal Wars.

It is not until the Byzantine period that the gathering of intelligence for both Rome and Persia by paid agents or merchants is mentioned as a mater of routine. Procopius, *History of the Wars of Justinian* 1.21.11–13 tells a story of a spy who went over to the Romans and returned to Persia to convey misleading information. See also 1.15.6 on bodyguards sent to spy out the enemy forces. He also says in *Anecdota*, 30 "It is an old custom among the Romans and the Persians that spies are paid by the state to travel secretly among the enemy in order to examine the state of affairs accurately and report on it to their rulers upon their return." One wonders how old a custom this really was.

533. Sheldon, Rose Mary, "Byzantine Counterintelligence and the Bulgarians," *Intelligence Quarterly* 1, 4 February 1986.

Re-telling of the intelligence coup pulled off by the leader of the Bulgars against Constantine V.

534. Sphenkas, K., "Ho demosios ton Byzantinon," *Nea Hestia* 47 (1950), pp. 374–376ff, 458ff, 539ff, 604ff, 656ff, 748–751ff.

Out of the *taxis* of the Logothete given by Philothetus we can positively identify *diatrechontes* (*cursores*, couriers) and *mandatores*. The job of the *mandator* is not completely clear. Presumably, he carried orders from the Emperor or his representatives. In this context he could either be a type of courier or an inspecting officer. This article does not add much to the discussion and is generally unreliable on the organization of the Post, its officers, and its connection with the Course. See instead, Bury, *The Imperial Administrative System in the Ninth Century* (no. **502**), p. 113 and Miller ("Logothete" no. **528**).

535. Theodosius, *The Theodosian Code* and Novels, and the Sirmondian constitutions; a translation with commentary, glossary and bibliography by Clyde Pharr, in collaboration with Teresa Sherrer Davidson and Mary Brown Pharr. With an introduction by C. Dickerman Williams, Princeton: Princeton University Press, 1952, 643 pp.

See I. 9, VI. 27, 28, 29; Novels of Valentianian 28 on the Master of Offices, and the *agentes in rebus*.

536. Theophanes, *The Chronicle of Theophanes*, trans. Harry Turtledove, Philadelphia: University of Pennsylvania Press, 1982, 201 pp.

The only source for an interesting intelligence story concerning the emperor Constantine V (741–775). In passage 448, he tells of Telerig, khan of the Bulgars, who claimed he wished to defect. He asked the emperor for a list of his secret agents so that he might contact them and use them as a network to escape to Constantinople. In an act of amazing naivete, Constantine turns over the list and Telerig has them arrested immediately. Theophanes gives us little detail about why Constantine was so easily duped, but then he is hostile to the emperor who was an iconoclast hated by Orthodox Christians. See also R.M. Sheldon "Byzantine Counterintelligence and the Bulgarians" (no. **533**).

537. Theophanes Continuatus, *Theophanes continuatus, Ioannes Caminiata, Symeon Magister, Georgius Monachus continuatus*, ed. I. Bekker (*Corpus Scriptorum Historiae Byzantinae*), Bonn, 1828–97, 1–481.

Among the many stories concerning spies, an interesting case of counterespionage is reported by the Emperor Constantine VII Porphyrogenitus in his biographical sketch of his grandfather, Basil I. The incident is reported in chapter 68 of the Continuator of Theophanes. It dates to the year 880. The Arabs decide to make a naval expedition against the Byzantines. First they send out spies to find out the enemy strength. They send an agent who wears Roman dress and speaks Greek. This spy, from Syria, reports back that the Byzantine navy was so large and in such a state of preparedness, that the Arabs call off the attack. There is the possibility that the spy was actually a dual agent.

See pp. 197–8 = *PG*, 109, col. 211 C-D on Byzantine signalling.

538. Treadgold, Warren, *Byzantium and Its Army 284-1081*, Stanford: Stanford University Press, 1995, 250 pp.

General history of role of the Byzantine army—chiefly its size, organization and pay. Three brief mentions of scouts are the only thing on intelligence.

539. Wessely, Carl, "Ein neues System griechischer Geheimschrift," *Wiener Studien* 26 (1904), p. 185ff.

The first example of the secret writing system mentioned in the title comes from Papyrus CXXI in the British Museum dating to the third century BC which Wessely published in his "Neue Griechischen Zauberpapyri (no. **242**). It is a type of numerical shorthand that Wessely works out and charts on page 188. He also gives a 12th century example.

540. Wirth, Peter, "Wie lange kannten Byzantiner die griechische Tachygraphie?" *Archiv für Diplomatik, Schriftgeschichte Siegel-und Wappenkunde* 39 (1993), pp. 269–271.

Wirth discovers documents which show that Byzantine officials were familiar with classical Greek tachygraphy because they noted it in their commentaries on classical works. There are also examples from their own diplomatic correspondence.

541. Zonaras, Johannes, ed. L. Dindorf (Teubner, Leipzig) IV 1871, p. 16 (=M. Pinder, *Corpus Scriptorum Historiae Byzantinae*, Bonn) III (1897) pp. 404–406 = *PG* 135, 28B–29A.

A Byzantine chronicler who lived from the latter part of the eleventh century to about the middle of the twelfth. Under the Emperor Alexis Comnenus he was commander of the imperial body-guard and first secretary of the imperial chancery. Later he became a monk at Hagia Glykeria where he wrote a compendium of history: *Epitome ton istorion*, superior in form and contents to most other Byzantine chroniclers. His work was extensively used in the Middle Ages and is a chronicle of the world from its creation to the accession of John Comnenus in 1118.

His work is of special value for its excerpts from the lost books of Dio Cassius, and it is a source on the Byzantine signalling system.

Greek Fire

One of the main goals of counterintelligence is to keep one's secrets safe from the enemy. No secret was better kept than the recipe for Greek fire. Constantinople was the main military goal of the Muslim armies, but the great Byzantine capital repulsed a series of Muslim attacks between 670 and 680. The Byzantine defense was aided by a secret weapon known as Greek fire, a liquid containing quicklime that ignited on contact with water and could only be extinguished by vinegar or sand. The original recipe has never been discovered.

542. Berthelot, M., *La chimie au moyen age*, Paris, 1893.

543. Bradbury, Jim, "Greek Fire in the West," *History Today* 29 (1979), pp. 226–331.

544. Byrne, M. and Haldon, J., "A Possible Solution to the Problem of Greek Fire," *Byzantinische Zeitschrift* 70 (1977), pp. 91–99.

545. Cheronis, "Chemical Warfare in the Middle Ages: Kallinikos' 'Prepared Fire'," *Journal of Chemical Education* 14, 8 (1937), pp. 360–5.

546. Dain, A., "Appellations grecques du feu grégeois," *Mélanges offerts à Alfred Ernout*, Paris, 1940, pp. 121–27.

547. Ellis-Davidson, H.R., "The Secret Weapon of Byzantium," *Byzantinische Zeitschrift* 66 (1973), pp. 61–74.

548. Korres, Th. K., *Hygron Pyr*, Thessalonika, 1985 (in Greek).

549. Lalanne, Ludovic, *Recherches sur le feu grégeois*, et sur l'introduction de la poudre à canon en Europe; memoire auquel l'académie des inscriptions et belles-lettres à decerne une medaille d'or, le 25 Septembre 1840, 2nd ed. cor. et entièrement refondue, Paris: J. Correard, 1845, 96 pp.

550. Mercier, Maurice, *Le Feu grégeois*, les feu de guerre depuis l'antiquité, la poudre à canon. Ouvrage publié avec le concours du Centre national de la recherche scientifique, Paris: Guenthner, 1952, 641 pp.

551. Paaszthory, Emmerich, "Über das Griechische Feuer," *Antike Welt* 2 (1986), pp. 27–37.

552. Partington, James Riddick, *A History of Greek Fire and Gunpowder*, Cambridge: W. Heffer, 1960, 381 pp.

553. Partington, James Riddick, "Greek Fire," *Technology and Culture* 33, 4 (October, 1992), pp. 162–166.

554. Pentz, Peter, "A Medieval Workshop for Producing 'Greek Fire' grenades," *Antiquity* 62 (March, 1988), p. 89.

555. Roland, Alex, "Greek Fire," *Military History Quarterly* 2 (Spring 2000), pp. 16–19.

556. Roland, Alex, "Secrecy, Technology and War. Greek Fire and the Defense of Byzantium," *Technology and Culture* 33, 4 (October, 1992), pp. 655–679.

557. Theophanes, *Corpus Scriptorum Hist*oriae Byzantinae (ed. B.G. Niebuhr, Bonn, 1839), I, pp. 540–2. *Compendium Hist.* (ed. Bekker, Bonn, 1839) p. 765.

558. Vasojevic, Andreas & Nicolaus, "Naphtha," *Philologus*, 128 (1984), pp. 208–229.

An historical survey of the use of naphtha in antiquity, from Egypt to the Bible through Pliny and the Romans. In Latin.

559. Zenghelis, C., " Le feu grégeois et les armes à feu des Byzantins," *Byzantion* 7 (1932), pp. 265–86.

Medieval World

With the collapse of the western empire, literacy all but disappeared. The monks of Europe kept alive the Latin alphabet and amused themselves by signing their manuscripts or adding the occasional gloss in cipher to amuse themselves. The systems they used were simple. Phrases were written vertically or backwards; dots were substituted for vowels; foreign alphabets like Greek, Hebrew or Armenian were used with each letter of the plaintext replaced by the one that followed it. In the most advanced system, special signs substituted for letters. According to David, "for almost a thousand years, from before 500 to 1400, the cryptography of Western civilization stagnated."

And he does not see much progress within the Middle Ages itself: an "advanced system is as likely to appear in the 600s as in the 1400s." He does argue that the really simple systems do fade away by the end of the period. The brilliant monk Gerbert, who reigned as Pope Sylvester II from 999 to 1003 and whose learning became legendary, kept his notes in the syllabic system called Tironian notes (nos. **279–307**). He even wrote his name in it on two of his bulls. Then there is, of course, the enigmatic cipher of Roger Bacon.

Outside of cryptography, there are many traces of intelligence gathering beginning with Charlemagne's *Missi dominici,* the royal inspectors or "envoys of the sovereign," and going through the War of the Roses. Where there are historical sources, we find spies.

General

560. Alban, J.R. and Allman, C.T., "Spies and Spying in the Fourteenth Century," in C.T. Allman, ed. *War, Literature and Politics in the Late Middle Ages*, New York: Barnes & Noble Books, 1976, pp. 73–101.

An excellent survey of the evidence for spies in the fourteenth century. The wars of the late middle ages witnessed a developing attitude towards spies whose services were coming to be increasingly used on all sides. Governments were reticent about mentioning their agents so the sources are sometimes sketchy and vague. The distinction between spy and messenger was a fine one. The authors imply throughout that although necessary, this was an aspect of war that was in some measure ignoble, and not even proper for heralds. There is the implication on the first page that such sneaky arts might have been learned from the Byzantine or Islamic world. An Orientalist slur at best.

561. Allmand, C.T., "Les Espions au Moyen Age," *L'Histoire* 55 (1983), pp. 35–41.

A popular account of espionage in the Hundred Years War and its contribution to the building of the nation state of France. Allman believes espionage, both commercial and military, was a daily reality in the Middle Ages. Illustrated.

562. Allmand, Christopher T., "Intelligence in the Hundred Years War," in Keith Neilson and B.J.C. McKercher, *Go Spy the Land. Military Intelligence and History*, Westport, CT: Praeger, 1992, pp. 31–47.

The decline of chivalric values and traditional military values in the late Middle Ages gave rise to practices described in contemporary writers as deceit, fraud, deception, subterfuge, and the use of spies. Allmand sifts through the evidence and discusses the vocabulary for spying in the Middle Ages in both French and English. He rightly notes that too little is known about spies at the end of the Middle Ages for us to judge how much organized espionage there was during the period, but it seems clear that it was becoming an important part of warfare in the 14th century.

563. Amanelishvili, L.A., "Gruzino-Grecheskie kriptogramy v Gruzinskikh rukopiyakh Xv," in AD. Lyublinskyaya (ed.) *Problemy paleografii I kodokologii v SSSR*, Moscow: Nauka, 1974, pp. 403–408.

Georgian cryptograms appear in tenth century manuscripts. They were derived from Greek cryptograms and Hebrew *atbash*.

564. Arensberg, Walter C., *The Cryptography of Dante*, New York: Alfred A. Knopf, 1921, 494 pp.

In the Mendelsohn Collection.

According to Arensberg, *La Divina Commedia* contains a large number of cryptograms. As an allegory, the poem has a hidden as well as a manifest meaning. The hidden symbols represent an anthropomorphic universe in which Beatrice is to be identified with Bella, the mother of Dante, and an incarnation of the divine or universal mother and DXV and the Veltro are to be identified with Dante, conceived as an incarnation of the divine or universal son. Among the cryptograms Arensberg has found are acrostics, telestics, interior sequences, anagrams, irregular letter clusters, string ciphers and cabalistic spelling devices. Think what he might have done with a computer!

565. Arkhipov, A.A., "O proiskhozhdenii Drevbeslavianskoi toinopisi," *Sovetkoe Slavyanovedenie*, Akademiya Nauk SSSR 6 (1980), pp. 79–86.

On the origins of Old Slavonic cryptograms.

566. Arthurson, Ian, "Espionage and Intelligence from the War of the Roses to the Reformation," *Nottingham Medieval Studies* 35 (1991), pp. 134–154.

Arthurson believes that in the period between the War of the Roses and the Reformation, spies were used both in foreign and military affairs but also for domestic security. Unlike many scholars of the middle ages, he believes spies are neither difficult to locate nor to document. The literature of the period suggests that spies were an everyday part of military life. The chronicles of the period deal with espionage in a forthright way, presenting it with little or no comment, except where there was a contemporary controversy. Letters of the period give much evidence for the work of spies, and royal accounts state openly that rewards were given for spying and that there were many agents out "on the king's business."

Bacon cipher. See nos. **615–617** below.

Bamberg Cryptogram. c. AD 818. See *Dubthach Cipher* (nos. **600–608**).

567. Bischoff, Bernard, "Übersicht über die nichtdiplomatischen Geheimschriften des Mittelalters," *Mitteilungen des Instituts für Österreichische Geschichtsforschung* Band 62 (1954), pp. 1–27.

Magisterial work on the use of secret writing and diplomatic codes in medieval manuscripts. Includes the Bacon cipher (see nos. **615–617**), the *lingua ignota* of Hildegard of Bingen (no. **590**). Has extensive bibliography and charts.

568. Bonet, Honoré, *The Tree of Battles of Honoré Bonet*, an English version with introduction by G.W. Coopland, Liverpool: Liverpool University Press, 1949.

In the late 1380s Honoré Bonet (alternative spelling, Bouvet), the prior of a monastic community in the southeast of France and a canon lawyer by training, wrote this work. He was particularly concerned with the way war was affecting

French society at the time. He questions whether it is fitting for a king or a prince to overcome an enemy by deceit or trickery. He felt victory should not be gained over an enemy by craft or fraud because this amounted to deceit. Covert deeds that brought military advantage were immoral.

See: Allmand, Christpher T., "The Tree of Battles of Honoré Bouvet and the Laws of War," in C.T. Allmand, ed. *War, Literature, and Politics in the Late Middle Ages*, Liverpool: Liverpool University Press, 1976, pp. 12–31.

569. Brayshay, Mark, "Post-haste by port horse?," *History Today* 42, 9 (1992), pp. 35–41.

A popular article on the movement of information transfer by post in the Middle Ages. The operational mechanics of the merchant's postal system in the later fourteenth century is deduced, for example, from documents related to the affairs of Francesco di Marco Datini, a merchant in the town of Prato, near Florence, whose business empire was founded in Avignon in 1368. He discusses the mounted couriers who provided messenger service in the Venetian Republic from at least the ninth century, and the post-horse riders of the merchant adventurers of London.

For later periods, see Brian Austen, *English Provincial Posts 1633-1840*, London: Phillimore, 1978; Mark Brayshay, "Royal Post-horse Routes in England and Wales: the evolution of the network in the late-sixteenth and early seventeenth centuries," *Journal of Historical Geography* 17, 4 (1991); J.W.M. Stone, *The Inland Posts 1392-1672*, London: Christie's-Robson Lowe, 1987; R. M. Willcocks, *England's Postal History to 1840*, London: the author, 1975; Philip Harrison and Mark Brayshay, "Post-horse routes, royal progresses and government communications in the reign of James I," *The Journal of Transport History* 18, 2 (1997), pp. 116–134.

570. Chatelain, Emile, "La Tachygraphie Latine," *Revue des Bibliothèques* (January-March, 1902), pp. 1–40.

The system of shorthand writing called Tironian notes was supposedly invented by the slave of Cicero. (See Tironian Notes nos. **279–307**.) There were signs added to the system in later ages. These were attributed to Seneca, Saint Cyprian and Gregory the Great. There are examples dating to the Carolingian period, and a syllabic tachygraphy used in Northern Italy during the 10th century. Chatelain gives over seventy examples of its use from manuscripts in Verona.

571. Chaucer, Geoffrey, *The Equatorie of the Planetis*, ed. Derek J. Price, Cambridge: Cambridge University Press, 1955, 214 pp.

Appendix I "Cipher Passages in the Manuscript" pp. 182–187, 75, 77, 78, 79, 85, 87.

By far the most famous cryptographer of the Middle Ages was Geoffrey Chaucer. He was a customs official, an amateur astronomer, and literary genius. In this work, he describes the workings of an astronomical instrument, and it was meant as a companion piece to his *Treatise on the Astrolabe*. He includes six short passages in cipher. He uses a symbol alphabet in which "a" is represented by a sign resembling a capital V, and "b" by one looking like a script alphabet. The encipherments give simplified directions for using the equatorie. The cryptograms are in Chaucer's own hand, making them among the most illustrious encipherments in history.

The appendix provides a summary analysis of the method with parallels in the Roger Bacon cipher.

572. Cortes Escriva, Josepa, Pons Alos Vicente, "Una clau criptografica d'Alfons el Magnanim per a la guerra amb Castella (1429)," *Saitabi; Revista de historia, arte y arqueologia* 36 (1986), pp. 25–36.

The authors summarize the use of cryptography in different European chanceries that had become common by the end of the Middle Ages, and they describe the methods used and show that ciphered writings increase at the same time. They publish the key that is taken from the Mayan collection at the *Collegio de Corpus Christi*, in Valencia. It makes use of a ciphered alphabet as well as a series of arbitrary and ideogrammatic signs representing people, cities, and other abstract concepts. The text includes an abcedarius formed by 17 signs representing consonants and another five for vowels. A list of toponyms, personal names and military terms, and a set of nine signs with no importance, but introduced to make decipherment more difficult. It originated in 1429, under Alfons el Magnanim, at the time of the war with Castile. In Catalan with an abstract in Spanish and English. Illustrated.

573. Costamagna, Giorgio, "Scritture tachigrafiche e criptografiche nel simbolismo del segno tabellionato nell 'chartae' dell'Italia settentrionale (se. IX–XI)," *Graphische Symbole in mittelalterlichen Urkunden: Beiträge zur diplomatischen Semiotik.* Ed. Peter RÜCK (Historische Hilfwissenschaftn, 3), 831 pp. Sigmaringen Thorbecke, 1996, pp. 115–119.

Cryptographical symbols used in charters and diplomatic documents of the ninth to eleventh centuries.

574. Crook, David, "The Confession of a Spy, 1380" *Historical Research* 62 (1989), pp. 346–50.

Richard, Earl of Arundel, sent to the King's Bench one Geoffrey Broun of Staunton whom he had arrested in Sussex for spying. A transcript of his confession was copied into the roll of memoranda concerning the progress of Crown cases kept by the clerk of the Crown in King's Bench. The confession, in French, was made on Thursday 11 October 1380 in Arundel Castle in the presence of two inquisitors. He confessed to having served in enemy company at Harfleur for two and a half years. He was on an enemy barge and then let off in the vicinity of Winchelsea with the object of spying on the coastal defenses. He intended to be near Beaulieu in the New Forest in Hampshire by Christmastime to meet twenty-nine enemy barges there and inform them about the defenses.

Dubthach Cipher. See nos. **600–608**.

575. Enterline, James, "Cryptography in the Yale Vinland Map," *Terra Incognitae* 23 (1991), pp. 13–27.

Yale University published the Vinland Map in 1965. At first it was thought a forgery, based on testing of its ink, which appeared modern. Recent findings on the chemistry of the ink from the Vinland map have re-opened the possibility that it is authentic. One of the arguments concerning its authenticity involves its use of cryptography. Enterline re-examines and extends this line of inquiry. He believes the Vinland Map's inscriptions seem to be as much a vehicle for clever cryptography as a vehicle for factual information. The audience would have been other scribes. Still, he does not rule out the possibility of forgery.

Cf. T.A. Cahill et.al., "The Vinland Map Revisited: New Compositional Evidence on Its Inks and Parchment," *Analytical Chemistry* 59 (1987), pp. 829–833.

Walter C. McCrone, "The Vinland Map," *Analytical Chemistry* 60 (1988), pp. 1009–1018.

Kenneth M. Towe, "The Vinland Map: Still a Forgery," *Accounts of Chemical Research* 23 (1990), pp. 84–87.

576. Griffiths, R.A., "Un Espion Breton à Londres, 1425–1429," *Annales de Bretagne et des Pays de l'Ouest* 86 (1979), pp. 399–403.

The *Chronique de Grégoire* gives the details of a story of a Breton, Ivo Caret, killed on a street in London on May 27, 1429. He turns out to be a spy from Brittany.

577. Havet, Julien, "L'écriture secret de Gerbert," *Académie des Inscriptions et Belles-Lettres*: Comptes-Rendus, 4th series, XV (1887), pp. 94–112.

Gerbert of Aurillac in Auvergne, France was born around AD 940–950 of humble parents and lived to be crowned Pope Sylvester II. He was the first Frenchman to become Pope and was known for his scholarly achievements. He is said to have introduced Arabic figures into Western Europe and to have invented the pendulum clock. He devised a quasi-cryptographic form of writing that is described in this article (see pp. 97–8).

578. Havet, Julien, "La tachygraphie italienne du Xe siècle," *Académie des Inscriptions et Belles-Lettres*: Comptes-Rendus 4th series, XV (1887), pp. 351–374.

Havet discusses some tenth century documents which use Gerbert's system of cryptographic writing (see no. **577**), including three Bulls which he wrote as Pope Sylvester II from 999, 1001, and 1002. Some of the symbols were taken from Tironian notes (see nos. **279–307**).

Kahn, David, *The Codebreakers*: *The Comprehensive History of Secret Communication from Ancient Times to the Internet.* First edition: New York: The Macmillan Company, 1967, 1164 pp.; revised edition 1996, 1181 pp.

Page 89–90 discusses cryptographic systems in the Middle Ages. See no. **38**.

579. Kahn, David, "On the Origin of Polyalphabetic Substitution," *Isis* 71, 1: 256 (1980), pp. 122–127.

The most widely used cipher system in the world is polyalphabetic substitution. In 1940, Charles J. Mendelsohn traced this cipher's first appearance to Leon Battista Alberti (1404–1472). Kahn investigates the source of Alberti's idea. He suspects that the source was the medieval Catalan mystic Ramon Lull (c. 1232–1315) who devised a mechanism for combining letters that stood for philosophical concepts in groups of three. Kahn goes onto describe the system in detail. There is apparently no document stating that Alberti knew of Lull, but the close resemblance of their disk systems suggests there was borrowing. Kahn also discusses theories about where Lull might have gotten his inspiration.

580. Levison, Wilhem, *England and the Continent in the Eighth Century.* The Ford Lectures delivered in The University of Oxford in the Hilary Term, 1943, Oxford: The Clarendon Press, 1946, 347 pp.

Pages 290–94 and Appendix VIII are on "St. Boniface and Cryptography." A manuscript purported to be written by a student of Alcuin's and originating from the Fulda circle in the 9th century discusses the runes of the Marcomanni, abbreviations, monograms, and makes mention of cryptic writing and St. Boniface's part in its diffusion. Evidently, such methods of secret writing were used on both sides of the Channel during the Middle Ages. Levison gives examples from both England and the Continent. He says that no examples predating Boniface are known.

The system involves vowels superseded by the next consonant or by various numbers or dots.

581. Mallett, Michael E., "Diplomacy and War in Fifteenth-century Italy," in George Homes (ed.) *Art and Politics in Renaissance Italy*, British Academic Lectures, Oxford: Oxford University Press, 1993, pp. 137–158.

See pages 144 and following on the role of diplomatic agents as intelligence gatherers in the fifteenth century.

582. Marra, Charles Luigi, *La crittografia nel secolo XIV in Sicilia*, Catania: Accademia Gioenia, 1858, 24 pp.

Mendelsohn Collection 652M M348. Cryptographic writing used in 14th century manuscripts from Sicily.

583. Meister, Aloys, *Die Geheimschrift im Dienste der päpstlichen Kurie von ihren Anfängen bis zum Ende des XVI Jahrhunderts*, Paderborn: Ferdinand Schöningh, 1906, 450 pp. (Quellen und Forschungen aus dem Gebiete der Geschichte ... Hrsg von der Görres-Gesellschaft ... XI, Bd.)

Treatise on the origins of the use of cryptography in papal communications. Medieval papal letters to high church officials were generally encrypted. During the fourteenth century, we have knowledge of several Pope's personal ciphers as well as a complete code book of Pope Clement VII's cryptography specialist. This papal cryptography was generally in the form of substitution ciphers, where an alternative alphabet was used to spell out the message. Such a message cannot be read without knowing the cipher alphabet, but it is obvious on its face that it is gibberish and most likely a cryptogram.

Friedman Collection F 92; Mendelsohn Coll. 652 M M477.

584. Mongé, Alf, and O. G. Landsverk, *Norse Medieval Cryptography in Runic Carvings*, Glendale, Ca., Norsemen Press, 1967, 224 pp. Friedman Collection 1157.

Chapters on cryptographic puzzles in Runic inscriptions, Norse calendrical cryptography, seven medieval Norse cryptograms, the Kensington Runestone carving (photo on page 135), cryptography in the Vinland map, and the Benedictines in Norse cryptography.

Mongé's primary efforts were in a field he called calendrial cryptography. It aroused much criticism, much of it valid. See especially Aslak Liestol,

"Cryptograms in Runic Carvings—A Critical Analysis," *Minnesota History* 41 (1968), pp. 34–42 who points out among other things that certain markings on the stones they discuss were the result of working from bad xerox copies, and do not appear in the original inscription. See also Hans Karlgren, "Review of Mongé and Landsverk," *Scandinavian Studies* 40 (1968), pp. 326–330 who reviews the work that proved the Kensington stone a forgery and dismisses Mongé and Landsverk as a couple of amateurs.

585. Morosi, R., "I saiones. Speciali agenti di polizia presso i Goti," *Athenaeum* 58 (1981), pp. 150–165.

In the *Variae* of Cassiodorus, we read that under the Ostrogothic kings of Italy there existed a group of governmental officials called *Saiones*. They operated as a type of secret police with both military and civil authority. They were Gothic men chosen for their bravery and loyalty. Because of their devotion to the king they were often called *viri devoti*. They were organized in a corps much like the *agentes in rebus* before them, and terrorized the population in the same way. Both groups existed simultaneously, but the *saiones* were replacing the *agentes in rebus* and interfering in their areas of competence. (See Sinnigen, "Administrative Shifts of Competence Under Theodoric" no. **459**.) They guaranteed a certain Gothic presence in the central administration of the kingdom.

Morosi traces their recruiting, promotion and activities. They were used as postal inspectors, tax collectors, police officials and judicial officials. The Lex Visigothorum shows that they continued to be used in the Visigothic kingdoms, but only as *exsecutores* in the tribunals of the provincial governors.

586. Muñoz y Rivero, D. Jesus, *Palaeografia visigoda, método téorico-practico para aprender à leer los códices y documentos españoles de los siglos V al XII ... Obra ilustrado con 45 láminas dibujadas por el autor.* Madrid: Impr de la Guirnalda, 1881, 148 pp.

See Chapter 3, pp. 77–81 on encoded writing. Cf. Locard, *Bibliographie cryptologique* p. 928; Meister, *Die Anfänge der modernen diplomatischen Geheinmschrift*, (no. **583**), p. 8; Prou, *Manuel de paléographie latine et française*, p. 42.

587. Parkes, Malcom B., "Tachygraphy in the Middle Ages: Writing Techniques Employed for 'Reportationes' of Lectures and Sermons," *Medioevo e Rinascimento* 3 (1989), pp. 159–169.

Tironian notes were used as late as the tenth century, but by the twelfth century, this shorthand method had been more or less forgotten, as was classical Latin. From the late eleventh century onwards, manuscripts appear that contain texts of lectures delivered in schools. They are in shorthand systems that used some Tironian notes but had to make new accommodations. Parkes explains the systems.

588. Paterson, John, "Jeux des Moines," *Intermédiaire des Chercheurs et Curieux*, May 1958, col. 389–391.

A treatise on monks' word games.

589. Pavan, E., "Police des moeurs, société et politique à Venise à la fin du Moyen Âge," *RH* 264 (1992), pp. 241–88.

Espionage is often referred to as "the world's second oldest profession." Here is an article about the world's first oldest profession. Pavan discusses the policing of prostitution in medieval Venice. Policing morals also included stamping out homosexual activity. Repressive institutions such as the *Seigneur de la Nuit* patrolled nocturnal hangouts. They were aided by private informers who turned in their neighbors thus creating a double system of surveillance and a flourishing community of sycophants. Bounties were put on the heads of certain people for their behavior and a sliding scale of prices was paid when a culprit was discovered, arrested and convicted. Since Venice burned heretics, sorcerers and sodomites, the stakes were high for those caught and accused.

590. Portmann, Marie-Louise and Adermatt, Alois (edd.), *Wörterbuch der unbekannten Sprache* [*Lingua Ignota*] in der Reihenfolge der Manuskripte, sowie alphabetisch nach unbekannter Sprache, lateinischer Übersetzung, mittelhochdeutscher Übersetzung und moderner Übersetzung. Basel: Basler Hildegard-Gesellschaft, 1986, 82 pp.

Contains the text of Hildegard of Bingen's 1,000 word "secret" vocabulary. The eleventh century nun saw a vision of a cipher that she claimed came to her in a flash of inspiration. See Jeffrey Scnapp, "Virgin Words: Hildegard of Bingen's *Lingua Ignota* and the Development of Imaginary Language Ancient to Modern," *Exemplaria* 3 (1991), pp. 267–298. Berlin Staatsbibliothek, Preussischer Kulturbesitz has the original manuscript, cod. lat. quarto 674; and finally, *Lingua Ignota*, partially edited by Jean-Baptiste Pitra, *Analecta Sacra*, vol. 8 (Monte Cassino, 1882), 496–502. Bischoff (no. **567**).

591. Prestwich, John O., "Military Intelligence under the Norman and Angevin Kings," in George Garnett and John Hudson (edd.) *Law and Government in Medieval England and Normandy.* Essays in honour of Sir James Holt, Cambridge: Cambridge University Press, 1994, pp. 1–30.

Prestwich notes that the topic of military intelligence in the Middle Ages has been previously ignored. Yet he points out that it would be odd indeed "if military intelligence remained rudimentary during a period when administrative measures were increasingly marked by a concern for extensive, precise, and tested information." He finds, in fact, that spies and informers were part of the fabric of Anglo-Norman society. Prestwich gives examples of background intelligence being gathered, the collection of strategic and tactical intelligence, intelligence used to achieve surprise attacks, and the systems run by William the Conqueror, Henry I and Henry II. He concludes that the volume and variety of evidence is conclusive enough to state that the abler commanders had a great interest in gathering intelligence, assessing it and exploiting it.

592. Prestwich, John O., "A New Account of the Welsh Campaign of 1294–95," *Welsh History Review* 6 (1972), p. 94.

An account of the Welsh campaign of 1294–5 and the battle of Maes Moydog. On March 10, 1295, a Welsh spy in the English service tricked an army into advancing into a trap and, as a result, the Welsh were defeated.

593. Probst-Biraben, J. H., "Les Templiers et leur alphabet secret," *Mercure de France*, Paris, (August 1, 1939), pp. 513–532.

In the archives of the modern order of Templars is the 13th-century "Corsini manuscript" that contains among other things a chart of the transmission of power of the order listing all the grand masters, the rules of the order, and most interesting to us, the palaeographic tables of a secret writing system used to encode secret documents including their financial transactions. This includes a cryptographic system, explained on page 522, based on a red cross of St. André.

Microfilm 03611 Library of Congress.

594. Quaesitor, "Jeux des Moines," *L'Intermédiaire des Chercheurs et Curieux*, 8, no. 86 (May, 1958), cols. 389–391,

The use of substitution ciphers in the Bible (see *atbash* [no. **61**], *atbah* [no. **60**] and *albam* [no. **59**] in "Mesopotamia and Palestine") sensitized the monks and scribes of the Middle Ages to the idea of letter substitution. And from them flowed the modern use of ciphers—as distinct from codes—as a means of secret communications. See David Kahn, *The Codebreakers* (no. **38**), p. 79.

Quaesitor gives a broad description of scribes' word and letter games.

595. Thomas, Heinz, "Französische Spionage im Reich Ludwigs des Bayern," *Zeitschrift für Historische Forschung* (1978), pp. 1–21.

A discussion of French espionage in Germany during the reign of Ludwig IV of Bavaria (b. 1294–d. 1347). He begins with a discussion of espionage since the Middle Ages, and there is an interesting discussion on p. 17 n. 68 on what spies were called and how the word returned to *spion* at the time of the Thirty Years War in the 17th century.

596. Thorndike, Lynn, *A History of Magic and Experimental Science during the First Thirteen Centuries of Our Era*, New York: Columbia University Press, 1964–66, 8 volumes.

Volume II, pp. 659–661 on Roger Bacon's cipher.

597. Wilson, W. J., "An Alchemical Manuscript by Arnaldus de Bruxella," *Osiris* 2 (1936), pp. 220–405

Arnaldus of Bruxella, in a manuscript compiled at Naples between 1473 and 1490, uses five lines of cipher to conceal the crucial part of the operation of making a philosopher's stone. On page 345, the author describes where in the critical point of the operation, the text uses a special alphabet. Fortunately for us, the scribe also transliterated it into plain Latin in the upper margin of the same text.

Cf. David Kahn, *The Codebreakers*, p. 91.

598. Wilson, W.J. "Catalogue of Latin and Vernacular Alchemical Manuscripts in the United States and Canada," *Osiris* 6 (1939), pp. 1–836.

Passages in cipher on pp. 312, 316, 317, 433, and 545.

599. Zitzelberger, Otto J., "Medieval physiology encoded: An Icelandic samtal," *Medieval Scandinavia* 12 (1988), pp. 273–290.

Eleven extant Icelandic manuscripts, ranging in date from ca. 1700 to 1896, discuss matters of human physiology. One ms, number 4889, has a number of ciphers. The use of ciphers is sometimes found with personal names in Icelandic

MSS, but otherwise is a relatively rare phenomenon. This seems to be an example of scribes having fun, or is reminiscent of scribes in Old High German who encoded vernacular equivalents of Latin *lemmata*. In this case, as with the German examples, we have a displacement cipher, a rather simple patterned reshuffling of the alphabet. Zitzelberger provides the key.

Dubthach Cipher and the Bamberg Cryptogram

In the early 800s, an Irishman named Dubthach concocted a cryptogram while at the castle of the king of Wales. It functioned as "a kind of malicious IQ test" (Kahn, no. **38**) for visiting compatriots. He apparently wanted to embarrass them in revenge for some humiliation he had suffered at home, and was confident that "no Irish scholar, much less British" would be able to read it. Four Irishmen eventually broke the code: Caunchobrach, Fergus, Domminnach, and Suadbar. They solved the cryptogram by discovering the secret: it was a short Latin plaintext written in Greek letters. They then sent the answer back to Ireland lest any other visitors get embarrassingly stumped.

The cryptogram is preserved in the so-called Bamberg manuscript. Attached to the cryptogram is a letter from a certain Irishman on the continent to their teacher Colgu in Ireland:

> "This is the inscription that was offered as an ordeal by Dubthach to the learned Irishmen at the castle of Mermin King of the Britons. For he so far thought himself the best of all the Irish and the Britons as to believe that no Irish scholar, much less British, would be able to interpret that writing before King Mermin. But to us, Caunchobrach, Fergus, Dominnach and Suadbar, by the help of God it did not remain insoluble." Then follows the interpretation of the cryptogram—"mermin rex Conchen salutem" and the explanation of the method by which it was composed. It is a substitution cipher and a table is given showing how Greek letters were substituted for Latin. They then suggest the cipher be given to any Irishmen sailing to Britain lest they be embarrassed in the presence of Mermin if they cannot solve the riddle.

The key set forth in this text can also be used to decipher a marginal entry in the 8th or 9th century MS of Juvencus in the Cambridge University Library.

600. Connop, Thurwell, "The Welsh Glosses and Verses in the Cambridge Juvencus," *Transactions of the Philological Society* (1860–61), p. 221.

601. Derolez, René L.M., "Dubthach's Cryptogram," *L'Antiquité Classique* 21 (1952), pp. 359–375.

Derolez examines the Brussels Ms. Bibliothèque Royale 9565–9566, dating to the 10th century and comments on Dubthach's cipher. It had been previously discussed for its runic material. See E. Raucq, "Die Runen des Brusseler Codex No. 9565–9566," *Mededeelingen van de Konicklijke Vlaamsche Academie voor Wetenschappen, Letteren en Schoone Kunsten van België. Klasse der Letteren.* Jaargang III, No. 4, Brussels, 1941.

602. Gougaud, Louis, *Les Chrétiennes celtiques*, Paris: J. Gabalda, 1911, pp. 244–45.

603. Heiberg, J.L., "Et lille Bidrag til Belysuing af Middelalderens Kendskab til Graesk," *Bulletin de l'Academie royale de Cohenhague* (Oversigt over det Kongelige Danske *Videnskabernes Selskab.* Forhandlinger og dets Medlemmers Arbejder) (Oct., Dec. 1889), pp. 198–204.

It is Heiberg who identifies Mermin with Mervyn Vrych, King of Wales (d. 844).

604. Kenney, James F., *The Sources of the Early History of Ireland*, New York, Columbia University Press, 1929), Vol. 1 Ecclesiastical, 807 pp.

See page 556 on the Bamberg Cryptogram with full bibliography and commentary.

605. Loth, J., "Étude sur le cryptogramme de Bamberg," *Revue Celtique* 14 (1893), p. 91, p. 352.

606. Loth, J., "Un Nouveau Cryptogramme," *Annales de Bretagne* 8 (November 1893), pp. 289–293.

607. Stokes, W., "The Cryptogram in the Cambridge Juvencus," *Academy* 42, no. 1062 (1892), p. 215.

The solution to the Dubthach cryptogram in the Bamberg MS can also be used to decipher a marginal entry in the eighth or ninth century MS of Juvencus in the Cambridge University Library.

608. Stokes, Whitley M., "On a Medieval Cryptogram," *The Academy* 42 (July 1892), pp. 71–72.

Oghams

Ogham is form of Celtic writing that occasionally used cryptographic forms. Ogham survives chiefly in inscriptions on tombstones. Its alphabet consists of five groups of five letters, represented by one to five lines extending away from a horizontal line. In the first group, the lines extend above the horizontal line; in the second group, below it; in the third, perpendicularly above and below; in the fourth, diagonally above and below; the fifth group is heterogeneous. Methods for enciphering them are catalogued in the *Book of Ballymote*, a fifteenth century compilation of historical and genealogical information. See the three articles by Charles Graves (nos. **366**, **367**, **368**).

One of the most charming things about ogham is the name it uses for its systems. One is called "the ogham that bewildered Bres" that comes from a story about a message written in this script that was given to the ancient hero Bres who was going into battle. He was so confused by the message, that he lost the battle while trying to figure it out. "Sanctuary ohgam" puts a stroke between every pair of letters. "Serpent through the heather" runs a wavy line above and below the successive letters. "Great speckle" has a single mark of appropriate slant and length for the letter, followed by as many dots, less one, as there are strokes in the letter. In "twinned ogham" each letter is doubled; in "host ogham" it is tripled. "Vexation of a poet's heart" reduces the lines to short marks extending beyond an empty rectangle. In "point against eye," the alphabet is reversed. In "fraudulent ogham" the letters are replaced by symbols one step further on. There is even a system in which the chaotic order of the substitutes seems to have resulted from an infuriated Irishman's knocking them about with a shillelagh, called "Outburst of rage ogham." David Kahn does not believe any of these actually enciphered ogham but were just dreamed up for fun.

On the bottom of one of the pages of the *Book of Ballymote*, there is written in another system called Bricrui's ogham, what seems to be the fragment of an ancient Druidic liturgy—probably the only one known to the modern world, and appropriately, the one type of document that might have used encipherment to conceal the text. See David Kahn, *The Codebreakers* (no. **38**), p. 88, and p. 990n.

609. Anders Ahlqvist, *The Early Irish Linguist*, Commentationes Humanarum Litterarum 73 (1982), Helsinki: Societas Scientiarum Fennica, 81 pp. esp 7ff on the ogham alphabet.

610. Atkinson, Robert (ed.), *The Book of Ballymote* [a facsimile], Dublin: Royal Irish Academy House, 1887, pp. 311–314.

611. Calder, George (ed.), *Auraicept na n-eces; The Scholar's Primer*, Edinburgh: John Grant, 1917, pp. 272–299, 300–319.

612. Diringer, David, *The Alphabet, a key to the history of mankind*, New York: Philosophical Library, 1949. Appendix to Chapter IX, Runes and Oghams.

613. Macalister, Robert Alexander Stewart, *The Secret Languages of Ireland*, with special reference to the origin and nature of the Shelta language, partly based upon collections and manuscripts of the late John Sampson, Cambridge: Cambridge University Press, 1937, pp. 18–19, 28, 38–59.

Pages 37–61 are entirely on Celtic cryptology.

614. MacCarthy, Bartholemeo, *The Codex palatino-vaticanus, no. 830*, Dublin: Academy House, 1892, 450 pp. 121 ff. is the Book of Ballymote.

Bacon Cipher

Roger Bacon, the English monk, was the only writer in the Middle Ages to describe cryptography but never actually use it. In this Epistle, written around the middle of the 13th century, he stated: "A man is crazy who writes a secret in any other way than one which will conceal it from the vulgar." He then lists seven deliberately vague methods of doing so. Among them are the use of consonants only, figurate expressions, letters from exotic alphabets, invented characters, shorthand, and "magic figures and spells."

Some believe Roger Bacon to be the author of the Voynich Manuscript (nos. **623–631**), but this is neither proven not generally accepted, especially by those who think it is a 16th century and not a 13th century manuscript. The works below will get one started on an investigation into the subject.

615. Bacon, Sir Roger, *Roger Bacon's Letter Concerning the Marvelous Power of Art and of Nature and Concerning Nullity of Magic*, trans. Tenney L. Davis, Easton: Chemical Publishing Company, 1923, pp. 39–41.

616. Newbold, William Romaine, *The Cipher of Roger Bacon*, edited with foreword and notes by Roland Grubb Kent, Philadelphia: University of Pennsylvania Press, 1928, 224 pp.

One of the most extensive discussions of the so-called Roger Bacon cipher, but it convinced no one.

617. Thorndike, Lynn, *A History of Magic and Experimental Science during the First Thirteen Centuries of our Era*, New York: Columbia University Press, 1964–66, Volume 2, Chapter 41, pp. 659–661.

Runes

A form of writing that flourished in Scandinavia and in Anglo-Saxon Britain during the seventh, eighth and ninth centuries. Runes were nearly always used for religious purposes. A stark, angular script, its alphabet was divided into three groups of eight runic letters. The letter thorn, for example, which looked something like a modern *þ* and represented the initial sounds of "thin" and "then," was the third letter of the first group. All systems of runic cryptography replaced runic letters by groups of marks indicating the number of a letter's group and the number of its place in that group. *Isruna* used the short *I* rune, a short vertical stroke named "is," to give the number of the group, and the long *I* rune to give the place number. Thus thorn—group 1, letter 3—would be replaced by a single short vertical mark and three longer vertical marks.

Another system of runic cryptography, *hahalruna*, attached diagonal strokes representing these numbers to a vertical shaft, putting the group marks on the left, the place marks on the right. Sometimes shafts were crossed.

Other variations on this theme were *lagoruna*, *stopfruna*, and *clopfruna*. Cryptographic runes occur in many places, most profusely on the Rök stone, a 13-foot high slab of granite standing at the western end of the Rök churchyard in Sweden. It includes among its more than 770 runic letters, a veritable catalogue of runic cryptography.

There are over 517 articles on runes listed in the *International Medieval Bibliography* from 1971–1996.

618. Antonsen, Elmer H., "Runes and Romans on the Rhine," *Amsterdamer Beiträge zur älteren Germanistik* 45 (1996), pp. 5–13 who rejects the Roman influence theory. Good bibliography and summary of the state of our knowledge.

619. Derolez, Rene, *Runica Manuscripta: The English Tradition*, Bruges: De Tempel, 1954, 60, 89, 133–146.

620. Diringer, David, *The Alphabet, A Key to the History of Mankind*, New York: Philosophical Library, 1949. Appendix to Chapter IX, Runes and Oghams with extensive bibliography.

621. Elliott, Ralph W.V., *Runes: An Introduction*, Manchester: Manchester University Press, 1959), pp. 1–2, 43–44, 85, 107; 9 (1981 edition published by Westport, Conn.: Greenwood Press).

Kahn, David, *The Codebreakers*. See entry **38**.

622. Stephens, George, *Handbook of the Old-Northern Runic Monuments of Scandinavia and England*, Edinburgh: Williams and Norgate, 1884, Vol. 3, pp. 42–47.

The Voynich Manuscript

Dubbed "the most mysterious manuscript in the world," this work is described by David Kahn as: "The longest, the best known, the most tantalizing, the most heavily attacked, the most resistant, and the most expensive of historical cryptograms…" The book is a large octavo of 6 × 9 inches, containing 204 pages (another 28 are lost). Its cover is missing, and the vellum pages are filled with drawings of tiny female nudes, astrological diagrams, and about 400 drawings of fanciful plants colored in blue, dark red, light yellow, brown, and an especially vivid green. The book resembles an herbal, like the ones common in the Middle Ages, that listed plants with medicinal properties and recipes for extracting drugs from them. But this is where any resemblance to a normal Medieval manuscript ends.

Palaeographers do not recognize the script; linguists do not recognize the language; Cryptanalysts have performed frequency counts and come up with little. Scholars from the Vatican, specialists in botany and chemistry, Medievalists, professors of anatomy, and Bacon scholars have all failed. We do not know its author, its date, or even if it is authentic.

Among the most noted public attempts to solve the mystery were some made by the following authors:

Newbold, William Romaine, *The Cipher of Roger Bacon.*

His interpretation was at first accepted by John Matthews Manly in "The Most Mysterious Manuscript in the World," *Harper's Magazine*, 143 (June 21, 1921) pp. 186–197, but Manly later attacks it in: *Idem*, "Roger Bacon and the Voynich Manuscript," *Speculum* 6 (July 1931), pp. 345–391. Newbold is also attacked by J. Malcolm Bird, "The Roger Bacon Manuscript," *Scientific American Monthly* 3 (June 1921), pp. 492–496.

The French scholar of Francis Bacon, Raoul Carton, accepted Newbold's theory.

623. Carton, Raoul, "Le chiffre de Roger Bacon," *Revue d'histoire de la Philologie* (August 1928), pp. 31–66, and 165–179.

624. O'Neill, Hugh, "Botanical Observations on the Voynich Manuscript," *Speculum* (January 1944), pp. 126–7.

A discussion of the plant drawings in the manuscript.

The manuscript's history and a description of the various decryption attempts can be found in David Kahn, *The Codebreakers* (no. **38**) pp. 863–872. The manuscript now resides in the Beinicke Rare Book Room and Library at Yale, Ms 408. There is an entire website devoted to the manuscript that also contains a history, and an up-to-date bibliography: www.voynich.nu/history.html.

625. Strong, Leonell C., "Anthony Askam, the author of the Voynich Manuscript," *Science* N.S. 101, no. 2633 (June 15, 1945), pp. 6–8–9.

Dr. Leonell C. Strong, a highly respected cancer research specialist, believed that Anthony Ascham, an English scholar and author of an herbal, is also the author of the Voynich Manuscript. He does not explain his method of cryptanalysis and this conclusions have been severely attacked on philological grounds.

626. Brumbaugh, Robert S., *The World's Most Mysterious Manuscript*. Carbondale: Southern Illinois University Press, 1978. London: Weidenfeld and Nicholson, 1977.

627. D'Imperio, M.E. (ed.), *New Research on the Voynich Manuscript*: Proceedings of a Seminar, 30 November 1976. Privately printed pamphlet, Washington, D.C., 1976.

628. D'Imperio, M.E., *The Voynich Manuscript: An Elegant Enigma*, Fort George G. Meade, Md.: National Security Agency, 1978. (Reprinted by Aegean Park Press, Laguna Hills, Ca., 1980.)

629. Feely, J.M., *Roger Bacon's Cipher*, Rochester, New York, self published, 1943.

An unconvincing attempt to decipher the cipher of Roger Bacon and the Voynich Manuscript.

630. Guy, Jacques, "Statistical Properties of Two Folios of the Voynich Manuscript," *Cryptologia* 15 (1991).

631. Reeds, Jim, "William F. Friedman's Transcription of the Voynich Manuscript," *Cryptologia* 19 (1995).

The Islamic World

The Arab empires copied the Roman example and set up intelligence networks throughout their territories that allowed them to monitor their subjects and their enemies alike. Al-Omari in his treatise on government and statecraft entitled *al-Tarif* refers to the state intelligence system as: "The wings of Islam which cannot be trimmed and the tip of its wings which cannot be cut off" (Dvornik p. 227). Such networks were set up for the exclusive use of the Sultan as a rapid information service. It had no commercial or economic ties, but was exclusively military or administrative in character. The sultan, as supreme commander of the army and chief of state, demanded to be informed of all enemy movements, and all subversive movements.

Cryptography was actually invented by the Arabs. They were the first to discover and write down methods of cryptanalysis. In fact, the word cipher is an Arabic word. Arabic literary works included riddles, rebuses, puns, anagrams, and similar word games. Grammar study became popular, and with it secret writing. Moslem states used ciphers in some rare cases for political purposes, but they did not have codes. They may have derived the practice from the Persian empire, upon which they modeled much of their administration. The general lack of continuity in Islamic states, however, and the consequent absence of a permanent civil service and to permanent embassies in other countries militated against cryptography's more widespread use.

A system called *qirmeh* was a special cryptography used by tax officials. It first appeared in Egypt in the 16th century, and most of the financial records in Istanbul, Syria and Egypt until the latter part of the 19th century were written in *quirmeh.* It was used only in documents pertaining to tax affairs, in order to keep revenue information secret.

General

632. Abu Bakr Muhammed b. Yahya as-Suli, *Adab al-kuttab*, Beirut, Lebanon: Dar al-Kutub al'Ilmiyah, 1994, 328 pp.

This list encompassed, for the first time in cryptography, both transposition and substitution systems, and, moreover, gave, in system 5, the first cipher ever to provide more than one substitute for a plaintext letter.

633. Bosworth, C.E., *The Ghaznavids*, Edinburgh University Press, 1963, p. 95.

A few documents with cipher text survive from the Ghaznavid government of conquered Persia, and one chronicler reports that high officials were supplied with a personal cipher before setting out for new posts.

See also: Baihaqi, *Tarikh I Mas'udi*, ed. Ghani and Faiyad, Tehran, 1324/1945–6), pp. 654–655, 688. David Kahn, *Codebreakers* (no. **38**), pp. 95 and note.

634. Bosworth, C.E., "The Section on Codes and Their Decipherment in Qalqashandi's Subh al-a sha," *Journal of Semitic Studies*, 8 (Spring, 1963), pp. 17–33.

A commentary on Arabic cryptography followed by large portions of the text in translation.

Qalqashandi attributed most of his information on cryptography to the writings of Taj ad-Din Ali ibn ad-Duraihim ben Muhammad ath-That alibi al-Mausili who lived from 1312 to 1361 and held various teaching and official posts under the

Mamlukes in Syria and Egypt. Except for a theological treatise, none of his writings is extant, but he is reported to have authored two works on cryptology. One was a poem, "Urjuza fi l'mutarjam," in a loose meter often used for didactic poems and perhaps chosen for mnemonic purposes. The other work consisted of a prose commentary on the poem "Miftah al-kunuz fi idah al-marmuz." David Kahn lists this as one of the lost books on cryptology, and believes most of its information is preserved in Qalqashandi. (*The Codebreakers*, p. 95).

There are scholars however, like John R. Walsh of the William Muir Institute in Edinburgh, who believe there never was a science of cryptology among the Arabs and uses the fact that Qalqashandi has no first hand information himself and that documents cannot be produced in archives that use his system. (See Davif Kahn, *Codebreakers*, [no. **38**], p. 992.)

This is certainly the best article on cryptography and cryptanalysis in the Islamic world. David Kahn considers it "the most important single article on the history of cryptography" (*The Codebreakers*, p. 992).

635. Casanova, M., "Alphabets Magiques Arabes," *Journal Asiatique*, 11th series, Vol. 17 (July–September, 1921), pp. 37–55.

In 1076, the copyist of a treatise on magic operations enciphered such words as "opium" using the alphabet called *dawoudi*. (ben Wahshiyya an-Nabati]. It was considered the magic alphabet par excellence, and was sometimes called *rihani*, a form of a word meaning "magic."

636. Colin, George S., "Note sur le système cryptographique du Sultan Ahmad al-Mansur," *Hesperis* 7 (1927), pp. 221–228.

In 1600, the Sultan of Morocco, Ahmad al-Mansur, sent an embassy headed by his confidential secretary, Abd al-Wahid ibn Mas'ud ibn Muhammad Anun, to Queen Elizabeth of England to ally himself with her against Spain. The ambassador reported back in a mono-alphabetically enciphered dispatch, which shortly thereafter apparently fell into the hands of an Arab, evidently intelligent, but as evidently ignorant of his great cryptological heritage. In a memorandum, he wrote:

"Praise be to Allah! Writing of the secretary 'Abd al-Wahid ibn Mas'ud Anun. I found a note written in his hand in which he had noted in secret characters some information destined for Our Protector Abu l'Abbas al-Mansur.... This information relates to the Sultana of the Christians (May God destroy them!) who was in the country of London in the year 1009 (= 1600–1601). From the moment when the note fell into my hands, I never stopped studying from time to time the signs which it bore.

"...About 15 years more or less passed, until the moment when God (Glory to Him!) did me the favor of permitting me to comprehend these signs, although no one taught them to me...."

Kahn notes that Ibn ad-Duraihim could have solved this in a few hours. *The Codebreakers* p. 99.

637. Decourdemanche, M.J.A., "Note sur quatre systèmes turcs de notation numérique secrète," *Journal Asiatique*, 9th series, XIV (September–October, 1899), pp. 258–271.

See pp. 267–269 that describe one of the classic substitution alphabets. This one survived as late as 1775, when it was used in a spy letter to the regent of

Algiers. This script is known in Turkey as "Misirli" ("Egyptian"), in Egypt as "Shami" ("Syrian"), and in Syria as "Tadmuri" ("Palmyrene").

Dvornik, Francis, *The Origins of Intelligence Services*, New Brunswick, N.J. Rutgers University Press, 1974, 334 pp. Dvornik's chapter 4, pp. 188–261, has an excellent discussion of the postal services of the Arab Muslim empires. See entry **3**.

638. Hartmann, R., "Politische Geographie des Mameluckenreichs," *Zeitschrift der deutschen Morgenländisches Gesellschaft* 70 (1916), pp. 1ff, 477ff.

Two-part article on the political geography of the Mameluk empire. Part one, p. 81 has a section on signalling and relay stations. The second part, pp. 477–511, discusses the state post using camels, sea transportation, carrier pigeons, and fire signals.

639. Hartmann, R., "Zur Geschichte der Mamlukenpost," *Orientalische Literaturzeitung* 46 (1943), col. 266–270.

Review of Sauvaget's work, *La Poste aux chevaux dans l'empire des Mamelouks*, Paris, Adrien-Maissoneuve, 1941 (see no. **648**). A study of the postal service (*barid*) in the empire of the Mamelouks (1250–1517).

640. Hugounet, Paul, *La Poste des Califes et la Poste du Shah*, Paris: Union Générale de la Librairie, 1884.

Hugounet begins with a discussion of the communications systems of Alexander the Great and the Romans then moves quickly to the caliphs and shahs of Persia, Arabia and Turkey under the Sultans up to the nineteenth century.

French translation of K. Thieme's essays on Arab post in *Archiven für Post Und Telegraph*, pp. 54–103.

641. Ibn ad-Duraihim ben Muhammed ath-Tha alibi al-Mausili,Taj ad-Din Ali.

Author of two works on cryptography. Neither is extant, but the contents are supposedly summarized in Qalqashandi who attributes to him seven systems of cipher. As described by David Kahn, *The Codebreakers*, p. 96, they are:

1) One letter may replace another.

2) The cryptographer may write a word backward. Muhammad in the consonantal Arabic alphabet would become DMHM.

3) He may reverse alternate letters of the words of a message.

4) He may give the letters their numerical value in the system in which the Arabic letters are used as numbers and then write this value in Arabic numerals. Muhammad becomes 40+8+40+4, and the cryptogram looks like a list of figures.

5) The cryptographer may replace each plaintext letter with two Arabic letters, whose numerical value adds up to the numerical value of the plaintext letter. Qalqashandi adds that: other letters can be used, so long as they add up to the number of the original letter.

6) He may substitute for each letter the name of a man or something like that.

7) The cryptographer may employ the lunar mansions as substitutes for the letters, or list the names of countries, fruits, trees, etc. in a certain order, or draw birds or other living creatures, or simply invent special symbols as ciphertext replacements.

The similarity of this list to Ibn Khaldun's suggests that both writers took their information from a 10th century manual for secretaries by Abu Bakr Muhammad ben Yahya as-Suli who gave both the bird and lunar substitutions, reporting that they are Persian in origin.

642. Kazem-Zadeh, H., "Les chiffres Siyak et la Comptabilité Persane," *Revue du Monde Musulman* 30 (1915), pp. 1–51.

Describes ciphered forms of numerals in Persian financial accounts called siyak. Compare to the Arabic system, *qirmeh*, el Mouelhy (no. **645**).

643. Ibn Khaldun, Abd al-Rahman, *The Muqaddimah: An Introduction to History*, trans. Franz Rosenthal, Bollingen series 53, New York: Pantheon Books, 1958, 3 volumes.

Vol. 2, pp. 391–392 notes that officials of the government tax and army bureaux used a very special code among themselves, which is like a puzzle. It makes use of forms different from the accepted forms of the letters. Such a code is agreed upon by the correspondents between themselves, in order to be able to convey their thoughts in writing. The names of the birds recalls the Persian system that also used them, and points to a Persian origin for at least this cipher, and by implication for others.

cf. David Kahn, *The Codebreakers*, p. 94–95.

644. al-Khalil ibn Ahmad ibn Amr ibn Tammam al Farahidi al-Zadi al Yahmadi, Abd al-Rahman.

Kitab al-mu-amma ("Book of Secret Languages").

The Arab world's first great philologist, and the first man to conceive the idea of a comprehensive dictionary was "the shining light of the school of Basra" (Kahn). He lived in AD 718/719 to between 786 and 791. His secret book is now lost. In it, was a solution to a cryptogram in Greek sent to him by the Byzantine emperor. When he was asked how he managed to solve it, he answered: "I said to myself, the letter must begin "in the name of God or something of that sort. So I worked out its first letters on that basis, and it came right for me."

This description, and the fact that it took him a month before he could solve it, suggests that the Arabs had not yet formulated the more analytical techniques of cryptanalysis based upon letter-frequency. By the time Ibn Ad-Duraihim came along 600 years later, these studies had become sophisticated enough to enable others to apply them and used them to find the solution to ciphers.

Kahn believes that Durahim's discussion of cryptanalysis as reflected in Qalqashandi is so mature, that it implies a fairly long preceding period of development. See David Kahn, *The Codebreakers* (no. **38**), p. 97–98.

645. el Mouelhy, Ibrahim, "Le Qirmeh en Égypte," *Bulletin de l'Institut de l'Égypte* 29 (1946–47), pp. 51–82.

Qirmeh was a special cryptography used by tax officials. It simplified the forms of the Arabic letters, reduced the size of their bodies and elongated their trails. It dropped diacritic points, ran words together, and sometimes imposed or intermingled them, and abbreviated many words. It first appeared in Egypt in the 16th century, and was used only in documents pertaining to tax affairs in order to keep revenue information secret.

646. al-Qalqashandi, Shihab al-Din abu l'Abbas Ahmad ben Ali ben Ahmad, Abd Allah.

Qalqashandi lived in Egypt. His work, the *Subh al-a 'sha*, is an enormous 14-volume encyclopedia written to afford the secretary class a systematic survey of all the important branches of knowledge. It was completed in 1412 and evidently succeeded in its task.

He considers espionage "an important part of the basis of kingship and a pillar of the kingdom." He names the head of the Chancery as the pivot of espionage, and his is the task of choosing tasks and assigning men.

The cryptologic section "concerning the concealment of secret messages within letters" has two parts. One deals with symbolic actions and allusions, the other with invisible inks and cryptology. This section falls under a larger heading "On the technical procedures used in correspondence by the secretaries in eastern ands western lands and in the Egyptian territories, ranging over the whole period from the appearance of Islam up to our own time," which in turn, is within a unit headed "On the forms of correspondence."

Bosworth (no. **633**) Kahn (no. **38**). See most recently Bernard Lewis, *A Middle East Mosaic*, New York: Random House, 2001, p 283.

647. Sabbagh, Michel, *La colombe messagère plus rapide que la mouse*, transl. from the Arabic by A.I. Silvestre de Sacy, Paris, 1805, 95ff.

The history of the carrier pigeon. Starting with the variety of pigeons used, Sabbagh gives the history of their use from the earliest times, how to raise them train them and use them, and passages from literature mentioning them.

This is a rare book. Harvard University library has one of the few copies on microfilm.

648. Sauvaget, J., *La Poste aux chevaux dans l'empire des Mamelouks*, Paris, Adrien-Maissoneuve, 1941, 100 pp.

A study of the postal service (*barid*) in the empire of the Mamelouks (1250–1517). The word *barid* is derived from the Latin *veredus* (horse), meaning the horses used in the state post that the Arabs copied from the Romans. Our knowledge of the Mamelouk intelligence system because it is described in the Sirat of al-Quadi Muki al-din and in the treatise of al-Tarif composed by al-Ouari in 1348. Chapter six of this treatise, translated by Hartmann (no. **638**), is devoted to the history of the Arab post and its re-creation by Baybars. Baybars ruled over Egypt and Syria as far as the Euphrates. He appointed a vizier and expressed a desire for frequent information on the situation at the earliest date, especially on the movements among the Mongols and Franks. He is alleged to have said: "If you can achieve it I will have to pass not one morning and not one night without receiving a report from you...."

Good maps and illustrations of the routes as they were set up in Mamelouk territory.

649. Scanlon, George T., *A Muslim Manual of War*, ed. & trans. of Umar Ibn Ibrahim, Cairo: American University in Cairo, 1961, 97 pp.

The author was at first anonymous because no name appeared on the Istanbul manuscript that was thought to be unique until another copy was found in the Yahudah collection catalogued by Princeton. That later copy lists the author as Umar b. Ibrahim al-Awsi al-Ansari written in the reign of the Mamluk Sultan Faraj B. Barquq.

Some have described it as "reeking of the library and the court" rather than the camp and the battlefield, but it has much useful information on running spies. Book I, ch. 3 covers intelligence collection and transmission. It discusses fire signals, carrier pigeons, couriers on foot and on mounts and the use of informers and spies. Book II, ch. 1 tells how to judge the qualifications of good agents and spies—trustworthiness, keen intelligence, well-traveled sophistication. Chapter 2 tells how to honor and treat them. Chapter 3 talks of the management of spy networks and counterintelligence. Book III covers envoys, Book IV deceptions and stratagems, Book VIII discusses scouting parties, and Chapter XV scouting parties. One can see that the military supremacy of the Mamluks and Ottomans did not rely entirely on their use of weapons and tactics.

650. Siddiqi, Iqtidar Husain, "Espionage System of the Sultans of Delhi," *Studies in Islam* Vol. I, No. 2 (April 1964), pp. 92–100.

India has a long history of intelligence activities (Trevedi, no. **679**). Siddiqi writes about a previously neglected period of medieval Indian history, the Sultanate of Delhi (c. AD 1555). The intelligence system in the Mauryan Empire was known, but it was not the well-organized institution it became under the Sultans of Delhi. Their system included couriers, both mounted and on foot. They also used private informers who were placed in the houses of nobles both great and minor.

The Sultans were evidently equal opportunity employers since women seem to have played a large part in their system. They used slave girls, maid servants, perfume dealers and women of all sorts in disguise.

There are noble-born spies and slaves, and even an interesting group called "charming smilers" that suggests a certain amount of personal persuasion was involved. Among other things, spies were used to enforce the prohibition against wine. Most importantly they were used to prevent uprisings against the throne. Overthrow would mean anarchy, and with the administrative machinery paralyzed, the intelligence network would suffer a setback.

651. Sprenger, Aloys, *Die Post- und Reiserrouten des Orients* (Abhandlungen der Deutschen Mordenländischen Gesellschaft, III Band, No. 3) Mit 16 Karten nach einheimischen Quellen, Leipzig: F. A. Brockhaus, 1864, 159 pp.

The most complete study of the postal system and travel routes of Syria, Mesopotamia, Persia, Iraq, Armenia, and the sea communications of the Near East with India and Persia. A very useful set of maps showing the routes accompanies the text.

652. Ibn Wahsh iyah, Ahmad ibn Ali, *Kitab shauq al-mustaham fi ma'rifat rumuz al-aqlam* ("Book of the Frenzied Devotee's Desire to Learn About the Riddles of Ancient Scripts"). This book has been translated by Joseph Hammer as *Ancient Alphabets and Hieroglyphic Characters Explained*, London: W. Bulmer & Co., 1806, 136 pp.

A ninth century text on ancient alphabets and hieroglyphic characters. He included several traditional cipher alphabets used for magic. One alphabet, called *dawoudi*, meaning "Davidian," from the name of the King of Israel, was developed from Hebrew letters by changes in cursive form, by adding tails to letters, or by dropping parts of them.

A difficult book to find. The Peabody Library in Baltimore has a copy, and the Library of Congress has it on microfilm plus two copies in the Rare Book, Special Collections Division.

653. Wiet, G. "Les communications en Égypte au Moyen Âge," *L'Égypte contemporaine*, 24 (1933), pp. 241–264.

Wiet examines various means of communication in Egypt during the Middle Ages. He starts with the roads used by the agricultural population to get from one village to another. He then goes on to discuss commercial traffic along the Nile, pilgrimage routes for those going to Mecca, and finally the postal system

We see quickly that the communications system took on a political character. The Egyptians inherited the Byzantine system called the *veredus*, which becomes *barid* in Arabic. The head of the *barid* was an important governmental official who ran essentially an intelligence service. Wiet compares them to the Carlingian *missi dominici*. He traces the system through the first caliphs and finally to the Mamluks. He ends with a discussion of carrier pigeons for very special communications.

For a further discussion of the Mamluk postal system, see Francis Dvornik, *The Origins of Intelligence Services* (no. **3**) chapter 4; on carrier pigeons, see Hans Fischl (no. **25**).

654. Wüstenfeld, F. "Eine arabische Geheimschrift," *Nachrichten von der Gesellschaft der Wissenschaften und der Georg-Augusts-Universität (Göttingen)* (1879), pp. 349–355.

In a manuscript on the art of war, probably dating to the 14th century and of Egyptian origin, there is a cipher concealing the crucial ingredients of compounds to be hurled into besieged strongholds. Reproduces the original Arabic text. See also Greek fire (nos. **542–559**).

Yezidis

This obscure sect of about 25,000 people in northern Iraq use a cryptic script in their holy books because they fear persecution by their Moslem neighbors. The following books will give the reader a general idea of their beliefs, the documents we use to study their practices, and their use of cryptography.

655. Ahmed, Sami Said, *The Yazidis, their life and beliefs*, edited by Henry Field, Miami: Field Research Projects, 1975, 485 pp.

Chapter 4 is about the Yazidi holy scriptures, and the appendix contains translations of the important Yazidi scriptures, prayers, and public documents.

656. Diringer, David, *The Alphabet: A Key to the History of Mankind*, 2nd ed. New York: Philosophical Library, 1949.

657. Guest, John S. *The Yezidis: a study of survival,* London and New York: Routledge and Kegan Paul, 1987, 299 pp.

Chapter 10 discusses the sacred texts and their publication. There is a good bibliography at the end.

658. Layard, Austen Henry, *Nineveh and Its Remains*, New York: G.P. Putnam, 1849.

Russia, China India, Africa

The East has produced some interesting intelligence organizations, beginning with postal communications services and including secret services. These are just a few of the works describing them. My own lack of eastern languages prevents a more thorough collection from China, Japan, or Southeast Asia.

Russia

659. Alef, G., "The Origin and Early Development of the Muscovite Postal Service," *Jahrbücher für Geschichte Osteuropas*, N.F. 15 (1967), pp. 1–15.

Travel and the movement of information in 16th century Russia was aided by a postal service that included a road system, horses and couriers. The government demanded speed of its messengers and a rather brisk pace for ambassadors. Travel was hazardous especially on the southern steppe where reports of assault, robbery, ransom and murder were common. Travel along approved roads with the proper documents was safer, suggesting a higher degree of internal order on policed roads.

Alef gives a good summary of the postal services in western Europe and concludes that by the end of the 15th century, the Muscovite government had established one of the best systems of internal communication to be found in Europe. In time, the post service would be extended along the main roads to every corner of the developing empire.

660. Amanelishvili, L.A., "Gruzino-Grecheskie kriptogramy v Gruzinskikh rukopiyakh Xv," (Georgian-Greek Cryptograms in Georgian MSS 10th c," *Problemy paleografii kodokologii v SSSR*, 1974, pp. 403–408.

Georgian cryptograms appear in tenth century manuscripts. They were derived from Greek cryptograms and Hebrew *atbash*.

661. Arkhipov, A.A., "O proiskhozhdenii Drevneslavianksoi toinopisi" (The origins of Old Slavonic Cryptograms," *Sovetskoe Slavyanovedenie*, Akademiya Nauk SSSR 6 (1980), pp. 79–86.

There were two types of Old Slavonic Cryptograms, all of them of Greek or Hebrew origin. The author believes they had their origin in Hebrew cabalistic methods (*atbash*, no. **61**). They were used to emphasize the significance of important parts of the text. It was a kind of "angel language" and they used it to get magic strength for exorcisms and charms. Sometimes it was used to pass secret information.

662. *Armenia.*

In Armenia in the 16th century, two scribes employed a Polybius-like checkerboard to inject an air of special hidden knowledge into religious texts. A third scribe composed his ciphertext by writing two letters, whose numerical value equaled that of the plaintext letter-z, with value 6, became GG, each G having a value of 3. See David Kahn, *The Codebreakers* (no. **38**), p. 85, p. 989n. Werner Winter, "Armenian Cryptography: Notes on Some Samples in the Collection of H. Kurdian, Wichita, Kansas," *The Armenian Review*, 8 (Autumn, 1955), pp. 53–56.

663. Brückner, A., "Russisches Postwesen im 17 und 18 Jahrhundert," *Zeitschrift für allgemeine Geschichte* vol. 1 (1884), pp. 881–907.

Précis of J. P. Chruscova, *K istorii russkich post* II (St. Petersburg, 1884) (*Zur Geschichte der russischen Post.* Die Fahr- und Briefpost von den ältesten Zeiten bis zur Regierung Katharinas II). He cites another work by Fabricius entitled *Die Post und die Volkswirtschaft in Russland im 17 Jahrhundert*, (St. Petersburg, 1864) (in Russian). The Russian postal system resembled eastern models (Persia? Byzantium?) in that it was a system for sending and gathering information by the rulers of the Russian state. Evidently the postal system could do the 900 kilometers from Kiev to Moscow in 15–20 days.

China and Southeast Asia

664. Chao, Y. R., "Eight Varieties of Secret Language Based on the Principle of Fanchieh," *Bulletin of the Institute of History and Philology*, Academia Sinica II (1931) 312–354.

An article on oral secrecy, in Chinese.

665. *Malaya.*

In Malaya, natives call their secret script or cryptographic alphabet the *gangga malayu.* It consists of the slightly altered or inverted characters of the Malayan Arabic alphabet, with some Javanese marks.

See David Kahn, *The Codebreakers* (no. **38**), p. 85, and p. 989n.

R.A. Kern, "A Malay Cipher Alphabet," *The Journal of the Royal Anthropological Institute of Great Britain and Ireland*, 38 (1908), pp. 207–211 and plate xvii explains the system well but includes no further bibliography.

666. Needham, Joseph, *Science and Civilisation in China*, Cambridge: Cambridge University Press, 1971, Volume IV, part 3.

See pp. 34–38 on the Post-station system that Needham rightly says is exactly what a government does once it "attains an imperial level of organization." He argues that such governmental intelligence systems existed in China as far back as the Shang Dynasty. The most common form and the terminology that goes with it date to the Han Dynasty.

667. Olbricht, P., *Das Postwesen in China unter der Mongolenherrschaft im 13 und 14 Jahrhundert*, Göttinger asiatische Forschungen, vol. I, Wiesbaden, 1954, 111 pp.

The largest land empire in the world could not have functioned without a communications system to carry military intelligence. Post-horse stations along the imperial highways became a major task of the Mongol Empire. The organization was initiated by Jenghiz Khan and is mentioned in his *Yasaq*. Each station or *jam* was erected at a distance of a day's journey and had to be provided with as many as twenty horses. They also provided fodder for the animals and food and drink for the travelers. Officials made an annual inspection of each *jam*. The service was free for the use of ambassadors and the khan's messengers. The Khan levied post service taxes and duties, and a levy of cattle and forage on local residents. The imperial messengers, called "arrow-messengers," rode with bandaged head and trunk in order to make known their character and the importance of their message. Subotai is said to have ridden 1,200 miles, using this system, in a little more than a week.

668. Sawyer, Ralph and Mei chün-Lee, *The Tao of Spycraft; Intelligence Theory and Practice in Traditional China,* Boulder, CO: Westview Press, 1998. Notes. Index. Pp. xvi, 617.

As the authors themselves point out "No nation has practiced the craft of intelligence or theorized about it more extensively than China..." and yet so little has been written about it. Except for Richard Deacon's *Chinese Secret Service* that deals mostly with internal security matters in modern China no treatments exists of ancient Chinese espionage. The Sawyers have collaborated on the daunting task of scanning China's military classics and its twenty-five dynastic histories to produce the first thorough discussion of the theory and practice of intelligence operations. While most western readers, and especially military scholars, are familiar with Sun Tzu's *Art of War*, the Sawyers' discussion includes theoretical military manuals previously unknown in the West. REVIEWED BY: R.M. Sheldon, *Journal of Military History*, vol. 63, No. 2 (1999) pp. 432–435.

669. *Siam* (Thailand).

The cryptography of Thailand developed under Indian influence. An embryonic study of the subject even appears in a grammatical work entitled Poranavakya by Hluang Prasot Aksaraniti (phe). One system, called "the erring Siamese," substitutes one Siamese letter for another. In another system, consonants are divided into seven groups of five letters; a letter is indicated by writing the number of its group and placing vertical dots under it equal in number to the letter's place in its group. A system called "the hermit metamorphosing letters" writes the text backwards. See David Kahn, *The Codebreakers* (no. **38**), p. 85, p. 989n, and O. Frankfurter, "Secret Writing in Siamese," *The Journal of the Siam Society* 3 (1906), pp. 62–72.

670. Sun Tzu, *Art of War*, translated and with introduction and commentary by Ralph D. Sawyer and Mei-chün Lee Sawyer, Boulder, Co.: Westview Press, 1994, pp. 375.

A classic work on the art of war. First translated into French by a missionary roughly 200 years ago, it was reportedly studied and used effectively by Napoleon. For two thousand years it remained the most important military treatise in Asia and was studied by Chinese, Japanese and Korean military theorists and professional soldiers. Chapter 13 on "Employing spies" describes five kinds of spies: local, internal, double agents, dead (expendable) and the living spy.

671. *Tibetans.* The Tibetans use a kind of cipher called "rin-spuns" for official correspondence. It is named for its inventor Rin-c'(hhen)spuns(-pa), who lived in the 1300s. David Diringer, *The Alphabet: A Key to the History of Mankind*, 2nd ed. New York: Philosophical Library, 1949, chapter 6.

India

672. Akhtar, Jamna Das, *Pak Espionage in India*, Delhi: Oriental Publishers, 1971.

Only chapter one deals with ancient espionage—a mere 16 pages. In that small space he discusses references in the *Rig Veda* and the *Avesta*, Indian spies in Asia Minor, training spies in ancient Taxila, Chandra Gupta and Kautilya and spies mentioned in the *Arthasastra* and even a section on beautiful girls as spies.

673. Basham, A. L., *The Wonder That Was India*, 1954 Reprinted New York: Grove Press, 1959, pp. 121–22.

Describes ancient India's espionage system as "the least pleasant feature of political life." This section summarizes the sections of the Arthasastra of Kautilya who describes the country as riddled from top to bottom with secret agents and spies. They were organized through "institutes of espionage" to which they delivered information, sometimes in cipher, and from which they received their orders.

The Indian intelligence establishment was an equal opportunity employer. Spies were recruited from all walks of life and such work was open to both genders. There was even a special class of spy called a satr, an orphan trained from childhood for the work, and usually masquerading as a holy-man or fortuneteller, two professions whose members were especially trusted by the public.

674 Bayly, C. A., *Empire and Information: Intelligence Gathering and Social Communication in India, 1780-1870*, Cambridge, 1996, 412 pp.

Bayly examines British political intelligence in north India between the 1780s and 1860s. It describes the networds of Indian running-spies, newswriters and secretaries whom the officials of the East India Company recruited and employed in their efforts to secure military, political and social information. It also considers how the colonial authorities interpreted and misinterpreted the material derived from these sources. It is particularly good on the gaps, distortions and panics about "malignant native plots" that afflicted the system of imperial surveillance within north India and also outside its borders in Nepal, Burma and beyond the northwestern frontier. Finally, the book examines the extent to which intelligence failures and successes contributed to the course of the Rebellion of 1857–9, the collapse of the East India Company's government and the form of the following pacification.

675. Chakrabotry, Gayatri, *Espionage in Ancient India from the Earliest Time to the 12th century A.D.*, Calcutta: Minerva Associates, 1990, 153 pp.

A systematic survey of espionage in ancient India from the earliest times to the downfall of the Hindu dynasties with special reference to northern India. The author makes no reference to Trivedi's 1984 work (no. **679**) that actually deals with the material from Kautilya's *Arthasastra* in more detail. Chakraborty begins his history with the Indus Valley civilization. A chapter is devoted to espionage during the historical period (400 BC to AD 1200) and follows with a chapter each on military espionage and ambassadors and diplomatic intelligence. There is even a small section on espionage in Buddhist works.

676. Ganguly, Anil Baran, *Sixty-four Arts in Ancient India*, New Delhi: The English Book Store, 1962, pp. 168–174.

Ganguly lists three branches of the art of secret communication from ancient India. The first involves telegraphing signals by means of pre-arranged codes. The second is secret speech. The third is hand signals.

677. Kautilya, *The Arthasastra*, edited, rearranged and introduced by L.N. Rangarajan, London: Pengiun Books, 1987, 868 pp. See also Narasingha P. Sil, *Kautilya's Arthasastra. A Comparative Study*, New York: Peter Lang, 1985, 173 pp.

Kautilya was the Brahman minister of the emperor Chandragupta Maurya (321–297 BC). He ranks as the first great Indian empire builder. His minister, Kautilya may rival his fame. Known as the "Indian Machiavelli," he may have been the real architect of Mauryan rule. He was probably not the real author of this work on the art of government, but it is attributed to him. Lost to historians, the text was only rediscovered in 1909. It has many sections on spying, covert operations, running agents, and disguises.

678. *Maldive Islands.*

This isolated area in the Indian Ocean actually has two kinds of secret writing. *Harha tana* involves reciprocal substitution between consecutive letters of their alphabet, the *gabuli tana*, so that h = rh and rh=h, and so forth, the first equivalent perhaps giving rise to the name of the system. "De-fa tana" effects substitutions between the halves of the *gabuli tana*. David Kahn, *The Codebreakers*, p. 85, and p. 989n, and David Diringer, *The Alphabet: A Key to the History of Mankind*, 2nd ed. New York: Philosophical Library, 1949, chapter 6.

Siddiqi, Iqtidar Husain, "Espionage System of the Sultans of Delhi," *Studies in Islam* Vol. I, No. 2 (April, 1964), pp. 92–100. See entry **650**.

679. Trivedi, S. I., *Secret Service in Ancient India*, New Delhi, 1984, 291 pp.

Spying is mentioned in the Vedas, the most ancient of Indian texts. Trivedi, a police officer, has a master's degree in Ancient Indian History and Archaeology, and did his D.Phil. thesis on "The Organization and Role of Police in Ancient India." Here he expands his work to include secret services. He draws mainly on Kautilya's *Arthasastra* (no. **677**). It is a gold mine of information on spies and spying, internal security, counterintelligence and covert operations.

680. Vatsyayana, *The Kama Sutra,* translated by Sir Richard F. Burton, New York: Barnes and Noble Books, 1993.

This famous textbook on erotic subjects is the last place one would expect to find a treatise on cryptography. Yet the author lists secret writing as one of the 64 arts or yogas that women should know and practice. It is 45th in a list that begins with vocal music and runs through prestidigitation, the solution of verbal puzzles, and exercises in enigmatic poetry. One of the methods is letter substitutions based upon phonetic relations—the vowels become consonants, etc. Another kind of cipher alphabet called *muladeviya* existed in a written form and a spoken form that figures in Indian literature and was used by traders with geographical variations.

Africa

681. *Nsibidi*

A secret society in Nigeria that uses pictographic writing to keep it hidden from Europeans. It is used chiefly to express love in rather direct imagery, and samples appear to be at least as pornographic as they are cryptographic. See David Kahn, *The Codebreakers* (no. **38**), p. 85, and David Diringer, *The Alphabet: A Key to the History of Mankind*, 2nd ed. New York: Philosophical Library, 1949, chapter 9.

An Unsolved Cryptogram: The Sator Rebus

S A T O R		R O T A S
A R E P O		O P E R A
T E N E T	or	T E N E T
O P E R A		A R E P O
R O T A S		S A T O R

This word square is one of the oldest unsolved cryptograms in the world. Efforts to discover a solution for the sator-formula date as far back as the fourteenth or fifteenth century. The Bibliothèque Nationale in Paris possesses a manuscript of Byzantine origin with an attempt at a translation (see Seligman, *Satorformel* [no. **813**], p. 174). Serious modern investigation of its origin and nature began in 1881 with Köhler's article in *Zeitschrift für Ethnologie* (see no. **775**), and after almost 120 years of archaeological, philological and religious investigation, and much controversy, no conclusive solution has ever been found for this "magic square." I have given it its own section since the bibliography is so large and it spans both centuries and continents.

When Dornseiff wrote his study, the earliest text was thought to be a Coptic papyrus of the fourth or fifth century AD. However, archaeological excavations at Dura Europas on the Euphrates conducted by Rostovtzeff for Yale University in 1931–32 and by the French Academy of Inscriptions and Letters, turned up three more specimens on the walls of a military office that had originally been a Temple of Azzanathkona. This dated the square firmly to the Roman period. In the following year, a fourth specimen was found at Dura, and it was suggested that they must have been inscribed there before the Persians destroyed Dura soon after AD 256.

Five years after the Dura discoveries, Della Corte (no. **721–724**) while conducting excavations at Pompeii, came across a version written on a column near the amphitheater. With this example he was then able to restore a fragmentary example of the square found in 1929 from Pompeii, discovered in the house of Publius Paquius Proculus. In 1954 another specimen was found in Altofen, Budapest, which dated to the third century and was published by Szilagi.

Examples after the Roman period date from the sixth to the nineteenth century and were found spread over Europe, Africa and America (Jerphanion, *Recherches des Sciences Religieuses*, no. **769**). In France alone, it goes through an amazing history of having magical powers attributed to it. At first, the square simply appears in religious contexts. The earliest example is found in a Carolingian Bible of AD 822, which belonged to the monastery of Saint-Germain-des-Près (although there is a distinct possibility the formula is a gloss). In the twelfth century the formula is inscribed on the masonry of the Church of St. Laurent near Ardèche and in the keep of Loches. In the thirteenth century parchment of Aurillac, however, it apparently intercedes for those women in labor. By the fifteenth century the formula had become a touchstone against fire in the Châteaux of Chinon and of Jarnac and in the courthouse at Valbonnais. By the sixteenth century, it had become a cure for insanity and fever. The device has been found in a walled-up section of the chapel of Saint-Laurent in Rochmare,

Ardèche, the ruined convent of Santa Maria in Campomarzo in Verona, the church of Santa Lucia of Magliano in Aquila, the cathedral at Sienna, and the church of San Pietro ad Oratorium in Capestrano. (See Jerphanion, *La Formule Magique* no. **769**).

By the end of the Middle Ages, the prophylactic magic of the square was firmly established in the superstition of Italy, Serbia, Germany, Iceland and even North America. In Cappadocia in the time of the emperor Constantine VII Porphyrogenitus (913–959) the shepherds of the nativity are called Sator, Arepon and Teneton (Jerphanion, no. **771**). A Byzantine Bible of an earlier period interprets the square to contain the baptismal names of the three Magi—Ator, Sator and Peretoras (Jerphanion, no. **769**). Nor was the square confined to Europe alone. Examples have been found in Abyssinia and Nubia. The Nubia example was interpreted according to a Coptic phrase denoting the names of the nails of Christ's cross (Crum, *EEF*, no. **713**), and in the eleventh century, the five words were used in Abyssinia to denote the five wounds of Christ (Ludolf, no. **785**). In Germany it was used to put out fires—the formula was written on a disk that was thrown into the fire to extinguish it. An edict in 1743 by Duke Ernest Auguste of Saxe-Weimar ordered that all towns and villages should manufacture such fire disks to serve as a means of quenching conflagrations that endangered the community. In Bosnia the formula was used as a remedy for headache and for hydrophobia, and in Iceland it was scratched on the fingernails of patients as a cure for jaundice. The most recent examples come from nineteenth century South America where it was in used to cure dog-bites and snake-bites (Gardner no. **747**). Also enclaves of Germans in the Allegheny Mountains in the eastern United States used it to prevent fire, stop fits, and prevent miscarriages. (See J. Hampden Porter, no. **801**.)

The discovery of the *Pater Noster* solution led to general acceptance by the majority of reputable scholars. See Grosser (no. **751**), Agrell (no. **683**), and Frank (no. **742**) who were the first. Earlier attempts to pierce the secret of the square had either divided the individual words more or less arbitrarily or had rearranged the individual letters in anagrams ranging from pious prayers to diabolic incantations.

There seems to be no end to the attempts to interpret it. To paraphrase Atkinson (p. 419), in the mysterious region where religion, superstition, and magic meet, where words, numbers and letters are believed, if properly combined, to exert power over the processes of nature, the so-called Sator-formula will occupy a distinguished place.

682. _____, "A proposito della formula medioevale 'Sator arepo'," *Bibliofilia* 25½ (1923/1924), pp. 42–43.

Notes several medieval examples of the square and notes that often the author hides his own name in the enigma. Augusto Gaudenzi suggested *arepo* was really *aretro* and relates it to *alepe* in Dante's verse: *PapeSatan pape Satan aleppe*.

683. Agrell, S., "Runornas talmystik och dess antika förebild," *Skrifter utgivna av Vetenskaps Societeten i Lund*, 6 (1927), pp. 31ff.

Agrell thought that the *sator* formula represented an early Christian mysticism, and by calculating geometrically the numerical value of the letters of the figure (A=1 to X–21), he obtained the sum of 303, i.e. 3 × 101, the ternary number as a symbol of the Trinity. The theory met with some skepticism, since unlike Greek letters, Latin letters are not used as numbers. He also came to the *pater noster* solution independently of Grosser (no. **751**) and Frank (no. **742**).

684. Alcock, A., "A Coptic Magical Text," *Bulletin of the American Society of Papyrologists* 19 (1982) pp. 97–103.

The formula is found on an amulet believed to cure fevers.

685. Andrieu, "Le 'Carré Sator' étude nouvelle," in *Mémoires de l'Académie des Sciences, Arts et Belles-Lettres de Dijon* (1934 31ff; (1935) 15ff; (1937) 30ff.

Not available at press time.

686. Atkinson, Donald, "The Origin and Date of the 'Sator' Word-Square," *Journal of Ecclesiastical History* 2 (1951), p. 1–18.

Demolishes Carcopino's dating of the square to AD 177. The two texts from Pompeii show that the square was known by the late seventies of the first century. He believes *arapennis/arapennis*, on which the Celtic *arepo* depends may well be Italic. He suggests *arepo* is simply the palindrome of *opera* and, as such, a nonsense word. That both the wheeled plow and the wheeled harvesting machine are attested for Gaul strengthens the Gallic provenience.

687. Atkinson, Donald, "The Sator-Formula and the Beginnings of Christianity," *Bulletin of the John Rylands Library* 22 (1938), p. 419–434.

The oldest example of the *sator* formula was discovered on a fragment of wall plaster from a Roman house in Cirencester, Glos and is now in the Cirencester Museum. Atkinson includes a photograph of the fragment with this article. Atkinson reviews the immense bibliography on the subject and divides the main areas of investigation and evidence into five headings 1) place of origin of the amulet (Rome), 2) the Christian origin 3) the *pater noster* solution (see Grosser, no. **751**, p. 4) evidence from St. Mark's Gospel, 5) the alpha and omega abbreviations and 6) its use as a Christian amulet. He believes the odds against this solution being accidental are astronomical. The article provides a good discussion of the "state of research" up to 1938.

688. Baar, T. van den, "On the Sator Formula," In J.J. van Baak (ed.) *Signs of Friendship*. To Honour A.G.F. van Holk, Slavist, Linguist, Semiotician, Amsterdam, 1984, pp. 307–16.

Discusses the Russian *sator* squares. See also:

A.I. Sobolevsky, "Perevodnaya literatura Moskovskoi Rusi XIV–XVII vekov," *Sbornik Otdeleniya russkogo yazyka I slovesnosti Akademii nauk*, 74/1 (1903), p. 226.

D. Rovinsky, *Russkie narodnye kartinki*, Spb. 1881, iii, 87; iv, 581ff and the appended atlas iii, no. 798.

689. Bader, Richard-Ernst, "Sator arepo: Magie in der Volksmedizin," *Medizinhistorisches Journal* 22 (1987), pp. 115–134.

A discussion of the many forms of the *sator* formula used as charms to ward off evil or illness, or used as a cure for diseases or animal bites. Brings together much of the 19th century literature by Treichel and colleagues (nos. **818–828**). Interesting illustrations of disks containing the *sator* formula from Nuremberg.

690. Baines, William, "The Rotas-Sator Square: A New Investigation," *New Testament Studies* 33 (1987), p. 469–476.

Baines uses the computer to dispute the *pater noster* interpretation of the famous square. He concludes that it is possible to abstract a number of pseudo-Christian formulae from the word square, and that this proves nothing about its original use. There may well be no explanation called for other than the inclination of people to construct word games and the fascination that this particular arrangement of letters held for those people.

691. (Bastian) for Erman, Adolph, "Die Sator Arepo Formel," *Zeitschrift für Ethnologie*, 13 (1881), p. 35–36.

Erman describes a Coptic ostrakon in the Berlin Museum, No. 7821 bearing the *Sator* acrostic and refers to Hiob Ludolf, *Ad historiam Aethiopicam commentarius* (Osnabrück: Biblio Verlag, 1982 reproduction of the 1691 edition) p. 351 who discovered these five words in an Ethiopian manuscript. The five words are identified as names of the five wounds of Christ: *sador, aroda danad adera rodas.* Budge (no. **698**) *Zeitschrift für Ethnologie.* Verhandlungen der Berliner Gesellschaft für Anthropologie, Ethnologie und Urgeschichte, 13 (1881), p. 35.

See also by the same author, *Aegypten und Aegyptisches Leben in Altertum*, Tübingen: Mohr, 1923 p. 486.

692. Bauer, J.B., Die SATOR-Formel und ihr Sitz im Leben, *ADEVAMitteilungen* 31 (1972), pp. 7–14.

A Stoic interpretation of the square.

693. Becker, Albert, "Die Sator-Arepo-Formel patentamtlich geschützt," *Zeitschrift für Volkskunde* 44 (1934), p. 66.

The *sator* formula was copyrighted as a business trademark in the imperial patent office in 1921, and was renewed in 1931. The company defended its right to the logo in court several times charging copyright infringement.

694. Beltz, Walter, "Noch Zwei Berliner Sator-Amulette," *Archiv für Papyrusforschung* 24/25 (1976), pp. 129–134.

Two examples of the *sator* square appear on P(apyrus) 982 and P 8096, two papyri at the Staatlichen Museum in Berlin. They are examples of Greek versions of the formula dating to the seventh century.

Cf. Krall (no. **779**).

695. Biedemann, Hans, "SATOR AREPO TENET OPERA ROTAS," in *Handlexicon der magischen Künste von der Spätantike* bis zum 19 Jahrhundert. Graz: Akademische Druck und Verlagsanstalt, 1968, pp. 320–321.

Short encyclopedia entry on the *sator* square. He gives both Christian and Jewish interpretations. The *sator* square appears on the cover of the book. It is also illustrated with an example of the square found in the church of Pieve Terzagni in Cremona, Italy.

696. Bodman, Jr., H. J., "The Sator Formula: an Evaluation, in *Laudatores Temporis Acti. The James Sprunt Studies in History and Political Science* 46 (1964), pp. 131–141.

Bodman believes that no solution embodying a translation of the formula's words can be accepted without a reasonable interpretation of *arepo*. Yet it still seems impossible to find one. The author gives a good summary of the state of knowledge in 1964 but adds little to the interpretation except agreeing with Grosser.

697. Boris, Rolland and May, Louis Philippe, "Le Pythagorisme Secret du Sator Arepo. Lettres et nombres," *Recueil des Notices et Mémoires de la Société Archéologique, Historique, et Géographique du Département de Constantine* 69 (1955–1956), pp. 95–117.

A Pythagorean interpretation of the square.

698. Budge, E. Wallis (ed. and trans.), *The Bandlet of Righteousness, an Ethiopian Book of the Dead*, London, 1929, pp. 37, 75, 101.

The phrase descriptive of the nails of the cross in association with the *sator*-formula occurs in an Ethiopic work, the *Lefafa Sedek* or "Bandlet of Righteousness," where the formula is repeated four times in garbled but identifiable form and preceded once by the sentence: "in the five nails of the Cross of Our Lord Jesus Christ, I thy Servant Stephen have taken refuge." Another introduction to the formula in the same work is "I demand this by the five nails that were driven into Thy Body on the Glorious Cross, being ... [*sator* formula]." The garbled form of the formula is Sador, Alador, Danat, Adera, Rodos. It is clear that the Ethiopians borrowed it from the Copts and that neither people knew what the words really meant. REVIEWED BY: J. Simon, *Analecta Bollandiana* 49 (1931), p. 163–168.

699. Budimir, M., "Quadratum magicum retractatur," *Ziva Antika* 8 (1958), pp. 301–304.

Budimir suggests a pagan Orphic interpretation of the symbol.

700. Carcopino, Jérôme, "Le Christianisme secret du carré magique," *Museum Helveticum* 5 (1948), pp. 28ff.

Carcopino believes the Pompeian examples of the square were written by treasure hunters among the ruins many years after the eruption in AD 79, perhaps even as late as the third century AD. This is contradicted by Atkinson's article (no. **686**) which shows that the square was known by the seventies of the first century. He holds that there must have been a Celtic word *arepos* from which the Latin word *corpus* was derived and he cites scholars of Latin and Celtic languages in support of his stand that AREPO was either an "ablative instrumental" or a *datif d'intérêt'* of a word meaning plough. He dates it to AD 177. See Moeller (no. **793**), p. 9–10 who finds Carcopino's interpretation strained, Guarducci (nos. **752**, **753**), Hugh Last *Journal of Roman Studies* 44 (1954) pp. 112–115.

See also Carcopino, Jérôme, *Études d'histoires chrétiennes. Le christianisme secret du carré magique; les fouilles de Saint Pierre et la tradition.* Paris, 1953, pp. 11–91. Reviewed by Hugh Last, *Journal of Roman Studies* 44 (1954), pp. 112ff.

701. Carcopino, Jérôme, "Encore le carré magique," *CRAI* (1955), pp. 500–507.

On the square found at Aquincum.

702. Carcopino, Jérôme, El lenguaje cifrado de los primeros cristianos," *Boletin de la Academia Nacional de la Historia*, Buenos Aires, 9 (1936), pp. 261–271.

Christians in the early Roman empire often had to hide their religious practices or even their identity from the intermittent persecutions by the authorities. Many of their inscriptions, therefore, had to be written in code. Most people are familiar with the fish symbol; the Greek letters of the word *ichthus* stood for the phrase: Jesus Christ, son, God and savior. The familiar pagan funerary heading DMS (standing for *Dis Manibus Sacrum*) when appearing on a Christian headstone might stand for *Deo Magno Sacrum*. One of the most puzzling symbols, however, is the so-called SATOR rebus that has never been fully explained. It appears numerous times in ancient and medieval contexts and was used as a magical talisman.

703. Carcopino, Jérôme, "Une note du R. P. Jerphanion sur de nouveaux exemplaires du carré magique SATOR récemment découverts à Pompeii," *CRAI* (1937), pp. 84–93.

Carcopino comments on the four inscriptions found at Dura Europas. He points out that the earlier the Christian community, the more likely they would have had access only to the Greek text of the Gospels and therefore the *pater noster* should be in Greek. He does not believe the rebus has a Celtic origin. He also believed there were enough examples to suggest the rule that magic cube, when found in the Roman world, was read ROTAS OPERA but when it is found in a Christian context it reads SATOR OPERA. He wants to wait until there are more pre-Christian examples before making a judgment on its ultimate origin.

704. Cardan, Jerôme, *De Rerum Varietate*, Milan, 1557.

The square as a cure for fever or insanity.

705. Caviness, Madeleine H., "Images of Divine Order and the Third Mode of Seeing," *Gesta* 22 (1983), pp. 99–120.

A brief discussion of the *sator rebus* in the context of medieval artistic patters—i.e. expressing divine order through abstract structures including perfect geometrical forms, symmetrical schemata, palindromes and monograms. Such forms provided the underlying structure for images of heavenly beings, of those who are spiritually enlightened, and of man's position in an ordered universe.

706. du Choul, Jean, *De Varia Quercus Historia*, Lyons, 1555.
In the section "De veteribus Gallorum Magis" he discusses the square as a cure for insanity and fever. It was used by the ancient Gauls as a febrifuge; used to awaken love or to obtain favor. As one example: A citizen of Lyons recovers from insanity after eating three crusts of bread, each inscribed with the magic square. The meal was punctuated by the recitation of five paternosters im remembrance of the five wounds of Christ, and of the five nails of the cross: *pro quinque vulneribus Christi, quae moriendo accepit, nec non pro clavibus*. This local association with the Lord's Prayer may go back to the second bishop of Lyons, St. Irenaeus, who himself had a devotion to the five summits of the cross: *et ipse habitus crucis fines et summitates habet quinque, duas in longitudine et duas in latitudine et unam in medio in quo requiescit qui clavis affigitur*. Irenaeus, *adv. Haer* 2.24.4.

707. Cipolla, Carlo, "Per la storia della formula Sator Arepo," *Atti della Reale Accademia delle Scienze di Torino* 29 (1893–1894), pp. 209–212.

708. Collingwood, R.G., *The Archaeology of Roman Britain*, London: Methuen & Co., 1930, 293 pp.
Many interpretations of the square founder on the word *arepo* which has never been satisfactorily explained. On p. 176. Collingwood as did Haverfield (nos. **759**, **760**) treats the word *arepo* as a proper noun, though admittedly one of no known connotation.

709. Corte, E.C., "Le carré magique de Pompeii," Humanités. *Revue d'enseignement secondaire et d'éducation* 27 (1954–55), pp. 5ff.
Not available at press time.

710. Couchoud, P. L. and Audin, A., "Le carré magique. Une interprétation graphique," *Latomus* 17 (1958), pp. 518–27
The authors believe the square is pre-Christian.

711. Crozet, Léo, "Credo secret antique dans un carré magique," *Bulletin de l'Association Guillaume Budé,* 4th series, No. 2 (June, 1960), pp. 572–578.
Crozet is doubtful about Carcopino's interpretation of the *sator* square. He interprets it as Christian, the product of a great mind, created to be obscure. His solution: "Le Créateur, depuis qu'a eu lieu une Restauration Parfaite, retient l'action du destin." He proceeds, then, to show how it fits in perfectly with Catholic doctrine about the early Church.

712. Crum, Walter Ewing, *Coptic Monuments. Catalogue générale des Antiquités Égyptiennes du Musée du Caire*, No. 8001–8741, Cairo: Imprimerie de L'Institut français d'archéologie orientale, 1902, p. 42.
Another Coptic example of the *sator*-formula which ties it to the alpha-omega, a device used as a good luck charm in the same manner, in connection with the cross. One of the inscriptions is clearly a part of a prayer for the healing of a foot.
Cf. Stegemann, "Zaubertexte," (no. **814**) 18, 38, 52, 78.

W.E. Crum, *Catalogue of the Coptic MSS in the British Museum*, London, 1905, No. 524, p. 254, col. 2, vii.

713. Crum, Walter Ewing, "Coptic Studies," *Egypt Exploration Fund* (1897–98) p. 63.

The anagram spells out SADOR, ALADOR, DANET, ADERA, RODAS—the Names of the nails of Christ's cross. F.L. Griffith, (no. **750**).

714. Cumont, Franz, Atti della *Pontificia Accademia Romana di archeologia, Rendiconti* 13 (1937), pp. 7–8.

Cumont rejects the *pater noster* cryptogram. He interprets the cube according to the meaning of the words themselves. He believes they refer to various passages in the visions at the beginning of Ezekial (I.15–17; X.2.9–22). These passages use words that appear in the square "rotae, opera" and the meanings of the words *tenet, sator*" but nothing corresponds to the word *arepo* and this word remains unexplained. See Cumont, Franz, *CRAI* 1937, 93 ff.

715. Curvers, Alexis, "Le carré magique," in: *Itinéraires* Part I: 120 (1968) 33ff; Part II: 121 (1968) 168ff.; Part III: 122 (1968) 329ff.; Part IV: 123 (1968) 876ff.; Part V: 124 (1968) 93ff.; Part VI: 125 (1968) 258ff.; Part VII: 126 (1968) 117ff.; Part VIII: 128 (1968) 111ff.

An eight-part overly-labored piece of research that was unedited and was ultimately meant to appear in a book called *De La Subversion*. A very Catholic interpretation, ultimately unconvincing.

716. Dain, A., "Au dossier du mot carré 'Sator'," *Revue des Études Latines* 29 (1951), pp. 84–85.

Text of a sator square found in the 15th century legal manuscript (Parisinus Suppl. gr. 1238) in Greek characters.

717. Daniélou, Jean, *Primitive Christian Symbols,* trans. by Donald Attwater, Baltimore: Helicon Press, 1964 pp. 99–101.

Danéliou suggests that Irenaeus of Lyons knew of the cryptogram and spoke of Him "who joined the beginning with the end, and is the Lord of both, and has shown forth the plough at the end" (*Adv. haer.* 4.34.4). Irenaeus was refuting the Gnostics who interpreted John 4.37, "One sows, another reaps," as an opposition between the Demiurge, who created, and Christ, who redeemed. He maintained that the creator and the redeemer are one, and the passage refers to the cross, symbolized by the plow, which was shown forth at the beginning or seed time, and in the end at the final weeding.

718. Darmstaeder, Ernst, "Die Sator-Arepo-Formel und ihre Erklärung," *Isis. Quarterly Organ of the History of Science Society* 18 (1932), pp. 322–329.

Still another author who attributes a religious meaning to the famous palindrome. His solution to the formula: *Sator Tenet Opera Rotas Arepo* is: "The Sower holds with (for) his sheep the wheels." Symbolically, *Sator* = God, *Rotas*: the constellations, Sun and Moon, *Arepo*, which has never been translated. He unscrambles *arepo* into *pareo* (I appear, am visible, show myself) or "I command, lead me."

719. Daube, David, "Arepo' and the 'Sator' Square, *Expository Times* 62 (1951), pp. 316.

Daube discussed the mysterious and unexplained word AREPO in the square. He believes it is Hebrew or Aramaic for alpha omega (aleph o), and thus gives a Jewish-Christian origin to the square.

720. Delatte, A., *Anecdota Atheniensia*, Liège-Paris: E. Champion, 1927.

The author includes a number of magic spells that contain garbled versions of the *sator* formula as well as several magic texts attributed to Solomon. These two elements are not found combined. Metal talismans called seals of Solomon are known in Byzantium, but they do not contain the *sator* square. Ryan (no. **805**).

721. Della Corte, Matteo, "I cristiani a Pompeii," *Rendiconti Accademia di Archeologia, Lettere e belle arti di Napoli,* 12 (1936), pp. 394–400.

In 1936 a version of the *sator arepo* square was found on the column of a building cleared near the amphitheatre at Pompeii, and this led Della Corte to recognize that in 1929 he had already published fragments of a similar text from the house of P. Paquius Proculus in the same city. The examples found in the palaestra may have been done by military personnel because the *palaestra* was used as a barracks. The examples at Cirencester (Haverfield, nos. **758–759**) and Dura Europas (Rostovtzeff, nos. **803–804**) were also found in military contexts.

See *Notizie delle Scavi*, Ser. 6, vol 5 (1939), p. 449, no. 112.

See also, "Il crittogramma del Pater Noster," *Rendiconti Accademia di Archeologia, Lettere e belle arti di Napoli*, 17 (1937), pp. 96ff.

722. Della Corte, Matteo, " I Cristiani a Pompei," *Rendiconti Accad. di Arch., Lettere e belle arti di Napoli* 19 (1936), pp. 5–30.

Basing his conclusions on a thorough study of the Pompeii graffiti, Della Corte is certain that Christians were present at Pompeii, although probably not in great numbers. He defends Grosser's *Pater noster* solution against the criticism of Jerphanion. Among his proofs he offers the epigraph Cristiani found in the atrium of the Hospitium and a cross in a bas relief over a corner shrine in the house of Pansa (p. 6). Both Della Corte and Atkinson believe that the Lord's Prayer was recited immediately by all Christians and was translated into Latin at an early date.

723. Della Corte, Matteo, Reale Istituto di Archeologia e Storia dell'Arte. *Atti della Reale Accademia Nazionale dei Lincei, Notizie degli Scavi di antichità* 6, 5 (1929) p. 449, no. 112; 15 (1939), pp. 263, no. 139.

The discovery at Pompeii of two specimens of the *rotas-sator rebus*. These are the earliest examples so far discovered and confirm that the original version began with *rotas* rather than *sator*. One fragment was found in a private home, and the other is a complete version of the square scratched in a column in the *palaestra*, both of them beginning with the word *rotas*. They may be dated between 50 and 79 AD because the decoration of the house is in a style generally agreed to have been developed after AD 50, and Pompeii was destroyed in AD 79.

724. Della Corte, Matteo, *Rendiconti Accademia di Archeologia, Lettere e belle arti di Napoli* 19 (1939), pp. 28–30.

Discussion of the *pater noster* theory of the Rotas-Opera square, its earliest appearance, whether the formula is Christian, and the Christians at Pompeii.

725. Deonna, W., "Talismans Magiques trouvés dans l'Ile de Thasos," *Revue des Études Grecques* 20 (1907), pp. 364–382.

Page 365 illustrates an example of the *sator* square on a bronze disk from Thasos. Deonna suggests that the formula should be read in a line, separated into words at other points that every fifth letter, or that it should be read *boustrephedon* that is, the first line from left to right, the second from right to left, etc. This solution supposes a transitional phase in writing between cultures with writings in opposite directions. Although this condition existed between Semitic languages and Latin, it would imply that the formula was evolved in a Semitic culture. There is no evidence at this point to suggest that this was the case.

726. Dieterich, Albrecht, "ABC-Denkmaeler," *Rheinisches Museum für Philologie* 56 (1901), pp. 77–105.

Thinks the *rotas rebus* is a "giuoca di parole" i.e. simply a word game.

727. Dinkler, E., "Sator arepo," in *Die Religion in Geschcihte und gegenwart. Handwörterbuch für Theologie und Religionswissenschaft*, 3rd rev. edition, 1961, vol. 5 1373–74.

728. Doignon, Jean, "Le carré magique et Sainte Irénée," *Bulletin de la Faculté des Lettres de Strasbourg* 34 (1955–1956), pp. 232–234.

Doignon focuses on the translation of *arepo* and relates it to a passage in Saint Irenaeus, *Adv. haer.* 4.34.4 as did Carcopino. He feels that the number five is privileged in the text, and that the Gnostics played around with the symbolism of the number five. This square may have been Gnostic propaganda later turned into a Christian symbol by St. Irenaeus.

Duplicated in *Revue des Études Latines* 33 (1955), pp. 82ff.

729. Dornseiff, F., *Das Alphabet und Mystic und Magie*, 2nd ed. Leipzig: B.G. Teubner, 2nd edition, 1925, 79 & 179.

Discusses the *satorformel* along with other acrostics and magic formulas from antiquity. He accepts the *pater noster* arrangement.

Reviewed in *Gnomon* 6 (1930), pp. 361–368 by Otto Weinreich.

730. Dornseiff, Franz, "Martialis IX, 95 und das Rotas Opera Quadrat," *Rheinisches Museum für Philologie* 96 (1953), pp. 373–378.

Dornseiff finds in the Alfius-Olfius transformation in Martial's epigram an echo of the Alpha-Omega in the *rotas-sator* square.

731. Dornseiff, Franz, "Das Rotas-Opera-Quadrat," *Zeitscrift für neuetestamentlische Wissenschaft* 36 (1937), pp. 222–238.

Dornseiff accepts Cumont's explanation of the *rotas* formula being based on Ezekiel, but believes that the prophecy of Ezekiel is a secondary influence, and that the primary root of the square is the *pater noster*. This makes it primarily a

Christian-Judaic manifestation in Pompeii. He suggests that the "rotas" figure was conceived in Judaic or Christian- Judaic circles in Pompeii for the purpose of condemning Rome by practicing black magic. Dornseiff also proposes that the formula had a prophylactic sense, and indicates the four T's that can be explained like the sign *tav* in the vision of Ezekiel (IX 4–6). Not convincing. For the counter argument, see Sundwall (no. **815**), p. 13.

732. Eitrem, S., "The SATOR AREPO-formula once more," *Eranos* 48 (1950), pp. 73ff.

Suggests an orphic interpretation and believes it is of local Italian origin.

733. Emminghaus, J. H., "Satorformel," *Lexicon für Theologie und Kirche* 9 (1964), pp. 343–344.

A short encyclopedic entry on the *sator* formula with bibliography divided into Christian, Jewish and other interpretations.

734. Erman, Adolf and Krebs, Fritz, *Aus den papyrus der Könglischen Museen*, Berlin: W. Spemann, 1899, p. 262.

The earliest example of the *sator* square found on a papyrus in Egypt dated to the fourth or fifth century. It shows no evidence of a Christian association. It is merely a formula inscribed in Coptic letters on papyrus. There was a two-century gap in the evidence in this area before several Coptic and Ethiopic examples were found in strikingly Christian contexts dating to the 6th or 7th centuries.

735. Euringer, Sebastian, "Das SATOR-AREPO-Quadrat: Aberglaube oder Arkandisziplin?," *Historisches Jahrbuch* 71 (1952), pp. 334–353.

Another survey of the discussions on the square, plus his spin on the theory that words stand for the name of the nails used to crucify Jesus and how this secret information was passed on through the ages.

736. Ferrua, A., "Sull'esistenza di cristiani a Pompei," *Civiltà Cattolica* 3 (17 July 1937), pp. 127–139.

Ferrua gives a brief review of the discussion over the *rotas-sator* square found at Pompeii. He considers whether the origins are Christian, pagan or Jewish, considers Grosser's theory on the *pater noster* solution, and then comes up with the best explanation for what the cryptogram means: "Esattamente quello che si vuole"(!) E basta di questo argumento. (It means exactly what you want it to mean. And so much for that argument!).

737. Fishwick, Duncan, "An Early Christian Cryptogram?,"*Report-Canadian Catholic Historical Association,* 1 (1959), pp. 29–41.

A good summary of the state of research in 1959. Fishwick believes that the square consists of five words ingeniously evolved from the *pater noster* charm which, when properly combined, form a square that can be read in four different directions. The 'magic' of the square is basically the perfect symmetry of its component letters. These also contain cryptic Jewish symbols to those who know their origin and secret. Constructing such a square from the *pater noster* is, according to the author, "a technical achievement of the highest order." He believes those who require that the individual words (including the palindrome for *opera* that is not even a Latin word) also be meaningful when read concurrently, is to ask the impossible. Any superficial meaning that can be wrung from them is, therefore, purely superficial. The final verdict on the origin of the Rotas-Sator square is clearly dependent on future archaeological discoveries. In the form we have it now, it should be described as a charm that originated with Latin-speaking Jews settled in Italy in the period immediately prior to the Christian era.

738. Fishwick, Duncan, "On the Origins of the Rotas-Sator Square *Harvard Theological Review* 57 (1964), pp. 39–54.

Fishwick asks the question: "Is it or is it not sheer chance that the letters of the square can be rearranged in two intersecting *pater noster's* with two A's and two O's remaining to be positioned at will?" He sides with Cumont and Jerphanion in believing the origin of the squares from Pompeii have a Jewish origin. He believes the form we now have originated with Latin-speaking Jews in the period immediately preceding the Christian era. It fell out of use, only to be revived as a Christian symbol at Dura Europas, Aquincum, and Cirencester. From the Middle Ages on it won fame as a reliable talisman against fire, tempest, theft and sickness.

739. Focke, F., "Sator Arepo: Abenteuer eines magischen Quadrats," in *Würzburger Jahrbücher für Altertumswissenschaft* 3 (1948), pp. 366–401.

Focke maintains that it is a mere accident that the square contains letters that can be arranged as to intersecting *pater nosters*, together with two As and two Os rather than having the square deliberately constructed to contain these letters so as to serve as a sign which might be recognizable by Christians without arousing the suspicion of pagans.

740. Forbes, T. R., "Word Charms and the Sator Mystery," in *The Midwife and the Witch*, New Haven-London, 1966, pp. 80–93.

Examples of how the *sator* square was used as a spell against fire, to prove whether a person was a witch or not, against poisonous air and pestilence and against sorcery.

741. Franco, Marchese P., "Sator Arepo Formel," *Zeitschrift für Ethnologie* (Organ der Berliner Gesellschaft für Anthropologie, Ethnologie und Urgeschichte) 13 (1881), p. 333–334.

The anagram is solved as: *Pater, oro te, pereat Satan roso. Roso* comes from *rodere*, to bite as in dog bite. Thus another example of the charm being used as a preventative or cure for dog bites.

742. Frank, Chr., *Deutsche Gaue* 25 (1924) p. 76.

Frank stumbled upon the *pater noster* solution independently of Grosser and Agrell.

743. Fritsch, H., "Die Bedeutung des Sator-Spruches," *Zeitschrift für Ethnologie* (Organ der Berliner Gesellschaft für Anthropologie, Ethnologie und Urgeschichte) (1883), p. 535.

Fritsche rearranges the letters and finds in them an invocation to Satan: *Satan oro te pro arte a te spero.*

744. Fritsch, G., "Sator Tenet Opera Rotas," *Zeitschrift für Ethnologie* (Organ der Berliner Gesellschaft für Anthropologie, Ethnologie und Urgeschichte) (1917), pp. 144–145.

He reviews an article by Alexander Moskowski in the *Vossischen Zeitung* about "Buchstabenspiele" and uses it to give to the *sator* square a numerical value that translates to an invocation of Satan.

745. Frugoni, Arsenio, "Sator Arepo Tenet Opera Rotas," *Rivista di Storia e Letteratura Religiosa* 1 (1965), pp. 433–439.

Frugoni surveys the literature and then concludes that the square meant different things to different people, but probably originated as a piece of word play and cites its appearance in the *Carme delle scolte modenesi* where it is written in the margin next to another famous palindrome: *Roma muro luceas summus saeculorum amor.*

746. Fuchs, M. Harald, "Die Herkunft der Satorformel," *Schweizerisches Archiv für Volkskunde* 47 (1951), pp. 28–54.

The most astonishing feature of the solutions to the mystery is the number of purportedly meaningful texts that can be wrung from this extraordinary word square. Fuchs lists over thirty anagrams. The article also contains an excellent bibliography. Fuchs sides with a Jewish interpretation of the square.

747. Gardner, George, *Travels in the Interior of Brazil, principally through the Northern Provinces and the Gold and Diamond Districts during the years 1836-1841*, New York: AMS Press, 1970, 562 pp.

Pp. 52–53 give the most recent example of the square being used as a cure for dog-bites and snake bites. Each line of the acrostic is to be written separately on a slip of paper and then rolled into the form of a pill. All five are to be given to the patient as soon as possible after the person (or animal) has been bitten.

748. Germain, Gabriel, "Contemplation et Interprétation du 'carré magique'," *Bulletin de l'Association Guillaume Budé*, 4th series, No. 1 (1966), pp. 124–132.

Written in response to the publication of Jerome Carcopino's *Études d'histoires chrétiennes. Le christianisme secret du carré magique; les fouilles de Saint Pierre et la tradition*. Paris, 1953. Another translation that revolves around the Jesus as sower motif.

749. Griffith, F. L. (ed.), *Egypt Exploration Fund: Archaeological Report,* London, 1897–98, p. 63.

In the desert west of Faras in Nubia, an inscription in a tomb consists of a prayer dated AD 739 for the soul of a certain Theophilus. The *sator*-formula is included in columns of inscriptions among which is a Coptic version of the apocryphal letter from Jesus to Abgar V, King of Edessa, a letter widely employed by the Copts as a prophylactic against illness. Another list records the names of the forty martyrs of Sabaste, also a talisman against disease. The final lists consists of the *sator*-formula in linear form preceded by the phrase: "These are the names of the nails of Christ." The names are SADOR, DANET, ADERA, RODAS.

See also, A.H. Sayce, "Gleanings from the Land of Egypt," *Rec Trav* 20 (1898), p. 176.

750. Griffiths, J. Gwyn, "'Arepo' in the Magic 'Sator' Square, *Classical Review* 80 (1971), pp. 6–8.

Gives a plausible explanation of the word *arepo* as a personal name derived from the Egyptian *Hr-Hp*. He proposes an Egyptian, specifically an Alexandrine origin where there was a Gnostic tradition that used acrostics.

751. Grosser, Felix, "Ein neuer Vorschlag zur Deutung der sator-Formel," *Archiv für Religionswissenschaft* 24 (1926), pp. 165–169.

Grosser, a German priest, caused a furor when he published this article in 1926. By rearranging the letters of the Sator rebus, he created a Christian cryptogram of two *pater nosters* crossing on the common N and with A and O at the ends of the cross. This referred to the Apocalypse's symbolism of God as the Beginning and the End. He believed the *Sator rebus* was invented during the persecutions of the Christians. Unbeknownst to him, a Swedish scholar working simultaneously and independently came to the same conclusion. Agrell (no. **683**). Cf. Rostovtzeff (nos. **803**, **804**), and Sundwall (no. **815**).

752. Guarducci, Margherita, "Ancora Sul 'Quadrato Magico," *Archaeologica Classica* 19 (1967), pp. 9–10.

La Guarducci compares the Rotas/Opera/Tenet/Arepo/Sator palindrome to another which reads Roma/Olim/Milo/Amor. There are examples of this word game from Ostia, Pompeii, and another found at Bolonia (Belo in the province on Cadice) found during the 1917–21 excavations there.

753. Guarducci, Margherita, "Il misterioso 'Quadrato Magico': L'interpretazione di Jérome Carcopino e documenti nuovi," *Archeologia Classica* 17 (1965), pp. 219–270.

Guarducci successfully puts to rest Carcopino's shaky interpretation. She cites the work of Amedeo Maiuri on the excavations at Pompeii where two examples of the Sator rebus were found. This work was overlooked by Carcopino. She concludes the formula is a simple word game.

754. Gunn, Charles Douglas, *The Sator-arepo Palindrome. A New Inquiry into the Composition of an Ancient Word Square.* Unpublished Dissertation, Yale University, 1969.

Gunn examines the idea that the *sator* formula is simply a gibberish *abracadabra*. He was one of the first scholars to use the computer to prove his case.

Available on microfilm at Yale; non-circulating.

755. Handelmann, H., "Diskussionsbemerkung," *Zeitschrift für Ethnologie* 12 (1880) pp. 216–217.

756. Handelmann, H., "Satorformel," *Zeitschrift für Ethnologie* 18 (1886) p. 315. Another dog bite formula.

757. Hardenberg, Kuno von, *Damstädter Tageblatt*, 1935 no. 69.

Another ingenious anagram. Hardenberg believed he had found in the square a reference to the comfort the Rose of Sharon is said to have brought to St. Peter for his sin in denying Christ. *Petro et Reo Patet Rosa Sarona.* i.e. "For Peter even [*sic*] guilty the rose of Sharon is open." The interpretation is dubious since the authority given for this incident (Acts 9.35) is dubious, and there is no reference to the Rose of Sharon, at least in the Vulgate. The incident is probably apochryphal and merely a poetic tradition. Both the incident and the Latinity of von Hardenberg's solution have been questioned (Fishwick, *CCHA*, 1 [1959] p. 34, no. **738**).

758. Haverfield, F., "Notes on the Roman Origin of a Medieval Charm," *Journal of the Anthropological Institute of Great Britain and Ireland, 22* (1899), p. 306ff.

759. Haverfield, F., "A Roman Charm from Cirencester," *Archaeological Journal* 56 (1889), pp. 319–23.

At the time the Cirencester inscription with the *sator* square was found in 1868, Haverfield considered it to be the first Roman example of the charm to be found. His theory was discounted at the time because no other instances were known that could be dated before the 8th or 9th century. Haverfield based his interpretation on the forms of the letters and the general Romano-British character of the find spot. The article contains a full-size photo of the inscription. Haverfield is clueless as to the meaning although he rehashes a few of the older interpretations.

Haverfield, F., *Ephemeris Epigraphica. Corpus Inscriptionum Latinarum Supplementum,* Vol. IX, fasciculus quartus. *Addimenta quinta ad Corporis volumen VII*, p. 519, no. 1001, Berlin 1913.

760. Hepding, Hugo, "Die Satorformel," *Hessische Blätter für Volkskunde* 34 (1935), pp. 111–113.

A short notice on the discovery of four new examples of the square found in Dura Europas.

761. Hepding, Hugo, "Die Sator-Formel," *Hessische Blätter für Volkskunde* 36 (1937), pp. 175–176.

Short notice on the discovery of the *sator* formula in Pompeii.

762. Hoffman, Heinz, *Pauly-Wissowa, Realencyclopädie der Classischen Altertums Wissenschaft*, Supplementband XV (Munich, 1978), col. 477–565.

Hoffman provides historians of Graeco-Roman religion with an exhaustive, 87 column account of the attempts to solve the puzzle since 1823. He adopts and strongly defends the position taken by Hildebrecht Hommel in 1952, that the square has a Stoic-Pythagorean origin.

763. Hommel, Hildebrecht, "Satorformel," *Lexicon der Alten Welt,* Zürich & Stuttgart: Artemis Verlag, 1965, 2705.1969, p. 2706.

Short summary of the formula and its history.

764. Hommel, Hildebrecht, *Schöpfer und Erhalter*, Studien zum Problem Christentum und Antike, Berlin: Lettner Verlag, 1956, pp. 32–79.

Following an old French anonymous suggestion going back to 1854, he assumes that the Sator square was written boustrephedon (zigzag), and that the middle word *tenet* should be read twice—*Sator opera tenet: (tenet) opera Sator*, which he translates, "Der Schöpfer (Sämann, Vater) erhält seine Werke" or "The Creator preserves his works." He believes the *sator* square derives from a Stoic-Pythagorean setting.

765. Ihlenfeldt, Margaret, "Bread-wrapper Palindrome," *Classical Journal* 49 (1953), p. 100.

A high school student in Springfield, Illinois found the *sator* formula on the back of a bread wrapper. The students not only noticed that the sentence reads the same backwards as forwards, but the initial letter of each word spells the first word, the second letter of each word spells the second word, the third letter of each word spells the third word and so for the other two words. It was billed as "The World's Most Amazing Sentence." They translated it as "God, the Creator, rules the motion of the Universe," which will not hold up to scrutiny.

766. Jagor, "Die Formel Sator Arepo," *Zeitschrift für Ethnologie* 14 (1882), p. 415–416.

Jagor finds an example of the *sator* square in Charles Davillier's *Voyage en Espagne*, (1872, vol. 2, p. 376). In the book, Davillier reports that at the Chateau Rochemaure on the banks of the Rhone, there is an inscription that contains the *sator* rebus.

767. Jagor, Hr., "Die Formel Sator Arepo," *Zeitschrift für Ethnologie. Verhandlung der Berliner Gesellschaft für Anthropologie* 14 (1882), pp. 415.

A short notice suggesting a plausible translation of the famous formula. An inscription found at the Chateau de Rochemaure on the Rhone: *Sator opera tenet* ... he translates as*: le sémeur tient son ouvrage, ou comme on sème on recolte.*

768. Jerphanion, G.A. de, "A propos des nouveaux exemplaires trouvés à Pompeii, du carré magique 'Sator,' par le R.P. Jerphanion," *CRAI* (1937), pp. 84–94.

The discovery of two specimens of the square in Pompeii that could be reasonably dated as earlier than AD 79 caused Jerphanion to recant his previous views. He gives five reasons:

1) That it would be surprising if there had been Christians at Pompeii before the destruction.

2) That if the square had originated among Christians of the first century, one would expect the writing to be in Greek.

3) That A and O as a description of God passed into Christian parlance in the Apocalypse which hadn't yet been written in AD 70.

4) That the intersecting arrangement of the double pater noster would require the cross to have become a Christian symbol by the date of the composition, though it is not found earlier than the Epistle of Barnabas for which Jerphanion accepts a Hadrianic date.

5) That the use of a *crux dissimulata* as an esoteric sign of Christianity is again a practice otherwise unknown before the second century.

769. Jerphanion, Guillaume de, "La formule magique: Sator Arepo ou Rotas Opera. Vieilles théories et faits nouveaux," *Recherches de science réligieuse,* 25 (1935), pp. 188–225. REVIEWED IN: *Analecta Bollandiana* 53 3/4 (1935), pp. 382–385 by H.D.

Jerphanion discusses the *sator rebus* as it is found in the Roman world—from the inscriptions at Dura Europas, Cirencester. etc. and discusses its possible Gallic origin. He compares it to various palindromes. There is a section on the *sator* formula among the Copts and the Ethiopians, and in the Byzantine world in Cappadocia. In these traditions, the square is sometimes linked to the names of the Magi and the fives nails of the cross (Griffith, no. **750**). Jerphanion believes these names were derived from the square and not the square from the names. A good inventory of the various anagrams that can be made from the letters in the square.

770. Jerphanion, Guillaume de, "Du nouveau sur la Formule magique: Rotas Opera (et non SATOR AREPO)," *Recherches de science religieuse,* 27 (1937), pp. 326–35.

Its original Jewish meaning was related to a passage in Ezekiel but then changed (at a time still unknown) by Christians to the symbolism of the cross and the Alpha-Omega.

771. Jerphanion, Guillaume de, *Une Nouvelle Province de l'Art Byzantin: Les Églises Rupestres de Cappadoce*, Haut Commissariat de la République Française en Syrie et au Liban. Services des Antiquités et des Beaux Arts. Bibliothèque Archéologique et Historique. Tome VI. Paris: Librairie Orientaliste Paul Geunthner, 1934.

I.78 and 158 and plate 38, figure no. 1. Shows a representation of the nativity from a church in Cappadocia which dates to the time of the Emperor Constatine VII Porphyrogenitus (913–959).

In Cappadocia, the words of the *sator*-formula became the names of the shepherds of the Nativity. In the rupestral churches of the Ürgüp region there are several nativity scenes, classifiable roughly into two categories. An early group, ninth to eleventh centuries, of frescoes with strong eastern influence, and a later group, dating from the eleventh century, in which the paintings reveal a decided Byzantine influence. The words of the formula occur primarily in the first group. In the Church of St. Eustathius, the shepherds are named SATOR for the young man, AREPO for the old man, TENETO for the musician. The words are placed next to the head in the oriental fashion so the intention of the artist cannot be misunderstood.

At Toqale Kilissé, the young man is named AREPON and TENETON seems to designate the musician while the old man is unidentified. Vol. I, pt 1, 78 and pl. 38, figure 1; and above Jerphanion, *RecSciRel* 25 (1935) p. 202, n. 35. In anther case the musician is entitled PEREROTAS, a composite of opera and rotas. Vol. II, pt. 1, p. 155 and plate 152, fig. 2. Among the second group of frescoes the shepherds are usually unnamed. In one case, however, only the musician is named and he is SATOR. Vol. I, pt. 2, p. 411 and pl. 104, figure 3. Thus there is a definite link between the words of the *Sator* formula and the shepherds of the Nativity but no tradition appears to exist connecting a specific shepherd with a particular word of this formula.

772. Jerphanion, Guillaume de, "Osservazioni sull'origine del quadrato magico," *Rendiconti della Pontificia Accademia di Archeologia* 12 (1936), 401ff.

Jerphanion becomes an early agnostic over the *pater noster* solution to the *sator* puzzle.

773. Karner, K., "Die Sator-Inschrift von Aquincum," *Theologische Literaturzeitung* 82 (1957), pp. 391–394.

Karner discusses the *sator* inscription found at Aquincum (Szilagi, no. **817**). At the time of its discovery, it was the second oldest example of the formula found.

774. Kilian, Werner, "Gedanken zum Grossen Palindrome," *Forschungen und Fortschritte* 32 (1958), pp. 272–277.

Kilian is not interested in translating the five words of the square. Rather he is interested in the use of the letters to form the *pater noster* anagram. He rearranges the *pater nosters* in endless forms, proving nothing, but is convinced of the genius of the author in creating this palindrome that bonded together the *cognoscenti* while warding off their enemies.

775. Köhler, Reinhold, "Sator-Arepo-Formel," *Zeitschrift für Ethnologie*, 13 (1881), p. 301–306 and *Kleine Schriften* 3, p. 564.

In the latter article he collects many of the early examples of the *sator* square. He discusses one scratched on the marble above the chapel of St. Laurent in Rochemaure, France, one in Cirencester, England (Atkinson, no. **686**), on the mosaic pavement of a church in Pieve Terzagni from the end of the eleventh century, in an Oxford Latin Ms. of the thirteenth century; in a Greek manuscript in the Bibliotheque Nationale in Paris; in the marginalia of a Munich manuscript. In fifteenth century writing (du Choul, no. **706**). It was used to extinguish fires and to protect against the bite of mad dogs. It was used by the natives of northern Brazil to protect against and heal snake bites.

Köhler does not attempt to interpret the meanings of the words, but concludes that with the exception of *arepo*, which has not been satisfactorily explained, they are all well-known Latin words.

776. Kolberg, *Verhandlung der Berliner Gesellschaft für Anthropologie*, 1887, p. 69.

He regards the letters of the Sator acrostic as abbreviations of Latin words. He refers to the Nuremberg meal or plate described in *Verhandlung der Berliner Gesellschaft für Anthropologie*, 1883 p. 354 and interprets it as a paten or communion plate. On the outer circle are the words: + Deo Honorem + Et Patria + Liberationem + Mentem Sanctam + Spontaneam, and the *sator* acrostic, which he arranges rather arbitrarily as follows:

SAT ORARE
POTENter ET OPERAre
RatiO (oder auch ReligiO) TuA Sit.

He interprets: Viel beten
Und kräftig arbeiten
Das sei Deine Lebensweise (oder Religion)

He believes it is an ancient rule of the Benedictines.

777. Kraeling, C. H., "The Sator Acrostic," *Crozer Quarterly* 22 (1945), pp. 28–38.

He disputes Grosser's *pater noster* solution for the reversible, four-way acrostic. It originated as a word game, but once it was established as a magic formula, its perpetuation in Christian circles is readily explicable without the hypothesis of Christian origin.

778. Krall, V., "Koptische Amulette," *Mitteilungen aus der Sammlung der Papyrus Erherzog Rainer* 5 (Wien, 1882), pp. 115ff.

Coptic amulette with the *sator rebus* on it.

779. Krall, V., "Sator Areto Tenet Opera," *Mitteilungen aus der Sammlung der Papyrus Erherzog Rainer* 5 (Wien, 1889), pp. 99–122.

Discusses a Greek version of the *Sator-Arepo* square found on a Coptic papyrus (kopt. Perg. Nr. 2434–2436).

780. Last, Hugh, Review of Jerome Carcopino, *Études d'Histoire Chrétienne. Le Christianisme Secret du Carré Magique: Les Fouilles de Saint-Pierre et la Tradition*, Paris: Albin Michel, 1953, in *Journal of Roman Studies* 44 (1954) pp. 112–115.

Last does not accept the *pater noster* solution as does Carcopino.

781. Last, Hugh, "The Rotas Sator Square: Present Position and Future Prospects," *Journal of Theological Studies* n.s. 3 (1952), pp. 92–97.

A 1,500 word article on the present state of opinion (in 1952) on the famous 25-letter square by a respected classicist. He suggests having scholars compose twenty-five letter squares of the *sator-rotas* variety and see how many of them can in fact be made with Latin words. This would help to determine the degree of probability that Cumont was right when he described the square as "la plus ancienne inscription chrétienne connue et la premiere qui établisse l'existence d'un christianisme latin."

782. Leclercq, H., "Sator Arepo," *Dictionnaire d'Archéologie Chrétienne et de Liturgie,* Paris: Letouzey et Ané, Vol. 15 (1950), col. 913–915.

After a discussion of some of the more popular interpretations, Leclercq traces the origin of the rebus to folklore and doubts its connection with either Hebraic or Christian symbolism.

783. Letonnelier, G., "Une interprétation du carré magique SATOR AREPO," *Bulletin Archéologique du Comité des Travaux Historiques* (1951–1952), pp. 168–69.

Letonnelier suggests some of the words are actually abbreviations. His reading: Sat Orare Poten(tia) et Oper(a) A Rota S(ervant). "Prier beaucoup est notre force, et son effet préserve (ou sauve) de la roue." Prayer is our strength and will save us from the wheel (of fate?). The formula is thus a Christian call to prayer.

784. Letonnelier, G., "Note sur l'inscription de Valbonnais," *Cahier d'histoire et d'archéologie* (Nîmes), no. 13, 1932, pp. 291–299.

A medieval French example of the *rotas-opera* formula. It was inscribed long after anyone comprehended the meaning, but was used as a magical talisman.

785. Ludof, Hiob, *Ad Historiam Aethiopicam Commentarius*, Osnabrück: Biblio Verlag, 1982 reprint of the 1694 edition, p. 351.

In the eleventh century, the five words from the square were used in Abyssinia to denote the five wounds of Christ. They are reported here as Sador, Aroda, Danad, Adera, Rodas, a corruption of *Sator, Arepo, Tenet, Opera, Rotas*, the text of which they had probably never seen. The Ethiopian text is included.

786. McBryde, J.M. Jr., "The Sator-Acrostic," *Modern Language Notes* 22 (1907), pp. 245–249.

McBryde discusses much of the earlier German literature on the magical and curative powers of the formula, and concludes that the *sator* square is related to the Jewish Kabbalah, but at the same time is also related to magic squares where letters and words are reduced to numbers with definite fixed values. These are older than the Kabbalah and may be traced back through the Pythagorean philosophy to ancient Babylon.

He adds many examples that he found in manuscripts but had been previously unpublished.

787. Maresch, Gustav, "Zur Sator-Formel," *Commentationes Vindobonenses,* Vienna 1 (1935), pp. 94–97.

Rather than the *pater noster* solution, he prefers an early version with Pater-Soter and a gnostic interpretation.

788. Markovich, M., "Sator Arepo = Georgos Harpon (Knoyphi) Harpos," [Greek Arpo(cra), Harpo(crates)," *Zeitschrift für Papyrologie und Epigraphik* 50 (1983), pp. 155–171.

Markovich attacks the interpretation advanced by Hommel and defended by Hoffman in Pauly-Wissowa that interprets the square as emanating from a Stoic-Pythagorean setting. Marcovich gives one of the best clues to the meaning of the word *arepo*. The author believes it is a Latinized nickname for the god of good luck in Graeco-Roman Egypt—Harpon (Knuphi). The translation of the charm would be: "The sower Horus/Harpocrates checks, toils, and tortures."

789. Marques-Rivière, Jean, *Amulettes, Talismans et Pentacles dans les Traditions Orientales et Occidentales*, Paris: Payot, 1938, pp. 167–70.

Cites examples from Cappadocia where the words of the formula are connected with the names of the shepherds who worshipped the infant Jesus at the Nativity.

790. Mestorf, J., *Zeitschrift für Ethnologie. Verhandlung der Berliner Gesellschaft für Anthropologie*, 14 (1882), p. 555–558.

Mestorf describes a cup of "oriental workmanship" found on the island of Gotland. It has Runic letters engraved upon it which spell out the *sator*-acrostic, together with the five-pointed star or wizard pentagram. The cup is said to date to the fourteenth century.

791. Metzger, Bruce M., "Rotas-Sator Square," (supplement), *Twentieth Century Encyclopedia of Religious Knowledge*, Grand Rapids, Mi, 1955, vol. 2, p. 983.

A short summary of the theories on the *sator* square with a bibliography almost as long as the entry.

792. Meysing, J., "Introduction à la numérologie biblique. Le diagramme Sator Arepo," *Revue des Science Religieuse* 40 (1966), pp. 321–52.

A planetary, astrological, cosmological interpretation of the famous square. Rarely has so much been made of so little.

793. Moeller, Walter O., *The Mithraic Origin and Meanings of the Rotas-Sator Square*, Leiden: E. J. Brill, 1973, 53 pp., plates.

Moeller believes that SATOR was Saturn and that the Mithraic triad is present: Saturnus-Aion, Sol Invictus and Mithra. The square transmitted a direct message concerning sowing and reaping. There are indications of a connection between the square and the Apocalypse of St. John. And finally, the square is a number square from which many numbers can be calculated including 666. Not convincing, but contains an excellent bibliography.

794. Omedeo, A., "La croce d'Ercolano e il culto preconstantiniano della croce," *La Critica* 38 (1940) 46, n. 3.

A Mithraic interpretation of the square. He bases his interpretation on a graffito containing the square found in the Pompeian palaestra which he believes suggests a Mithraic origin because the area was used for military exercises for the *Iuvenes*. For a Mithraic interpretation based on other grounds, see Walter O. Moeller, *The Mithraic Origin and Meanings of the Rotas-Sator Square* (no. **793**).

795. Ooteghem, J. van, "Le Rébus Sator," *Études Classiques* 3 (1934), pp. 557–558.

A short description of the square, its history and a discussion of other scholars' work. He accepts the Christian interpretation and rejects Suys (no. **816**).

796. Orcibal, Jean, "Dei agricultura': Le carré magique Sator Arepo, sa valeur et son origine," *Revue d'Histoire des Religions* 146 (1954), pp. 51–66.

Orcibal concentrates on the concept of Christ as the Sower and the meaning of Sator. He takes examples from the Gospels and Christian writers. He believes it was used for its magical powers long before it was Christian. He discusses the mathematical possibilities of the *pater noster* solution being just chance. He feels that the magic which pagans saw in the square rested purely on the symmetry of the words. One might find the formula in a collection of pagan magical papyri had Diocletian not had such magical papyri burned.

797. Palma, J., "Une curieuse inscription," *L'Intermédiaire des Chercheurs et Curieux* 3, 57 (1866), pp. 476–477.

The author takes *arepo* to be a proper name, that of the "sower," and produced: "An indefatigable sower, the worker Arepo, holds the works, the wheels." He then interpreted the translation to mean "God, the creator, holds in his hand both his vases of clay known by the name of man and all the force of the round machine." This solution required the interpolation of additional letters to derive a meaning.

798. Pennington, Anne E., "South Slavs in Malta," in *Byzance et les Slavs. Études de civilisation*. Mélanges Ivan Dujcev, Paris, 1979, pp. 333–5.

A previously unpublished Serbian version of the square. It was used as the antidote to the bite of a mad dog (p. 334, n. 3).

799. Picard, Charles, "Sur le carré magique à l'Eglise odorante" (Kokar Kilise, Cappadoce," *Revue Archéologique* 1 (1965), pp. 101ff.

In the region of Hasan Dagi in Cappadocia (Turkey), two French scholars found on the wall of a church a series of musicians next to a figure being baptized. Underneath appears the enigmatic *sator* formula. The figures are wearing pointed Phrygian caps and oriental dress. Picard, of course, accepts a Christian interpretation of the square.

800. Polge, H., "La fausse énigme du carré magique," *Revue d'Histoire des Religions* 175 (1969), pp. 155–163

Polge (and Gunn, no. **755**) were among the first to use the computer to solve the *sator-arepo* mystery. He calls the *sator* square "une construction phraséomorphe anacyclique à quadruple entrée." He has the computer calculate the 625 applicable combinations of the 25 letters of the square and concludes that none of the combinations is linguistically viable. He concludes that *Arepo* is "un anthroponyme imaginaire," "un artifice lexicale," "une option irrationelle." Any attempt to link it to a person or thing in the Graeco-Roman world is fruitless.

801. Porter, J. Hampden, "Folklore of the Mountain Whites of the Alleghenies," *Journal of American Folklore* 7 (1894), pp. 105–117.

On p. 113 he describes an example of the *sator rebus* he found that was used as a talisman. It was written on parchment, in ink that was "dim with age" and was surmounted by an indistinct device that looked like an equilateral triangle inscribed in a circle. It was used for "almost everything to carry with you to be safe any place or to keep in your house to keep it from burning down or stop fits or prevent miscarriage. If convulsions occur in consequence of injuries, no benefit follows the use of this remedy, but a copy of the formula swallowed or taken in the form of an infusion will certainly prevent a mad dog's bite from causing hydrophobia, and the same methods of administration prove effectual in cases of continued fever."

802. Ricci, V., "Sator Arepo," *Catholic Encyclopedia*, New York: The Encyclopedia Press, Inc., 1917, p. 1098.

Ricci believes a possible transliteration is: *sator*, the sower; *arepo*, with his plow, *tenet*, holds; *opera*, with purpose; *rotas*, the wheels. The five words can be read consecutively either horizontally or perpendicularly; and while the disposition of the words varied in both East and West during the Middle Ages, the device was traced to the fourth century AD and considered of Christian origin.

803. Rostovtzeff, M.I., *The Excavations at Dura-Europus*: Preliminary Report of the Fifth Season, New Haven, 1934, pp. 159–161; and *op. cit.* Sixth Season, New Haven, 1936, p. 482–6.

The original excavation reports for the discovery of the four examples of the *sator* formula found in the Temple of Artemis Azzanathcona at Dura-Europas, the Syria city that for the last years of its existence (ca. AD 165–256) was an important fortress in the Roman military defenses against Parthia and then Sassanian Persia. The camp of the Romans was located in the section of the city in which the formula inscriptions were found. It is apparent that the rooms of the temple were taken over by the military probably at the beginning of the third century when the garrison was considerably increased by local Semitic recruits.

A number of the inscriptions are of cabalistic character: alphabets, magic signs and symbols, pentagrams, evil eyes, a magic animal, and several hermetic texts in mystic alphabets (see p. 482). The room in which the *sator*-formulae were found also contained a large number of graffiti relating to military affairs and indicate that it was a clerical office for the garrison. Many of the inscriptions are Latin written in Greek alphabet. Two of the three *sator*-formulae substitute Greek letters for the Latin, the earliest example of this common practice.

The *terminus ante quem* of the Dura examples seems to be fixed again by the destruction of the city c. AD 256 by the second Sassanian attack. They massacred and carried away its inhabitants into slavery. The *terminus post quem* is harder to establish, but if the *sator*-formulae are associated with the military inscriptions, which seems plausible, then the date would be around AD 200. The author also assumes that the inscriber or inscribers of the Dura formulae were members of the Roman military more familiar with Greek than Latin, probably local recruits.

804. Rostovtzeff, M. I., "Il rebus 'Sator,'" *Annali della Reale Scuola Normale Superiore di Pisa,* Lettere, Storia e Filosofia, Ser. 2, Vol. 3, fasc. 1 (1934), pp. 103–105.

Rostovtzeff uncovers two more examples of the SATOR rebus (see Carcopino, nos. **700–703**). These are graffiti scratched by soldiers of the two auxiliary cohorts stationed at Dura Europas: T he II Ulpia and the XX Palmyrenorum into the wall off the cortile of the Temple of Azzanathcona. Since Dura was abandoned in AD 256, we now have examples dating before the middle of the third century.

Since the vast majority of the *sator-rebus* inscriptions are in Latin, Rostovtzeff believes they originated in the West, possibly in Gaul. These inscriptions support the idea that the rebus was invented much earlier than the fourth century.

He follows Grosser (no. **752**) in believing they began during the great persecutions. J. Dölger, *Antike und Christentum*, III (1932), p. 278 disagrees.
Cf. F. Haverfield, *Ephemeris Epigraphica* 9, no. 1001
R. Collingwood, *The Archaeology of Roman Britain,* p. 176, fig. 174.

805. Ryan, W.F., "Solomon, Sator, Acrostics, and Leo the Wise in Russia," *Oxford Slavonic Papers*, n.s. 19 (1986), pp. 46–61.
Ryan has found Cyrillic examples of the *sator* formula in Russian manuscripts where it was usually titled "Seal of King Solomon the Wise." Russian scholars have not discussed the *sator* square in the context of the more general history of the subject, and there are some aspects of it which Ryan thinks deserve comment. In particular, its possible Jewish connections, its associations with divinatory, computistic and 'Solomonic' texts, and the acrostic text ascribed to Leo the Wise which goes with some specimens. Ryan lists twenty-nine examples of the Russian *sator* square known to him. Illustrated.

806. Sabbadini, R., *Rivista di Filologia* 47 (1919), p. 34.
Jesus as sower or Sator as God the creator.

807. Schmöger, A., *Katholische Kirchenzeitung* (Salzburg), no. 21 of May 24, 1917, p. 173.
This is the earliest attempt to interpret *sator* as Jesus the Sower (Matthew 13:3; Mark 4:3; Luke 8:5), or as God the Creator.

808. Schneider, Wolfgang Christian, "Sator Opera TenetPoros Aras. 'Der Sämann erhält die WerkeDu aber pflügst' Eine Deutung des Sator-Quadrats," *Castrum Peregrini* 189/90 (1989), pp. 101–124.
Schneider believes the *sator* square is the key to an important philosophical concept that joins the tradition of Etruscan/Roman religion and philosophy to the Stoic and Academic Greek traditions of philosophy.

809. Schulenberg, W. von, "Formel 'Sator Arepo'," *Zeitschrift für Ethnologie,* (Organ der Berliner Gesellschaft für Anthropologie, Ethnologie und Urgeschichte) 13 (1881), p. 85–86.
Tells the 16th century story of several women with eye maladies who had them cured by wearing a parchment around their neck that had the *sator* square written on it. The *sator* square was also found on a lead tablet that was nailed to the oldest house in Pösneck to protect it from fire.

810. Schulenberg, W. von *Zeitschrift für Ethnologie* (Organ der Berliner Gesellschaft für Anthropologie, Ethnologie und Urgeschichte) (1881), p. 167.
An attempt to translate *arepo* as "Areben."

811. Schwartz, J., "À propos du carré SATOR chez les Éthiopiens," *Annales d'Éthiopie* 2 (1957), pp. 219–223.
Schwartz discusses a graffito found at Touna el-Gebel on the wall of a funerary monument from Hermopolis. It is the *sator rebus* but in Coptic with a few

changes in consonants due to the language difference. He relates the words to the names of the five nails of the cross and the use of these names and symbols in Coptic amulets.

812. Schwartz, Paul, "Sator arepo Formel," *Zeitschrift für Ethnologie*, (Organ der Berliner Gesellschaft für Anthropologie, Ethnologie und Urgeschichte) 13 (1881), pp. 131–132.

Schwartz was the Gymnasiallehrer in Salzwedel and reports on an example of the *sator* formula being used as a cure for dog bites.

813. Seligman, Dr. S., "Die Satorformel," *Hessische Blatter für Volkskunde* 13(1914), pp. 154–183.

A complete study of the *sator rebus*. The oldest one found was patently Christian in character, found in Asia Minor, originating perhaps in Egypt, and dating to the fifth century. He believes the inventor of the magic formula wanted to join the traditional names of the three kings of the OrientAtor, Sator and Peratoras in the form of two squares, one inserted into the other, a very *recherche* explanation that the discovery in Pompeii (Sundwall, no. **815**) completely refutes.

He gives an interesting survey of the German examples of the formula. The majority of these are to be found on medals and plaques generally accompanied by epithets of God. These are in Latin, Hebrew and pseudo-Hebrew. One in the numismatic collection of Gotha is a silver medallion on which the formula is encircled with the words Saraot (Sabaot), Emanuel, Soter, Helian, Usion, Tetragrammaton, Onagia and Ealuaet. On the reverse is a heart in which is engraved Javneh and Schadai in Hebrew and INRI. Emerging from the heart are the hands and feet of Christ, marked with wounds, arranged in a manner suggestive of a cross. Encompassing these are Adonai, Eloy, Eloah, Elohim, Ehohrah, Seday and Zebaot.

814. Stegemann, Victor, "Die Koptischen Zaubertexte der Sammlung Papyrus Erzherzog Rainer in Wien," *Heidelberger Akademie der Wissenschaften. Sitzungsberichte.* Philosophisch-historische klasse 1 (1933–34), pp. 26, 74–75.

An example of the *sator* square in Coptic of the Sa'idic dialect, dated by its orthography to the sixth or seventh century. It is preceded by three crosses.

Also V. Krall (no. **779**).

815. Sundwall, John, "L'enigmatica inscriziones ROTAS in Pompeii," *Acta Academiae Aboensis Humaniora* XV, 5 Abo, (1945), pp. 3–17.

Another example of the famous *sator rebus* was found during the 1935–1939 excavations in Pompeii in the portico of the large palaestra near the amphitheater. The inscriptions from the palaestra date before the year AD 63 when the palaestra was partially destroyed by an earthquake. Both students at the palaestra and spectators inscribed dozens of "enthusiastic greetings" and in this case, a protective symbol to a Christian. Sundwall is one of the few who suggest a pagan interpretation of the symbol. He believes it is Orphic.

#852 Friedman Collection; 852.1 English translation.

816. Suys, E., "La formule SATOR est-elle chrétienne?," *Études classiques* 4 (1935), pp. 291–294.

Suys discusses the formula and debates whether it is Christian or pagan, and whether its origin is Gallic and whether it was used by Christians during a Roman persecution. He was one of the first writers to reject the widely-accepted *pater noster* solution to the square.

817. Szilagi, J., "Ein Ziegelstein mit Zauberformel aus dem Palast des Statthalters in Aquincum," *Acta Antiqua Academiae Scientiarum Hungaricae* 2 (1954), pp. 305–310 = *Année Epigraphique* (1956) no. 63.

On the square found at Aquincum on a roof tile from the villa publica, the residence of the imperial governor of Pannonia Inferior. The inscription contains the *Roma tibi sub(ito motibus ibit amor)* palindrome, and the *sator* square in the *Rotas, Opera, Tenet, Arepo, Sator* version.

Commentary in German and Russian.

818. Treichel, A., "Beiträge zur Satorformel und zur Tolltafel," *Zeitschrift für Ethnologie* 14 (1882), p. 264.

The *sator* square was used as a talisman against rabies. Wooden molds were made out of two pieces of pear wood carved like castinets. Dough was squeezed between them and the resultant cookie was baked. One piece was fed to the bitten person and one to the dog as a cure against rabies.

819. Treichel, A., "Nachträge über die Tolltäfelchen," *Zeitschrift für Ethnologie* (Organ der Berliner Gesellschaft für Anthropologie, Ethnologie und Urgeschichte) 12 (1880), pp. 276–284.

Treichel suggests another interpretation. *Sator* = Father, Nourisher, Supporter. *Rotas* = Wheel of fate. Hence, "Der gütige Vater hält mit Mühe auf das verderbliche Rollen der Schicksalräder." (With effort, the kind father holds on to the ruinous rolling wheels of fate). He still finds, however, no satisfactory explanation for the word *arepo.*

He cites examples of the use of the *sator* acrostic to cure toothaches. The letters are supposed to be written in butter or on a piece of bread and butter that is then to be eaten. The idea is to swallow the magic words so that they may expel the sickness. Instances are given where the acrostic was used to extinguish fires.

820. Treichel, A., "Nachträge zu den Tolltafeln und zur Satorformel," *Zeitschrift für Ethnologie* (Organ der Berliner Gesellschaft für Anthropologie, Ethnologie und Urgeschichte) 13 (1881), pp. 258–260.

Albrecht Dürer's famous "Melancholie" shows a figure holding a tablet with numbers. Some believe the numbers can be related to the *sator* formula.

Treichel also relates stories about *tolltafeln* as rabies cures. One baked a rye flour "cookie" that contained pieces of the heart, liver and spleen of the dog that had bitten someone (and was now presumably dead). The *sator* square was pressed on the outside of the cookie. The bitten person ate the cookie, but just to be sure, the wound was also cauterized.

821. Treichel, A., "Nachtrag zur Satorformel," *Zeitschrift für Ethnologie* 15 (1883), pp. 354–55.

An example of the *sator* rebus that appears in the middle of an elaborate series of concentric circles with Christian inscriptions. It is in the German National Museum in Munich.

822. Treichel, A., "Sator Arepo Formel und Tollholz," *Zeitschrift für Ethnologie* (Organ der Berliner Gesellschaft für Anthropologie, Ethnologie und Urgeschichte) 13 (1881), pp. 162–167.

Treichel refers to an article by Frischbier on " Hexenspruch und Zauberbann" (Berlin, 1870) who gives an imperfect acrostic, apparently a corruption of the *sator*-acrostic, which reads thus:

NATOR
AUTNO
TERUT
AUTNO
ROTUR

823. Treichel, A., "Satorformel," *Zeitschrift für Ethnologie* 19 (1887) pp. 69–74.

A series of examples of the *sator* square in different contexts. One use involves taking a copy of the square and adding various herbs and marine plants, then sealing them in a leather bag and wearing them around the neck as a cure for vertigo.

824. Treichel, A., "Tolltafel aus Jeseritz," *Zeitschrift für Ethnologie. Verhandlung der Berliner Gesellschaft für Anthropologie* 12 (1880), pp. 215–217.

An inscription on a *tolltafel* (charm against rabid dog bites) with a very garbled version of the *sator* square found in Jeseritz.

825. Treichel, A., "Das Tolltäfelchen aus Wahlendorf," *Zeitschrift für Ethnologie. Verhandlung der Berliner Gesellschaft für Anthropologie* 12 (1880), pp. 42–47.

Brief communication in which the author describes a curious *Tolltafel* or small wooden tablet containing the *sator* formula, and used as a charm against the bite of a mad dog or other rabid animal. He can find no translation for Arepo and so treats it as a proper name. The translation is "Der Säemann Arepo hält mit Mühe die Räder. (The Shaman, with effort, holds the wheels). Later in the same issue (p. 215) he reports the discovery of another little tablet, inscribed with an acrostic containing several letters of the *sator* formula, but including other letters in different order.

826. Treichel, A., *Zeitschrift für Ethnologie* (Organ der Berliner Gesellschaft für Anthropologie, Ethnologie und Urgeschichte) (1884), p. 66–70.

The author considers a Celtic interpretation of the formula.

827. Treichel, A., *Zeitschrift für Ethnologie* (Organ der Berliner Gesellschaft für Anthropologie, Ethnologie und Urgeschichte) 18 (1886), p. 349.

Treichel suggests the god Saturn for SATOR and takes ROTAS to refer to the wheels of the sun chariot, translating: "Saturnus mühevoll die Räder (das Sonnenrad) lenkt." For *Arepo* he suggests a derivation from the Finnish *Aurinko*, die Sonne.

828. Treichel, A., "Zur Satorformel und Tolltafel," *Zeitschrift für Ethnologie* (Organ der Berliner Gesellschaft für Anthropologie, Ethnologie und Urgeschichte) 13 (1881), pp. 306–307.

Treichel reports examples of the *sator* formula being used to cure the bite of a rabid dog.

829. Ussani, Vincenzo, "Per un esemplare cassinese di 'Rotas Opera'," *Studi Medievali* n.s. 16 (1943), pp. 237–241.

Ussani discusses three medieval examples of the *sator* square. One is from Codex 384 from Monte Cassino dating to the 9th or 10th century, one was found inscribed in the church of San Pietro all'Oratorio di Capestrano, and the third is written in the margin of a work entitled *Versus de cavenda Venere et vino* found in Codex I.4 of the *Capitolare di Modena.* There are illustrations of all three.

830. Valentiner, Theodor, "Arepo, "*Römische Mitteilungen. Deutsches (rraeologischen Instituts, Rom,* 57 (1942), pp. 250.

Proposes new explanation of the word *arepo* with the argument that it might be an "acrostic," that is a summary of the first letters of a line of words "*A r(erum) e(xtremarum) p(rincipio) o(mni).* The meaning of the *rotas* formula would be: "The Creator from the very beginning to the last moment of eternity holds (in his hand) the celestial movement (of the stars) and events." Rejected by Wendell (no. **836**).

831. Vendryès, Joseph, "Une hypothèse sur le carré magique," Comptes Rendus de l'Académie des Inscriptions et des Belles-Lettres (1953), pp. 198–208.

Vendryès accepts a Christian interpretation of the square. He then goes on to discuss the word *arepo* which he believes is a Celtic adverb and the square is therefore Gallo-Roman.

832. Veyne, Paul, "Le carré Sator ou beaucoup de bruit pour rien," *Bulletin de l'Association Guillaume Budé,* 4th series (1968), pp. 426–60.

In a somewhat over-argued but perceptive article, Veyne applies the theory of probability to prove that the anagrams drawn from the square are *posteriori* events and are therefore in no way remarkable. The square is purely a palindrome. For discussion see Moeller (no. **793**), p. 37, n. 1.

833. Wehling-Schücking, H., "Zum Deutproblem der Sator-Inschrift," *Album philologicum voor Th. Baader,* Tilburg, 1939, pp. 197ff.

A fanciful explanation that treats the central N as the abbreviation for Nazarenus. He follows Cumont and Jerphanion in thinking the Pompeian squares are Jewish.

Word magic, alphabetic acrostics, and gematria, by which a numerical value was ascribed to individual letters of a word, were very important in Jewish exorcism, cosmogonic theories, and the symbolic representation of divine powers. On this, see M. Simon, "Versus Israel," *Bibl. des écoles française d'Athenes et de Rome,* fasc 166, Paris, 1948, pp. 394–431.

834. Weinreich, O., "Zweifel an der Richtigkeit der Lösung unmöglich," *Gnomon* 6 (1930), pp. 365–367.

Review of Grosser's article.

835. Welz, Ed. von., "Sator Arepo," *Societas Latina* 5 (1937), pp. 55ff.

Discusses the anagrams that came be made from the letters of the *sator* square.

836. Wendel, C., "Das Rotas-Quadrat in Pompeji," *Zeitschrift für neuetestamentlische Wissenschaft* 40 (1941), pp. 138–51.

Tries to substantiate the theory of the *pater noster*, stating that the magic formula of the Pompeian square is explained as an expression of faith of the masses in spirits and also of the faith of the new Christian community, faith of a different nature from that of the Apologists and the Apostolic Fathers. Decisively refutes Valentiner's acrostic theory. He includes a detailed bibliography.

837. Wescher, C., "Note sur l'Interprétation d'une inscription (Provenant de Rochemaure [Ardèche])," *Bulletin des Antiquitées de France* 1874, p. 153.

The *sator* formula was found in a walled-up section of the chapel of Saint-Laurent in Rochemaure, Ardèche. Wescher uses the Byzantine manuscript's hypothetical Greek equivalents of the words and comes up with the solution: "The sower is at the plough; the work (of plowing) occupies the wheels."

838. Wulff, Oscar and Volbach, W.F. (eds.), *Die Altchristlische und Mittelalterlischen Byzantinischen und Italienischen Bildwerke* (Könglische Museen zu Berlin, "Beschreibung der Bildwerke der Christlischen Epoche," 3 Band; Berlin: Walter de Gruyter & Co., 1909. I, 317 no. 1669.

An example of the *sator* square from Cappadocia dated by the author to the fourth or fifth century AD. It has definite Christian associations: the fish and the formula IC + XC. There is some question whether the dating is accurate for this bronze amulet, since the minuscule *pi* in the Greek transliteration of *arepo* and *opera* is rendered as an *omega* with a line above it and the *tau* in two of the four times it occurs in the formula, is written as a 7. According to leading authorities on the alphabet, these forms of the letters were not used until the ninth century and the twelfth and fourteenth centuries, respectively.

See: David Diringer, *The Alphabet, a Key to the History of Mankind* (no. **612**) p. 457, columns 8 and 10 of table. If we accept Bodman's objections (no. **696**, p. 134), then the earliest Christian use of the formula, indicated by associated formulae, must be the Coptic examples of the sixth to the eighth centuries.

839. Zatzman, V., "Die Sator-formel und ihre Lösung," *Hessische Blätter für Volkskunde* 24 (1925), pp. 98–105.

Sees the square as an apotropaic formula against the devil. The acrostic should read *Satan Adama Tabat Amada Natas*. He believes the original formula was Hebraic/Aramaic.

Index

References are to entry numbers.